VOICES IN BRONZE AND STONE

Kansas City's World War I Monuments and Memorials

JAMES J. HEIMAN

VOICES IN BRONZE AND STONE

Kansas City's World War I Monuments and Memorials

By James J. Heiman

Editor: Diane McLendon

Design: Tom Dolphens

Published by Kansas City Star Books
1729 Grand Blvd.Kansas City, Missouri 64108
All rights reserved.
© 2013 by James J.Heiman

First edition: Second Impression

ISBN-13 Print: 978-0692409282
ISBN-10: 0692409289
Library of Congress Control Number: 2013952626
Printed in the United States.

To order copies, go to www.amazon.com

On the cover: Detail from American Legion I, Budd Park Esplanade, Van Brunt at Anderson, Kansas City, Missouri, Robert Merrell Gage, Sculptor, 1921.

KANSAS CITY STAR BOOKS

"The best who could do the most
        to rebuild *Europe*
                had gone down.
The best that we who were left could do was
        to refuse
        to forget
and
        to teach *our successors what we remembered*
in the hope that they,
              when their own day came,
would have more power
        to change *the state of the world*
than this   *bankrupt,*
                shattered
                generation."

– After Vera Brittain, *Testament of Youth,* 1933

Otto P. Higgins, *The Kansas City Star* War Correspondent with the 35th, 42nd and 89th Divisions. England, Ireland, France and Germany. Served 6 April 1917 - 8 April 1919.

Sheila Scott, OPH Collection

James J. Heiman

Cpl. Louis I. Drackert
163rd Aviation Repair Depot
Dallas, Texas.
Served 30 Aug. 1918 - 29 Mar. 1919

Sgt. Aloysius M. Drackert,
HQ Company Quartermaster
Repair Shop 303.
Nevers, France.
Served 17 Jan. 1918 - 11 Sept. 1919

Mary Keeven

Dedications

To my grandfather, Cpl. Louis I. Drackert,
his brother, Sgt. Aloysius M. Drackert,
and his brother-in-law, Pvt. George M. Schollmeyer,
and to my War Correspondent mentor,
Otto P. Higgins
–all of whom served
with their buddies in the Great War;

To my son, Jamie,
who visited
the American Legion I Fountain and Lt. Fitzsimons'
Memorial
with his dad;

And to my grandson, Jeremy,
who climbed Liberty Memorial Hill
with his grandfather.

**Pvt. George M. Schollmeyer
Co. E., 354th Infantry,
89th Division.
Wounded in gas attack
7 Oct. 1918,
St. Mihiel Sector.
Served 27 April 1918 -
22 May 1919. Died of
war-related complications
in 1928.**

James J. Heiman

Table of Contents

Acknowledgments

A number of people and institutions have provided valuable assistance to support this study. Ann McFerrin, archivist for Kansas City Parks and Recreation, made available to me her own collection of articles and notes about Kansas City monuments and from the very beginning helped to orient me to their study. From there, the staff of the Missouri Valley Room of the Kansas City, Missouri, Public Library located unique materials pertaining to the "lost monuments." The library's microfilm collection of *The Kansas City Star* newspapers was a primary source for information on the building and dedications of the monuments, as well as for the stories of those whose service is commemorated by them. The Library of Congress photo archive proved to be an invaluable resource for period photographs, and the Midwest Genealogical Library an easily accessible source for newspaper microfilm and biographical information. The dedicated volunteers at the Raytown Historical Society Museum assisted in my efforts to locate the original Richards Flying Field marker and provided a variety of materials to tell its story.

I am indebted to a number of other museum professionals, who provided access to people and resources to support the work. Stacie Petersen, National World War I Museum registrar, patiently located and formatted high quality images of many of the subjects whose stories appear here. Lora Vogt, Educational Director of the National World War I Museum, and Rebecca Schroeder, Curator of Education at the Kansas City Museum, sponsored the first Trolley Tour of Kansas City World War I Monuments. Joining them were 25 intrepid participants who braved a rainy Saturday in October 2012 to take the tour and hear my presentation. The opportunity for a live audience allowed me to explore a way to put my research to practical use.

I am also very indebted to Jonathan Casey, archivist for the National World War I Museum at Liberty Memorial, who originated the idea for the trolley tour, worked to support it, and participated in it. He and senior curator Doran Cart made the unique resources of the archives available to me and were willing to spend time assisting me with their use. Their creative thinking, encyclopedic knowledge of the Great War, extensive knowledge of the archives themselves, and resourceful networking have nourished this research and enriched it immensely.

A number of other colleagues, friends, and family members have encouraged me to write. My daughters, Marla and Katie, and Marla's husband, Brent, proved to be willing audiences. My grandson, Jeremy Lowry, and his dad and my son, Dr. James R. Heiman, toured the monuments with me, found interesting materials in used and rare book stores, and always took the cue to ask me how the project was going. Sara Crump, my co-teacher in the creative writing courses for the George Caleb Bingham Academy of the Arts, and her parents, Dick and Dixie, took an early interest in the work and have been loyal to it throughout. Fellow Vietnam War veteran Michael Brady patiently listened to my latest piece during Thursday morning breakfasts. His wife, retired speech and debate teacher Georgia Brady, and our good friends and colleagues, history teacher Jan Rush and English teacher Kathy Wiley, offered encouragement, advice, and suggestions along the way. Dr. Dan Wright, another colleague and good friend, encouraged me to write in my own voice and, once I had found it, patiently read and commented on the result. Katie Kline, Director of the Greater Kansas City Writing Project at UMKC, and the many colleagues who participated in its annual writing retreats offered me the opportunity to write and receive feedback in a professional and supportive setting.

I am very indebted to Doug Weaver, publisher of Kansas City Star Books, for accepting the book proposal, offering valuable advice about focus and fluidity, and remaining flexible throughout. From the outset, he recognized my passion for the project, guided me through the publication process, en-gaged an expert editor and a talented design artist, and is largely responsible for any success the book might enjoy. Because I depended so much on *The Star*'s war reporting while I was writing, I appreciate being able to publish with *The Star* now. Any shortcomings, omissions, or errors are, however, entirely my own.

Also especially supportive of the work are Sheila Scott, granddaughter of *The Kansas City Star* World War I correspondent, Otto P. Higgins, and members of her extended family. They generously shared access to family history and to their grandfather's records and war memorabilia. To Otto himself and to his wife, Elizabeth, I owe a special debt of gratitude for their friendship and inspiration.

To my wife and fellow English teacher, Dr. Maridella Carter, I owe my greatest thanks. Besides patiently enduring my frenzy for collecting war-related material, she paid for a seat on the trolley tour, read the manuscript of the book, suggested valuable edits and revisions, offered professional advice, toured the battlefields with me and truly believed that the project, its author, and the war-related material were worth tolerating for a while.

Independence, Missouri
June 3, 2013

Introduction:
The Rest of the Hill

Halfway up the steps so steep from Pershing Road to the deck of Liberty Memorial, I became winded.

"Let's rest," I said, motioning to an area where we could sit just in front of the frieze.

A nod from my grandson acknowledged the 47 years between us. He had taken the steps completely in stride – one of the surest signs of intergenerational difference.

The trip down to the dedication wall had been easy enough for both of us, and as I took pictures of the corroding medallions of Pershing, Foch, Beatty, Jacques, and Diaz, I chatted away about the five commanders who, early in November 1921, had met together for the first time to dedicate the site in Kansas City.

Now, trying to catch my breath, I had little to say.

That was not the case for my grandson, who, with just a few more words, took my breath completely away.

"Why are you glorifying war?" he asked.

He had me there. Before coming to the Liberty Memorial, we had recited the inscriptions on the Rosedale Arch and the Soldiers and Sailors Memorial Hall in Kansas City, Kansas; together the inscriptions were steeped enough in glory, and now the grander scale of Liberty Memorial had heaped the

mountain of glory even higher, making a good answer that much more difficult.

I couldn't afford my usual long-windedness, and by that point in our monumental tour, I could sense that his youthful patience was wearing thin. But the question so direct and fundamental to my purpose deserved an answer, however inadequate.

"It's not so much about the war," I gasped, "as it is about the human spirit. At the point between life and death."

I was breathing harder now. "People do extraordinary things. Say extraordinary things."

"Do you have to have a war for that?" he countered.

"No. Just a test of character. What you do for family, a buddy. What you do when you share hardship."

"Why not just do it instead of making such a big deal about it?" he concluded.

"I think it's because we're so surprised, so hurt, so confused about the senselessness of what happens. We just don't know what else to do but tell the story."

I was getting my breath back now.

"Why not just let it go? You have to do that anyway."

"This is a way we let it go." I gestured up to the frieze and the tower. "Where we can go on without feeling guilty about going on. Where we can go on and still be reminded that life is more than ordinary."

We talked about two of his friends, older men my age with whom he had worked side by side, whose expertise he had grown to appreciate, and who now had experienced trauma. One was in the hospital, recovering slowly. He was positive, hopeful, acknowledging the pain but appreciating the chance to heal. The other was similarly confined and had a chance to reflect about how his life would be different. Both had shared their stories with my grandson. He honored them.

"And now I think I can go on," I said, breath enough restored.

"Yes," he said. "Let's go on."

Together we made up time and the rest of the hill.

Independence, Missouri
July 25, 2012

Maridella Carter

Jeremy (right) and his grandpa resting on the steps in front of the frieze at Liberty Memorial.

Putting this Book to Use

This book was developed to serve a variety of purposes and audiences. By following the Table of Contents, a general reader can pursue the story of how Kansas City remembered its 440 men and one woman who died in the Great War. Beginning with two Kansas City memorials that list the dead, and continuing with the story of the exhumation of bodies from French cemeteries for reburial in Kansas City, the reader then arrives at the dedication of the Liberty Memorial, the most visible and comprehensive World War I monument and museum in Kansas City, the nation, and perhaps even, the world. From there, the reader is introduced to the roles played by those whose lives were profoundly affected by the Great War: the nurses and doctors in the base hospitals; the women at home; and the men and women abroad in hospital, Naval, aviation, infantry, engineer, artillery, field signal, and ammunition train units.

To establish a context for 19 of the most prominent Kansas City World War I memorials, the book focuses especially on the international and national commemorations of Unknown Soldiers in 1921, at the same time that the newly formed American Legion held its national convention in Kansas City and the commanders of the five Allied nations appeared together for the first and only time in history. It was during the convention that the first three Kansas City Great War memorials were dedicated: Liberty Memorial, American Legion I Fountain, and American Legion II Fountain. From the lists of war dead, the first American Legion Posts in Kansas City adopted names for their posts. Those names appear on the American Legion I Monument dedicated during the 1921 American Legion Convention. The stories of those 12 men and the units in which they served form the core of this book of war remembrance.

Besides reading the book as a history of Kansas City's remembrance of the Great War, a reader can also use the book as a resource guide tied directly to visits to the memorials themselves. To that end, the stories can stand on their own and be read independently of one another. In the section of the book entitled "Monumental Conversations," the "related readings" help the reader identify those stories directly related to the featured monument, and the reader can pursue one or more of the stories before or after visiting the monuments themselves. "Monumental Conversations" also organizes the monuments into groups of five tours by proximity and/or theme. Each tour identifies and describes the featured monuments and gives their locations. A map and a legend serve as guides to the tours.

Also provided for each monument are discussion questions inviting the participation of young people at the elementary (grades 4-5), middle school (grades 6-8), and high school (grades 9-12) levels. The questions are aligned to the new "Common Core Standards." Adults – parents, youth group leaders, teachers, or anyone else interested in war memorials or in Kansas City's participation in the War – can use the questions to stimulate observation, interpretation, and reflection.

Finally, the book can be read as an inquiry into why Kansas City remembers the Great War and continues to struggle for peace. Located in the heart of the nation, Kansas City is the center of a unique history of war and peace. The Kansas-Nebraska Act of 1854 managed to recreate in local physical and geographic terms the national political extremes that tested the very concept of American freedom, equality, and justice. Consequently, by some accounts, more battles were fought along the Kansas-Missouri border than anywhere else in the country, and the scars of Civil War still linger here.

So it is not surprising that this region gave birth not only to commanding generals of the First and Second World Wars, but also to two American Presidents who served during and immediately after those wars to bring the country and the world back to peace after the use of what was considered at the time to be weapons of mass destruction. Nor is it surprising that the consciousness of war continues in our midst, even as we – a portal of trails to American dreams – look in a different direction with hope to the Southwest, the West, and the Northwest, to Santa Fe, California, and Oregon.

In all, 38 reading selections provide a detailed account of how Kansas City remembers the ideals and sacrifices of its own very best hopes – the World War I dead honored in 19 different memorials scattered throughout the city.

Sources for the reading selections include division and regimental histories, contemporary accounts by eyewitnesses, and most especially, contemporary newspaper articles describing the dedications of the memorials themselves and the stories of the men and women whose lives are commemorated in the memorials.

Although the reading selections contain a good deal of military and social history, they are not intended as an historical study of the war. Nor is the list of Kansas City war memorials exhaustive. The list does not, for example, contain the many plaques commemorating the World War I military service of members of civic and professional organizations, or the war commemoration tablets erected in the vestibules of churches or other semi-public buildings.

The selections that are here reflect, perhaps, the most visible aspect of Kansas City's remembrance of the Great War and the stories of some of the men and women whose lives were most affected by it.

Most of all, the book is meant to serve the next generation in the hope that retelling the story in personal terms and in a familiar and concrete setting might enable the young to learn to live long enough without war to hand the story of it on to the generation that follows them.

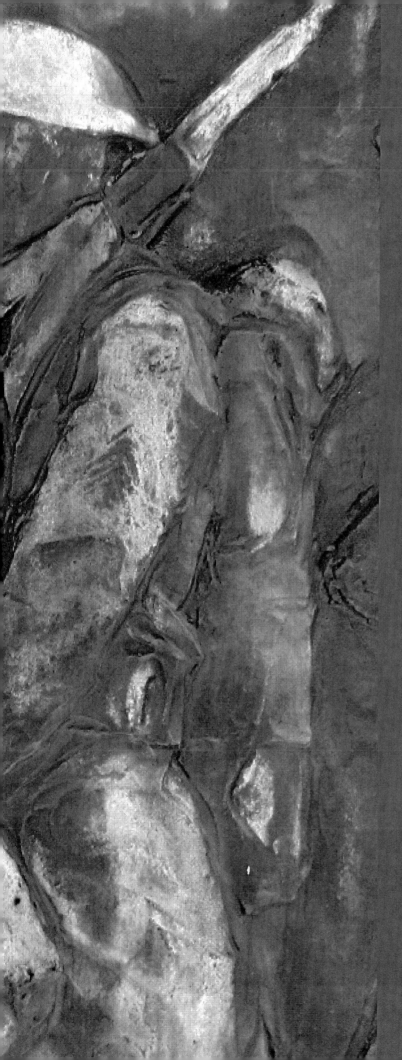

"Lafayette, we are here!"

—Col. Charles E. Stanton with General John J. Pershing at the tomb of Lafayette, Paris, France, July 4, 1917

Detail from American Legion Fountain II, West Entance, Swope Park, Kansas City, Missouri, Robert Merrell Gage, Sculptor, with the assistance of architects Wilson & Crans and G. B. Franklin, 1921

Photo courtesy of National World War I Museum Archives.

Armstead E. Swearingen.

"The hearts of those at home were torn by strong emotions rivaling even the crushing knowledge of their own losses. 'Shall I bring my boy home? Or, shall I leave him where he has sacrificed?'"

—*Armstead E. Swearingen.*

In Memory:
"We Are the Dead"

"Shall I Bring My Boy Home?"

Armstead Swearingen faced a dilemma no parent should ever have to face. Both of his sons, Ernest and Hewitt, served in World War I. Ernest returned; Hewitt did not. "From the hour of the first casualty reports bringing the message that our boys were dying in the trenches and on the battle line," Mr. Swearingen wrote, "the hearts of those at home were torn by strong emotions rivaling even the crushing knowledge of their own losses. 'Shall I bring my boy home? Or, shall I leave him where he has sacrificed?'"[1]

Swearingen noted that many shared the sentiment of Theodore Roosevelt, who preferred that his son Quentin, who died when his plane was shot down in France, remain where he had fallen. "Where the tree falls, there let it lie," the ex-President said.[2] Swearingen also noted, however, that 60 percent of those next of kin who had lost family or friends were afraid that Europe would be torn up again by war and that the graves of their loved ones possibly desecrated or even completely obliterated by further strife. These bereaved wanted to bring their boys home. At home, families and friends could watch over their graves, and the boys would be surrounded by the scenes of their boyhood.

However, for as much as the American State Department pressed the French government to permit disinterment from that area where most of the battles had been fought, now called the "Zone of the Armies," the French were either unable or reluctant to do so – at least for the present.

"The transportation facilities of France have suffered terribly during the war and even yet remain practically non-existent in the devastated areas," Secretary of War Newton D. Baker's private secretary, Ralph Hayes, explained to Mr. Swearingen.[3] "The spirit of the French population so fearfully tried by the years of warfare on French soil was strained almost to the breaking point and is now beginning to pass through the first stages of reconstruction and rehabilitation. The French government feels that the disinterment of these millions of bodies and the vast funeral processions that would start across France to the Western ports would have a very grave effect upon the morale of the people, who since 1914 have borne such a heavy burden."

Writing from Coblenz, Germany, on April 30, 1919, *Chicago Daily News* syndicated correspondent Junius B. Wood reported that the first large American cemetery in France had been laid out at St. Mihiel, a few kilometers north of Thiaucourt. It had a capacity for 4,000 graves and received Americans who had fallen east of Verdun. Just east of Romagne-sous-Mont Faucon was the largest American national cemetery with a capacity of 25,000 to 30,000. Room for 1,000 additional American graves was made available at a third cemetery in France, Beaumont, near Sedan. Romagne and Beaumont became the sites for the large number of American fatalities suffered in the Battle of the Meuse-Argonne.[4] In all, approximately 50,000 American soldiers had died in the war.[5] "Adding statistics on other casualties, roughly 50 per cent of the men who served were captured, wounded or killed."[6]

Most of the American dead in the French cemeteries were re-burials from the battlefield. The process of their disinterment from where they had died was a grim task that fell to thousands of African-American soldiers. Junius Wood continued: "Thousands of negro soldiers are now digging up the dead from the scattered graves, wrapping them in burlap, placing them in rough wooden coffins, loading them in trucks and bringing them to these cemeteries. On an average 250 bodies are reburied each day. All of the battle front has been carefully scoured and probably not a single American now remains unburied."[7]

After reburial from the battlefields, American dead remained in the French cemeteries, despite the efforts of the U.S. Department of War and the Department of State to permit their removal. It wasn't until June of 1920 that the American war dead were disinterred once again and began coming home.[8] When they finally did arrive in the United States, their return had a "grave effect" upon the morale of the American people, just as their movement to the French ports affected the French people. From ports along the Atlantic Coast, long funeral trains stretched across the eastern United States to St. Louis and Omaha, the

KEEP THE HOME FIRES BURNING

HELP

KANSAS CITYS

flag-draped caskets of soldiers visible whenever the freight cars opened, finally returning the boys to the cities and towns from which they had come.

In Kansas City, the Gold Star League of Jackson County, Missouri, was formed in March 1920 to facilitate the return of the dead. President of the League was William B. Davis, who, like Armstead Swearingen, gave two sons to the war. One of those sons, Maj. Murray Davis, did not return. W. B. Davis appointed Swearingen Chairman of the Committee on Service, and he and his committee met the trains arriving at Union Station. The Committee made funeral arrangements, being careful to provide full military honors. In some cases, the Committee was the only reception the boys received. "In instances where there were 'no relatives' reported," Swearingen observed, "did the Gold Star League find its fullest expression of service in paying honor to a friendless soldier."

Throughout the city, flags flew at half-mast as multiple processions of dead crept through the streets to Forest Hill, Mount St. Mary's, Mt. Washington, and Elmwood. Police furnished motorcycle escorts; funeral homes resumed Sunday burials. "Members of the League with cars," Swearingen recalled, "put them at the service of the organization for almost daily use: to take parents to the station to meet a son, or to drive to some family in the suburbs; to deliver Gold Star wreaths in the County, as was done on sufficient notice."[9]

Throughout the war, as men died in the training camps and their bodies were returned home, military honors were discharged by the Home Guards, later the 7th Regiment, or the Veterans of Foreign Wars. Spanish-American veterans also volunteered to perform taps and to render the rifle salute. But now that the war was over and the bodies of the dead were streaming back home in significant numbers, these organizations struggled to keep pace with the number of funerals needed each day. At that point, the Kansas City American Legion, which was newly formed in 1919, stepped up. The dead would be honored by the comrades who had served with them.

The Posts themselves had taken on the names of the Kansas City dead, sometimes hyphenated to remember two men: Joseph Dillon, Murray Davis, Robert T. Clements, William J. Bland, Hedrick-Shackleton, Wayne Miner, William T. Fitzsimons, James Cummings, Arthur Maloney, Hewitt J. Swearingen, Joseph Liebman, Montgall-Richards, and Sanford M. Brown.[10]

The first man returned to Kansas City from a French grave was William Sudduth, son of Lee Sudduth, 6613 East 13th Street.[11] William was killed in action on October 13, 1918, in Brest, France,[12] and a year and a half later on June 12, 1920, was finally brought home to rest in Mount Washington. More than 67 reburials followed in Kansas City. Among those was Armstead Swearingen's son, Hewitt, a private with the 117th Ammunition Train, who was killed on the night of July 1, 1918, after helping deliver ammunition to the front. Hewitt's father, Armstead Swearingen, had finally resolved the dilemma of whether to bring his boy's body home from the grave that had been dug for him and his three companions the day after they were killed. Hewitt Swearingen was reburied at Mount Washington Cemetery in Kansas City.

Of the 21 African-American soldiers from Kansas City who lost their lives in the war, only one, Clifton Waller, was returned for final interment in Kansas City.[13]

A total of 58 of the 1,419 men lost in the 89th Division were from Kansas City.[14] Approximately 100 of the 960 men lost in the 35th Division called Jackson County home. Eight Kansas City boys were killed on the very last day of the war. In all, the plaques on the Meyer Circle Gateway at Meyer Circle and Ward Parkway and on the west wall in Memory Hall of the Liberty Memorial record the names of 441 Kansas City dead from all branches of the service.

Some lie in Kansas City, some in outlying areas of Kansas and Missouri. Some lie in France; a few lie in Arlington. All had made the supreme sacrifice.

Starting on the next page is the list of Kansas City's 441 World War 1 dead.

ARMY OFFICERS   N=48

Major William John Bland
Major Murray Davis
Major Mark Hanna
Capt. Sanford M. Brown, Jr.
Capt. William T. Fitzsimons
Capt. Arly Luther Hedrick
Capt. E. Burton Hocker
Capt. Rolla Berry Holt
Capt. Rufus Ford Montgall
Capt. Philip V. Sherman
Capt. Fielding M. Wilhite
Capt. Stanley Willis Wood

Lt. Lloyd O. Beaton
Lt. Fayette E. Blachert
Lt. William Ewing Boone
Lt. Wilfrid C. Bourke
Lt. William O. Briggs
Lt. Drury Albert Brink
Lt. Jefferson U. Brumback
Lt. Otto Carlson
Lt. Alan Campbell Clark
Lt. Joseph C. Conway
Lt. Carl C. Cramer
Lt. John M. Darrough

Lt. Georg H. Edwards, Jr.
Lt. Richard J. Fuller
Lt. Clark B. Hannah
Lt. Amos D. Johnson
Lt. Roscoe W. Kingrey
Lt. Homer M. Lee
Lt. Arthur T. McAllister
Lt. James MacKenzie
Lt. Guy E. Morse
Lt. Oscar G. Ressel
Lt. John F. Richards, II
Lt. Elmer O. Rugh

Lt. Joseph W. Sanborn, Jr.
Lt. William E. Scott
Lt. James J. Sexton
Lt. John K. Sloan
Lt. Frank L. Stauver
Lt. James J. Swofford, Jr.
Lt. Guy Austin Tull
Lt. William F. Ward
Lt. Marion L. Willis
Lt. John R. Wingate
Lt. Charles P. Woodbury
Lt. Arch Dixon Worsham

CANDIDATE OFFICERS   N=4

Robert B. Carson

Allan J. Hughes

William T. Law

Grover Metzger

NONCOMMISSIONED OFFICERS   N=80

Sgt.Major Roswell B. Sayre
Sgt. Fred H. Ainsworth
Sgt. William D. Bateman
Sgt. Francis A. Burton
Sgt. Melville G. Bussey
Sgt. Joseph C. Carson
Sgt. Harry O. E. Christ
Sgt. Joseph Dillon
Sgt. James W. Donaldson
Sgt. Clarence C. Dry
Sgt. Carl C. Holland
Sgt. Robert P. Hopkins
Sgt. George L. Huff
Sgt. Axel W. Johnson
Sgt. Leo P. Keenan
Sgt. Eudell M. Lusher
Sgt. John Joseph Lynch
Sgt. Harry D. Magness
Sgt. Harry C. Monday
Sgt. Clinton E. Moss

Sgt. Almo E. O'Kell
Sgt. Arthur S. Olsen
Sgt. Fred Ridley
Sgt. William A. Sauer
Sgt. William M. Seiler
Sgt. Fred J. Shackleton
Sgt. Drury R. Sherrod
Sgt. Eddie S. Smith
Sgt. Ralph P. Tanner
Sgt. Chester A. Waltman
Sgt. Harold E. Weber
Sgt. Everettt A. Weeks
Sgt. James W. West
Sgt. Elmer E. Wickline
Cpl. Lloyd L. Adams
Cpl. Arthur B. Baughman
Cpl. David E. Blackburn
Cpl. Tracy S. Blair
Cpl. Fred D. Byard
Cpl. Stuart Carkener, II

Cpl. Clyde C. Chilson
Cpl. Diller O. Clouse
Cpl. Lanier Cravens
Cpl. Frank W. Dabney, Jr.
Cpl. Paul Dancy
Cpl. Earl J. Douglas
Cpl. Robert E. Fitzmaurice
Cpl. Edgar Fuqua
Cpl. Francis W. Greene
Cpl. Rufus S. Greene
Cpl. George W. Halin
Cpl. Virgil L. Hammontree
Cpl. Jack Harris
Cpl. Thomas Grover Hay
Cpl. Leonard N. Holbert
Cpl. Harry Ward Hunter
Cpl. Claude C. Jackson
Cpl. Otis I. Jones
Cpl. Ralph Blondon Kyle
Cpl. Merle T. Lewelling

Cpl. Fred C. Lott
Cpl. Burl McClure
Cpl. Lee. L. McGee
Cpl. Daniel P. McGrath
Cpl. Arthur P. Mahaney
Cpl. Charles Manfre
Cpl. Starr S. Merrill
Cpl. Clarendon I. Miller
Cpl. Dorsey E. Mitchell
Cpl. Claude D. Moreland
Cpl. Samuel P. Nickells
Cpl. Walter L. Pelter
Cpl. Scott W. Richards
Cpl. Dudley W. Sawyer
Cpl. William L. Scott
Cpl. William C. Setliff
Cpl. David Ray Staley
Cpl. Harrison A. Tinker
Cpl. James I. Tucker
Cpl. Earl L. Wiseman

ENLISTED MEN   N=252

Paul Dean Adamson
Thomas Agar
Charles E. Ainsworth
Frederick D. Allen
Guy W. Allen
Arthur Anthony

Byron E. Ashbrook
Raymond M. Ashurst
Thomas Atkins
George Aumann
David Donald Baker
William C. Balke

A.C. Barkhurst
John T. Barnby
Louis L. Barnett
John F. Bascom
Richard Dodd Beck
Morris A. Blacker

Frank Blackwell
Charles Blair
George J. Blanchard
Rector Guy Boyce
Luther M. Boyd
George W. Boyle

Alfred S. Brabant

Edwin T. Brandell

Vawter W. Bratton

Frank M. Broaddus

Lewis F. Brotherton

Warren A. Brown

Walter O. Brueckmann

Harry M. Brummer

Cortez M. Campbell

Eugene O. Campbell

Fred C. Campbell, Jr.

Fred Campo

J. Cantrell

August L. Carlson

William Emmett Carry

Edgar C. Cary

James Henry Caylor

Neely O. Chaquette

George B. Cheshire

Virgil Omar Clark

Claude E. Clement

Robert T. Clemments

Baker B. Cleveland

Bernard E. Cole

Harry Russell Cole

Asa L. Collins

G. W. Collins

Francis Lester Conboy

Joseph L. Connelly

Harry Connors

Edgar B. Cook

Walter W. Cowgill

Fred Cox

Robert B. Craig

Roger K. Cramer

Albert R. Creasey

Everettt A. Crenshaw

Ernest Crowder

Milton R. Cummins

Raymond Currier

Charles V. Curtis

Harry J. Dabner

Glenn W. Davis

Henry Davis

A. Delephine

Arthur W. DeWald

Samuel DeWitt

Leroy Dickerson

Ernest Dinsmore

Louis J. Dolbow

Frank H. Donaldson

Peter Dover

James H. Downing

Bertie L. Dubuque

Jean Louis Ducret

Hugh L. Dumas

Arthur D. Fellman

Joseph Frankowski

Earl P. Freyermuth

John Eugene Friel

Lawrence W. Fulton

Edward Joseph Garin

James T. Garvin

George E. Gerber

George Benjamin Gohl

James D. Goodwin

Palmer Gordon

Joseph A. Graham

Lloyd Chester Green

Fred H. Griffin

Thomas M. Griffiths

Walter John Gruer

Antone G. Hake

Lawrence A. Handel

Paul Hansen

Petros D. Hantzon

William H. Harrah

Cleo Heavener

Anthony Henkel

Alexander P. Henritze

William H. Hensley

James A. Holden

Gustaf E. Holmstrom

Anthony J. Holterman

William S. Hopper

Roland R. Hosterman

Benjamin M. Howard

T.A. Howell, Jr.

John Henry Huff

Benjamin H. Hutsell

Claude Isom

Arthur J. Jackson

Charles W. Jackson, Jr.

Gustave Janzen

Arthur L. Johnson

Ben Johnson

Michael Karratt

Roland R. Karstetter

Henry H. Kasha

Harry H. Keiser

James Kelley

Harry F. Kennedy

Thomas J. Kiely

Lloyd Kingery

Joseph F. Kinney

William E. Kirtley

Henry M. Kopp

Abraham Kotelov

Walter R. Kren

George A. Krumrak

William Harry Langan

Flavel E. Law

Ray Layman

William A. Leach

John L. Leahy

Jacob W. Leavitt

Herbert Lee

Isadore H. Levin

Verne D. Lewellen

Joseph Liebman

Charles Lindsay

Samuel G. Lindsey

John Linton

James W. Littlefield

Jorgen P. Lock

John C. Lowder

James A. M'Anally

G. MacMahon

Thomas McArthur

Cornelius B. McCabe

Jay W. McCammon, Jr.

Charles Holmes McCoun

Ralph A. McCurry

John McGuire

Joseph E. McVey

Joseph A. Mack

Addison D. Madeira, III

Edwin W. Mall

James A. Maloney

Burley Manuel

Jacob Martin

Albert Maxwell

Robert G. Meador

Guy Ora Meily

Lee Mettler

David Miller

Dewey Miller

Harry N. Miller

Leonard R. Miller

Thomas H. Miller

Wayne Miner

George E. Monehan

James W. Morrow

Lynn M. Murray

Ernest H. Neeley

James H. Noble

Stephen R. O'Bannon

Charles E. Olson

Ray McKay Oliver

John F. O'Rourke

Frederick G. Parke

Milton Payne

Herbert P. Payson

Adelbert Penney

Paul E. Peters

Victor E. Peterson

Cyrus E. Phillips

Jesse N. Phillips

Harry A. Pierce

Glen A. Pinkerman

Bennis Powers

Frederick O. Rees

William J. Rogerson

Raymond J. Rolls

Carl C. Schmidt

Alonzo V. Scott

Charles Walter Scott

Paul Duke Scott

Fred H. Seaman

William A. Seevers

George M. Shaw

William C. Shields

Otto W. Shiffert

George L. Shiffler

William A. Short
Frank Shrontz
Charles P. Sievers
Robert M. Simpson
David L. Smith
Arthur L. Sprague
Harry B. Stein
Rowland H. Stevenson
Albert J. Stoenner
George A. Stokes
William Sudduth

Hewitt J. Swearingen
Mayo E. Taggart
Bert K. Talbot
Fred N. Tennis
Charlie Thomas
Morris H. Thomas
Thomas Harold Thompson
Forest A. Tillery
Alfred C. Toense
Jules J. Truss
Jasper Turman

Clinton H. Underwood
Walter J. Van Briggle
Carld B. Vance
John Wade
David F. Walker
Clifton Waller
William H. Warren
Earl Webb
Jacob A. Weis
Louis James Welsh
Robert Welsham

Rogers C. West
Jack A. White
Meredith H. White
Travis B. White
George Widlansky
Russell A. Wilson
Burley Woodward
James R. Woodworth
Floyd M. Worley
Chandler Porter Wright
James M. Wright

MARINE CORPS N=1

Lieut. Palmer Ketner, Jr.

ENLISTED MEN - MARINE CORPS N=16

William Eugene Bush
John J. Bush
Renick H. Carson
Robert H. Cowdrey, Jr

Cyrus Thurston Dorr
Frank J. Ehrenhoffer
Harry Hoggatt
Leslie Frank Jones

D.J. O'Connell
Robert B. Peebles, Jr.
James Young Simpson, Jr
Henry Clayton Smalley

Edward G. Warren
Edward Henry Wells
Henry Clayton Smalley
Edward G. Warren

NAVY N=1

Lieut. Benjamin J. Worrall

ENLISTED MEN - NAVY N=38

Edward C. Armstrong
Thomas William Brew
James M. Burbridge
Vernon Butts
Richard B. Campbell
William A. Comfort
Mearl Ralph Cox
James Cummings
James G. Daniels
Clinton Dunn

Oscar Lloyd Evans
William Harry Fort
Dale A. Geoghegan
Bernard Vance Giffin
John T. J. Gillespie
William F. Gove
Joseph W. Hopkins
Edward J. Hughes
John Braden Kerr
William Port Leach

George McFarlane
Thomas M. McGrath, Jr.
Earl W. Malone
Clinton H. Mettlestadt
Charles H. Milburn
Earle Myers
Oscar Duval Oakley
Leslie Pfaff
Lawrence H. Price
Thomas Reed

David John Ritchie
Leo M. Schaaf
Benjamin F. Thompson
Gilbert B. Thompson, Jr.
Cornelius O. Torjuson
Elmer Felix Trueke
Francis Joseph Werner
Otto Wolf

NURSE N=1

Loretto Hollenback

M-1 **Memory Hall—Liberty Memorial**
100 West 26th Street, Kansas City, Missouri

Tinted by the first rays of sun in the morning, these stones will take up the light of a full day. Then turning gray in the dusk that follows, the glories of sunset will stand a silent guard through the night, the million stars overhead solemn reminders of the glory of the gold stars that hang in Memory Hall."[15] So did Kansas City Mayor Albert Beach reference Memory Hall to the 150,000 people gathered for the dedication of Liberty Memorial on a cold November 11, 1926.

Memory Hall, Liberty Memorial.

Photo by James J. Heiman

President Calvin Coolidge also reminded the audience of the obligation to those whose memory is enshrined here. "Those dead whose sacrifices we are commemorating have placed their trust in us," the President said. "Their living comrades have made their sacrifice in the belief we would not fail. In the consciousness of that trust and belief, this Memorial stands as our pledge to their faith, a holy statement that our country will continue to do its duty under the guidance of Divine Providence."

In affirmation, "We are the Dead" proclaim in unison the columns of names listed on bronze tablets on the west wall inside Memory Hall. In all, 440 men and one woman – the very last name – are listed in nine groups: "Army Officers, Candidate Officers, Non-commissioned Officers, Enlisted Men, Marine Corps, Enlisted Men-Marine Corps, Navy, Enlisted Men-Navy and Nurse."[16]

Photo courtesy of National World War I Museum.
Mural by Daniel MacMorris on the south wall of Memory Hall.

M-2 Meyer Circle Gateway Avenue of Trees
Meyer Boulevard and Ward Parkway, Kansas City, Missouri

The Gateway at Meyer Circle looking south is made up of four bronze tablets mounted on natural stone walls. The names of all 440 Kansas City men and one woman are inscribed on the tablets in double columns.

The dedication on the 2nd tablet reads: "Placed by the K.C. Chapter Daughters of the American Revolution and the K.C. Chapter Sons of the Revolution, Armistice Day 1930."

A dedication band also appears on the flagpole: "Kansas City Chapter Daughters of the American Revolution to honor K.C. heroes, the World War 1914-1918, Dedicated Armistice Day, 1940."

At 2:00 p.m. on the Indian summer afternoon of Armistice Day, November 11, 1930, nearly 1,000 people gathered in the grassy area between the north and south-bound lanes of Ward Parkway immediately across from Meyer Circle. Protecting them on both sides of the road and stretching out for nearly a mile south to 76th Street, 441 newly planted elm trees raised their bare branches in two columns, single file on either side. Each tree represented one of the men and the single woman whose names were inscribed on bronze tablets, but the trees would be dedicated to more than the valorous spirits of those who had lost their lives.

"The World War was not won by material forces," Dr. G. Charles Gray, wartime chaplain of the 89th Division, told the gathering that day. "America's balance of power was not the power of munitions nor of the numerical force of men. We won the war with spirit, the spirit of the soldier," he said. "We dedicate these trees not to individual records of valor. We dedicate them to the spirit of American youth."[17] Both soldiers and youth testified to those spirits on the 12th anniversary of the Armistice.

Colonel Edward. M. Stayton represented the soldiers. He echoed Chaplain Gray's dedication when he referred to the spirit of the soldiers, who, at 9:30 that morning, had marched from 9th and Grand Avenue south to 27th Street and west to Liberty Memorial. The men were, he said, "a parade of fighters to testify to America's well-being". Twelve years earlier at noon on September 29, 1918, Colonel Stayton had formed the line of his 110th Engineers to protect the mangled and scattered units of the 35th Division as they struggled back from their advance in the Meuse-Argonne.

Now throughout the dedication ceremony, veterans from that same line of Engineers stood at attention in their new dress blues until representatives of the spirit of Ameri-

Photo by James J. Heiman

Meyer Circle Gateway eagle.

can youth could play their part. Eagle Scouts and a group of girls from the Betsy Hall chapter of the Children of the American Revolution pulled the veils from the bronze tablets of Kansas City's service dead. Then, roaring in the skies above the trees that represented the spirit of those American youth, two airplanes dropped poppies that floated to the ground below.

Ten years later, on Monday, November 11, 1940, another group of people, much smaller than the previous gathering, came together at the same spot. The mood was very different, and the weather very cold. The clouds of war gathered as the 200 people stood in an icy wind to dedicate a flagpole to Kansas City's war dead. In a little more than a year, America, too, would once again be at war[18].

The day before, the 22nd anniversary of the Armistice, Dr. Edward Bishop, pastor of the Broadway Methodist Church, reminded his congregation why America would have to go back to war. Besides the spirit of the soldiers that had brought victory, another spirit had attended the Armistice of 1918. "Hate of the bitterest kind was evident at the treaty table," he said. "It was the hate that blinded diplomacy to the best interests to be served by the treaty. There was no armistice for revenge at the council table," and "the spirit of revenge" was allowed to dictate the terms of the treaty, he concluded[19].

Two soldiers who had fought for the Armistice and spoken at the 1930 dedication spoke again. Edward. M. Stayton of the 110th Engineers, now a Major General, joined Dr. G. Charles Gray, now the pastor of Westminster Congregational Church. He urged those

Photo by James J. Heiman

Meyer Circle Gateway, looking south.

in attendance to rededicate themselves to the principles of freedom, equality, and fraternity. Chair of the Memorial Trees Committee, Miss Lucy Stowe Bigelow, presented the memorial, and Park Board president John A. Moore accepted.

Young people were there, as well. Boy Scouts from Troop 34 raised the flag 62 feet to the top of the pole while the Southwest High School band played the national anthem. No planes flew overhead and no poppies were dropped on the trees – only the flag cracked and snapped in the cold wind as the same generation of American youth whose spirit had been recognized in the earlier dedication prepared for yet another war.

Inscription on flag-pole at Meyer Circle Gateway.

Endnotes

1 Armstead E. Swearingen, *World War Soldier Dead Memorial: Annals of Kansas City, Missouri.* Vol. II, No. 1. Kansas City: Missouri Valley Historical Society, 1926, p. 53.

3 Ibid. p. 54.

4 Junius B. Wood, "The Dead Rest at Last," The Kansas City *Times*, May 2, 1919, p. 13.

5 H. P. Wilmot, *World War I.* New York: DK Publishing, 2007, p. 307.

6 Jay Winter and Blaine Baggett. **The Great War and the Shaping of the 20th Century.** New York: The Penguin Group. 1996, p. 362.

7 Wood, p. 13.

8 Lisa Budreau refers to three chronological stages in the development of American identity as a world power after the war, "repatriation, remembrance, and return." Budreau defines "repatriation" as "the process of democratic choice regarding the disposition of remains." Lisa M. Budreau, *Bodies of War.* (New York: New York University Press, 2010), pp. 4-5. Her book offers a very important and thorough investigation of the politics of commemoration. As the country tried to make sense of a controversial war, a fresh vocabulary for mediating grief attempted to transform grief into glory. What emerges, she says, is a new myth of the war experience and a new identity for America in an "era of discontinuity" that continues to this day.

9 Swearingen, p. 55.

10 Ibid. p. 56.

11 Ibid.

12 Ibid. p. 29, p. 57.

13 Ibid. p. 89.

14 Ibid. p. 91.

15 "Throng of 150,000." *The Kansas City Star.* November 11, 1926, p. A1.

16 "Kansas City War Dead." National World War I Museum at Liberty Memorial. http://www.theworldwar.org/s/110/new/index. aspx?pgid=1108 accessed January 7, 2012. Also see Donovan, Derek. *Lest the Ages Forget: Kansas City's Liberty Memorial.* Kansas City, MO: Kansas City Star Books, 2001, pp. 96-97.

17 "Dedicate the 441 Trees." *The Kansas City Times.* November 12, 1930, p. 13. Also see "At the Dedication of the Avenue of Memorial Trees" pictures in *The Kansas City Times.* November 12, 1930, p. 13, and "The Gateway to the Avenue of Trees Which Will be Dedicated Today as a Monument to the War Dead," picture in *The Kansas City Times.* November 11, 1930, p. 5.

18 "Dedicate a Flagpole." *The Kansas City Times.* November 12, 1940, p. 3.

19 "Hate in the Armistice." *The Kansas City Times.* November 11, 1940, p. 6.

CHAPTER 1

"We Died Saving Lives"

Lt. W. T. Fitzsimons: "That the Americans Might Not Forget. . ." (William T. Fitzsimons American Legion Post No. 8)

From the very outset of its entry into the war, America was not prepared for the fight. Kansas City Dr. William T. Fitzsimons, however, was prepared. He had already served a tour in Europe, had returned to Kansas City, and, when America entered the war, was ready to return to the battle zone once more. Lt. Fitzsimons was the first American officer to die in the war, and his name became a rallying cry to prepare America for the fight and, after the fight was over, to serve as the name of one of the very first American Legion posts in Kansas City.

By early September 1917, hundreds of men began pouring into the 16 cantonments, or training camps, scattered throughout the country. At Camp Funston on the Fort Riley, Kansas, military reservation, the first draft quota of traveling salesmen, clerks, foremen, real estate men, insurance men, mechanics, and laborers stood in line to be screened for contagious diseases and have their names checked off the quota lists. After bathing, they were issued what clothing the quartermaster had in stock and were allowed to become familiar with their barracks. But the camp was not quite ready for them. *Kansas City Star* war correspondent Otto P. Higgins relayed a message from camp authorities: "All who come here should be sure and bring plenty of towels and soap."[1]

The next day, OPH reported that "even the overalls have run out now, and many of the national army men are drilling in their civilian clothing. They are given underclothing, shoes, socks, hats, and hat cords. More overalls may be here by tomorrow morning, and the breeches and shirts are expected in a day or two. They are being shipped by ex-

press in carload lots."[2] Men shivered without blankets, he reported,[3] and later, as the men began drilling, he observed that they had to use wooden replicas of rifles because real rifles were not available[4]. Camp construction continued around them. Five months after Congress had declared war on Germany, the country was still not prepared for the fight.

Such was not the case for William T. Fitzsimons, a 28-year-old doctor from Kansas City, who, by the same time in early September 1917, had already spent 14 months ministering to the war-wounded in Europe. Born in Burlington, Kansas, on April 18, 1889, Fitzsimons attended the Jesuit-sponsored St. Mary's College in St. Mary's, Kansas,[5] and transferred to the University of Kansas in 1908. In 1910 he earned a bachelor's degree, and two years later, a medical degree from the University of Kansas. Following graduation he spent a year at St. Mary's Hospital in Kansas City, and in June 1913, went to New York to work for 14 months as a surgery intern at Roosevelt Hospital[6]. On September 13, 1914, shortly after the war in Europe began, he departed for England as a

Red Cross volunteer, serving six months at a hospital in South Devon under the direction of Sir William Osler, and then, going where the need was greatest, served seven months in Belgium. He returned to the United States on December 10, 1915.

In a summary of Fitzsimons' work written for the University of Kansas *Graduate Magazine*, Associate Dean of the School of Medicine, Dr. Mervin T. Suddler, noted that "in general, he described his experiences abroad as largely hard work, a great deal of it routine in character, which he was glad to do, and yet the professional knowledge gained had not been in proportion to the amount of energy and time expended."[7]

Photo courtesy of National World War I Museum.
Lt. William T. Fitzsimons.

Still, he was dedicated to the cause. Back in Kansas City, Fitzsimons talked about the war at a noon luncheon of the City Club and many other meetings, showing stereopticon scenes of the field hospitals in France. He established his own offices in suites 810-15 of the Rialto Building and took up the practice of medicine there.[8] He also took charge of surgical work in the outpatient department at Kansas University hospital two mornings a week and assisted with teaching a lecture course there.

But he couldn't get the scenes in the field hospitals out of his mind, so he joined the Medical Reserve Corps, was commissioned on March 27, 1917, and three weeks after the United States had declared war on Germany, resigned from his appointments to enter active duty on April 27, 1917.

The Star reported that Lt. Fitzsimons "left on his second trip to the front June 15 with Lieut. C. A. McGuire," another Kansas City doctor.[9] Both Lt. McGuire and Lt. Fitzsimons were looking forward to meeting a third Kansas City doctor, Dr. Paul Wooley, already in France.

On August 16, shortly after his arrival at the Hotel du Nord, Boulogne-sur-Mer, France, Fitzsimons wrote to his mother, Mrs. Catherine Fitzsimons, 517-A Knickerbocker Place, Kansas City:

Dear Mother:

I suppose you received my cable from Liverpool. We arrived there on August 13, after having been at sea twenty-one days.

We left New York – went direct to Halifax where we laid in the harbor without shore leave for a solid week. We landed in Liverpool, went direct to London and then here.

Doctor McGuire and myself have been stationed here temporarily for a few days and then we do not know just where we will be sent, but probably to a hospital similar to the one I was in Belgium. We are detailed with the British forces for the present.

Doctor Wooley is stationed near here, but have not been able to see him yet.

We had several submarine scares on the way over, but nothing happened.

We expect to be able to see the paymaster in a day or two and we certainly need to as we have received no pay since July 1.

Continue to send my mail in care of the American Express, Paris, and as soon as I know where I am to be stationed definitely I will send for it.

Suppose I will get news from you when I receive some of my mail.

Best regards to all of my friends and love to you and the kids.

Your loving son,
Will[10]

On August 27, he joined the staff of the Harvard Unit of Base Hospital No. 5, near Dannes-Camiers in Pas-de-Calais, France,[11] where he was appointed adjutant and company commander under Colonel Robert U. Patterson. Base Hospital 5 cared for 2,000 sick and wounded patients in what has been described as a "hospital city" that included a British component and a total capacity of 12,000 beds.[12] Nearby were the cement plants of Dannes-Camiers, and in the sand flats, ammunition dumps.[13]

Typically, a hospital would not be considered a legitimate military target. But on September 4, around noon, a German observation plane appeared over the hospital camp. In the words of one observer on the ground, "the weather was clear and the air crisp, thus making ideal conditions for photographic work. The anti-aircraft guns, both mobile and stationary, did valuable work in keeping the plane at a very high altitude. Some criticism was heard concerning Colonel Patterson's desire to have the Stars and Stripes flying over the hospital area from such a tall flagpole. It is believed by some to be possible that a photograph of this camp, showing the United States flag flying overhead, was secured and that, as a warning to other Americans who were to follow us into the battlefields of France, we should be made the objective of an aerial attack in spite of the fact that we were a hospital unit and therefore classified as non-combatants."[14]

Earlier in the evening, the Germans had attempted a raid on the English coast, just 20 miles across the English Channel, but their attempt was thwarted. Then, "at ten-thirty

Picture from Concerning Base Hospital No. 5: France, 1917-18-19.

Colonel Robert U. Patterson Commanding Base Hospital No. 5.

we received a warning that enemy planes were approaching along the coast. The anti-aircraft guns at Sainte Cecile Plage and at Neufchatel were actively employed for a few minutes but were soon quiet and the all-clear was sounded. At ten fifty-five p.m. without any warning whatsoever, and while all lights in the vast twelve thousand-bed hospital area were illuminating the camp, an enemy aeroplane suddenly swooped down over the brim of the circle of high hills from the direction of Étaples. A few minutes prior to this incident a loud report as of the crashing of a bomb had been heard from that direction, but by those who had heard it, it was mistaken for the report of an anti-aircraft battery."[15]

The Base Hospital No. 5 history noted that "Lieutenant William Fitzsimons, who had recently been appointed adjutant of Base Hospital No. 5, was among those who heard the first report, and fearing the possible approach of enemy planes had summoned the sentry, Private Hiram Brower, to ascertain the cause of the violent explosion. Having answered the question of the adjutant, the guard resumed the patrol of his post. Scarcely a minute had elapsed when another more violent explosion occurred, caused by the dropping of an aerial torpedo on General Hospital No. 18. Fortunately, no damage was done as it dropped in the center of the athletic field, tearing a deep hole several yards in diameter. Then swinging his plane in a semicircular course," the pilot dropped a smaller bomb "into the reception tent of No. 4 General Hospital, followed almost immediately by two bombs that dropped within eighteen inches of each other in front of Lieutenant Fitzsimons' tent, two others at each end of Ward C-6 and another in the reception tent of No. 11 General Hospital."[16]

In another account, Lieutenant Fitzsimons "heard the signal warning of the raid at midnight Tuesday night and came to the door of his tent. Just as he stepped out two bombs fell, striking the ground no more than six feet apart. One of them landed and exploded within two feet of the Lieutenant.

"Fragments of the bombs flew hundreds of yards, one piece passing through the Harvard officers' mess hall. When one of the Boche bombs struck a tent filled with wounded, the legs of one of the wounded men were blown off ... A fifth bomb killed another man who was standing in the door of another hospital tent ... One nurse was blown off her feet by the explosion of a bomb. She was wounded slightly about the face and her clothing was torn to shreds, but she went on with her duty ... Nurses and officers alike ignored all personal danger. They cared for those wounded by the bombs immediately and gave no heed to the explosions."[17]

The Base Hospital No. 5 unit history recorded that "Lieutenant William Fitzsimons was instantly killed by the first two bombs to be dropped on Base Hospital No. 5, while the flying fragments wounded Lieutenants Rae Whidden, Thaddeus Smith, Clarence McGuire, and Private Hiram Brower. Fragments from the two bombs which were dropped on Ward C-6 killed Private Oscar Tugo and several patients, while other patients were wounded and large portions of the ward were wrecked."[18]

Nurse Louise McCloskey described the scene in the operating room after the explosions: "Words are futile to describe that night," she wrote. "The scenes in the operating room ... the dead, dying, and wounded lying on the floor, and only a flickering candlelight ... Someone whispered, 'Lieuten-

Photo by James J. Heiman

1917 German Pfennig pieces brought back from the war by Otto P. Higgins, *The Kansas City Star* war correspondent.

ant Fitzsimons has been killed' ... Scenes of anguish lasted all night. In one corner was a dying lad moaning, his abdomen torn open. Knelling by him, like a guardian angel, was a Jesuit college lad, who pressed the crucifix of his rosary to the lips of his dying comrade and recited an Act of Contrition."[19]

Louise worked tirelessly through the night, and as she emerged into the daylight, a grim scene confronted her. "Before my misty eyes were the coffins side by side, holding the lifeless bodies of soldiers killed that night. Some were draped with the Stars and Stripes, others with the British Union Jack. Silently, before the lifeless remains of Lieutenant Fitzsimons, I stood dazed."[20] Then at breakfast time, Louise watched incredulous as ambulances delivered, under the covers of their blood-stained canvas, 200 more wounded, fresh from the front.

The Star reported that "of the sixteen wounded at the Harvard unit's hospital, five were members of the American staff, and eleven were patients." The report continued: "In addition to the American hospitals, a British military hospital was bombarded. The raids occurred Tuesday night, and like the bombardment of hospitals nearer the front the last few days the attacks were deliberate. ... German aviators dropped bombs every twenty minutes for several hours of daylight on a hospital at Vandelaincourt. Nineteen persons were killed and twenty-six wounded."[21]

Reporting from the scene of the Harvard

Unit Base Hospital No. 5 bombardment the next day, September 8, United Press staff correspondent William Philip Simms affirmed the deliberate nature of the attacks, adding an especially poignant detail: "The raids upon hospitals were deliberate. That the Americans might not forget, the Boches dropped German coins over the camp, as souvenirs. These souvenirs were pfennig pieces. The officer in command of the Harvard Hospital unit, which suffered most in the raid, showed me one of the coins. The survivors of the raid, indignant and bitter at the display of barbarity in the attack on the defenseless hospitals, all declared they believed the German pilot deliberately dropped the coins as 'souvenirs' of his visit," but, the report continued, "the first American unit to be under enemy fire carried out the work they had to do with the utmost bravery."[22]

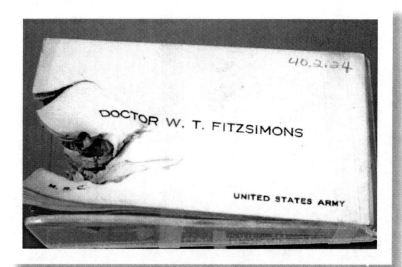

Photo courtesy National World War I Museum.

Evidence of shell fragment damage from the bombing that killed Lt. William T. Fitzsimons. The punctured stack of cards remain as silent testimony to the mockery of the scattered pfennig pieces.

On Friday morning, the casualties of the bombing were buried in the British Military Cemetery among the sand dunes of Dannes-Camiers and Étaples. In a letter to Mrs. Catherine Fitzsimons, Major Roger I. Lee described the services: "We all went to the funeral services and never have I attended a more impressive service. Delegations from all the surrounding encampments were there. Nearly all the Allies were represented. There were over 100 British officers, a number of French, some Portuguese and of course all the Americans from far and near. The priest was very moving in the service as he spoke of the consecrated life, the consecrated ideal and the consecrated ground. We miss Fitz, as we called him." [23]

Reaction to the news of the bombing and the sacrifice of lives was immediate and profound, spreading rapidly throughout the entire country. *The Star* was especially concerned that the Fitzsimons family be informed in person. "A reporter for *The Star* went to the Fitzsimons apartment before the news appeared in an early edition of *The Star*, so as to forestall the sudden shock to the relatives of learning first of Dr. Fitzsimons' death through publication. Mrs. Fitzsimons bore the shock bravely. She had heard yesterday one of the officers was killed but had been told it was Lieut. Paul W. Wooley, also of Kansas City."[24] The next day *The Star* reported that in Washington, D.C., the Army's Medical Department was "boiling mad." One medical officer remarked: "Isn't it typical of what we are fighting that the first American who should fall should be a doctor on an errand of mercy in France – helping the wounded and killed by a deliberate attack on a hospital that should know no foe?"[25]

Dr. J. F. Binnie was especially affected by Dr. Fitzsimons' death. He was a Medical Corps Reserve major, co-commander of Hospital Unit No. 28, a Kansas City unit soon to be deployed in Limoges, France. When he heard the news, Dr. Binnie was in Washington attending a conference at the Medical Department. As soon as he confirmed the early press dispatches, Dr. Binnie sent a telegram to Dr. Fitzsimons' mother, which she received Saturday evening, September 8.[27]

"When the call was made for young doctors for immediate service in France, Doctor Fitzsimons was the very first one to respond. 'I enlisted him,' Doctor Binnie said ... 'He was a good boy – a good boy.'"[28]

Only six days before the bombing, Saturday, September 1, Dr. Binnie had recommended Lt. Fitzsimons for promotion to captain. On September 10, Congressman Borland, representing Kansas City's congressional district, introduced a bill in the House authorizing the President to issue the promotion.[29]

The bill was passed, and President Wilson signed it into law.

Meanwhile at Kansas City's Cathedral of the Immaculate Conception, preparations were underway for a Solemn High Mass of Requiem sung by Reverend L. Curtis Tiernan, Chaplain of the Second Missouri Field Artillery, who later served in France as Chaplain of Cpt. Harry S. Truman's Battery D, 129th Field Artillery, and even later as Colonel, Chief of Chaplains in Europe during World War II.[30] Like Dr. Fitzsimons, Monsignor Tiernan was also a former student of St. Mary's College in St. Mary's, Kansas, where, on the same day, September 12, Father C. J. Scott celebrated a High Mass of

Photo courtesy National World War I Museum Digital Archives.

Maj. J. F. Binnie enlisted Lt. Fitzsimons.

Maj. Henry Lyman of Base Hospital 5 sent Lt. Fitzsimons' mother this picture of Lt. Fitzsimons' grave in a British cemetery at Camiers in northwestern France. Base Hospital 5 nurses decorated the grave and the English Women's Auxiliary Corps care for the cemetery.[26]

Requiem in the Immaculata Chapel.[31]

Back at the Immaculate Conception Cathedral in Kansas City, Bishop Thomas F. Lillis delivered a stirring sermon. "The people of Kansas City have gathered here today through the outpourings of the profoundest sentiment of the human heart," he said. "We, as citizens, have come here as proof of our appreciation for one of our own young men whose loyalty and great sacrifice endear his memory to all. He volunteered for service for our country in a far distant land. He made the greatest of human sacrifices. He gave his life. Such sacrifice may come in time to others of our sons.

"We show our appreciation for this first of the martyrs and his work in life; we feel it on our bended knees in this church today. Let us arise and go forth to show and live our continued appreciation by a deeper patriotism and a greater love for our flag and our Nation.

"He is the first martyr to the cause of American patriotism. Let his blood not be shed in vain.

"You young men wearing the insignia of the United States Army today must feel more strongly than ever the love of cause and the devotion to duty which brought sudden death to this young man.

"We at home must better know the sacrifice and anguish our boys must face.

"And yet let us not forget that the sorrow and anguish of mind of the soldier, while not to be excelled by any other thing, is equaled, if not surpassed, by the sorrow and anguish of mind of the mothers who gave their boys to the United States and to God."[32]

> "The people of Kansas City have gathered here today through the outpourings of the profoundest sentiment of the human heart. We, as citizens, have come here as proof of our appreciation for one of our own young men whose loyalty and great sacrifice endear his memory to all. He volunteered for service for our country in a far distant land. He made the greatest of human sacrifices. He gave his life."
>
> — *Bishop Thomas F. Lillis*

The Bishop's words rang in the ears of the men in uniform gathered for the occasion. "Before the service began, the two batteries of the Second Missouri Artillery, part of a company of the Third Missouri Infantry, Base Hospital Unit No. 28, with the officers of the respective organizations and a number of unattached commissioned men, gathered at Convention Hall and marched to the Cathedral. There they were joined by a group of Navy officers and the various consular agents stationed here … A large delegation of the Knights of Columbus attended the service. Reservations for all the delegations, military and civil, were filled to overflowing. Part of one of the batteries was unable to enter the Cathedral, so great was the crowd.

"The battery buglers entered with the first unit artillerymen. They gave the final military touch to the impressive service by playing taps slowly at the close of the Solemn Requiem High Mass. After the service when the military units had marched out, the big crowd lingered, heads bowed, deeply impressed by the service and the display."[33]

This was the funeral of the first American officer to fall in the war.

During the next 14 months, America would return with interest the mockery of the pfennig pieces the German pilot had scattered with his bombs that day in September 1917 when he brutalized 16 lives at Base Hospital No. 5 in Dannes-Camiers, Pas-de-Calais, France. But for now, news of Lt. Fitzsimons death shocked Americans and steeled their resolve to strike back at the brutality of an enemy who would attack with impunity men already suffering from the wounds of war and slaughter the unarmed men and women who were trying to save their lives. The attack on Hospital No. 5 and the death of a doctor as the first American officer to fall in the war had done more to prepare the American spirit for war than the enemy could possibly imagine. If America was not yet prepared in rifles, ammunition, artillery or uniforms, the effort to be so would be redoubled and joined to a spirit even more resolved to fight back.

No. Americans did not forget.

M-3 **William T. Fitzsimons Memorial Fountain**
The Paseo at 12th Street, Kansas City, Missouri

The same day as Dr. Fitzsimons' funeral mass, plans were being made for a permanent memorial "to the first American in the service of the United Stated Army to be killed in Europe in the line of duty" as *The Star* designated now Cpt. Fitzsimons. Thomas M. Finn, former head of the Hospital and Health Board and a close friend of Dr. Fitzsimons, chaired the memorial fund.

Reverend Robert Nelson Spencer, rector of Trinity Episcopal Church, suggested a bronze tablet or medallion to be placed on the Federal Building. Catholic Diocese Bishop Thomas F. Lillis suggested a simple marble marker or shaft similar to the granite shaft commemorating the city's policemen who died in the line of duty. "A monument of this kind, simple but effective," he said, "would be most appropriately placed in one of the parks, on a much-traveled boulevard or other public place."[34] The Bishop offered a rationale for a more visible memorial, especially important now for its effect on other young men who were about to enter the conflict. "The young lieutenant's service and death in the service is an inspiration to the young men of the city and the Nation," he pointed out, "an encouragement to them to make any sacrifice to which the needs of the Nation may put them. This is really an American affair, but it is up to Kansas City to see that it is done."[35]

With a donation of $100, *The Kansas City Star* was among the first three subscribers to the memorial fund.[36] By mid-September, a total of $700 had been collected, with more donations anticipated. "The interest taken in the erecting of the memorial is greater than I expected," Chairman Finn said. "In fact, the people seem to be carried away with the idea. Everyone seems to realize the duty of Kansas City to pay a lasting honor to the memory of the first American officer to give his life so honorably in France."[37]

It wasn't until May 30, 1922, however, almost four years after the war, that the memorial in Kansas City became a reality as a fountain embedded in the wall of the south terrace at 12th and the Paseo. As some groups had done nearly five years earlier on their way from the Convention Center to the funeral mass at the Cathedral of the Immaculate Conception, the Knights of Columbus, Kansas City physicians, and war veterans who comprised the William T. Fitzsimons Post of the American Legion, marched north on the Paseo and formed in front of the terrace, where the memorial stood veiled and Fitzsimons family members were seated: the doctor's mother, Catherine Fitzsimons; his brother, G. K. Fitzsimons; and his sisters Julia, Helen, and Catherine Fitzsimons, and Mrs. J. H. Green.

One of many speakers to address those gathered, Bishop Lillis reminded his listeners, "Our first duty is to God and our second to our country. Religion and patriotism walk hand in hand. Patriotism is inspired in time of war by religion. Patriotism should not discriminate against religion in time of peace."[38]

"It is a privilege to be present at these ceremonies," the Bishop continued. "We owe all gratitude to the thousands, and hundreds of thousands, of boys who gave their lives that this country might remain intact forever. When we do honor to the memory of William T. Fitzsimons we pay tribute to all of them. But we pay a special tribute to this boy, because he was ours, because he reflected the spirit of the people of Kansas City."[39]

Then Dr. Paul Wooley, Dr. Fitzsimons'

THIS FOVNTAIN IS ERE
IN MEMORY OF
WILLIAM T. FITZSIMONS
1ST LIEVT MEDICAL CORPS V.S.A.

* * * * *

KILLED IN FRANCE * * *
SEPTEMBER SEVENTH
NINETEEN HVNDRED
SEVENTEEN * THE FIRST
AMERICAN OFFICER TO
GIVE HIS LIFE IN THE
GREAT WORLD WAR
* * * FOR LIBERTY.
ANNO DOMINI

MCMXXII

Lt. William T. Fitzsimons Memorial Fountain, 12th & Paseo, Kansas City, MO.

colleague and commander of the William T. Fitzsimons American Legion Post, rose to unveil the memorial and to remind his audience of the strong desire Fitzsimons had to serve those suffering the brutality of war. Dr. Wooley briefly recounted Lt. Fitzsimons' service. "His was a life of sacrifice to humanity from a very early date," Dr. Wooley said. "From the time of his graduation in medicine, this sacrifice of self for the benefit of the afflicted dominated his life. This desire to serve humanity caused him to forego his desire to practice his profession for a time after finishing his internship at Roosevelt Hospital. For at this time war broke out in Europe in 1914. He realized that the call of humanity was greater from across the water than it was at home, and he went to the aid of the British Army, serving as a medical officer in a

Red Cross unit for eighteen months …

"Those eighteen months were spent in the main on very active fronts. He was spared from serious injury during this first service in France and returned to Kansas City, where he entered the practice of medicine. Not long after, our own country was compelled to declare war on Germany. His recollections of his own hardships and experiences at the front while with the British did not for a moment cause him to hesitate. He volunteered for immediate service in the United States Army and was among the first to don our Army uniform and report ready for duty.

"We are here today to dedicate this fountain which was built in memory of a true American who was the first officer of our Army to make the supreme sacrifice for his country."[40]

■ ■ ■

Besides reporting on the tributes to Dr. Fitzsimons made that day and being among the first to contribute financially to the W. T. Fitzsimons Memorial, *The Kansas City Star* was also instrumental in memorializing Dr. Fitzsimons in an even greater way in its pages. *The Star*'s founder, William Rockhill Nelson, was a good friend of the Colonel and former President Theodore Roosevelt from the days of the Spanish-American War until April 1915 when Nelson died. During a chance meeting with the Colonel on a westbound train from New York early in June 1917, Nelson's son-in-law, Irwin Kirkwood, proposed the idea that the Colonel write editorials on the war for *The Star*. The newspaper would syndicate them for a minimum transmittal fee to any other newspapers interested in the Colonel's opinion.

Managing editor Ralph Stout observed, "Daily momentous problems of the war were coming up. Mr. Kirkwood felt strongly that the American people were eager to know what Theodore Roosevelt felt on those questions. If he could reach the public quickly, great good would result to this country's cause."[41] The Colonel readily agreed, and the arrangement was set to begin in October,[42] but with Dr. Fitzsimons' death, Kirkwood recognized the impact that a Roosevelt editorial on the subject would have on the nation at a time when the first selective service draft had just been set in motion and recruitment was foremost on the minds of Americans. Kirkwood proposed the subject to Colonel Roosevelt, who produced the first of his 114 editorials for *The Star*.[43]

"There is sometimes a symbolic significance in the first death in a war," Roosevelt wrote. "It is so in this case. To the mother he leaves, the personal grief must in some degree be relieved by the pride in the fine and gallant life which has been crowned by the great sacrifice. We, his fellow countrymen, share this pride and sympathize with

this sorrow. But his death should cause us more than pride or sorrow; for in striking fashion it illustrates the two lessons this war should especially teach us – German brutality and American un-preparedness.

"The first lesson is the horror of Germany's calculated brutality," Roosevelt continued. "As part of her deliberate policy of frightfulness she has carried on a systematic campaign of murder against hospitals and hospital ships. The first American in our army to die was killed in one of these typical raids." The Colonel went on to decry not only German brutality but "the base or unthinking folly of those Americans who aid and abet the authors of such foul wickedness; and these include all men and women who in any way apologize for or uphold Germany, who assail any of our allies, who oppose our taking active part in the war, or who desire an inconclusive peace."

"The second lesson is our un-preparedness," Roosevelt declared. "We are in the eighth month since Germany went to war against us; and we are still only at the receiving end of the game. We have not in France a single man on the fighting line. The first American killed was a doctor. No German soldier is yet in jeopardy from anything we have done.

"The military work we are now doing is work of preparation. It should have been done just three years ago. Nine-tenths of wisdom is being wise in time," the Colonel concluded.[44] His words resonated with the news articles *The Star*'s own correspondent, Otto P. Higgins, was writing from Camps Funston and Doniphan within the very week that Kansas City native Dr. Fitzsimons became the first American Army officer to die in the Great War.

With the aid of Roosevelt and its own front pages, *The Star* created a living memorial to the slain doctor, urging the country to action not only to avenge his death but to recruit its own forces and get them trained and deployed with proper equipment as quickly as possible. Doing so was the best way to commemorate and to continue Dr. William T. Fitzsimons' work of saving lives.

■ ■ ■

Designed by Kansas City architect, John Van Brunt, and carved by Kansas City sculptor Jorgen C. Dreyer, the William T. Fitzsimons Memorial Fountain is made of Dakota limestone and includes a central tablet with decorative columns on both sides.[45] The tablet is topped by a crescent-shaped lunette with an eagle in its center. Below the lunette and at the top of the tablet is the Army Medical Corps emblem in bronze – a caduceus consisting of two serpents entwined around a pole with a ball or knot on top and wings projecting from either side.[46] The caduceus was the staff carried by Aesculapius, the Greek and Roman god of healing. In ancient times, the snake was associated with healing because of its ability to shed its skin and restore itself. The caduceus is also as-

Photos by James J. Heiman

Detail of Lt. William T. Fitzsimons Memorial Fountain, 12th & Paseo, Kansas City, MO.

sociated with the staff of Hermes, the Greek messenger of the gods. Its wings symbolized peaceful communication and represented influence over the living and the dead.[47] Beneath is the inscription, 12 feet by 5 feet, which reads:

"This fountain is erected in memory of William T. Fitzsimons, 1st Lieut. Medical Corps U.S.A. killed in France September 7, 1917. The first American officer to give his life in the great World War for liberty. Anno Domini MCMXXII."

Centered at the bottom of the tablet is a bronze lion's head, which serves as a spout for a jet of water directed into a semi-circular basin. The lion, the snake, and the eagle remind us of the courage, the humanity, and the dignity of the first American officer to give his life in the Great War.

M-4 Fitzsimons-Battenfeld at Kiely Park
The Paseo at Cleaver II Boulevard, Kansas City, Missouri

The granite monument, 9 feet by 4 feet, was erected by the Fitzsimons-Battenfeld American Legion Post No. 8. The inscription reads:

"For God and Country
Fitzsimons-Battenfeld
Post No. 8

William T. Fitzsimons
Lieut. U.S. Army
Medical Corps World War I

James R. Battenfeld, Jr.
Lieut. SR. GD. U.S. Navy
Flight Surgeon, World War II"

The Fitzsimons-Battenfeld Monument commemorates the service of two physicians – one from WWI and the other from WWII. The site was originally dedicated to a WWI infantryman from Kansas City, Thomas J. Kiely, who was an enlisted man in Company E, 354th Infantry, 89th Division. On liaison to the 356th Infantry, he was killed on the 3rd day of the battle of St. Mihiel on September 14, 1918.

A French 75 mm cannon stood at this location when the site was dedicated May 25, 1941, under the sponsorship of the Thomas J. Kiely Post of the American Legion. Kiely's 75-year-old mother, Mrs. Julia T. Kiely, was in attendance that day,

James J. Heiman
Fitzsimons-Battenfeld Monument at Paseo and Cleaver II Boulevard.

as were Rev. Thomas E. Donnelly, assistant pastor of St. James Catholic Church, and H. J. Haskel, editor of *The Kansas City Star*.[48] The cannon, an artifact of the Great War, was removed later in 1941 as a danger for children who, as children are inclined to do with war memorials, converted it to a teeter-totter.[49]

Now, besides the name of the triangular piece of ground on which the memorial stands, no other public reference occurs here to remember Thomas J. Kiely or the members of the American Legion Post who commemorated his memory in 1941. Only the names of two physicians, Lt. Fitzsimons and Lt. Battenfeld, remain. Lieutenant William T. Fitzsimons was the first American officer to be killed in World War I, a native of Kansas City and the victim of a German bomber who strafed American Base Hospital No. 5 in Dannes-Camiers, Pas-de-Calais, France on September 7, 1917. A separate memorial fountain is dedicated to Lt. (later Cpt.) Fitzsimons at 12th and Paseo. Jesse R. Battenfeld, Jr. was a Lieutenant Senior Grade U.S. Navy Flight Surgeon killed in World War II.

The names of Thomas J. Kiely and William T. Fitzsimons are also commemorated, along with 439 other names of Kansas City World War I casualties, on the plaques at Meyer Circle Gateway and in Memory Hall at Liberty Memorial.

Kansas City Women at War: The Nurses of Base Hospital No. 28 and the Red Cross Nursing Service

Kansas City nurses responded quickly to the rallying cry for war. Under the direction of Miss Eleanor Keely, 72 nurses departed Kansas City for training in New York and then for deployment overseas in Limoges, France, as part of Base Hospital No. 28. Back home, Miss Cornelia Seelye, Chair of the Red Cross Nursing Service, recruited 246 nurses – 69 to serve at home and the rest in the training cantonments and later overseas. No other city of its size in the United States gave the military service so many volunteer physicians and nurses as Kansas City did.

have just these few directions to give you," Miss Eleanor Keely[50] told the women assembled at the Christian Church Hospital, 2625 West Paseo. "Don't talk too much."[51]

Keely was speaking to 72 of the 100 nurses in Base Hospital Unit No. 28. These 72 were about to be sworn into the service of the United States and join the other 28 who were already Miss Keely's responsibility. She was ready for them. Before the war, she had been nurse superintendent at St. Luke's Hospital and on Thursday afternoons had taught girls at Westport High School 12 weekly lessons on the fine points of surgical dressing. For good measure, she had also supplemented their instruction with two hours of military drills per week.[52] She was used to keeping her girls in line.

This time it was noon on Thursday, May 23, 1918, and the women, who were not that much older than Miss Keely's high school girls, almost all from Kansas

City hospitals, had gathered to take the oath and receive their orders.[53] For more than three months, they had lived under a 10-day departure order, eagerly awaiting the call that would put them on a train bound for New York City, and from there, to an eastern port for embarkation to France.[54]

"Your orders will tell you how much you may eat and drink," Miss Keely said, "and when you have signed your application blank and been sworn," she concluded, "you will belong to the United States service, and your pay starts."[55]

The next day, Friday, May 24, the women assembled again, this time at 5 p.m. before the check stand in the west wing of Kansas City's Union Station. There, dressed in their distinctively white dress uniforms, they deposited their luggage, only the bare minimum for travel, and clustered into small groups around their men, some of whom were dressed in khaki, but all of whom held in their arms a wife, a sweetheart, a sister, or a daughter about to depart for war.

In front of the Red Cross booth in the station lobby, Judge Arba S. Van Valkenburgh presented the unit with a service flag – a large red cross surrounded by 106 stars, each representing one of the nurses and their six civilian attaches.[56]

Then it came time for the train to depart. Roll was taken; one of their numbers was found missing, but they couldn't wait. They were military now, and the order had been given. It was time to go.

Suddenly as the train pulled away, Miss Grace Flack burst through the crowd and sprinted along the platform, racing after the train as it receded into the distance. But for all her training, she could not keep up. On the observation platform, friends who had missed her earlier cheered the effort.

"There's another train tomorrow, Gracie," they called in consolation.[57]

In disgrace, she turned back and through her tears explained, "I had to say goodbye to Daddy, and he couldn't get away to come down here."[58]

Meanwhile, more cheers went up from the platform; the rest of the crowd were intent on thoughts of those aboard, and as the train picked up steam in quickening chugs, tears and a few sobs matched the rhythm of increasing distance.

The train almost out of sight now, a husky corporal caught the pull of emotion tugging at the moment. He turned suddenly behind him to the soldiers in his squad.

"Boys," he said, "that's nerve."[59]

■ ■ ■

Once in New York City, the "feminine battalion of the Army of Mercy," as *The Kansas City Star* dubbed the nurses,[60] detrained and took up temporary residence in one of several hotels the government had requisitioned to house nurses while they completed their training. A large armory, formerly the training site for New York boys now in the trenches, became the site for morning drills in military formation conducted by a young lieutenant. A local New York City church volunteered space for the nurses to study French, a necessary skill for their work, even though most of them would serve overseas in American units. In off-duty hours they saw the sights, many of the nurses East for the first time.

Besides the time spent in training and sightseeing, the nurses also spent a good

Photo author's collection

Christian Church Hospital, 2625 Paseo, Kansas City, Mo. 1916.

deal of time being outfitted. They used government vouchers to procure their own shoes, fitting themselves as well as the prescribed regulations. They received grey uniforms for hospital work, a government issue of waists, pairs of stockings, and "most of the other garments that make up a woman's wardrobe … Uncle Sam is thorough about it," *The Star* reported.[61]

For parade and street appearances, they wore dark blue serge and a "chick hat" like aviators wore – only in dark blue – and were issued another hat in a velour style similar to those worn in the telephone units. Instead of the old time "Red Cross Cape," they wore a cloak that was much warmer. Finally, after the government issue was completed, the nurses sent all their other clothes back home.

Overseeing the outfitting and training on and off-duty, Miss Keely kept the records, made the reports, and saw to any other needs the nurses had. "It takes efficiency and ability to do it," *The Star* observed, "but to hear the way the nurses of the unit feel about it, they would back Miss Keely against any one in the army."[62]

■ ■ ■

Meanwhile, President Wilson directed the Surgeon General to issue a call for 25,000 additional nurses nationwide; Kansas City's quota was 200.[63] To achieve that goal, Miss Cornelia Seelye, Chair of the Red Cross Nursing Service Committee, created 12 teams – each was comprised of nine nurses and a captain. Each team, in turn, operated from one of the city's hospitals or nursing associations:

Team No. 1 at Research Hospital, Miss Mary Burns, captain;
Team No. 2 at Swedish Hospital, Miss Lillie Nelson, captain;
Team No. 3 at South Side Hospital, Mrs. Phoebe Neidenberger, captain;
Team No. 4 at University Hospital, Miss Olive M. Bayer, captain;
Team No. 5 at Wesley Hospital, Miss Bertha Loomis, captain;
Team No. 6 at Mercy Hospital, Miss Mary Burman, captain;
Team No. 7 at St. Luke's Hospital, Miss Clara Tullos, captain;
Team No. 8 at Christian Hospital, Miss Charlotte Forrester, captain;
Team No. 9 at St. Joseph's Hospital, Mrs. Alllie Curran, captain;
Team No. 10 at Independence Sanitari um, Miss Sarah M. Rogers, captain;
Team No. 11 at the Visiting Nurses As sociation, 117 Railway Exchange Building, Miss Alma M. Barr, captain;
Team No. 12 at the Kansas City Gradu ate Nurses Association, 3031 Char lotte, Miss Ella Dunham, captain.

Eligibility was limited only to nurses who had completed a 3-year training course. After enrolling in the Red Cross Nursing Service, nurses were then assigned to duty in one of the training cantonments for men. Later, the nurses would have the opportunity to serve overseas if they so desired.[64] The registration campaign, which lasted six days, from Monday, June 3, to Saturday, June 8, was an unqualified success. A total of 177 nurses signed up for active service, 69 additional nurses, mostly married, to serve at home, for a grand total of 246.[65] Although the campaign had closed, Cornelia Seelye wanted to continue enrollment until every nurse in Kansas

City was listed. Her efforts and those of the medical community in Kansas City earned the recognition of Surgeon General Rupert Blue, who acknowledged that "no other city of its size in the United States gave us so many volunteer physicians and nurses, both for overseas service and for service during the influenza epidemic at the various camps, as did Kansas City."[66]

■ ■ ■

While the Red Cross recruitment was going on in Kansas City, Eleanor Keely and her 99 Kansas City nurses were completing their training in New York and were on their way to Limoges, France, the site of Base Hospital No. 28, which began receiving patients on July 23, 1918. On that day, 30 victims of gas were transferred from Base Hospital No. 24, one other of three base hospitals in Limoges. On the night of July 27, even more cases arrived at Base Hospital No. 28.

Nurses and officers set up beds in 12 wards and processed more than 600 patients in five hours, at the rate of two patients per minute. Eventually, the number of wards was extended to 23 with 64 beds each, a total of 1,472 beds in a number of single-story temporary barracks buildings. In addition, 1,136 beds were located at neighboring Bellaire Seminary, and Miss Nell R. Roberts from Muscotah, Kan., had charge of 300 beds located in tents near the barracks buildings[67] – for a grand total of 2,908 beds.[68]

The greatest strain on hospital facilities and personnel, however, came in October 1918, during ten days of the battle of the Meuse-Argonne, when 12 train-car loads of wounded were brought into the hospital. Several of the Base 28 officers, numbers of its enlisted men, and 30 of its nurses had already been detailed to other hospital work, but the other 70 nurses and the men remaining in Unit 28 met the test and worked around the clock to save the trainloads of wounded.[69]

After six months of continuous operation, Base Hospital No. 28 shut down and submitted its final report, noting that it had received 9,954 cases – 6,087 of which were medical and 3,867 surgical. Only 69 deaths were recorded in-hospital: 46 of these were ascribed to medical conditions and 23 from battle wounds that surgery could not fix. The hospital released its last patient and ceased operations completely on January 31, 1919.[70] "How the nurses held up is hard to understand," Base Hospital No. 28 co-commander, Ltc. Lindsey S. Milne said when he returned to the states on May 1, "but they did."[71]

"The spirit of the nurses was magnificent," he continued. "In spite of handicaps and work of the most trying type, they gave everything they could in care for the benefit of patients. It was only by their loyal support and professional skill that Base 28 was able to make the record it did in returning its patients, fit and sound, in such large percentage.

"I don't like to go in for heroics," he added, "but it is only their due to recall the cheerfulness and brightness they brought to the hospital wards. That cheer, when they couldn't have felt cheerful under the strain they were working," he concluded, "meant many a life."[72]

The 72 nurses who had departed from Kansas City that Friday evening in May 1918, could finally think of com-

Photo courtesy of National World War I Museum Archives.

Ambulance delivery at Base Hospital No. 28, Limoges, France, 1918.

Photo courtesy of National World War I Museum Archives.

Ltc. Lindsey S. Milne, Co-Commander of Base Hospital No. 28.

Photo courtesy of National World War I Museum Archives.

Personnel from Base Hospital No. 28.

"The spirit of the nurses was magnificent. In spite of handicaps and work of the most trying type, they gave everything they could in care for the benefit of patients. It was only by their loyal support and professional skill that Base 28 was able to make the record it did in returning its patients, fit and sound, in such large percentage."

— *Base Hospital No. 28 co-commander,*
Ltc. Lindsey S. Milne

29

ing home, but they did not return to the states as a single unit. Military nurses in those days did not travel on the regular troop transports, but instead shipped in small groups aboard passenger vessels. Many of the nurses, however, did not leave right away after the base hospital closed. Twenty of them remained to tend German prisoners at a hospital in Bordeaux. One of those nurses, Miss Opal Jackson, described the experience.

"At first I felt like I wanted to slip the German wounded a pill that wouldn't help them recover at all. But I got over that – they were just big boys, and they were patient, too," she said. "After they had recovered enough to be about they were put to work, and many times when I would pass them they would uncover [take off their hat out of respect]; sometimes when there was a muddy place a prisoner would toss a rock or a board over the spot so that I could cross without wetting my feet.

"It is hard to hate people like that," she reflected, "even when one remembers all the horrible things they did."[73] The nurses who tended the German prisoners at Bordeaux were under orders to proceed to Brest for the trip home. Miss Nell Roberts, who had charge of the tent

hospital at Base Hospital No. 28 and had later been transferred to Base Hospital No. 1 in Nantes, accompanied them. They were the very last of the Base 28 nurses to leave France – except for Miss Keely who, true to form, remained there as a regular army nurse.[74] She transferred to Base Hospital No. 98, which was located in Limoges.[75]

Gracie Flack returned home too. This time she was not late, and although it is not recorded, most likely her father was able to meet her when she arrived at Union Station.

"It was not so unpleasant as I had expected," Opal Jackson said, summing up her ten months overseas. "There were many disagreeable features I had prepared myself to face that I did not encounter.

"I would not have missed it for anything – and yet I wouldn't go to France again – even on a honeymoon."[76] She wouldn't need to. In the words of the corporal who had watched her and the rest of her unit depart from Kansas City that day in May a year earlier, she had already proved that she had plenty of nerve

Head nurse Eleanor Keely, "Unit 28 Head Nurse Chose to Stay in France," *The Kansas City Star*, May 4, 1919, p. 14A.

Nurse Opal Jackson of Hospital No. 28, Limoges, France.[77]

Lottie Ruth Hollenback:
"She Died That Others Might Live"

One of the nurses who had enlisted in Kansas City Base Hospital No. 28 was Lottie Hollenback. Because of the shortage of nurses at the Base Hospital at Fort Riley, she was sent there for two months and was preparing to leave with the rest of the Kansas City nurses for deployment to France when she was stricken with influenza and died. She had taken the oath of enlistment from Major J. F. Binnie, the same medical officer who had enlisted Lt. Fitzsimons, and now she was the first Red Cross nurse to die in the service since war had been declared, and she was the only woman whose name appears on the list of 441 Kansas City war dead – the very last name on the list.

Clo J. Willard had been working his shifts as a regular Army attaché in the sterilizing department of the Base Hospital, Fort Riley, Kan., when on Thursday, January 3, 1918, he was asked to help remove one of the many "rough boxes," as they were called – coffins containing hospital victims who had succumbed to illness.

Glancing down at the tag affixed to the coffin, he suddenly drew back in horror. "LOTTIE HOLLENBACK" the tag read. Miss Hollenback had been his teacher some 20 years earlier at the Ridge Summit country school he had attended, northeast of Wilmore, Comanche County, Kan., where Clo had grown up in the 1890s. For as long as Miss Hollenback had lived in the county, "there was between them," a later account recalled, "that warm interest which usually exists between teacher and pupil."[78] But as time went on and the Hollenback family moved away, Clo lost contact with his former teacher and had no idea that she was among the contingent of Red Cross nurses working

along with him at the Ft. Riley Base Hospital – until, that is, the day he had to carry her body out of the hospital. She was 36, a victim of lobar pneumonia.

Lottie Hollenback was stricken at 5:00 in the morning of Wednesday, January 2nd, and after an illness of only 42 hours, died at 11:00 Thursday night, January 3rd. "She died in the work – in the work that was given her to do," the *Olathe Daily Mirror* wrote, "and was as truly a soldier fighting for world democracy as if she had fallen on the battle field. She was to leave for France in about six weeks."[79]

Lottie Hollenback was among the first of the nearly 60 doctors, nurses, and hospital attendants who died at Camp Funston in 1918. In addition, between 16,000 and 17,000 cases of influenza among the men had been treated at Fort Riley that year, 900 of whom died. "Most of the deaths were from pneumonia of a virulent type," camp commandant Major General Leonard Wood, a physician himself, wrote later that December. "In many ways, it was worse than a battle," he observed.[80]

Lottie Ruth Hollenback was born in Paola, Kan., January 31, 1881, to George W. and Charlotte Ranney (Dunbar), who were married on November 21, 1877, in Manhattan, Kan.[81] She moved with her family to Comanche County in 1885 and lived in the eastern part of the county for about 17 years until they moved in 1905 to northeastern Kansas. Her father was a member of the 1891 Kansas House of Representatives from Comanche County. She attended school in Salina and in 1905, at the age of 24, entered nurse's training. She took a two-year training course at General Hospital in Kansas City and graduated from there in 1907. She worked for ten years as a nurse in Kansas City before joining the Red Cross.[82]

During the summer of 1917, she enlisted with Kansas City Base Hospital Unit 28 under the command of Major John F. Binnie and took her oath of office on November 20, 1917.[83] She lived at 2627 Chestnut, Kansas City, Mo.[84] Because of the shortage of nurses, she was sent on temporary duty to the Base Hospital at Fort Riley, served there for two months, and had just been appointed head of her ward. At the time of her death, she "was considered one of the most efficient nurses at the hospital."[85] The Base Hospital serving Camp Funston could accommodate 3,000 patients and was located three miles west of the Cantonment, near Fort Riley.[86]

A military escort accompanied her remains to the station at Fort Riley, and a delegation of Red Cross nurses met them at Union Station, Kansas City. At 2:00 Sunday afternoon, January 6, 1918, Rev. Gale, assisted by Major Binnie, conducted funeral services at Bethel Church, Bethel, Kan., from which the remains were interred in the little cemetery on a knoll near her parents' home. She was buried in a soldier's casket in her Red Cross uniform, on which was affixed her Red Cross pin, permission for which had been wired from Washington. Her parents, her brothers, George and Ben, and her sister, Martha, survived her.

Lottie Ruth Hollenback was the first Red Cross nurse to die in the service since the beginning of the war.[88] Less than four months before, Major Binnie, the co-commander of Lottie's unit, Base Hospital No. 28, had attended the funeral of the first American officer to be killed in the war, a physician whom he had inducted into the service, Lt. William T. Fitzsimons. Both Nurse Hollenback and Dr. Fitzsimons were from Kansas City, both had been enlisted by Dr. Binnie, and both were the first American health professionals to die in the war. In Kansas City, at Memory Hall of the Liberty Memorial and also at the Meyer Circle Gateway Avenue of Trees, 441 names commemorating war deaths from Kansas City are listed on bronze plaques.[89] Loretto Hollenback is the only woman whose name appears on the lists.[90] On the stone marking her grave in the Bethel Cemetery was the emblem of the Red Cross, with the inscription, "She Died That Others Might Live."[91]

Photo by author, 10 January 2012.
The grave of Lottie R. Hollenback and her parents in Bethel Cemetery, 78th Place and Leavenworth Road, Kansas City, Kan.

The Nurses' Quarters at Fort Riley, 1918. Photo from *Cantonment Life Camp Funston, Illustrated*, 1918, p. 21.[87]

Base Hospital at Ft. Riley, 1918. From *Cantonment Life Camp Funston, Illustrated*, 1918, p. 21.

Endnotes

1   Otto P. Higgins, "Class of Men a Surprise," *The Kansas City Times*, September 6, 1917, p. 1.

2   Otto P. Higgins, "A Happier Attitude Now," *The Kansas City Times*, September 7, 1917, p. 3.

3   Otto P. Higgins, "Men Shiver at Funston," *The Kansas City Times*, September 21, 1917, p. 1.

4   Otto P. Higgins, "Big Shortage of Rifles," *The Kansas City Times*, September 15, 1917, p. 2.

5   Jeanine Dredger, "St. Mary's and the War," Alma Mater, Winter, 1991, http://www.smac.edu/?StMarys and the War, accessed May 18, 2011.

6   John H. McCool, Department of History, University of Kansas, (http://kuhistory.com/proto/story-printable.asp?id=66, accessed by the author on May 18, 2011).

7   Mervin T. Suddler, *Graduate Magazine*. University of Kansas. www.kuhistory.com.

8   "Bomb Kills Local Doctor," *The Kansas City Star*, September 8, 1917, p. 1.

9   Ibid.

10 "War Martyr Wrote Home," *The Kansas City Star*, September 9, 1917, p. 11A.

11 "Unveil Memorial Fount," *The Kansas City Star*, May 30, 1922, p. 1 and "William T. Fitzsimons," (Wikipedia (http://en.wikipedia.org/wiki/William_T._Fitzsimons, May 18, 2011.

12 Adolph A. Hoehling, *The Fierce Lambs* (Boston: Little, Brown & Company, 1960), p. 116.

13 Ibid, p. 117.

14 Philip J. Hatch, Ed., *Concerning Base Hospital No. 5: A Book Published for the Personnel of Base Hospital No. 5, France 1917-18-19* (Boston: The Barta Press, undated). (http://www.ourstory.info/library/2-ww1/hospitals/bh5a.html accessed by the author on May 19, 2011).

15 Ibid.

16 Ibid.

17 William Philip Simms, "Raiders Mocked Their Victims," *The Kansas City Star*, September 9, 1917, p. 11A.

18 Hatch, unpaginated.

19 Hoehling, p. 122.

20 Ibid.

21 "Bombs on U.S. Hospitals," *The Kansas City Star*, September 7, 1917, p. 2.

22 William Philip Simms, "Raiders Mocked Their Victims," op. cit.

23 Hoehling, p. 124.

24 "Bomb Kills Local Doctor," *The Kansas City Star*, September 8, 1917, p. 1.

25 "Medical Officers 'Boiling' Mad," *The Kansas City Star* September 9, 1917, p. 11A.

26 "Lt. Fitzsimons' Grave in a British Cemetery at Camiers in Northwestern France." Photo from *The Kansas City Star*, February, 4, 1919, p. 4.

27 "War Martyr Wrote Home," *The Kansas City Star*, September 9, 1917, p 11A.

28 "Medical Officers 'Boiling' Mad," *The Kansas City Star,* September 9, 1917, p. 11A.

29 "Captaincy as a Tribute," *The Kansas City Star*, September 11, 1917, p. 2.

30 "The President's Old Outfit, Famed Battery D, Back in the News as Inaugural Nears," *The Kansas City Star,* undated, in *Battery D Pvt. Jack Naulty's Scrapbook of Truman's Inauguration*, author's collection, page 1.

31 Jeanine Dredger, "St. Mary's and the War," *Alma Mater*, Winter, 1991, http://www.smac.edu/?StMarysandtheWar, accessed by the author on May 8, 2011.

32 "Throng at Military Mass," *The Kansas City Star*, September 13, 1917, p. 2.

33 Ibid.

34 "Memorial Plans Take Form," *The Kansas City Star*, September 12, 1917, p. 1.

35 Ibid.

36 "Start a Fitzsimons Fund," *The Kansas City Star*, September 14, 1917, p. 2.

37 "Add to Memorial Fund," *The Kansas City Star*, September 16, 1917, p. 3A.

38 "Unveil Memorial Fount," *The Kansas City Star*, May 30, 1922, p. 1.

39 Ibid.

40 Ibid.

41   Ralph Stout, *Roosevelt in the Kansas City Star: War-Time Editorials by Theodore Roosevelt* (Boston: Houghton Mifflin, 1921), p. xxvii.

42   Ibid, p. xxxi.

43   Ibid, p. xxxii and "Theodore Roosevelt Writes of Doctor Fitzsimons' Death," *The Kansas City Star*, September 17, 1917, p. 1.

44   Stout, pp. 1-2.

45   Lillie F. Kelsay, *Historic & Dedicatory Monuments of Kansas City* (Kansas City, MO: Board of Parks & Recreation Commissioners, 1987), p. 20.

46   Sherry Piland and Ellen J. Uguccioni. *Fountains of Kansas City: A History and Love Affair.* (Kansas City, MO: City of Fountains Foundation, 1985), p. 126.

47   Oskar Seyfert, *Dictionary of Classical Antiquities* (New York: Meridian Books, World Publishing Co., 1964), p. 288.

48   "Thomas J. Kiely Park is Dedicated." *The Kansas City Times*, May 26, 1941, p. 8.

49   Kelsay, p. 21.

50   Miss Eleanor L. Keely's name is also spelled "Keeley" in some sources. I have preferred the "Keely" spelling because it is the spelling used in the official historical report.

51   "Mobilize Unit No. 28 Nurses," *The Kansas City Star*, May 23, 1918, p. 4.

52   *Annual Herald 1917.* Westport High School, Kansas City, MO. US School Yearbook. [Ancestry.com database on-line]. Provo, UT. Accessed by the author on February 25, 2012.

53   "Nurses to Leave Soon," *The Kansas City Times*, May 24, 1918, p. 4.

54   "Our Nurses on the Way," *The Kansas City Times*, May 25, 1918, p. 18.

55   "Mobolize Unit No. 28 Nurses," op. cit.

56   "No. 28 Nurses Away Tonight," *The Kansas City Star*, May 24, 1918, p. 2.

57   Ibid.

58   Ibid.

59   Ibid.

60   "Our Nurses on the Way," op. cit.

61   "Nurses Train for War," *The Kansas City Star*, June 16, 1918, p. 3A.

62   Ibid.

63   "City's Nurse Quota, 200," *The Kansas City Times*, June 4, 1918, p. 3.

64   Ibid.

65   "Nurse Roster Now at 246," *The Kansas City Star*, June 9, 1918, p. 11A.

66   Floyd C. Shoemaker, *Missouri and the War* (Columbia, MO: The State Historical Society of Missouri, 1919), p. 40.

67   "Base 28 Minus Nurses," *The Kansas City Times*, May 2, 1919, p. 7.

68   Anthony Kovac, Nancy Hulston, Grace Holmes & Frederick Holmes. "'A Brave and Gallant Company': A Kansas City Hospital in France during the First World War," *Kansas History: A Journal of the Central Plains* 32 (Autumn 2009), p. 177.

69   "Base 28 Minus Nurses," *The Kansas City Times*, May 2, 1919, p. 1.

70   Kovac et al., p. 177.

71   "Base 28 Minus Nurses," *The Kansas City Times*, May 2, 1919, p. 1.

72   Ibid.

73   "Nurses from Unit 28 Tell of Hero Patients," *The Kansas City Star*, May 4, 1919, p. 5B.

74   "Base 28 Minus Nurses," *The Kansas City Times*, May 2, 1919, p. 7.

75   Special Orders 31, Headquarters, Headquarters Company, Limoges, France, 3 Feb 1919, p. 4 and Special Order 49, HQ, HQC, Limoges, France, 17 Feb 1919, p. 4 from "Report of Changes Nurses Base Hospital No. 28 From Month of July [1918] to Month of March 1919," *Historical Report.* Base Hospital No. 28 Collection, National World War I Museum Archives.

76   "Nurses from Unit 28 tell of Hero Patients,"op. cit.

77   Ibid.

78   "How Things Will Sometimes 'Happen," *The Western Star.* April 22, 1921. http://www.rootsweb.ancestry. com/~kscomanc/hollenback-willard.html accessed by the author on January 9, 2012.

79   *Olathe Mirror*, Olathe, Kansas, January 10, 1918.

80   Hermann Hagedorn, *Leonard Wood: A Biography, Vol II* (New York: Harper & Brothers, 1931), p. 315.

81   George Martin, Ed., *Transactions of the Kansas State Historical Society, 1907-1908, Vol. X* (Topeka, KS: State Printing Office, 1908), p. 105. See also "An Old Timer Dies." *The Western Star.* May 8, 1925 http://www.rootsweb. ancestry.com/~kscomanc/hollenback_c.html, accessed by the author on January 9, 2012.

82   "Local Red Cross Nurse Dead," *The Kansas City Times.* January 5, 1918, p. 6.

83   "Nurses Who Died in the War," Kansas State Historical Society.

84   Loretta R. Hollenback, *Missouri Digital Heritage: Soldiers' Records: War of 1812 – World War I.* http://www. sos.mo.gov/archives/soldiers/details.asp accessed the author on January 9, 2012.

85   "Death of Lottie R. Hollenback." *Olathe Mirror.* Olathe, Kansas, January 19, 1918. http://rdk1.com/rdkfour/ LottieRuthHollenback.html accessed by the author on January 9, 2012. Also see "Miss Lottie Hollenbeck Dies at Ft. Riley." *The Western Star.* January 18, 1918. http:www.skyways.org/genweb/Comanche/library/obits/hollenbe.html accessed by the author on January 9, 2012.

86   *Cantonment Life Camp Funston Illustrated* (Camp Funston, KS: Department of Camp Activities and Amusements, 1918), pp. 20-21.

87   Pictures of Fort Riley Base Hospital from Department of Camp Activities and Amusements, Camp Funston, Kansas. *Cantonment Life Camp Funston, Illustrated.* (Kansas City, MO: Baird Company Engravers, 1918).

88   *Olathe Mirror* , Olathe, Kansas, January 10, 1918.

89   *World War Soldiers Dead,* Vol II. No. 1. (Kansas City: Missouri Valley Historical Society), 1926.

90   Note on spelling: "Hollenback" appears on the gravestone as well as in contemporary newspaper accounts in *The Western Star*, the *Olathe Mirror, and Transactions of the Kansas State Historical Society, 1907-1908, Vol. X.* These sources also record the first name as "Lottie," as does *The Kansas City Star* notification of her death on January 5, 1918. However, *The Star* spells the last name as "Hollenbeck." The memorial plaques at Memory Hall at the Liberty Memorial and at the Meyer Circle Gateway Avenue of Trees list her name as "Loretto Hollenback." Her service record on file with the archives of the Missouri Secretary of State lists her name as "Loretta R. Hollenback." I have preferred the spelling that appears on Miss Hollenback's grave marker.

91   Joan Kusek, *Wyandotte County, Kansas, Cemetery Records, Vol. I* (Published by Joan Kusek, October 1993), p. 10. Bethel Cemetery is located at 78th Place and Leavenworth Road, Kansas City, Kan. For reasons unknown, the Red Cross emblem and inscription "She Died that Others Might Live" have been removed from Lottie Hollenback's headstone.

CHAPTER 2

"We Gave the Work of Our Hands and the Men of Our Lives"

Suffrage and Service: "Needles are Guns, Wool is Ammunition, the Soldiers are Kansas City Women"

Kansas City nurses were not the only volunteers to serve the cause of war. The women of Kansas City served in the canteens, sold war bonds, made bandages, and knitted caps, gloves and sweaters. They also worked in munitions plants, operated telegraph sets, and drove and repaired motor vehicles. At a time when state legislatures were voting on the 19th Amendment to give women the right to vote, women's roles were undergoing dynamic changes that would have profound influence on how America prepared for both war and peace.

Women's influence and work will be a far-reaching and almost determining factor in the conduct of the war if we play our part as we should and as we will," Louise Wood said to an audience of women who filled the Kansas City Grand Avenue Temple on Friday, May 17, 1918. The women's committee of the Jackson County Council of National Defense sponsored the meeting. Jane Addams of Hull House, Chicago, and Katherine Davis, the former Commissioner of Corrections of New York, shared the podium with Mrs. Wood, the wife of the Major General in command of the training camp at nearby Camp Funston.[1] Preparation for war was occurring at the same time as many state legislatures were considering ratification of the 19th Amendment that would finally give women the right to vote. Exercising that right would, in the opinion of many, give women the best weapon for preparing for war and preserv-

ing the peace once the war was won. Consequently, women did not hesitate to use the language of war to press their campaign for suffrage, but they were careful to avoid appearing overly militant, preferring instead, to emphasize their traditional roles of nurturing life and preserving peace. Their voices would be heard for suffrage, for preparedness, and at last for peace.

"Women must, now that in many states they have full political responsibilities, see to it that the country be always ready in spirit and in material preparation to play its part in making the world safe for democracy and a safe place to live in," Mrs. Wood continued. "If we want a righteous peace we must be so prepared that our voice will be listened to, because it will be a voice not only of a just but of a strong people."

Similar concerns were voiced a week earlier by speakers before the Jackson County

Louise Wood and her husband, Major General Leonard Wood.

Photo Library of Congress.

Louise Wood at Hope Farm Fair.

Photo Library of Congress.

Federal Suffrage Amendment Campaign Committee. "Suffrage must not wait until after the war," *The Star* quoted from the proceedings. "Rather, conditions must be changed so that women will have a voice in the determination of peace terms."[2] To that end, the committee met to organize its campaign urging the Missouri legislature to ratify a 19th Amendment to the Constitution, which had just passed the U.S. House of Representatives and was expected to meet the approval of the U.S. Senate before being submitted for a vote of the state legislatures, two-thirds of whose approval was needed before ratifi-

cation became a reality and women had the vote in fact. Recognized Kansas City leaders Mr. W. T. Kemper, Dr. Burris A. Jenkins, and Rabbi H. H. Mayer were among the male members of the advisory board lending their voices in support of the cause.

However, the issue of militancy was a major concern for the local Jackson County Federal Suffrage Amendment Campaign Committee. The speakers at the May 17 meeting did not want their committee or their cause to be confused with the more militant Congressional Union, "a suffrage organization committed to militant methods, among which has been the picketing of the White House." After all, the Jackson County speakers pointed out, the militant Congressional Union had "applied for membership in the National American Suffrage Association but the membership was denied them on the ground that rules of the national organization forbade the use of militancy."[3]

Even so, although the local suffrage amendment committee did not want to be associated with the militancy of marching in protest before President Wilson, the committee still insisted that suffrage was needed now, before the war ended, to ensure a viable peace. Otherwise, the women reasoned, the cessation of hostility, when it did come, would simply lead to further war. History had amply demonstrated that men just couldn't be trusted to keep the peace. That was why, the women insisted, that the 18th Amendment (Prohibition) and the 19th Amendment (Women's Suffrage) were being considered by Congress at the same time.[4] For now, the Jackson County Federal Suffrage Amendment Campaign Committee women would moderate their persuasive voices with the argument of peace.

Louise Wood, on the other hand, was not at all hesitant to associate the voice of women's suffrage with war or peace. After all, she had been married to the General for more than 25 years and was the product of a military family. Her father, Colonel Condit-Smith, was the Quartermaster General of the Army of Tennessee and had served on the staff of General William Tecumseh Sherman.[5] Although not directly hostile to President Wilson, Louise Wood was not afraid to take him on, however subtly.

Like her husband, Major General Leonard Wood, and his close friend and fellow Rough Rider, Colonel Theodore Roosevelt, Louise Wood strongly advocated for preparedness, which was sorely lacking at that point in the war, and, if the lack of preparedness for war was any indication, would be sorely lacking in the peace, as well. So, Louise Wood was

not afraid to associate women's suffrage with President Wilson's own rallying cry, "to make the world safe for Democracy." Nor was she afraid to align the voice of women's suffrage with the prosecution of what she termed a "righteous peace," urging women to prepare their voices to be heard because those voices were authoritative expressions of justice and strength.

Louise Wood was not alone in associating women's concerns with the demands of war. At the Jackson County Council of National Defense meeting where Mrs. Wood spoke, famed social worker Jane Addams raised her voice to speak on "The World's Food Supply – America's Responsibility" and urged more careful conservation of food to meet global demands seriously threatened in the prosecution of the war.[6] In addition, former New York corrections commissioner Katherine B. Davis also spoke to preparedness, urging the women to spend at least two days studying material from the commission on training camp activities to improve the physical, mental, and moral well-being of the men now in the cantonments but soon to be in the trenches.

Other women in other venues spoke out about the social significance of women's roles and the absolute dependence the nation had on them for its survival. "Wives and mothers have never lacked opportunity for war service," popular author Mary Austin observed in an article that appeared in *The Star* the day after Louise Wood, Jane Addams, and Katherine Davis spoke in Kansas City. "But this war calls for qualities in woman which transcend her sex and establish her social value on her power to do, rather than on her power to give."[7] In other words, women's work and their roles in the war went beyond the categories traditionally assigned to them.

Women certainly *gave*: they wrote letters, made bandages, served as nurses, visited the cantonments, cut sandwiches at the canteens, canvassed for the Liberty Loans, volunteered for the Red Cross, and sent packages to their men after they had kissed and cried them off to war. Women also *did*: they drove tractors on farms, harvested crops, wrote books and articles on the war, worked in munitions plants, served as accountants, operated telegraph sets and wireless devices, as well as drove and repaired motor transports.

Pointing out how much these working women and their male counterparts in uniform depended upon the culture of organizations to support their efforts, Austin used military marching metaphors to observe that "Young men are captained and generaled. Expert supervision of their patriotic service is at their elbows. They have the splendid inspiration of togetherness, music, banners, shoulder touching shoulder. Even wage-working women have a sense of direction: they see the work that passes through their hands pushed steadily to an end."[8] But what can the lone, single woman do?

"What shall she do," Austin asked, "the young woman at home, who is neither the mistress of the house nor a wage earner? How shall she turn back to the general account the care and schooling she has had, and how satisfy the hungry desire to serve her country, which is, thank God, as characteristic of our young women as our young men?"[9]

Austin answered her rhetorical question by asserting, "the young woman of brains and education and leisure must captain herself. She must find her own job herself. More

> *"So it was the woman's work of the war, and especially the single woman's work, to take it upon herself to learn and do men's work, not only to free up a man for the work of combat, but to preserve and develop the skills that men themselves had built up before they had to leave their occupations to learn and execute the skills and arts of war."*
>
> — *Mary Austin*

than any war that was ever fought," Austin proclaimed, "it is a lone woman's war."[10]

On her own, the single woman must find mentors on-the-job to help her acquire skills like accounting in banks, bookkeeping in stores, card cataloguing and filing in a local Carnegie library, performing clerical work in a county seat, or operating a wireless telegraph set. She must seek out drivers to teach her about makes of cars, techniques of automotive repair and maintenance, the topography of roads, and the operation of farming implements. In short, Austin advised, "apprentice yourself to your chosen trade in the person of the most skilled workman you know. If you do not know how to choose, make a census of the skills of your town. Find out the most valuable skill and save that for your country."[11]

In the pages of *The Kansas City Star*, Austin urged a new type of thinking for single women. "Make it your business to capture and retain some of the things that men have learned. Nobody will refuse to teach you. A man owes his knowledge and skill to his country as much as he owes his life, all the more if he loses his life." If the skill of the men is lost, then civilization itself is most surely lost. "Women are the natural conservers of civilization," Austin argued. "It is our duty to gather up and hold fast every bit of gain. Women are only just learning what it costs men to be proficient, and even if there is no definite objective in view, we would not go far wrong in attempting to save something of the proficient man's purchase."[12]

So it was the woman's work of the war, and especially the single woman's work, to take it upon herself to learn and do men's work, not only to free up a man for the work of combat, but to preserve and develop the skills that men themselves had built up before they had to leave their occupations to learn and execute the skills and arts of war. "One of the terrible things about war," Austin observed, "is the loss of this accumulated skill. Men spend years in school and years more in practice, and then at their most useful time are cut off."[13]

Not only, then, did it fall to women to ensure the survival of civilization in a just and secure peace by acquiring the political and social power of the vote, but it also fell to women to ensure the survival of civilization by acquiring the skills of men who were forced to leave their jobs to fight, and who, if they were lost in combat, would no longer be able to resume their work – a double loss for national survival.

What was urgently needed for women was something akin to the draft registration for men. So, in the summer of 1917, the Council of National Defense began registering women for the work occasioned by the war – not only jobs left open by a shortage of men but also needs specific to the conduct of the war itself. In Kansas City, the women's committee of the Council of National Defense created files and indexes for 10,000 of the 24,000 names it received. "The files have been so arranged," *The Star* reported, "that any call for women in war work can be answered immediately. If knitters, ambulance drivers, stenographers or workers in any line are called for, they can be had."[14]

The Kansas City Times also provided a weekly bulletin board easily recognizable with its "Home Fires" logo. Here women could find all manner of announcements, hints, inspirational vignettes, brief exhortations, and pleas for help. At a glance, women could find items available and needed at the Red Cross Salvage store. They could find out when and where the knitting circle of the Daughters of the Confederacy planned to meet, where they could register their babies for birth certificates, and who was planning to go to Paris for work with the Fatherless Children of France.[15] In the "Home Fires" column of June 12, 1918, women learned that the Food Administration had estimated that 30 million bushels of potatoes were available in the United States and that, consequently, the week of June 10 had been designated as Potato Week, where potatoes should substitute for wheat on breakfast and dinner tables. Women also learned that the Worth-While Club had adopted a French baby and that it was a good idea to cultivate the garden after a rain.[16] If you needed a Shetland pony "harnessed to a cart and ready for a ride," you could get one "with a convincing pedigree" at the Red Cross Salvage Department at 2608 Main.[17] But you better get your knitting done, first.

Nowhere, perhaps, was the crisis of skill application and preservation and the biases that still prevailed against women more dramatically portrayed than in the work of the medical profession itself, especially in the contrast between American and French responses to the roles of women in that work. In the May 15, 1918, edition of the newspaper, *The Kansas City Times* reported on a presentation Mrs. Charles L. Tiffany made to the local suffrage league at the Hotel Statler in St. Louis. A unit recruited from among the women physicians on staff at the pioneer women's hospital in New York City "offered their services to one recognized authority after another, only to be rejected," Mrs. Tiffany told the women in her audience.[18]

The Red Cross turned them down, and so did the War Department in Washington. "We were referred to various committees, and on these committees there were one or two very funny and very ignorant men. They told us they did not know there were any women doctors capable of performing surgical operations.

"There was no way in which the government could use these women, some of the most skilled in their profession, many of them giving up yearly incomes of tens of thousands and willing to accept the pay of a captain or lieutenant, and only anxious to serve as near as possible to the firing line. It was hopeless," Mrs. Tiffany said.[19]

Relying on the experience of a Scottish group of suffragists working in France, the American physicians offered their unit directly to the French government. They were accepted immediately. "Nowadays our nurses are used everywhere as anesthetists," Mrs. Tiffany continued. "Doctor Finley is in complete charge of a pavilion devoted to shock cases, than which there are no more difficult or puzzling, and our surgeons are operating wherever they are needed."[20]

Not only were the physicians and specialists women, but working with them were "women dentists, women pharmacists, women dietitians, women X-ray experts, women chauffeurs, a woman plumbing expert and women mechanics and carpenters." Their work "was largely what is called 'reconstructive' among the suffering civilians and repatriates with special care over women and children."[21]

"Reconstruction" had a special meaning. After almost four years of intense warfare on their own soil and the calling off of the great April 1917 offensive that was to bring about a decisive Allied victory, the morale of the French *poilu* was so seriously jeopardized that the French high command pledged itself to taking care of every family of a French *poilu* until the end of the war.[22]

Thus, because of their dire need, the French readily accepted the offer made by the American women physicians and even requested the American Red Cross to forestall the reconstruction of French villages destroyed by the Germans and to direct its efforts instead to the care of French women and children most seriously compromised by the war. With the loss of an entire generation of men in the offing, the preservation of the morale and lives of the men remaining became absolutely critical to the very survival of France. In the extremities of those circumstances, the observations that Mary Austin, Louise Wood, and Jane Addams made about the value of women's work were underscored all the more.

Across the Midwest, at least part of the message was being heard. *The Star* reported on an Army ordnance department survey made by Florence King, president of the National Association of Business Women. She had visited war plants in Minnesota, Wisconsin, and Indiana, where 2,000 women had taken over the jobs once worked by men now drafted for war. King found that "the women were performing their work as well or better than men."[23]

"The kinds of work run almost the entire gamut of operations in foundries, machine shops and munitions plants," King said.

The "Home Fires" logo. The Kansas City Times, June 13, 1918, p. 5.

"Their wages range from $2.25 to $5 a day, with overtime for all work in excess of eight hours, and the work is no harder than that many had previously performed for from $7 to $10 a week. I found women from 16 years to 40 and more employed. War plants offer an excellent opportunity for women of middle age." King further observed that the work of women in munitions plants was rapidly expanding; women were registering for such work in Chicago and 24 other large industrial centers.[24]

Locally, women worked at a variety of industrial jobs including packing houses, creameries, and dress-making and millinery concerns. The Kansas War Industries Board recommended that the minimum wage for women employed in the factories of the state should be $9 per week after a six-month apprenticeship. The Board also recommended time-and-a-half for overtime beyond the eight-hour day.[25]

"Insignia for the cars and uniform for the drivers in the Women's Motor Car Corps."[27]

Industrial work was also offered to Kansas City women willing to relocate to the munitions industrial camp at Nashville for $40 a month with room and board. St. Louis munitions factories also advertised in Kansas City, offering women $1.70 per day for inexperienced workers and $18 per week for those with training.[26]

Besides serving in the medical field and doing factory work, Kansas City women also served in quasi-military organizations. Twenty-five women from Kansas City signed enlistments with the Motor Car Service, a branch of the National League for Women's Service. They were trained at the city's Polytechnic Institute not only to drive automobiles but to repair them as well. Mustered into active service on November 12, 1917, the Kansas City women drove their own cars and reported for daily work at the Women's City Club at 10th & Oak. They drove for the Red Cross, the American Fund for French Wounded, the Surgical Dressing Committee, and for various other relief organizations in the city.[28] The women wore khaki uniforms and worked under the command of Cpt. Evelyn Seavy and Lt. Sarah Morrison.

In just one month, the ranks of the Kansas City Motor Car Service had swelled to 70, and the drivers were deployed into six squads under the command of Sergeants Buechle Maxae, Teresa Chappell, Katherine Harvey, (Mrs.) R. D. Yates, Dorothy Deatherage, and Elizabeth Connor.[29] Their national corps commander, Helen Bastedo, could change a tire in 6 minutes, 45 seconds "flat," and was working to reduce that time to 5 minutes in order to enhance her credibility and to win the $1,000 reward offered by General Coleman Dupont.[30] Eventually, some of the women could be called to France for service with the American Fund for the French Wounded, but for the time being, at least, they served the war efforts of other Kansas City women who volunteered their time making surgical dressings, knitting scarves and socks, or working in the service canteens.

The demand for surgical pads and knitted

goods proved to be critical. Sixty-five thousand surgical pads were assigned to the Kansas City Red Cross and due before Christmas 1917.[31] The response equaled the demand: on just one day, Wednesday, December 13, Kansas City women made 3,500 pads, but the knitting was another matter. Because of deficient supplies of winter wear for the troops abroad, knitted mufflers, wristlets, sweaters, and socks were in high demand – 4,500 the quota for the Kansas City chapter of the Red Cross. For the most part, the knitting was done at home, but sometimes women gathered at the second floor of the Gordon & Koppel Building at 1005 Walnut, where instructors were available to explain the stitches and to offer knitting supplies[32] at cost – 65¢ a hank.[33]

On November 21, 1917, the plea went out in the morning *Times* for 500 knitters to transform 5,000 pounds of yarn, and when the plea fell short, *The Star* swung into action. The evening edition headline, "**AT LAST GERMAN LINE**," proclaimed in bold ½-inch type that British forces had struck through the Hindenburg defenses. Next to the huge headline in letters only half that size, the right-hand column of the first page shouted, "Need 500 Women to Knit." The juxtaposition was obvious; the embarrassment continued, the gauntlet flung down. The article complained that "an appeal published in *The Star* this morning for 500 knitters failed of such a response as was expected. Five thousand pounds of yarn at the headquarters is awaiting volunteer knitters. Of course, if the women do not respond" then the yarn could be sent to knitters at Lowry City, Missouri, who, a letter to *The Star* assured, "would gladly pay cash for the yarn and turn out the garments in short order"[34]

"Needles are guns, wool is ammunition; the soldiers are Kansas City women," *The Kansas City Times* proclaimed the next morning.[35] "The guns are ready, the generals are trained, the munition is on the field, but the soldiers are missing. If the allied attack is to be a success five hundred volunteers must step forward within a short time to answer the call of the country … If Kansas City boys in their Uncle Sam's army are to keep warm this winter, the women soldiers of the second firing line must respond to the call. Every sweater means a healthier soldier in Europe. Every knitter means more sweaters … Bales and bales of Yarn, ready to be held by some husband while wound into a ball, lie waiting for knitters."[36]

The Star got its point across, and the Red Cross got its knitters – 1,500 of them turned out to attack the gray yarn piled up at 1005 Walnut Street.[37] The battle engaged, the women fought furiously through the yarn. "We worked so desperately hard all week," one woman explained, "that it was absolutely necessary for us to close Saturday. We were worn out. And then the women just must have at least one day a week to spend at home."[38] Twenty instructors were at their posts; 100 women worked for five days at different times, officially from 10 am to 4 pm daily but usually an hour earlier and an hour-and-a-half later – for an 8½-hour day. On top of that, hundreds of volunteers picked up yarn and took it home to work. "As a result," *The Star* reported, "large quantities of yarn are being distributed. Knitting needles move faster. And there appears the assuring and satisfying picture of men fighting in the trenches for America – men warm and comfortable, and happier because of it."[39]

Victory. The women had done their part, and 4,500 boys would have sets of socks, sweaters, wristlets and mufflers by Christmas, making up in part for the government's own lack of preparedness. Louise Wood's prediction had been proved right: Women's influence and work had a far-reaching and almost determining factor in the conduct of the war.

American War Mothers: The Pilgrimage to France

After the war was over, women, especially the wives and the mothers who had lost husbands and sons in the fight, assumed a significant role in how America would remember the dead. These mothers formed local and national organizations to bring their dead men home, to advocate for the veterans who returned, and to mourn those who remained buried in the six World War I American cemeteries in France. In an unprecedented gesture of recognition, Congress passed legislation allowing 6,693 eligible women across America to make the pilgrimage from the United States to the American cemeteries in France at the expense of the federal government. Here are the stories of some of the women who made that pilgrimage from Kansas City and one from Tishomingo, Mississippi, who wrote about how it felt to leave her son's grave.

Women, especially war widows and mothers who had lost their sons, exerted great influence after the war was over, for it then became their charge to represent the nation in remembering the dead. First, however, the army of dead soldiers had to be militarized. The effort to report, identify, outfit, transport, relocate, verify, and dispose of dead soldiers was at least as complex as the effort to identify, draft, outfit, train, transport, relocate and engage them while they were alive.

Once the American Expeditionary Forces landed in France in June 1917, individual combat units immediately faced the gruesome task of burying their own dead. As soon as conditions permitted, burial details took up the work, either on the battlefield itself or in a local cemetery. A brief service was read and a marker was placed on the grave, but for most casualties, that grave was not to be the service man's or woman's final resting place. On August 7, 1917, War Department General Order 104 created a Graves Registration Service, which was responsible for taking care of the dead after their first burial.[40]

The Graves Registration Service collected information on each local burial and arranged for reburial in a cemetery set aside for American battle casualties. Members of the Graves Registration Service created a "Report of Disinterment and Reburial," listing the soldier's name, rank, serial number, and service unit. The report also indicated the site of the original burial and the exact location of reburial in the American military cemetery. The work of the Graves Registration Service continued until the service had accounted for all personnel who had died, sometimes as long as three years after the end of the war. Because of the decomposition of the bodies, identification had to be established through dental records, identification tags, grave markers, or other means that might even include information written on a piece of paper and sealed in a bottle buried in the coffin with the body. In all, the American

Battle Monuments Commission lists six World War I American military cemeteries in France: Aisne Marne (2,289 burials), Meuse-Argonne (14,246 burials), Oise-Aisne (6,012 burials), St. Mihiel (4,153 burials), Suresnes (1,541 burials), and Somme (1,844 American burials) – a total of 30,085 burials, all arrayed in military formation, rows upon rows of white crosses.[41] Of the 4,237,000 Americans mobilized for war,[42] the United States suffered approximately 50,000 killed (1.2%).[43]

Reburial in an American military cemetery may not have been the last burial, either. After the war, the Office of the Quartermaster General asked each family who had lost a service member whether they wanted the body to be returned to them or to remain in the American military cemetery in France. Some families opted to have the body returned home for reburial, but most families elected to have their sons and daughters buried with their comrades near the sites where they had given up their lives. Often, for families especially torn about the decision, receiving a picture of their loved one's gravesite – with hundreds of similar crosses in the background – settled the matter.[44] In that case, families saw the larger body of which their son or daughter was a part, and families began planning trips abroad to see for themselves where a son or a daughter had served, to know the place where he or she had died, and to touch the cross that marked the grave. For many fami-

Photo courtesy National World War I Museum.

The United States Steamship company presented the Gold Star Mothers with a medallion commemorating their Pilgrimage.

lies, however, the trip abroad was physically or financially impossible.

Even at that, their cause was not forgotten. Grace Darling Seibold, a mother who had lost her son, Lt. George V. Seibold, on November 4, 1918, just seven days before the war ended, reached out to other mothers who had lost sons. Not only did they offer each other comfort, but they also comforted veterans who had been hospitalized far away from their homes. Each mother displayed at her home a Gold Star Service Flag and wore on her left arm a black armband on which a gold star proclaimed the ultimate sacrifice that a son or a daughter had made in the service of the country. President Wilson himself had approved the designation of the Gold Star on May 28, 1918, at the suggestion of the Women's Committee of the Council of National Defenses. But that was not all. Throughout the 1920s, the women lobbied Congress for funds to send pilgrimages to the American cemeteries overseas so that mothers, who could not otherwise afford the trip, could visit the graves of sons and daughters lost in the war.[45]

The efforts of the women continued and became even more effective once they organized with an official charter and established a national organization. On June 4, 1928, 25 of the Gold Star mothers met in Washington, D.C., to form American Gold Star Mothers, Inc. Across the country, Gold Star Mothers organized in local chapters and affiliated with the national organization. Their lobbying efforts continued until, on March 2, 1929, Congress finally approved legislation authorizing the Secretary of War to arrange for "pilgrimages of mothers and widows who had lost a member of military and naval forces who had died in service between April 5, 1917 and July 1, 1921."[46]

In all, 6,693 out of 17,389 eligible women across America made the pilgrimage from the United States to the American cemeteries in France from 1930-1933 at the expense of the federal government.[47] On February 7, 1930, Congress appropriated $5,386,367 to fund the pilgrimages. Actual expenses were $2,561,792.34 for 1930, $1,546,998.47 for 1931, and $527,368.65 for 1932, leaving a balance of $750,207.54 available for 1933. The average cost per pilgrim in 1930 was $701.28, for 1931 the cost was $875.99, and for 1932 it was $931.71.[48]

From Kansas City, 16 war mothers and one war widow made the pilgrimage to the American cemeteries in France in 1930. The last Kansas City mother to make the pilgrimage and the only Kansas City mother to go in 1933 was the secretary to the Kansas City Chapter of the American War Mothers, Lenora Simpson, whose son, marine James Y. Simpson, was killed at Belleau Wood, June 6, 1918.[49] She sailed from New York on the *S.S.*

> *From Kansas City, 16 war mothers and one war widow made the pilgrimage to the American cemeteries in France in 1930. The last Kansas City mother to make the pilgrimage and the only Kansas City mother to go in 1933 was the secretary to the Kansas City Chapter of the American War Mothers, Lenora Simpson, whose son, marine James Y. Simpson, was killed at Belleau Wood, June 6, 1918.[49] She sailed from New York on the S.S. Washington, one day after the 15th anniversary of his death.*

Washington, one day after the 15th anniversary of his death.[50]

On the journey, each of the women wore a gold star to commemorate the loss she had endured in the service of her country. Once the women had accepted the government offer, the "War Mother Pilgrims," as they were known, came under the care of the U.S. Quartermaster Corps and of Col. Richard T. Ellis, the officer in charge of the American Pilgrimage Gold Star Mothers and Widows in Paris. His command coordinated travel and accommodations for the two-week trips to the cemeteries. Colonel Ellis noted that the trip "was in no sense a holiday or a pleasure trip, but on the other hand it was necessary to prevent over-emphasis of the sentimental side in order to prevent morbidness or hysteria."[51] To that end, the mothers were allowed time to do some sightseeing and shopping, but the focus remained on the cemeteries. One of those women was the mother of Corporal Ross Hadley of Kansas City.

Corporal Hadley enlisted in the United States Army in Cedar Rapids, Iowa, shortly after America declared war. He landed in France in the summer of 1917. Nearly a year later, on June 17, 1918, as he served with Headquarters Company, 16th Infantry, at Cantigny, the first American engagement in the war, he was hit by shrapnel and killed.

"'At first, we wanted to bring Ross home,'" his mother said. "'But then we decided the boy would wish to remain in France. So we started planning our trip to his grave.'"[52] Those plans were nearly extinguished in 1925 with another death. "Five years ago my husband died," Mrs. Hadley explained. 'Until our government offered us this trip I had given up hope. I am so happy now.'"[53]

On July 5, 1930, 12 years after her son was buried, Martha Hadley set out to visit his grave. She joined two other Kansas City women departing that day for the American military cemeteries in France. One of those women was Mrs. Catherine Fitzsimons, whose son, 1st Lt. William T. Fitzsimons, was the first American officer to be killed in the war. A physician with the Harvard hospital unit Base Hospital No. 5 near Dannes-Camiers, Pas-de-Calais, France, Lt. Fitzsimons was killed by shell fragments from bombs dropped on the hospital on September 4, 1917. Now Mrs. Fitzsimons was finally able to visit her son's grave, joined by her daughter, the Lieutenant's sister, Mrs. W. J. West of Gashland, Mo.

The third war mother from Kansas City to depart for France was Mrs. Barbara Meysembourg, whose stepson Harry was killed in action August 24, 1918. Like Mrs. Hadley and Mrs. Fitzsimons, Barbara Meysembourg was a widow; she had mixed feelings about going.

"'I want to go and yet I don't,'" Mrs. Meysembourg told a *Kansas City Star* reporter. "'My husband, before his death eight years ago, always wanted to go to Harry's grave. I know he would insist on my going if he were alive. So I am going.'"[54]

The three women were part of the eleventh contingent of 235 Gold Star mothers from across the United States who sailed from New York on July 9 on the *S.S. President Harding*.[55] They would return on the *S.S. President Roosevelt*, which set sail from France on July 29, 1930. The three were among 3,653 war mothers who visited the graves of their sons that year between May 16 and September 22, 1930.

Each woman prepared for the trip in her own unique way. Martha Hadley sorted through little remembrances of her son to take to his grave. Other women carried small boxes of dirt. "'Just earth,' one woman explained, 'from the window box where bloomed the flowers Jimmy liked – to sprinkle on his grave.' On returning she planned to bring a bit of earth from his grave."[56] Another mother brought tulip bulbs to plant around the cross marking her son's grave so that flowers would bloom when she could no longer tend it. At a tea given in honor of the Kansas City Gold Star Pilgrims on May 1, 1930, at the Hotel Muehlebach, the Gold Star League presented Mrs. Fitzsimons and Mrs. Meysembourg with poppies to place on their sons' graves.[57] At the time of the tea, the two mothers were the only ones of the 20 Kansas City applicants who had received sailing orders. By the time Mrs. Hadley received her sailing orders, she had accumulated 50 silk kerchiefs to take with her overseas, as tokens from the War Mothers at home.

Later, on August 19, 1930, a second troop of 16 mothers and one widow departed from Kansas City for their trip to the French cemeteries. They included widow Mrs. Martha Fair and mothers Mrs. Tenna Marie Caylor, Mrs. Maggie E. Hartman, Mrs. Viola Curry, Mrs. Maria Campo, Mrs. Stella Wright, Mrs. Lena M. Larson, Mrs. F. K. Scott, Mrs. Mabel C. Peebles, Mrs. Maggie D. Adamson, Mrs. A. A. Cleveland, Mrs. Margaret Fink, Mrs. Daisy Baughman, Mrs. Lula E. Brown, Mrs. Elizabeth Layman, Mrs. Sarah Lott, and Mrs. J. P. Langan.[58] Mrs. Euphemia Derby's name also appeared in another list of Kansas City Gold Star pilgrims.[59]

Many of the War Mothers who completed the Gold Star Mothers Pilgrimages of 1930 to 1933 kept diaries and journals of their time abroad. In particular, Julia C. Underwood, of Tishomingo, Mississippi, wrote a journal, dated from August 6 to September 10, 1932, that is now housed in the archives of the National World War I Museum at Kansas City's Liberty Memorial. Her son, Pvt. Henry A. Underwood, Company D, 26th Infantry, was killed at Chateau Thierry, July 21, 1918. After visiting his gravesite and the battlefield where he fought and died, she wrote, "We visited the cemetery (Chateau Thierry) and drove over the battlefields where our dear boys fought their last battle. Oh how sacred the ground is to me. I thank God for permitting me to visit here. I want my boy's body to rest here 'til God calls." Right before she left France for her return to America, she summed up her experience. "I had a wonderful trip," she said, "and [I have] seen so many wonderful sights, but oh how my heart did ache when I was on the battlefield."[60] What follows is an especially poignant expression of her feelings.

"When My Boy Fought His Last Battle"

Oh, France,
I can't leave you
for you hold my heart tonight.
Indeed the war is over,
but we mothers lost the fight.

I viewed the place where my boy lay,
where the crimson poppies grow,
but his soul rests in a fairer land
where the Easter lilies glow.

We knelt by their graves
and our eyes filled with tears.
Before us came a vision.
We looked back across the years

And thought of the day
when he said good-bye
as we held him to our breast,
and longed for the day
when he'd come back home,
but now in France he rests.

America – you can never know
what we mothers paid
when we gave our boys
for the liberty of our country
and [you] took us through that tragic war
with broken hearts.

No.
You will never know
the cost we paid
for you to say "We won"
–while we mothers only lost.

O, France!
I cannot leave you while they say
we must go home.
[But I know] we will meet our boys up yonder
–where we will never part.

–Julia C. Underwood[61]

Julia Underwood returned aboard the *SS. President Roosevelt*, leaving Cobh on September 2, 1932, and arriving in New York, September 9, 1932.

Two years earlier, on Sunday, August 10, 1930, 66-year-old Martha Hadley was the first of the Kansas City Gold Star Mothers to return home from the pilgrimage. Not knowing her exact arrival time, she did not telegraph her family to meet her at the station, but instead took a taxi home by herself to surprise her son, his wife, and their daughter. Martha brought with her four bags, two of which contained the mementos of her pilgrimage. In the diaries of her voyage and tour of the battlefields, she had carefully noted the names of places foreign to her but made especially dear and important to remember because they were now uniquely connected with her son.

In a piece of paper she had wrapped "crushed flowers from No Man's Land, a splinter of wood from a crumbling dugout and a few pebbles from the gravel path that led to her son's grave."[62] From Paris she had brought three dolls, one for each of her grandchildren. Granddaughter Martha Ruth Hadley, age 4 and named after her grandmother, lived at the home. Two other granddaughters, both age 3, lived out of town – one in Springfield, Mo., and one in South Dakota. After resting a minute on the porch, Martha rang the doorbell and was bustled in, much to her family's surprise and joy. Her son William, Ross' brother, carried in two of the four bags from the porch, then asked his mother, "Do you feel better now, Mother, since you've been there and seen his grave?"

"I feel as if a great load had been lifted," she said. "It was a beautiful cemetery. I am so glad I went. I feel now that Ross is resting in peace."[63]

Even before Martha had time to remove her hat, four-year-old Martha Hadley had another question for her grandmother – this one about the doll hinted at in letters her grandmother had written to the girl's parents. But when Grandmother Martha returned to

the porch to bring in the bag with the dolls, both of the other bags were gone. Neighbors, however, were alert; they had seen two men leap from a dark Ford roadster, spring up the walk and onto the porch to snatch the bags, and rush away before anyone could intervene. One of the neighbors, though, had written down the license plate number.

"I can spare the clothes in the grips," Mrs. Hadley explained, "But the other things – well, I simply can't understand how anyone would take them. The luggage was marked. One could see it belonged to a Gold Star Mother."[64]

It was as if Martha Hadley had lost her son again; even that little bit of his memory that she was able to bring back to share with his family had been taken from her. Granddaughter Martha was crushed.

Not much later, boys playing in a vacant lot some blocks away found the bags, now slit open with a knife and the contents spilled out, ransacked and mauled until they were barely recognizable. Everything of value had been pillaged, like a dead body on a battle-

"Sixteen Kansas City Women in Gold Star Pilgrimages to Graves of Loved Ones Overseas," *The Kansas City Star*, August 17, 1930, p. 5A.

field. Martha's son, William, took off work to claim the remains from the Flora Avenue Police Station. The 50 gift kerchiefs given to her in farewell showers before she left Kansas City were gone; all the clothes, including the lingerie, were gone; the white silk flag with the gold star emblem was soiled and rumpled; a small American flag lay spoiled, its slender shaft snapped; but the diaries remained, the travel notes still intact, despite being crumpled and violated with dirty finger marks.[65]

"Well, I'm not going to let it spoil my trip," Martha asserted. "It was too wonderful for that, and I'm glad for what I did get back. But how *could* anybody take those things?"

The question hung in the air and Martha continued to sort through her loss, when a tiny rag doll, its face smeared with dirt, peeped out from under the ruined heap, the only doll left of the three dolls Martha had bought in Paris for her granddaughters.

"It's mine!" shouted little Martha Hadley.

"Yes, dear," said the older Martha Hadley, "That one is yours."

■ ■ ■

Meanwhile, at 107 West Linwood Boulevard, the Gold Star League and its sponsor, the Missouri Valley Historical Society, kept in their museum quarters the memories of their Great War heroes. There the names and records of the men who had lost their lives were cherished along with their portraits and the pictures of the cemeteries where the men lay buried. There in the room was the white satin flag with 507 gold stars, each representing a member who had lost a son or a husband. And there also in the room, the stories were told of the national pilgrimages of Gold Star women to the soldier graves of France, pilgrimages without precedent in American history, in which mothers boarded trains and steamships and headed east to retrace the march of their sons overseas to the sites of their final resting places – and all at the expense of the national government, which had first taken their boys from their homes, armed them to fight, and left them dead in the fields and cemeteries of France.[66]

The great sacrifice the War Mothers made is also commemorated in three local American War Mothers memorials. The most prominent is the American War Mothers' Memorial Fountain at Meyer Boulevard and the Paseo. There in the very middle of the intersection, a square limestone monument rises 13 feet from the middle of a ceramic tile pool. At the top of the monument, carved eagles face out from all four sides, and below them is the insignia of the American War Mothers on one side and on the other three sides, in turn, a gold star for the mothers who lost their sons, a silver star for the mothers of sons who were wounded, and a blue star for the mothers of boys who saw service and returned home. The monument was dedicated on June 1, 1942,[67] three days before a significant American victory in World War II, the Battle of Midway.[68]

It took more than 23 years for the War Mothers to save the money to erect this monument to the sacrifices they had endured in World War I, and when they finally had enough to pay for its construction, the country was once again at war. This time for their grandsons and granddaughters, they placed the gold, silver, and blue stars in corners of their front windows or hung them suspended on a small banner on the front doors of their homes, still hoping that the generations of war could somehow, sometime stop. By this time, Martha Hadley was 78 years old, and her granddaughter, Martha, who had claimed the rag doll her grandmother had bought in Paris after she had visited Uncle Ross's grave, was 16.

Agnes Dora Fraas: The Journal of a Mount Washington Chapter War Mother's Voyage to France

One Kansas City mother, Agnes D. Fraas, also wrote about her experience of the pilgrimage to her son's grave in France. Her journal offers insight into the impact the journey had for many mothers who had never been abroad or who would otherwise have been unable to afford the expense of the trip. The journal expresses, in her own voice, how important sharing the experience with other mothers meant to those who made the journey.

In July 1931, three other Gold Star War Mothers from Kansas City set out on their pilgrimages. Mrs. Agnes D. Fraas had just turned 65 when she joined Mrs. Mary E. Trego and Mrs. J. McClure on their way to the American military cemeteries in France.[69] Thirteen years earlier, on September 29, 1918, in action against the Prussian Guard and Austrian Ulhan before Charpentry, Pvt. Frank X. Fraas, Battery C, 129th Field Artillery, 35th Division, reached for a shell to load into a French 155mm artillery piece.

"We laid down a barrage all night and the following day moved up behind the infantry," Willard J. Cleveland remembered. "All night long the Germans returned the fire, and the next afternoon, September 27, Frank was filled with shrapnel. We took him to the dressing station at Cheppy and he was evacuated from there. We never saw him any more."[70]

The shrapnel had left a slight flesh wound in Frank's left arm. More serious were the 3 or 4 places in his left buttock where shrapnel had cut deeply into his flesh. He was evacuated to Base Hospital 17 at Dijon, France, where, six days later, at 1:50 a.m. on October 5, 1918, he succumbed to lobar pneumonia in the lower left lobe of his lungs. He was buried initially in grave 37, Annex, Polygone (AA), Municipal Cemetery, Dijon, Cote-d'Or, France. Later, his remains were disinterred and reburied in Plot A, Row 23, Grave 32 at the St. Mihiel American Military near Thiaucourt, France, one of 4,153 burials there.[71]

At 6 p.m. on July 26, 1931, Agnes Fraas left Union Station in Kansas City on her way to her son's grave. "My family went to the depot with me," she wrote in her journal, "and a number of friends were there with gifts and good wishes, and [I] was more than impressed to see the Mount Washington Chapter of War Mothers, each of them assuring me that they would be with me in thought and spirit until I returned."[72] Among the gifts was a handsome green Moroccan leather journal with "My Trip" stamped in gold, framed in gold gilding, and inscribed by the Mount Washington Chapter of War Mothers. Inside were world maps in full color, sections devoted to day-trip itineraries and to details about the sailing, and 100 or more pristine white pages on which to record impressions and memories. Agnes, however, recorded on those pages only the names and addresses of 35 fellow pilgrims; she kept her own thoughts on notebook paper, reserving the smooth forest-green notebook as she might her good china – for her guests and only on special occasions, such as this.

Sharing the journey with other mothers who had also experienced the loss of their sons became a critical part of the pilgrimage, a living experience where care and camaraderie could assuage years of grief. "We found," Agnes continued, "there were three ladies on the train that were going in the same group that we were. Two of them were from Marysville, Kansas, and one from Hannover. We became very well acquainted by the time we arrived at New York." An Army officer met the ladies at the station and escorted them to the Hotel Pennsylvania, "and from then to the end of our journey," Agnes asserted, "we never had another care. When we would get to our hotel or also to our coming on board the steamships we would find our baggage there ahead of us. Everything that possibly could be done for our comfort and pleasure was done. At the hotel the large lounge was turned over to us for registration, to meet our friends in New York, to get acquainted with each other and especially to become acquainted with the Captain, the Doc, [and] the

Photo courtesy of National World War I Museum.
Pvt. Frank X. Fraas, Battery C, 129th Field Artillery, 35th Division American Expeditionary Forces, 1917.

nurse [Amy Hoover, RN] who were to have charge of us on the steamship."[73]

Friendship and time for expanding their horizons, free from care, continued to be an essential element of the pilgrimage. It was almost as if the War Mothers were experiencing a whole other world, a better place, perhaps alike in some ways to the place where their sons were, now that their struggles were over. "The next morning we were taken on a sightseeing trip in New York. Back to the hotel to lunch and the afternoon we were free, to give those who had friends [time] to visit them. Mrs. McClure and myself went to a show. After dinner a group of New York War Mothers, among them their president, Mrs. Birking, came to the hotel with greetings from their chapter and also greetings from the mayor, who was out of town and who sent each of the 96 mothers a lovely silk flag. The next day we were taken on another steamship bus ride back to lunch then the captain took our passports and [we] were given our return railroad tickets [that] were left with the officer at the hotel until we returned from France, so we didn't ever have to worry about losing our return railroad tickets."[74]

The experience was not without adventure and fanfare. "Left the hotel at 4 p.m. and had our first thrill of the trip. That was going over to Hoboken where the steamship was docked, through the Hudson River Tunnel. Just the thought of riding under the Hudson River for three minutes certainly was a thrill. On board the steam ship we stood on the deck and the War Mothers that came to see us at the hotel and a great many more mothers were on the dock to see us off. They waved flags and sang the Star Spangled Banner as the ship left and we did the same, using the flags that they had presented us with the morning before."[75]

Agnes, however, felt a tinge of anxiety. "With all the excitement and all the attention that was shown us, I for one, did not forget we were leaving the good old U.S.A. for a long six weeks. [After] our first dinner onboard ... we were taken to our cabins. I had just time to meet my roommate, a Mrs. Hamilton from Minnesota, when the steward came to the door with two large boxes of flowers, one from Dad and the Children, and one from our dear Mount Washington Chapter of War Mothers. They told me on leaving they would be with me in thought and spirit and it certainly looks as if they meant it. We could not keep all the flowers in our cabin so the steward brought me two vases. One I filled for our cabin, and one I took to Mrs. McClure and Mrs. Trego who shared the same cabin just across from us. The rest I gave to the steward of the

Photo courtesy of National World War I Museum.

The U.S. Government presented each of the Gold Star Pilgrim Mothers with a personalized identity badge.

dining room, who took care of them. And every day he would place some on our table in the dinning room. And the last day we still had two gladiolas left. We did not stay in our cabins long as everyone was anxious to see the last of New York and the Statue of Liberty. We sailed July 16, 9 p.m. on the S.S. *America* with 96 War Mothers, Captain Apgar of the U.S. Army, a Doctor, Nurses, and Hostess. There were 519 passengers; commander, officers and crew 467; total on board 986. The next morning we were out of sight of land on a beautiful calm sea."[76]

Once at sea, the mothers continued their society within a maritime routine. The sea itself had been a battlefield, and for the boys on board the troopships to England and France, the submarine menace had necessitated camouflaged destroyer escorts, a zigzag course, and a regimen of evacuation drills. Few troopships were attacked, but the menace was nevertheless real, and now the mothers experienced a reminder of that time in a tribute to those whose sons had died at sea. Following the tribute came the presentation of a special medallion designed by the United States Steamship Company expressly for all of the mothers whose pilgrimages they served. (See picture page 46.)

"The days were spent in getting acquainted," Agnes wrote, "taking our daily walks, and watching the games on deck. One day the crew had a fire drill, which was very exciting watching them answer the different signals, lowering the life boats and so forth.

On Sunday we had services on the boat deck for the boys that were lost at sea. Every pilgrimage has services for those lost at sea. We have with us a Mrs. Kuler from Philadelphia, who did not go with the group of mothers whose boys were lost at sea because of a broken ankle. She is just able to get around now with a cane. She was given the honor of casting the Gold Star wreath in the sea. She also cast overboard an armful of roses for her own dear boy, who was lost at sea. The ceremony was very impressive and was attended by our own Captain Apgar, the ship's officers, and all the passengers. Rev. Simpson opened the service with a prayer and Father Gillman gave a beautiful talk on mother-love sacrifice. Taps were sounded as Mrs. Kuler was dropping the flowers overboard. Then the band played the Star Spangled Banner as we were leaving the deck for the library. We were greeted by Mr. Chapman and given a lovely talk and were presented with a medal and a certificate on behalf of the steamship line that was taking the groups over to France."[77]

"Monday. A special entertainment was given in the social hall for the War Mothers, consisting of vocal and piano songs and duets. The songs were sung by the ship's Doctor, who has a wonderful voice. A composer of music – could not get his name – played a piece on the piano that he composed for the War Mothers. Slight-of-hand performances and lovely refreshments were served.

"Tuesday. We were shown all over the ship, though the tourist part, the kitchen, up on the captain's deck – shown all the mechanism that controls the working of the ship: how they measure distance by the sun, all are automatically controlled and so perfect they can change the course of the ship as easily as we can change the route of an automobile.

"Wednesday was field day [with] kinds of sports on deck, War Mothers taking part in some of them.

"Thursday night [at] the captain's dinner we were given comical caps and all kinds of souvenirs, and after dinner the Masked Ball. Of course we did not take part in the masking or dancing – only to look on.

"Friday everyone did just as they pleased. We were up early as we got our first sight of land about 6 o'clock, and it was the most beautiful sight I had ever seen – the sun coming up over the hills of Plymouth, England. A tender came out in mid-ocean, bringing passengers from England on their way to France and Hamburg, Germany. They also took the passengers of our ship that were going to England, among them the winners of the oratorical contest of *The Star* at Kansas City and nine hundred sacks of mail for England. By 10 o'clock we were out of sight of land again.

"Saturday morning we packed and were ready to leave the ship for Cherbourg. And I think I can safely say that every one of us were sorry to leave. We were told by the ship's crew that we had the most perfect voyage of any of the pilgrimages. The weather was perfect – cold but bracing, the sea so smooth that we seldom ever saw a white cap. Several of the younger mothers were sick the first two days, but after that everyone was in perfect health, everyone congenial, and it seemed that every one had the same mind, and that was to make the best of everything, to bear with each other's little peculiarities and get themselves in condition for what was ahead of us in France.

"Left the steamship at 4 p.m. We were taken to Cherbourg on the tender, *Atlas*. Arrived at six. Left immediately for France by railroad through a beautiful part of France – through Caen, Normandy. 'Apple Blossom Time in Normandy' was composed for this part of France. All the damage done to this part of France was done by air raids. There was no fighting through this part of France, but the damage was great, especially to forts and large buildings.

"Arrived France 1:30 a.m. at the *Gare de Invalides*. This station was used exclusively by the nobility of France. Pres. Wilson and Gen. Pershing used this station, the French extending the privilege to the U.S. to bring the Pilgrimage of War Mothers through this station. The people of France had planned a large reception for us, but we were a day ahead of our schedule so that was postponed for the next group. By bus to the wonderful Hotel Lutetia. The next morning we found we had been divided in groups, each group to different hotels to be closest to the cemetery they were going to visit. Mrs. McClure and I were separated from Trego. After two days of sight-seeing in Paris and our ceremony at the Tomb of the Unknown Soldier, our group was taken to Verdun." That was on Wednesday, July 29, 1931.[78]

At this point, Agnes Fraas ended the record of her journey from Kansas City to New York and across the Atlantic to France. Still remaining with the other mementos of her Pilgrimage are the printed itineraries of her time in France, but with them no other written record remains of her thoughts and feelings as she placed a spray of natural flowers over her son's grave and saw some of the sights of France.

From Thursday, July 30, to Saturday, August 1, the St. Mihiel Party L Group 3, of which Agnes Fraas was a part, visited Montsec, Metz, the Ossuary Fort Douaumont, and the Trench of Bayonets Loop. On Sunday, August 2, they left Verdun for St. Menehould, visited Suippes and Reims and arrived at Chateau Thierry. They were back in Paris on August 3 and the next day attended the Colonial Exposition and visited Napoleon's Tomb. On Wednesday, August 5, they were at Versailles, and spent Thursday shopping at Le Bon Marche. Friday was devoted to the Louvre before they departed from the *Gare des Invalides* on Saturday, August 8, for the trip home aboard the *S.S. President Roosevelt*, the thoughts of her family and the War Mothers from the Mount Washington Chapter with her still. Agnes arrived in New York on August 16, 1931. [79]

On April 25, 1932, less than a year after

Agnes Fraas returned to Kansas City from the pilgrimage to her son Frank's grave, a group of war veterans met in Gilmor Hall in the Fairmount district of Kansas City to form a new VFW post for veterans in Independence. The Frank Fraas VFW Post 1000, often referred to as the "Inter-City Post" because Fairmount was not a part of Independence at the time, was at one point the largest VFW post in the state of Missouri, with 1,400 members.[80] At the end of World War II in 1945, the name "Fain" was combined with "Fraas," and the post became "Fraas-Fain Post 1000" of the Veterans of Foreign Wars.

For the remaining 20 years of her life, Agnes continued to be devoted to the memory of her son. She served as president of the Mount Washington Chapter of the American War Mothers and with them was instrumental in erecting a stone monument to the boys from the Inter-City District who had given their lives in World War I and later others who died in World War II. Agnes survived the Second World War and died on May 26, 1951, in Montana, just a couple of weeks short of her 85th birthday. Her experience and the experiences of the other 6,692 World War I Gold Star Mothers who made the pilgrimage to France at the expense of the government would never be repeated, even though the war was.

Across from the entrance to Mount Washington Cemetery, the American War Mothers Mount Washington Chapter Monument and flagpole served as a physical reminder to Agnes of her son's death and later of her visit to his grave at St. Mihiel American Cemetery.

The flagpole came first, followed several years later by the stone monument. On Armistice Day, November 11, 1924, six years after Agnes had lost her boy and seven years before her pilgrimage to his grave, more than 600 people gathered around the flagpole in the center of a triangle of ground at the intersection of Brookside Drive and Independence Avenue. Troop 24 Boy Scout buglers played "To the Colors" and hoisted the flag

Mrs. Agnes Dora Fraas at the grave of her son, Pvt. Frank X. Fraas, St. Mihiel American Cemetery, Thiaucourt, France, July 1931.

Agnes Fraas stands beside the Mount Washington Chapter of the American War Mothers Monument across from Mt. Washington Cemetery.

to the top of the 50-foot pole. All assembled heard an address by Armstead E. Swearingen, 1st Vice-President of the Gold Star League of Jackson County and the man who played a key role in the reburials of so many of the Kansas City area boys whose bodies were brought back from the American cemeteries in Europe. Edwin S. Carroll, Commander of the Independence, Missouri, American Legion Tirey Ford Post, and Florence A. Latham, National Corresponding Secretary of the American War Mothers, also offered their remarks. The Reverend H. U. Campbell, pastor of the Mt. Washington Methodist Episcopal Church, delivered the invocation.

Surrounding the triangle in silent tribute with those 600 people were six trees planted two weeks earlier in memory of the Mount Washington boys who had sacrificed their lives: Reese Neeley, Minor Fixler, Francis Fraas, Robert Mayfield, Lawrence Trego, and Orlin N. Trego. A moment of silence followed the Reverend Campbell's benediction, and then the lone Boy Scout bugler closed the observance with the echoes of taps resounding in the distance.[82]

In the years that followed, on Armistice Day in the fall and Memorial Day in the spring, Agnes Fraas joined the Gold Star League and the American War Mothers as they continued to gather at the Mt. Washington flagpole, the last stop in their pilgrimage to the eight war memorial sites throughout the city.[83]

Included in their local pilgrimage was another American War Mothers monument and flagpole, this one for the Independence War Mothers Chapter — located on another triangle of ground at the intersection of 47th Street and Blue Ridge Boulevard. It is dedicated specifically to "Those heroic boys of Jackson County who gave their lives in noble sacrifice to our country in the World War."

The Jackson County Court deeded both properties to the War Mothers in recognition of the foreign ground where so many of their sons now lie. That ground is American soil, too.

M-5 Jackson County American War Mothers and Gold Star League Memorial

Blue Ridge Boulevard at 47th Street, Kansas City, Missouri.

This 7-foot, 1½-ton natural red granite boulder stands before a flagpole in a triangle of ground at the intersection of 47th and Blue Ridge Blvd. Embedded in the granite is an aging bronze plaque that reads:

In Memoriam
To Those Heroic Boys
Of
JACKSON COUNTY
Who Gave Their Lives
In Noble Sacrifice to Our Country
In the World War
1914-1918

"There is no death! The stars go down
To rise upon some fairer shore:
And bright in heaven's jeweled crown
They shine forever more.

And ever near us though unseen,
The dear immortal spirits tread:
For all the Boundless universe
Is life—there are no dead."

Erected by
The Kansas City Chapter
American War Mothers
And Gold Star League of
Jackson County, Mo.

The verses are the first and last stanzas of an 11-stanza poem, parts of which were composed in the spring of 1863 and revised 20 years later by John Luckey McCreery, who worked as a journalist in Iowa and served in various positions with the federal government in Washington, D.C. until his death in 1906. Originally published unsigned in

James J. Heiman

The Jackson County War Mothers "Boulder Memorial" at 47th and Blue Ridge Blvd.

Arthur's Home Magazine, July 1863, the same month as the Civil War battles of Gettysburg and Vicksburg, the poem was later falsely attributed to British novelist, politician, and poet Edward Bulwer-Lytton. The quality of the poem, its timely appearance at the turn of the Civil War, and the controversy surrounding its authorship made McCreery famous.[84]

The story of the source for the red-granite stone is equally distinctive. Mrs. Howard C. Boone, president of the Kansas City Chapter of War Mothers, selected the stone from among many others scattered about in fields near Graniteville, Mo. She selected this particular stone because she thought it especially suited to the message the monument would convey.[85]

James J. Heiman

Dedication plaque for the War Mothers' "Boulder Memorial," 47th and Blue Ridge Blvd.

The stone and its commemorative plaque were dedicated on October 4, 1923, during the fourth national convention of the American War Mothers held in Kansas City from September 29 to October 5, 1923.[86]

In a gesture symbolic of the nation for which the boys had sacrificed, a representative war mother from each of the 48 states poured soil from that state's capital around the base of the monument. Added to the soil was water brought from the Atlantic Ocean by Mrs. W. S. Titus, state War Mother of New York, and water from the Pacific Ocean brought by Mrs. B. V. Sargent, state War Mother of California.[87]

Adding to the symbolism of the monument's dedication was the special "Missouri Day" the War Mothers had planned as the highlight of their Fourth National Convention. The War Mothers invited General Pershing, Admiral Coontz, and General Enoch Crowder to address the convention on the last day, October 5.[88] General Pershing had commanded the American Expeditionary Forces in France; Admiral Coontz had commanded the Battleship Division in the Atlantic and had served as Chief of National Operations; General Crowder was chiefly responsible for writing the Selective Service Act of 1917 and, as Provost Marshal General, was charged with its administration during the war.[89] All three men were native Missourians, who had served with distinction during the war, and their presence at the convention would have added even more importance to the work of the War Mothers. However, the War Mothers' plans for the invitees apparently did not work out.[90]

A native Missourian who did figure prominently in the War Mothers Monument was Jackson County Presiding Judge Harry S. Truman, the chief executive officer of Jackson County government.[91] On August 5, 1929, the Jackson County Court deeded to the American War Mothers the land on which the monument resides and presented them with the flagpole and behind it the dedication plaque, to complete the patriotic spirit of the site.

There Is No Death

There is no death! The stars go down
To rise upon some other shore.
   And bright in heaven's jewelled crown
   They shine forevermore.

There is no death! The forest leaves
   Convert to life the viewless air;
The rocks disorganize to feed
   The hungry moss they bear.

There is no death! The dust we tread
   Shall change beneath the summer
showers
   To golden grain or mellow fruit,
      Or rainbow tinted flowers.

There is no death! The leaves may fall,
   The flowers may fade and pass away—
They only wait through wintry hours
   The warm, sweet breath of May.

There is no death! Although we grieve
   When beautiful familiar forms
That we have learned to love are torn
   From our embracing arms.

Although with bowed and breaking heart,
   With sable garb and silent tread,

We bear their senseless dust to rest,
   And say that they are dead—

They are not dead. They have but passed
   Beyond the mists that blind us here,
Into the new and larger life
   Of that serener sphere.

They have but dropped their robe of clay
   To put a shining raiment on;
They have not wandered far away,
   They are not "lost" or "gone."

Though unseen to the mortal eye,
   They still are here and love us yet;
The dear ones they have left behind
   They never do forget.

Sometimes upon our fevered brow
   We feel their touch, a breath of balm:
Our spirit sees them, and our hearts
   Grow comforted and calm.

Yes, ever near us, though unseen,
   Our dear, immortal spirits tread—
For all God's boundless Universe
   Is Life—there are no dead!

By John McCreery [92]

60

M-6 Inter-City American War Mothers Memorial
US Highway 24 (Winner Road) at Brookside

Eight miles north of the American War Mothers memorial to those Jackson County boys who sacrificed their lives during the war is the second of Kansas City's American War Mothers memorials, this one dedicated to the service dead who came from the "inter-city," that area between the city limits of Kansas City, Mo., and the city limits of Independence, Mo. This part of the metropolitan area includes Sugar Creek and Fairmount.

Directly across from the entrance to Mount Washington Cemetery, the 8-ton monument stands about six feet in height and is built of 15 layers of flat-trimmed Carthage limestone tapered from a four-foot square base. White marble tablets are recessed on both the front and rear. The front tablet states the purpose:

"Memorial to
Veterans of the
World War
Inter City District"

The rear tablet identifies the sponsor:

"Erected by the Mt.
Washington Chapter.
American War Mothers."

The War Mothers' medallion is centered at the top of the monument's front, and below it on either side of the marble tablet are metal plates. As the viewer faces the monument, the darker left plate bears the label, "Our Honored Dead," and includes the names of 16 men who lost their lives in World War I and World War II. Below that plate is another smaller but similar plate listing four additional names. The lighter right plate reiterates the monument's purpose, "In Memory of Those Who Served."

The Jackson County Court deeded the site of the memorial to the Mount Washington chapter of American War Mothers, and a flagpole was erected there by the community. Originally, seven trees were set out in memory of seven inter-city soldiers who died in World War I. The flagpole was dedicated on Memorial Day 1924, and the monument was erected several years later.[93]

JAMES J. HEIMAN

Mount Washington War Mothers "Inter-city" Memorial, US 24 (Winner Road) and Brookside.

OUR
HONORED DEAD
GEORGE BEAL
RICHARD CAVANAUGH
TRUMAN FAIN
ROBERT FRANCISCATO
FRANK FRASS
RICHARD HOLCOMB
ROBERT MAYFIELD
WILLIAM McINDOO
EDGAR McCORD
ARNOLD MORRIS
CECIL SOOTER
JOHN SRADER
FOREST TILLERY
JOSEPH THURMAN
SAMUEL VUKAS
IRVING WOODS
WORLD WAR I-II

IN MEMORY

OF

THOSE WHO

SERVED

Detail plaques on the Mount Washington War Mothers Memorial, U.S. 24 and Brookside.

Photos by James J. Heiman

AMERICAN WAR MOTHERS

M-7 Kansas City American War Mothers Memorial Fountain
The Paseo at Meyer Blvd., Kansas City, Missouri

Kansas City Architect Edward Buehler Delk designed this third War Mothers memorial, which rises 13 feet from a pool 24 feet in diameter. A single jet of water arcs from each side of the monument into the pool.

Stars appear on three sides of the monument: gold for sons that died, silver for sons wounded, and blue for sons who returned from the World War. The Insignia of the American War Mothers appears on the fourth side of the shaft.[94]

Erected in 1941, after the Kansas City Chapter of War Mothers worked for 20 years to collect funds and determine a fitting location, the monument was finally dedicated on Sunday, May 31, 1942. By that time, the country was again at war, a fact that R. Carter Tucker acknowledged in his dedicatory address. The mothers, he said, had the total unselfishness that must exist before the world's present total war can be ended. The Sanford Brown American Legion Post Auxiliary Choral Club and the Paseo High School Band provided the music, a living reminder that young people also pay the price of war.[95]

The Plaque reads:

1917   1918
Kansas City Missouri Chapter
American War Mothers
Building Committee

Mrs. V. V. Austin
Mrs. H. H. McCluer
Mrs. Howard C. Boone
Mrs. Arthur Schopper
Mrs. Louis S. Edwards
Mrs. Richard B. Teachenor

Erected 1941

Edward Buehler Delk — 1st Lieut. Air Service, A.F.F. Architect

James J. Heiman

Kansas City War Mothers Memorial Fountain, Paseo & Meyer Boulevard.

A star figures prominently on each of 3 faces of the Kansas City War Mothers Monument. On the face pictured here, the Gold Star honors those mothers who lost a son or husband in the Great War.

Endnotes

1   "Keep Worry from Men." *The Kansas City Times*, May 18, 1918, p. 7.

2   "Say Suffrage Can't Wait." *The Kansas City Times*, May 8, 1918, p. 5.

3   Ibid.

4   "Reports House Dry Bill." *The Kansas City Star*, Dec 11, 1917, p. 7.

5   Jack McCallum, *Leonard Wood: Rough Rider, Surgeon, Architect of American Imperialism* (New York: New York University Press, 2006), p. 48.

6   "Home Fires." *The Kansas City Times*, May 16, 1918, p. 6.

7   "The Lone Woman Goes to War." *The Kansas City Star*, May 19, 1918, p. 20C.

8   Ibid.

9   Ibid.

10   Ibid.

11   Ibid.

12   Ibid.

13   Ibid.

14   "Women Indexed for War." *The Kansas City Times*, November 16, 1917, p. 4.

15   "Home Fires." *The Kansas City Times*, June 13, 1918, p. 5.

16   "Home Fires." *The Kansas City Times*, June 12, 1918, p. 16.

17   "Home Fires." *The Kansas City Times*, May 28, 1918, p. 4.

18   "Women Doctors at Front." *The Kansas City Times*, May 15, 1918, p. 18.

19   Ibid.

20   Ibid.

21   Ibid.

22   Henry Wood, With the French Armies (By Mail), "Poilus' Morale Holds Up." *The Kansas City Times*, May 15, 1918, p. 18.

23   "U.S. Plans to Use Women." *The Kansas City Star*, May 17, 1918, p. 6.

24   Ibid.

25   "Fix Women's Wage in Kansas." *The Kansas City Star,* June 16, 1918, p. 5A.

26   "War Plants Call Women." *The Kansas City Star*, June 24, 1918, p. 3.

27   "Women's Corps to Work." *The Kansas City Star*, November 8, 1917, p. 8.

28   "Women in Motor Corps." *The Kansas City Star*, November 13, 1917, p. 7.

29   "Must Salute Girls Now." *The Kansas City Star*, December 23, 1917, p. 16A.

30   "Women's Corps to Work." op. cit.

31   "Women Must Rush Work." *The Kansas City Star*, December 14, 1917, p. 12A.

32   Ibid.

33   "Need Still More to Knit." *The Kansas City Star*, November 23, 1917, p. 4A.

34   "Need 500 Women to Knit." *The Kansas City Star*, November 21, 1917, p. 1.

35   "Women, The Yarn Awaits!" *The Kansas City Times*, November 22, 1917, p. 1.

36   Ibid.

37   "Need Still More to Knit." op. cit.

38   "Knitters are Yarn Weary." *The Kansas City Star*, November 25, 1917, p. 5A.

39   Ibid.

40   Constance Potter. "World War I Gold Star Mothers Pilgrimages, Part I, *Prologue Magazine*. Summer, 1999, Vol. 31, No. 2 *http://www.archives.gov/publications/prologue/1999/summer/gold-star-mothers-1html*, accessed by the author April 4, 2013.

41   American Battle Monuments Commission. www.abmc.gov/cemeteries/cemeteries.phd, accessed by the author on April 12, 2013.

42   "The losses suffered by the warring nations are not easy to compute." Martin Marix Evans. *Vital Guide: Battles of*

World War I (Ramsury, Marlborough, Wiltshire, UK: Corwood Press Ltd., 2004), p. 109.

43   H. P. Wilmot, *World War I* (New York: DK Publishing, 2007), p. 3

44   Potter, op. cit.

45   American Gold Star Mothers Inc. Website http://www.goldstarmoms.com/whoweare/history/history.htm. accessed by the author April 4, 2013.

46   Potter, Part 1, op. cit. and 71st Congress, 3rd Session. *Pilgrimage for the Mothers and Widows of Soldiers, Sailors and Marines of the American Forces Now Interred in the Cemeteries of Europe* (Washington, D.C., United State Government Printing Office House Document No. 140, 1930).

47   Potter, Part 1, op. cit.

48   Mrs. James Y. (Lenora) Simpson. *Kansas City Chapter American War Mothers Scrapbook 1932-1933.* Accession Number 76.268.11,Scrapbook #4. National World War I Museum Archives.

49   "Soldiers' Records: War of 1812-World War I," Missouri State Archives, service record for James Y. Simpson, http://www.sos.mo.gov/archives/soldiers/details.asp accessed by the author on April 29, 2013.

50   Mrs. James Y. (Lenora) Simpson, War Mothers Scrapbook #4, op. cit.

51   Col. Richard T. Ellis, "Report on the Activities in Europe of the American Pilgrimage Gold Star Mothers and Widows 1930." Gold Star, Record Group 92, National Archives.

52   "Mothers to War Graves." *The Kansas City Times.* July 2, 1930, p. 1.

53   Ibid.

54   Ibid.

55   "More Gold Star Mothers Off." *The Kansas City Times.* July 9, 1930, p. 1.

56   "On to Fields of France." *The Kansas City Times*, May 5, 1930, p. 5.

57   "Give Tea for War Mothers." *The Kansas City Times*, May 2, 1930, p. 4.

58   "Fourteen of the Twenty Kansas City Gold Star Women Who Sail this Summer to Visit Graves in France." *The Kansas City Times.* July 1, 1930, p. 6.

59   "Sixteen Kansas City Women in Gold Star Pilgrimage to Graves of Loved Ones Overseas." *The Kansas City Star,* August 17, 1930, p. 5A.

60   Julia C. Underwood, Untitled Journal of a War Mother's Pilgrimage to the Battlefields of France, August 6 to September 10, 1932. National World War I Museum Archives at Liberty Memorial, Kansas City.

61   Ibid.

62   "Rob Gold Star Mother." *The Kansas City Times*, August 11, 1930, p. 1.

63   Ibid.

64   Ibid.

65   "Gold Star Bags in a Lot." *The Kansas City Star*, August 11, 1930, p. 1.

66   "A Decade Ago the Gold Star League Was Started Here." *The Kansas City Star*, August 17, 1930, p. 5A.

67   Lillie F. Kelsay, *Historic & Dedicatory Monuments of Kansas City* (Kansas City: Board of Parks & Recreation Commissioners, 1987), p. 3.

68   Gorton Carruth, *What Happened When: A Chronology of Life & Events in America* (New York: Harper & Row Perennial Library, 1989), p. 301.

69   71st Congress, 3rd Session. *Pilgrimage for the Mothers and Widows of Soldiers, Sailors and Marines of the American Forces Now Interred in the Cemeteries of Europe.*
        (Washington, D.C., United State Government Printing Office House Document No. 140, 1930).

70   "V. F. W. Rolls Expand to 68." *The Inter-City News,* Fairmount, Missouri. May 13, 1932.

71   *World War I Honor Roll.* Ancestry.com Database On-line, Provo UT, USA., accessed by the author April 11, 2013.

72   Agnes Dora Fraas, Untitled Journal of a Gold Star Mother's Pilgrimage Voyage to France, July – August, 1931. National World War I Museum Agnes D. Fraas Archival Collection.

73   Ibid.

74   Ibid.

75   Ibid.

76   Ibid.

77   Ibid.

78   Ibid.

79   *New York Passenger Lists 1920-195.* Ancestry.com Database On-line, Provo UT, USA., accessed by the author April 11, 2013.

80   "In Memory of Veterans," undated and undocumented photocopy of a newspaper article with picture of Agnes Fraas and the Mount Washington War Mothers Monument in Agnes Fraas Gold Star Pilgrimage collection at the National World War I Museum archives.

81   Ibid.

82   "Flag Raising Honors Heroes." *The Kansas City Times*, November 12, 1924, p. 1.

83   "Wreaths for the Heroes." *The Kansas City Star*, May 30, 1932, p. 2.

84   Metcalf, Frank. "The Author of 'There is No Death." *The National Magazine*, Vol. 36, 1912, pp. 838-839. See the sidebar for the full text of the poem.

85   "Memorial to Soldiers." Great Bend *Tribune*, Sep 10, 1923.

86   "War Mothers Memorial to Jackson County's War Dead." *The Kansas City Star,* October 1, 1923, p. 4. A picture of the granite boulder monument accompanies the article.

87   "To Honor the War Dead." Undocumented newspaper clipping in War Mothers Scrapbook #1, National World War I Museum Archives.

88   "Cover of War Mothers Program Tells Story of Conflict." *The Kansas City Star,* September 7 1923, p. 2. A picture of the cover for the "Program [of the] Fourth National Convention,, American War Mothers Kansas City, Sep 29 Oct 5 – 1923" accompanied an article highlighting tentative plans for the convention.

89   Patterson, Michael Robert. "Enoch Herbert Crowder, Brigadier General, United States Army." Arlington National Cemetery Website. www.arlingtoncemetery.net/ehcrowder.net accessed April 14, 2013 by the author.

90   During the 1923 War Mothers convention, *The Kansas City Star* reviewed each day's activities and published an agenda of events scheduled for the next day. After the September 7 article ("Cover of War Mothers Program Tells Story of Conflict," op. cit.), none of *The Star's* reports mentions Pershing, Coontz, or Crowder. VFW national commander General Lloyd M. Brett, who commanded the 80th Division during the war, did, however, arrive in Kansas City on October 3, 1923, to attend the projected opening of VFW headquarters in Kansas City, Kan., and to address the War Mothers convention. See "V. F. W. Commander is Here," *The Kansas City Star*, October 3, 1923, p. 2. Also see "Mecca for War Mothers," *The Kansas City Star*, September 29, 1923, p. 2; "Loses 4 Sons, But Smiles," *The Kansas City Star*, September 30, 1923, p. 4A; "War Mothers in Session," *The Kansas City Star*, October 1, 1923, p. 3; "Keep Our Boys at Home," *The Kansas City Star*, October 2, 1923, p. 3; "Mothers Hit at Pardons," *The Kansas City Star*, October 4, 1923, p. 3; and "War Mothers End Sessions," *The Kansas City Star*, October 5, 1923, p. 2.

91   David McCullough, *Truman* (New York: Simon & Schuster, 1992), p. 173.

92   From *National Magazine*, Vol.36, 1912, pp. 838-839 http://books.google.com/books?pg=PA838&lpg=PA838&dq=John+L.+McCreery&id=B47NAAAAMAAJ&ots=wKMg48B66l, accessed by the author on April 14, 2013.

93   "In Memory of Veterans," undocumented newspaper photocopy in Agnes Fraas War Mother's Collection, National World War I Museum Archives.

94   Lillie F. Kelsay, *Historic and Dedicatory Monuments of Kansas City* (Kansas City, Mo.: Board of Parks & Recreation Commissioners, 1987), p. 3.

95   "A New Shrine to City." *The Kansas City Times*. June 1, 1942, p. 10.

Ltc. Ruby D. Garrett, 117th Field Signal Battalion, 42nd Division, with *Croix de Guerre.*

Photo Otto P. Higgins Collection, courtesy Sheila Scott.

CHAPTER 3

"We Remembered Buddies and Mothers"

The American Legion: To Continue the Fight for Democracy

Once the fighting had stopped, troop morale became an over-riding concern. More than a million men were under arms at the front, another million in support at the rear, and another million in the training camps ready to deploy. The million overseas had been drilled to fight, had endured the life-changing trauma of combat, and were anxious for release. Relationships were extremely important to the men, whose very survival had depended on one another, and even before the men left Europe, plans were being made for veterans' organizations to provide a means for the men to make the transition back to civilian life.

Suddenly silence. With one last drum roll of machine guns and one last chest-pounding thud of artillery fire, the killing stopped. Eleven, eleven, eleven, nineteen eighteen. Stopwatch stop. A profound quiet fell all along the Western Front. Many troops thought the silence was yet another trick to lure them out into the open, where the roar of slaughter would commence anew. Others replaced the din of battle with eerie shouts of joy. As quiet settled in once again, an uneasy loss of purpose took command. What would the troops do now, their energy pumped up, their nerves set on edge?

Some officers feared a Bolshevik-style mutiny. After all, that is just what had happened in Russia: non-military conscripts forced under arms could turn on authority itself. Now the enemy was boredom. The men wanted to go home …

now.

The incidence of desertion and dereliction of duty increased. Courts-martial counts rose. Venereal disease spread among the troops.

In counter-attack to the erosion of military discipline, officers increased military drills, but doing so just increased the tension. Before the Armistice, the drills had real purpose, but now their only purpose was to occupy the men, as if the very energy that had been harnessed to wage war was suddenly now the enemy itself. American soldiers had to be occupied just like German territory, and even at that, only a few divisions were assigned the long marches of occupation. Most units displaced the energy of the men into sports and staged entertainments. But officers everywhere worried; men grew increasingly anxious, and there were a lot of them.

Approximately one million American men

were under arms at the front, another million in the rear as part of the Service of Supply, and yet another million at home in the training camps, prepared to deploy.[1] The men in the training camps could simply be released and sent home by rail, but that wasn't so easily done with the men in Europe. They couldn't suddenly be released; land and sea transportation couldn't handle the volume, and what if the armistice itself failed to hold?

The situation posed a challenge unique to military strategy. No one had anticipated what would happen when hostilities ceased and so many non-professional military were left in the hands of the career professionals. Military procedure called for a reconnoitering, so AEF General Headquarters called a parley of field-grade officers, especially those who had seen service with the non-professionals – the National Guard units and the draftees in the National Army of the United States. The professional military needed to know how to improve morale before it deteriorated completely. "In particular, General Headquarters wanted to learn just what were the wants, needs, and desires of the non-professional soldiers that it had on its hands."[2]

The answer came back loud and clear. At the first morale conference held in Paris, February 15-17, 1919, 20 officers made the following recommendations:

1. Notify AEF units immediately of departure dates for return to the States;

2. Promote those personnel whose advancement had been earned prior to November 11 but had been frozen at the time of the Armistice; and

3. Reduce the number of maneuvers in the field.

A month later, the 20 officers who had attended the first conference held another meeting to implement yet another recommendation, this one made by Ltc. Theodore Roosevelt, Jr., the man "who was to do more than any other individual to combine the problem of raising the morale of the AEF with that of organizing a society of war veterans."[3]

Such societies had existed before in the history of post-war America. After the Revolutionary War, the Order of Cincinnati had been founded for officers of that war. Membership was hereditary. After the Civil War, the Grand Army of the Republic (the GAR) had been founded in 1866 to include all union soldiers of all ranks. Its counterpart for ex-Confederate soldiers, the United Confederate Veterans (UCV), was founded in 1889, but had little of the political impact of the GAR and even refused assistance from the federal government that had defeated them in the war.

The new veterans organization to follow the Great War, however, would be different from these previous veterans groups. Unlike the exclusionary Order of Cincinnati, the new veterans organization would be open to anyone who had served in the combat zone or in the states, regardless of rank. And unlike the politically active GAR, which had advocated for government pensions to Union veterans after the war, the new veterans organization would not be so aligned with a political party to achieve its own ends. Any new veterans group had to be non-partisan if it was to "convince the public that veterans were interested in more than raiding the treasury."[4]

Quite the contrary: instead of fighting for their own selfish interest, veterans wanted to continue the fight to which they had put their lives on the line, the fight "to make the world safe for democracy." During the war, national sentiment supported by George Creel's Committee for Political Information had created an image of the doughboy as a crusader in the cause of freedom, and, at least by some accounts, the doughboy took the idealism home with him to his own town and state to make it a better place in which to live. "For the World War veteran came from a simpler age, in which the ideals of honor, patriotism, and duty had been impressed upon him since childhood. For many of them only one thing set them apart from all of the other men that they had known back in their neighborhood, village, or farmland: service in the Great War. The desire to continue this crusading spirit in an organized fashion, to show the folks back home how a crusader behaved, was significant."[5]

So, to be at all viable, the new veterans association would have to offer the returning doughboy an opportunity to continue the bonds of brotherhood that combat had forged, to give purpose and mission to that brotherhood in improving the local community, and to do so in a spirit of egalitarianism and non-partisanship.

To that end, the original committee of 20 invited a larger group of enlisted men and officers for a caucus in Paris from March 15-17, 1919, to form a broad-based veterans organization. Among the delegates was Kansas City native Ltc. Ruby D. Garrett, field signal officer for the 42nd Rainbow Division and commander of the 117th Field Signal Battalion, the earliest of the Kansas City units to go overseas. Later, Ltc. Garrett became a member of the new organization's first national executive committee as well as the executive committee for Missouri, and he served as commander of Kansas City's William T. Fitzsimons Post, the largest in the state.[6]

Also among the delegates was another Missouri field-grade officer, Ltc. Bennett C. Clark, who was elected chairman of the caucus, in part "to dispel the suspicion of some that the new organization would have the political overtones of the GAR," especially its well-known association with the Republican Party.[7] Ltc. Bennett Clark was the son of Champ Clark, a leader in the Democratic Party and Speaker of the House.

While Ltc. Clark chaired the group of active soldiers in Europe, Ltc. Roosevelt chaired a parallel meeting in St. Louis for those servicemen who had already returned home or who had never left the United States. "Many concluded that it could hardly be a partisan organization if the son of the former Republican president [Ltc. Roosevelt] and the son of a well-known Democratic politician [Ltc. Clark] were to be leaders in this new Group."[8] To publicize the event in Paris, the *Stars and Stripes* emphasized the rank-less, non-partisan, and non-sectarian qualities of the organization whose main purpose was to continue the relationship formed among the men while in the service of their country.[9] Any enlisted man who happened to be in Paris at the time would be welcome to attend and participate even without a formal invitation, the popular

Photo courtesy Library of Congress.

L to R. Sen. Gerald P. Nye of North Dakota, Sen. Bennett Champ Clark of Missouri, and Sen. Arthur Vanderberg of Michigan discussing their neutrality bill, February 1, 1937.

paper said.

At the Paris meeting, Clark named committees to form a permanent organization, to determine the time and place of a national convention, to begin the draft of a constitution, and to propose a name. Committees met separately, then re-assembled at the Cirque de Paris theatre and auditorium to present their reports to an estimated attendance of about 500 servicemen.[10]

First to report was the committee on a constitution, which took as its model the Preamble to the U.S. Constitution to set forth the purpose of the new organization: "We, the members of the Military and Naval forces of the United States of America in the Great War, desiring to perpetuate the principles of Justice, Freedom, and Democracy for which we have fought, to inculcate the duty and obligation of citizens to the state, to preserve the history and incidents of our participation in the war, and to cement the ties of comradeship formed in service, do propose to found and establish an association for the furtherance of the foregoing purposes."[11]

Eligibility requirements in the proposed organization were simple: all who served between April 6, 1917 and November 11, 1918, with the exception of those who had not performed their full military duties (conscientious objectors) or those who had performed military service but who had refused to bear arms and those who had not received honorable discharges).

More difficult was the name by which the national veterans organization was to be

Photo courtesy of Library of Congress.
Maj. Theodore Roosevelt, Jr.

known. After considering some 15 submissions and unable to come to agreement, the committee submitted five favorites: "Legion of the Great War," "Veterans of the Great War," "The Legion," "Society of the Great War," and "The American Legion."[12] After a floor debate, the caucus chose the fifth-place choice, "The American Legion."

Ironically, "The American Legion" was also the name of an earlier organization formed in 1915 after hostilities had broken out in Europe but before America had joined the war effort. Theodore Roosevelt, Jr. had been a director. Believing that the United States would soon be at war, the organization sought to attract men with prior military service or special skills to assist in the preparation of a large U.S. military force. The organization supported the Plattsburg idea of military training for civilians. However, when President Wilson began the Preparedness Campaign of 1916, the purpose for the organization was no longer relevant. The government acquired the records of the former American Legion, and the old organization ceased to be.[13]

Meanwhile, preparations for the caucus in St. Louis were underway, and from May 8-10, 1919, delegates met at the Shubert-Jefferson Theater. Larger than the Paris caucus had been, the St. Louis caucus decided little beyond affirming the name "American Legion," re-writing its objectives, determining that the next meeting would be held in Minneapolis, and naming a permanent chairman after Theodore Roosevelt, Jr. had declined in favor of a political career.

The most important work of the St. Louis caucus was the revision of the objectives that had been composed earlier at the Paris caucus. With a strong emphasis on idealistic patriotism, the new document became the official Preamble of the Legion Constitution:

> For God and Country we associate ourselves together for the following purposes:
> To uphold and defend the Constitution of the United States of America; to maintain law and order, to foster and perpetuate a one hundred per cent Americanism; to preserve the memories and incidents of our associations in the Great War; to inculcate a sense of individual obligation to the community, state, and nation; to combat the autocracy of both the classes and the masses; to make right the master of might; to promote peace and good will on earth; to safeguard and transmit to posterity the principles of justice, freedom, and democracy; to consecrate and sanctify our comradeship by our devotion to mutual helpfulness.[14]

In the 50 years following its adoption, the only revision was that the word "war" was changed to "wars" to include those veterans of World War II and all other wars since the Great War.

Finally, the St. Louis caucus passed four resolutions advocating jobs for veterans, deportation of aliens who had refused to serve, denial of clemency for those serving jail sentences as conscientious objectors, and condemnation of Bolshevik attempts to take control of veterans organizations.

After the caucus adjourned, the various states set out to organize their own departments and plan for their first state convention. In Kansas, it was decided that a post, initially called a "billet," was to consist of at least 15 members and was not to carry the name of a living person but one who had died in the service of the country. Annual dues were set at 75 cents a year, and a charter was not to be issued to a local billet until all the dues had been paid. A major effort was made to assist veterans in converting their government war risk insurance to civilian coverage. The Legion also acted as an employment service for veterans. The initial dues were not at all sufficient to cover operating costs, and finances became an issue: Chair of the Kansas committee, Dr. W. A. Phares, and three other men co-signed a $1,000 note from a Wichita bank to put the new organization on its legs. At the national level, a large number of co-signers guaranteed a note of $300,000 for operating expenses.[15]

Now financially viable, the new American Legion held its first national convention in Minneapolis on the first anniversary of the Armistice. The convention declared that the Preamble crafted in St. Louis was the "best expression of the aims and principles of which was to become the largest veteran's organization in history."[16] With but a few modifications, the convention also adopted the constitution crafted by the St. Louis caucus.

Also significant for Kansas City was the proposal that the national headquarters be located there, but the proposal had to compete with bids from proponents of other cities – Washington, Indianapolis, Minneapolis, and Detroit. The Kansas City bid had much in its favor. Not only did Kansas City's central location make it conveniently accessible from anywhere in the United States, but the city could boast of a dedication equal to the patriotic spirit expressed in the Legion's newly adopted preamble and constitution. In the ten days between October 27 and November 5, 1919, more than 100,000 Kansas Citians raised $2.5 million dollars for the construction of a memorial to honor the service of those who had died in the Great War.[17] Further, the city was willing to accommodate in its construction the living presence of an American Legion National Headquarters at the site.

As appealing as the bid for Kansas City was, the appeals of Washington, Indianapolis and Minneapolis were stronger in the eyes of the delegates, and Indianapolis finally won out. Kansas City would go on to construct its Liberty Memorial, taking some consolation in the fact that the American Legion was not so much a national organization as it was local. "Policies might be decided upon at the national level or the department might proclaim a program to the entire state, but in the last analysis it has been at the community level that the Legion has had the most impact."[18]

Now at the local level, the energy devoted by the Kansas and Missouri delegates to Kansas City's bid for the site of national headquarters was replaced by competition for which local post would be designated as "first" in its state. Even after the numbers were assigned, the contention continues to this day because, at first, the assignment of post numbers was not consistent or centralized. Not completely confident that the fledgling organization would survive, the national headquarters sent 20 blank charters to each state with the provision that the state headquarters file the charter applications at national headquarters after the charter had been issued to the local post. This did not happen consistently.

Nor was the numbering of the posts consistent. In Kansas, for example, American Legion posts were numbered by counties, so that a number of Kansas posts bore the number "1." On June 16, 1919, ten posts were chartered in Kansas: Topeka, Newton, Columbus, Thomas Hopkins Post of Wichita, Emporia, Atchison, Fredonia, Garden City, Winfield, and Downs. Each could claim to be the first in the state. The "Withers Committee" was formed to consider the evidence for the various claims to priority, and an order was finally determined. Capitol Post of Topeka was designated as No. 1; however, other posts still disputed the claim and "controversy over the decision made by the Withers Committee still goes on."[19]

The city did attempt to contain the litter anticipated to accumulate from the exuberance of legionnaires. It purchased and set out 1,000 galvanized trashcans and closed down traffic from 10th to 13th streets between McGee and Baltimore. The city's good intentions were, however, politely ignored by uninhibited legionnaires, who turned the cans upside down and used them as drums, the lids offering a perfect opportunity for conversion to cymbals.

Although Kansas City was not designated as the official site for the national headquarters nor did one of its posts carry the coveted distinction as being the "first" in the state, the city was the site for the 1921 national convention hosted by both the Kansas and the Missouri Departments from October 31-November 2, 1921. It proved to be the convention that, according to at least one account, "set the pace for years to come."[20] With Kansas City's reputation of being a "wide-open city," the enforcement of prohibition possibly being less serious than in other cities, "the stage was set for a wild time."[21] The city did attempt to contain the litter anticipated to accumulate from the exuberance of legionnaires. It purchased and set out 1,000 galvanized trashcans and closed down traffic from 10th to 13th streets between McGee and Baltimore. The city's good intentions were, however, politely ignored by uninhibited legionnaires, who turned the cans upside down and used them as drums, the lids offering a perfect opportunity for conversion to cymbals.

Impromptu parades accompanied the instrumentation, and more than one legionnaire found himself rolling down one of the steeper inclines inside a galvanized container. Other activities contributed to a memorable Halloween night. A bread wagon that had somehow managed to enter the restricted zone found itself commandeered, its driver conscripted, and its contents immediately propelled to the eager crowd. The local police, who had previously agreed to "go easy" on the enforcement of local ordinances, was nowhere to be seen. In place of the local police, Legion guards had volunteered to regulate the parades and their related festivities. These friendly comrades, who acted less like military police and more like medics in the field, escorted their more obviously intoxicated brethren to a cold shower, soft bed, and bountiful breakfast in the rear – thus rehabilitating them for a "return to the front" of convention activities the next day. In the meantime, the impromptu parades continued, led by drum majors keeping time with mops turned upside-down, followed by off-beat rhythm sections and marchers noticeably imprecise in their mockery of military bearing.[22]

On a more serious note, the occasion of the American Legion convention also coincided with the dedication of the Liberty Memorial. In attendance at the dedication were Marshal Ferdinand Foch, Commander of Allied troops; General John J. Pershing, AEF Commander; Admiral Hugh Rodman, Commander of the U.S. battle fleet; General Armando Vittorio Diaz of Italy; Admiral David Beatty of England; Lieutenant General Baron Jacques of Belgium; and General John A. Lejeune who commanded American marines at Beleau Wood.[23]

At the same time, not to be outdone, the city itself dedicated two fountains, the first in what was anticipated to be a series of eight fountains, one for each of the city's eight American Legion Posts. Only two of the fountains, however, were actually constructed. The first, called American Legion Memorial II, cost $8,000 and was located at the Meyer Boulevard entrance to Swope Park. It was dedicated on October 30, 1921, and across the top bore the legend, "Dedicated by Kansas City to the American Legion Posts." Sixteen uniformed legionnaires uncovered the American flag, which draped the fountain. As the flag was removed, there appeared a bronze panel depicting 22 figures of American soldiers entering a French village and assisting wounded French soldiers and refugees. John W. Inzer, national chaplain of the legion, gave the dedication address.[24]

Two days later, on November 2, 1921, three Medal of Honor winners helped dedicate the second of the fountains, known as "American Legion I," originally placed at one of the city's most important intersections: "The Junction," at 9th and Main, at the time the center of the city's commerce. However, as vehicles replaced cable cars and pedestrians, the fountain's location created a traffic hazard and was finally moved to Budd Park Esplanade at Anderson Street, north of Independence Avenue on Van Brunt. One side of the pylon lists each of the American Legion Posts – the first eight and four others added later:

No. 8 William T. Fitzsimons
No. 10 Murray Davis
No. 50 William J. Bland
No. 81 Joseph Dillon
No. 93 Arthur Maloney
No. 124 Sanford Brown
No. 130 James Cummings
No. 148 Joseph Liebman
No. 224 Grover Metzger

No. 201 Hewitt Swearingen
No. 120 Hedrick/Shackelton
No. 149 Wayne Minor

On the opposite side is a quotation from President Theodore Roosevelt: "All daring and courage, all iron endurance of misfortune, all devotion to the ideal of honor and glory of the flag makes for a finer and nobler type of manhood." On the sides opposite of the inscriptions are bronze plaques depicting servicemen in combat: soldiers on one side, sailors on the other.[25] Also inscribed on the pylon are the words, "United Kansas City American Legion Posts October 31 – November 2, 1921," the dates for the American Legion convention in Kansas City and the Dedication of the Liberty Memorial.

From that day in March 1919 when Lieutenant Colonel Ruby D. Garrett attended the Paris caucus until today, the American Legion continues to honor all the men and women who have served in America's wars and who build the community with the same idealism and dedication the doughboys of 1917-1918 brought to the service of their country. Part of the Legion's legacy to Kansas City can be seen in the two fountains dedicated during the 1921 American Legion Convention.

Illustration for "In the Argonne," *The Kansas City Star*, **January 5, 1919, p. 12C.**

M-8 American Legion I Fountain
Budd Park Esplanade, Van Brunt at Anderson, Kansas City, Missouri

This fountain was originally installed at an intersection called "The Junction," located at Delaware and Main streets south of the old Westgate Hotel. Here, Main, Delaware, and 9th streets intersected in a point. A very busy intersection at the time, it was the heart of Kansas City's business district. The statue "The Muse of Missouri" occupies the spot today. At noon on Wednesday, November 2, 1921, Mayor James Cowgill presented the fountain in the name of the city to the American Legion, and Chairman of the Legion Americanism Commission, Alvin M. Owsley of Texas, delivered the dedication address.

"As Americans," he said, "we all can claim Missouri. From it came our General Pershing and Admiral Coontz. It belongs to us as a nation." Three Medal of Honor recipients – Major J. C. Dozier of South Carolina and Waldo M. Hatler and John Lewis Barkley of Missouri – accepted for the American Legion. Major Dozier introduced M. Waldo Hatler, who formerly accepted the memorial, noting that there were two kinds of memorials: one in stone and bronze, the other in

American Legion I Fountain Budd Park Esplanade, Van Brunt at Anderson, Kansas City, Missouri.

James J. Heiman

human hearts.

"This fountain," he said, "a gift of Kansas City that had so grandly poured out its heart to the American Legion, combined both".[26]

The sculptor, Robert Merrell Gage, was the same man who designed American Legion II. He was a native of Topeka, Kansas, and later became a Professor of Sculpture at the University of Southern California. The stone is Tennessee marble. The east panel, measuring 40" x 18 ½" in bas-relief, depicts two male figures carrying naval munitions. The west panel is also in bas-relief and contains three figures in a raiding party. The front figure holds his arm aloft, ready to throw a grenade. The central figure holds a rifle in his right arm.

The dedication side lists the names and post numbers of 12 American Legion Posts, each named after a Kansas City serviceman who lost his life in the war.

The side opposite of the dedication carries a quotation by Theodore Roosevelt: "All daring and courage, all iron endurance of misfortune, all devotion to the ideal of honor and the glory of the flag makes for a finer and

"*All daring and courage, all iron endurance of misfortune, all devotion to the ideal of honor and the glory of the flag makes for a finer and nobler type of manhood.*"

— *Col. Theodore Roosevelt*

Col. Theodore Roosevelt and Maj. Gen. Leonard Wood.

Photo courtesy Library of Congress.

nobler type of manhood."

The quote is especially poignant in the context of Roosevelt's own sacrifices. Each of Roosevelt's four sons – Theodore ("Ted"), Archie, Quentin, and Kermit – served in the war, and the Colonel himself applied to President Wilson to lead a division, but the President denied his request.

Kermit, the least military of the brothers, "gained access to the front through contacts in the British foreign office."[27] Ted served in both WWI and WWII. In WWI, Ted commanded the 1st Battalion, 26th Infantry, 1st Division. At one point, as a Lieutenant Colo-

nel, Roosevelt was assigned to Kansas City's 140th Infantry Regiment, but never reached the regiment, being reassigned instead to his former regiment.[28] Ted was instrumental in the formation of the American Legion, heading up the first large gathering of Legionnaires to be held in the states shortly after the boys returned home in 1919. Archie served as a captain in his older brother Ted's command.

Quentin, the youngest of Roosevelt's children, was a lieutenant in the 95th American Aero Squadron, First Pursuit Group. He was killed on Bastille Day, July 14, 1918, in single combat with a more experienced German pilot at Chamery, near Rheims. Three days before, he had won the *Croix de Guerre* in a daring exploit while scouting over German lines. He was separated from his comrades and, while dropping through a cloud patch, found himself in the rear of six German planes. Rather than retreat, he attacked, opening up with his machine gun and dropping one of the planes. Then he put his plane into a wide arc and flew toward Allied lines, pursued by the five remaining German planes. He dodged the bullets that day, but met his own end three days later. The Germans buried Quentin where he fell. Roosevelt's other three sons survived the war, and Roosevelt himself lived to see the Armistice, but died on January 6, 1919. When asked if he wanted Quentin brought back home for re-burial in the United States, Colonel Roosevelt is said to have responded, "Let the tree lie where it fell."

People who knew the former president said that he was never the same after his son's death, but the Colonel, himself sickly as a boy, espoused a life of vigor, like a "Bull Moose," he said, and he strongly supported U.S. involvement in the war, often berating Wilson for his "lack of preparedness." Losing his son Quentin was a great blow, and for the old Colonel of Rough Riders, his son, Quentin, is personified by his quote on the fountain, "All daring and courage, all iron endurance of misfortune, all devotion to the ideal of honor and the glory of the flag makes for a finer and nobler type of manhood."

The fountain was designed by Wilkinson and Crans and executed by Kansas City sculptor Robert Merrell Gage at a cost of $8,000. It consists of a 10-foot pylon of Tennessee marble rising from a bowl 7 feet in diameter. A glass dome containing an electric light was perched at the top of the monument. During the first winter of its operation, the pipes feeding the three drinking spigots froze and burst, so the water was perma- nently turned off.[29] Then in 1959, as part of the city re-development plan, the fountain was moved to the intersection of Van Brunt Boulevard and Anderson in a sliver of land called "Budd Park Esplanade."

In 2002, the fountain was struck in a motor accident and had to be removed and stored in pieces until the Parks Department allocated $25,000 in repairs to the masonry and plumbing.[30]

The names of the 12 American Legion Posts inscribed on the dedication side of the fountain include William T. Fitzsimons, No. 8; Murray Davis, No. 10; William J. Bland, No. 50; Joseph Dillon, No. 81; Arthur Maloney, No. 93; Sanford Brown, Jr., No 124; James Cummings, No. 130; Joseph Liebman, No. 148; Grover Metzger, No. 224; Hewitt Swearingen, No. 201; and Wayne Minor, No. 149. Most of these are no longer functioning as posts or have combined with others, but the stories of the men for whom they were named remain compelling and form the basis of this book on Kansas City War memorials.

James J. Heiman

Detail of eagle from the top of the American Legion I monument.

M-9 American Legion II Fountain
Swope Park West Entrance, Kansas City, Missouri

This working drinking fountain, dedicated during the 1921 American Legion Convention, is known as "American Legion II," but it was dedicated first, two days before American Legion I, at Budd Park Esplanade.

At 2:30 on Sunday afternoon, October 30, 1921, 16 uniformed legionnaires uncovered the fountain draped in an American flag. The fountain cost $6,000, and the City Council appropriated $20,000 to care for both American Legion I and II. Designed by Kansas City sculptor Robert Merrell Gage, the fountain is constructed of Tennessee marble. Its bronze panel contains 22 figures of soldiers, wounded, children, and elderly, 14 of which face right and eight to the left. American soldiers are entering a French village and wounded French soldiers and refugees greet them. Robert M. Gage designed and built the American Legion fountains with the assistance of architects Wilkinson & Crans and G. B. Franklin.[31] The larger story of the fountains, however, is grounded in the story of the Unknown Soldier.

James J. Heiman

American Legion II Fountain, Swope Park West Entrance, Kansas City, Missouri

Soldiers Known and Unknown: Marshal Foch, Admiral Beatty, and Generals Diaz, Jacques, and Pershing at the Liberty Memorial

Now that the survivors had been welcomed home and begun the transition back to civilian life, the process of national and local memorialization began in earnest. The "Unknown Soldiers" of England, France, Italy, and the United States focused international attention on the service of all who had fought and sacrificed. In Kansas City, the commemoration of the "Unknowns" coincided with the gathering of military commanders from the five allied countries – England, France, Italy, Belgium, and the United States – and their dedication of the site for the Liberty Memorial. At the same time, the American Legion held its national convention in Kansas City and dedicated the first of the Kansas City World War I monuments – American Legion I and American Legion II.

In the dead of the night on October 23, 1921, four U.S. Army trucks secretly transported to the Chalons hôtel de ville, the city hall at Chalons-sur-Marne, France, four bodies exhumed the day before – one each from the American cemeteries at Somme, St. Mihiel, Aisne-Marne, and Meuse-Argonne.[32] There in the city hall, a makeshift chapel had been constructed, and in the chapel, a quartermaster detachment of American soldiers from Coblenz, Germany, arranged the plain caskets in a row. Everyone left the chapel; only the dead remained.[33]

They were four of the 1,648 infantrymen who could not be identified from the 79,359 lost in the war.[34] And they were American. The location of their deaths, the circumstances of their original burials, and the character of their uniforms had established that fact. Nothing else was known. Before placement of the bodies in identical caskets, a team of

Corporal and later Sergeant Edward F. Younger. [38]

officers examined the bodies to verify that they could not, in fact, be identified. Even the four sets of paperwork distinguishing the transports had been burned upon arrival at Chalons-sur-Marne. In all respects, the dead were completely unknown. From that point on, by Congressional order, a new identity would be born from the hollow of a makeshift chapel in a French city hall along the River Marne.

On March 4, 1921, Congress directed the Secretary of War, who then delegated the Quartermaster Corps, to select an American Unknown Soldier for burial in the United States, at Arlington, on the third anniversary of the Armistice, November 11, 1921. To carry out that order, outside the makeshift chapel in Chalons-sur-Marne, stood the U.S. Quartermaster General, the Commanding General of American Forces in Germany, the Mayor of Chalons-sur-Marne, high officers of the French Army, and distinguished French and American civilians. In keeping with the order, the selection would be brief and simple.[35]

A French military band played the dead march from "Saul." A former member of the Chalons city council, M. Brasseur Bruffer, who had lost two sons in the war, gave Major R. P. Harbold, the officer in charge of grave registrations, a simple spray of red and white roses to honor the casket of the American Unknown. The Major selected six soldiers to act as pallbearers, one of whom, Sgt. Edward F. Younger, HQ Company, 2nd Battalion, 50th Infantry, a native of Chicago, designated the Unknown by placing the spray on his plain wood coffin.[36]

Alone with only the strains of a death march, Sgt. Younger passed through a line of French troops and entered the makeshift chapel. He walked around the four coffins three times. Then he stopped at the casket third from left facing the entrance. He placed the roses on the casket, turned, and marched back through the open doorway.

"It was as though something had pulled me," he later said. "A voice seemed to say, 'This is a pal of yours.'"[37]

Outside in the sunlight, Sgt. Younger turned to salute the casket. Then he reported to his officer that the mission had been accomplished.

Back inside, to completely ensure anonymity, the body of the Unknown was transferred to a new casket, and a body from one of the remaining three caskets was placed in his. The new casket was draped in the American flag, the single spray of red and white roses resting on it. The other three caskets were taken to the American Meuse-Argonne Cemetery and re-buried in plots designated 1, 2, and 3.

It was as if all of the deliberateness, ritual, secrecy, and privacy – the complete obliteration of any distinction remained only: the total reduction had created a new identity completely representational, completely Unknown, standing completely for all that is, in the final analysis, finally known about war.

At Le Havre, the port where so many Americans had landed and, after the war, departed France for home, the U.S. cruiser *Olympia* waited to convey the American Unknown back to his country.[40] Accompanying the body was a large box of earth taken from the American cemetery at Suresnes. It would be on a few inches of this French soil that the body of the Unknown would lay in its final resting place at Arlington.[41] The *Olympia* had been Admiral Dewey's flagship and was now accompanied by the American Destroyer *Rueben James*, DD245. Ironically, 21 years after 1921, the *Rueben James* would become the first American ship to sink in the Second World War. That same year, 1942, not far from the grave of the American Unknown, Sgt. Edward Younger would be laid to rest, too, in Arlington National Cemetery, the victim of a heart attack.

Meanwhile, in the central nave of England's Westminister Abbey, King George V of Britain, King Albert of Belgium, Marshal Foch of France, and others honored the grave of the

Sgt. Younger's right hand rests on the coffin of the American Unknown, next to the spray of roses he placed over the flag that drapes the Unknown's coffin. [39]

Unknown British Warrior.[42] On his marble gravestone, American General John J. Pershing laid the gold American Medal of Honor, then drew himself up to attention and stood in salute for the highest tribute the United States could offer its ally.[43]

In Paris, Marshal Foch, along with French Marshals Franchet d'Esperey, Petain, and Joffre, and American General Pershing, attended the dedication of the French Unknown, *Le Soldat Inconnu*. There, too, General Pershing offered his nation's tribute. He saluted *Le Soldat Inconnu* and then pinned the gold Medal of Honor to a velvet cushion on a small table before his grave.[44] *Le Soldat Inconnu* lies at rest beneath the Arc de Triomphe.

After the recognitions of the British and French Unknowns, both Foch and Pershing left separately for Kansas City at the invitation of the American Legion to attend its national convention and the dedication of the Liberty Memorial. In Washington, preparations were underway to receive the American Unknown where he would lie in state at the Capitol on November 10.[45]

Meanwhile, in the Atlantic, the French Liner *Paris*, on which Marshal Foch sailed, was ahead of the *U.S.A.T. George Washington*, the ship on which General Pershing was making

Photo courtesy Library of Congress.

Marshal Foch and General Pershing meet in New York.

the crossing. Consequently, the *Paris* was obliged to slow down,[46] and the American Legion requested the ex-servicemen working the boilers of the *George Washington* to "bend to the task" and pour on the coal so that Pershing would steam into New York an hour before the Supreme Commander of Allied Forces and be the first on American soil to salute his former commander and greet him with a handshake.[47]

General Armando Vittorio Diaz[48] Commander-in-Chief of the Italian armies; British Admiral Earl Beatty, Hero of the Battle of Jutland; and General Baron Jacques of the Belgian Army had already arrived in Washington from New York and were on their way to Kansas City too.[49]

In anticipation of their visit, 700 Kansas City women spread through downtown selling 15,000 medallions for a dollar each to help defray expenses for the Liberty Memorial dedication. Suspended from a red, white, and blue silk ribbon, the medallion featured, on the obverse, the design of the Liberty Memorial and, on the reverse, an explanatory engraving of the memorial's purpose.[5] However, their efforts were accompanied by less civic-minded intentions. Cpt. Harry S. Truman, Chair of the Decorating Committee for the American Legion Convention, reported the theft of 6,000 posters, which had been printed by the committee for free distribution, but were being sold illegally as souvenirs for five cents apiece. Truman requested that the police apprehend and prosecute the unscrupulous vendors posing as Legionnaires and warn the public not to buy the posters. Measuring 5" x 8", the posters pictured a doughboy and a sailor on a background of red, white, and blue, with the words "Welcome Legionnaire" prominently featured.[51]

More gracious was the hospitality extended to the honored guests. The American Legion Distinguished Visitors' Committee Chair Charles W. Bartlett offered 26 guests accommodations in the names of 21 prominent citizens.[52] Mrs. Laura Kirkwood, daughter of *The Kansas City Star* founder William Rockhill Nelson, and her husband Mr. Irwin Kirkwood, placed their entire home at 4620 Kenwood Avenue at the disposal of the committee. There, the committee billetted Marshal Foch and his party and General Pershing, who was accompanied by various U.S. government aides. The Marshal and the General quartered together.

Mr. Jacob L. Loose and his wife, Ella,[53] entertained General Armando Vittorio Diaz, commander-in-chief of the Italian armies, and his official party at their home at 101 East Armour Blvd.

Mr. Robert A. Long, Chair of the Liberty Memorial Association, and his wife, Ella,[54] hosted Admiral Earl Beatty, Commander of England's Grand Fleet, in their home, Corinthian Hall, at 3218 Gladstone Blvd. The Admiral's wife, an American, the daughter of Chicago department store mogul Marshal Fields, was unable to be with her husband during the Kansas City visit.

Mr. and Mrs. J. W. Perry hosted Lieut. Gen. Baron Jacques of Belgium and his party at their home at 1335 Santa Fe Road. General John A. Lejeune was the guest of Isaac P. and Bessie Ryland,[55] 3758 Washington, and Vice-President Calvin Coolidge and his entourage

The Liberty Memorial medallion.

In anticipation of their visit, 700 Kansas City women spread through downtown selling 15,000 medallions for a dollar each to help defray expenses for the Liberty Memorial dedication. Suspended from a red, white, and blue silk ribbon, the medallion featured, on the obverse, the design of the Liberty Memorial and, on the reverse, an explanatory engraving of the memorial's purpose.[50]

Welcoming posters distributed by Cpt. Harry S. Truman's Decorating Committee.

stayed at 5100 Rockhill Road, the home of Walter S. Dickey, whose wife Katherine had died the year before.[57]

Sixty-three-year-old Lieutenant General Baron Alphonse de Jacques of Belgium, aboard the Wabash from St. Louis, was the first to arrive in Kansas City, at 7:30 a.m. on Saturday, October 30, 1921. The hero of Dixmude and Liege was greeted on the platform by the national anthem of Belgium, "*LaBrabanconne*," and the "Star Spangled Banner" of the United States, in addition to several hundred legionnaires and Kansas City Belgians.[58]

Then as he moved from the train sheds through the long arcade and to the great lobby, out over the Station plaza, and up on to Liberty Memorial Hill, thousands more cheered.

"*Marveilleux*," the General said, tears welling in his eyes.

Missouri Governor Arthur M. Hyde and Kansas City Mayor James Cowgill extended the official welcome as General Jacques bowed and saluted the crowd. From Union Station, General Jacques proceeded south over Hospital Hill to Gillham Road, continuing south to Rockhill Road, to Brush Creek Blvd. and then to Wornall, across 51st Street to Sunset Drive and finally to Ward Parkway and to 1535 Santa Fe Road, the home of J. W. Perry.[59]

From there after breakfast, the General attended Mass at the Immaculate Conception Cathedral. Later in the afternoon, he appeared at an aviation meet and, in the evening, greeted the 89th "Middle-West" Division at Convention Hall.

General Baron Jacques of Belgium.[56]

The crowd could not forget that seven years earlier, in August 1914, as hordes of gray-coated Germans swept down into Belgium bound for Paris, Colonel Jacques threw the men of his 12th Regiment into the path of the onslaught at Vise and took the first devastating blow of the Great War. He led the 1st Battalion into the bloody battle of Sart Tilmant. Under heavy artillery and withering machine gun fire at Haecht and Over de Vaart, General Jacques led his men in attack, and at the Hansbrug bridgehead, detail after detail of his men stepped up to cover the retreat of the 11th Regiment as it attempted to pull back from the unrelenting German advance.

In a stirring Sunday feature article, *The Kansas City Star* summarized the character and heroic deeds of the man some called the "David of Belgium"[60]: "Liege and Namur fell, finally Antwerp. Colonel Jacques was at Antwerp with his regiment in the fourth sector between Fort Liezele and the flooded Reyndonck area. From here he was forced back by the strong attacks of the Germans toward the Blaesvelt bridgehead, and then came the memorable retreat from Antwerp to the Yser. In the region of Nieuport, the Meiser brigade, consisting of the 11th and 12th line regiments, together with the Ronarch marines, were given the task of defending Dixmude."[61]

Colonel Jacques rose to the task. "Upon him fell the maintenance of the bridgehead on the east bank of the Yser, which it was essential to hold at any cost. His post was in the city itself and here he took a solemn oath that so long as he remained alive, the enemy should not pass. Dixmude was under a storm of shells and soon became a vast heap of flame-swept ruins; the gallant battalions despite fearful losses and bleeding from a thousand wounds, held on. Although twice wounded himself, severely in the foot and again in the arm, Colonel Jacques refused to quit his post, knowing that his men would not weaken so long as their leader remained with them. When General Meiser had to be evacuated to the hospital, Colonel Jacques assumed command of the brigade and held out until his regiments, having reached the supreme limit of physical resistance and with the cross of the order of Leopold on their colors, were at last relieved."[62]

Colonel Jacques was promoted to major general in April 1915 and, less

General Armando Vittorio Diaz of Italy.[63]

than a year later, to lieutenant general, first commanding the 2nd Brigade and then the 3rd Division, known as "The Iron Division." As the lines of war dug in for months of trench fighting, General Jacques held various sectors along the Yser front, mingling daily with his troops, personally recognizing their bravery, and in his conduct and bearing, inspiring them all.

When the Germans launched their spring 1918 offensive, General Jacques' advance units were overrun, but in counterattack, the General drove the Germans back and regained the lost ground, taking nearly 800 German prisoners. Then in the last drive of the war, General Jacques assumed command of the central attack group for the offensive, re-took the Flanders ridge, and held at Stadenberg and Westroosebeke. Along with General Leman, the Defender of Liege, General Jacques "embodied in the eyes of the nation the loftiest military virtues" and was accorded the highest military honors by King Albert, who also entrusted his son, the heir apparent, Prince Leopold, to the 12th Regiment.[64]

Fifteen minutes after General Jacques' arrival at Union Station aboard the Wabash, a Santa Fe train from Chicago pulled alongside... Onto the platform stepped General Armando Vittorio Diaz, commander of the Italian armies.[65] There to greet him were 10,000 of Kansas City's Italian community. Like General Jacques, the governor and mayor welcomed General Diaz, and as he emerged from Union Station, an even larger crowd cheered the General. From Union Station, the General rode through Penn Valley Park, continuing south to Broadway, then east on Armour to the home of Jacob L. Loose at 101 East Armour.[66]

Later, Kansas City's Italian community more formally received General Diaz by presenting him with a diamond-encrusted golden sword.[67] The local Italian community also contributed $2,000 to decorate Fifth Street from Walnut to Campbell and from Missouri Avenue east to Washington Square.[68] Nineteen-thousand Kansas City Italians were eager to greet the man who had defeated the Austrians at the Piave, re-invigorated the morale of the Italian Army, and deemed by many to be the "Savior of Italy."[69]

After the Russian Revolution and the withdrawal of Russia from the war, the Central Powers were able to draw troops from the Russian front. As a result, the Italians were defeated at the Battle of Caporetto. Demoralized, the Army and the civilian population retreated for more than a week. It seemed that Venice would have to be evacuated and left to the enemy when Diaz halted the retreat and reformed the line at the Piave River.

Born of Spanish ancestry in Naples in 1861, Armando Vittorio Diaz began his military career as an artillery officer, was educated at military academies in Naples and Turin, and graduated a second lieutenant of artillery. Chosen as one of 60 for further military instruction, he proved his worth and joined the general staff as head of military personnel. In the field, he served as colonel of the 93rd Infantry Regiment during the Libyan campaign, where he delivered a critical bayonet charge in the first battle of Zanzur. The success of that charge and of the second battle of Zanzur brought Turkey to sue for peace within a few weeks. However, during the second battle, Diaz was wounded so critically that he requested to be wrapped in the Italian flag so that "he might die in the banner he had so valiantly served on the battle field."[70]

Gradually he recovered, and by the beginning of the Great War, he was head of the Supreme Command Office of Operations. Because of his superb leadership of the 18th Corps, 3rd Army at the Carso in 1915, he was promoted to command the 23rd Army on the Isonzo. Forced to retreat into the plains of Venitia as the Austro-German army bore down on Venice from Caporetto, Diaz took his stand at the Piave and held the enemy in a stalemate for almost a year as he rebuilt the strength and morale of his soldiers.

Then in October 1918, he struck, broke through the Austrian line, and created a wedge that sent the enemy into a rout with losses in the thousands. A week after the Italian offensive, the Austrians called for peace, and on November 4, an armistice was signed. Austria was eliminated from the war; General Diaz led a triumphant Italian Army into Trieste and was hailed as the savior of his people.

He won the heart of Kansas City, too. At Westport High School, students cheered the General after he had addressed them through an Italian interpreter. Then, in labored English, he said, "Boys and girls, I thank you from my heart." These were the first words of English he had ever spoken in a public address. The cheering lasted a full five minutes as he bowed to the students repeatedly, and it continued as he left the building for an appearance at Central High School, where he again spoke from his heart:

"On this platform today I occupy a place I should not occupy," the General said through an interpreter.

"I am not a speaker," he continued. "I only want to make an appeal to you for peace. Remember war only to keep far away from it. You have received a reward of sacrifices and abnegation. Grow up in the love of your country. In the name of the youth of America I will take back to Italy an expression of this manifestation of American youth."[71]

The morning of October 31, 1921, young people were also on hand to greet the next dignitary to arrive in Kansas City. Dressed in olive drab, cadets from Northeast High School waited patiently in the lobby of Union Station. A little more than two hours after Generals Jacques and Diaz arrived in Kansas City, British Admiral Earl David Beatty, hero of the Battle of Jutland, First Sea Lord and

Admiral of the Fleet, emerged from his Santa Fe railroad car onto the platform at Union Station to be greeted by a cheering crowd. Mr. R. A. Long, Chair of Kansas City's Liberty Memorial Association, was Admiral Beatty's host; Mr. Long welcomed the admiral, who graciously acknowledged Mr. Long's and Kansas City's hospitality.

"I'm very glad to have come," the Admiral said.

British Vice-consul Herbert W. Markirdy and reception committee chair Reginald Davidson then greeted the Admiral, and as Kansas City's 140th Infantry Band struck up the first bars of "Rule Britannia," the Admiral's tan-gloved hand snapped in salute. Anticipating the Admiral at the stairs ascending to the Union Station lobby, and now falling in behind him as he climbed the stairs, were two squads from Kansas City's Marine Club; 75 former members of famous British regiments lined the way on either side.

Admiral Earl David Beatty of Great Britain.[72]

Near the entrance to the lobby stood H. F. Haverstock of Kansas City, who had been on the Admiral's flagship, *Queen Elizabeth,* and who held in his hand the Admiral's flag, a red cross on a white field. Touched by the gesture, the Admiral responded to Haverstock and then turned to be greeted by Governor Hyde and Mayor Cowgill.

Meanwhile, 15,000 more people awaited the Admiral outside of Union Station. Fifty British soldiers in uniform raised three cheers for the Admiral as he emerged, and the words "Ypres," "Somme," and "Vimy Ridge" echoed in the air.

Acknowledging the crowd, the Admiral stepped into a waiting car with R. A. Long for the trip to his home, Corinthian Hall. Along the way, school children shouted and waved flags; the Admiral saluted a middle-aged woman who greeted him from a tenement porch, whose bare wood bore a single British flag.

As the motorcade swung from Independence Avenue onto Gladstone Boulevard, the chimes of Independence Boulevard Christian Church intoned "God Save the King." Suddenly the Admiral's car halted, and the Admiral rose to attention, saluting for two stanzas the tribute to his King and Country. On the move again, the Admiral waved to hundreds of school children who lined the way to the R. A. Long home. There in the library, he greeted the American Legion and expressed his hopes for the upcoming Washington Conference on the Limitation of Armaments.

An equestrian, breeder, and lover of fine horses, the Admiral was then the guest of Mr. Long and his daughter, Loula Long Combs, at a 2:30 horse show at Longview Farm.[73] Mr. Long had issued the invitation when he met the Admiral in England the previous summer. Now a crowd of more than 3,000 had gathered around the racetrack and in the grandstands at Longview to greet the Admiral and other guests, among whom was Vice President Calvin Coolidge, who, characteristically, had avoided the motion picture photographers by slipping in unexpectedly by a rear drive after the party had been seated. Mr. Long and his daughter then appeared in saddle on the track before the start of five races featuring prize-winning hackneys, which Long had purchased during his visit to England. After the race, the visitors were served tea at Longview and entertained by the 30-piece 140th Infantry band.[74] Later that evening, Robert A. Long and his wife hosted a dinner in honor of Admiral Beatty, U.S. Navy officers Rear Admiral Hugh Rodman, Admiral Robert E. Coontz and Captain Hayne Ellis. Also among the guests were Vice-President Calvin Coolidge; Mr. R. Pryor and Mrs. Loula Long Combs; Mr. Jacob L. Loose; Mr. Ford Harvey of the Harvey House chain; Mr. Marshall Field, III; Judge Edward L. Scarritt; and Mr. Hall.[75]

The son of an Army captain, David Beatty was born in Borodale, County Wexford, Ireland, in 1871 and, according to an account published in *The Kansas City Star* the morning of his arrival in Kansas City, Beatty entered the Navy "at the early age of 13."[77] As a young lieutenant of 25, he was sent to the Sudan where Kitchener assigned him the challenge of maneuvering gunships over the waterfalls of the Nile. With that successfully accomplished, Beatty assumed command of the flotilla when Commander Colville was wounded during the bombardment of the stronghold at Hafir. Awarded the D.S.O. ("Companion of the Distinguished Service Order") for his courage, he was promoted to commander

"Corinthian Hall," home of R. A. Long, host to Admiral Earl Beatty.[76]

in 1898 after distinguishing himself in further gunboat operations in the Sudan. Two years later, he was placed in command of the *Barfleur* during the Boxer Rebellion in China. On June 18, 1900, as head of a landing party, he was twice wounded during an attempt to capture two Chinese guns. Recognized for "conspicuous bravery," at the age of 29, he was promoted to Captain.

During convalescent leave in England, he met and married the former Ethel Field, daughter of Chicago multi-millionaire retailer Marshall Field and just recently divorced from Arthur Tree. After several commands in the Mediterranean, Beatty was appointed *aide de camp* to King Edward VII and introduced to life at court, where his wife gained particular notice for her charm and tact. At the end of two years, he was promoted to Rear Admiral, served as naval secretary to the First Lord of the Admiralty, and commanded the 6th and 1st cruiser squadrons.

It was said that twice he refused knighthood offered by King Edward VII and later by King George V, but was prevailed upon to accept Knight Commander of the Bath at the outbreak of the war in 1914. Just a few months later, he was promoted to Vice-Admiral and placed in charge of the first battle cruiser squadron, which participated in minor engagements while eagerly waiting for the German fleet to emerge from behind the protection of its mine fields and engage the Allies in open battle in the North Sea.

The chance finally came on May 31, 1916. *The Star* recalled the events of that day in what became known as the major sea battle of the war, the Battle of Jutland: "Late that afternoon Beatty was steaming along off the coast of Jutland well in advance of Jellicoe, who was following with the heavier and slower ships of the line. Unaware that the enemy had come out from behind the mine fields, he suddenly saw the fighting craft of Hipper, who, like Beatty, was in advance of the main fleet under Scheer, which followed behind him. Immediately Beatty went in, eager for a chance at the Germans. Hipper turned and ran, hoping to draw Beatty into a trap when they should meet Scheer. But Beatty suspected Hipper's plan and when sight contact was had with the powerful squadron under Scheer, he turned back on his track, fighting all the way, pursued now by both Hipper and Scheer and ready to reverse the tactic they had employed on him.

"It was what Beatty wanted, for he knew that Sir John Jellicoe with the remainder of the British grand fleet was to the north of them in the gathering mists. All four came together about 6 o'clock and the one great naval battle of the world war was fought. In point of ships involved, both in number and tonnage, it was the greatest naval battle in history, and it must be added the most indecisive. For both Germany and the allies claimed the victory. The British fleet was somewhat superior in tonnage and guns to the Germans, but the later had the advantage of position. The British were silhouetted against the yellow light of the western sky; the Germans to the eastward were shrouded in mists. Three times the British lost sight of the German fleet entirely for periods of as much as half an hour, and were obliged to fight with no target except the flashes of the German guns. Darkness ended the combat and the German ships slipped away from the British to the security of their base behind the mine fields. The British losses exceeded the German, both in men and ships and upon this Germany based her claim of victory, but the allied blockade of Germany was unshaken, the German high sees fleet and her merchantmen continued to rust in port. Great Britain still remained mistress of the seas.[78]

"That the British regarded it the victory it was may be inferred from the fact that Jellicoe was rewarded with a viscountcy and Beatty with an earldom. After Jutland, Beatty became commander of the Grand Fleet and as such finished the war. His elevation to the rank of Admiral came after the close of the war. It was to Beatty that the German high seas fleet surrendered shortly after the Armistice was signed."[79]

Beatty was, however, disappointed that he couldn't have more of an opportunity to engage the Germans. His daring was especially celebrated in a story told about the Battle of Jutland. When his flagship, the *Queen Elizabeth*, was damaged during the battle, he wouldn't wait for a ladder but leaped from the deck of his ship onto the deck of a destroyer, the *Attack*, which took him to another vessel to which he transferred his flag – the one that, five years later, H. F. Haverstock held in his hand and that Admiral Beatty stopped especially to recognize as he emerged into the lobby of Union Station.

A few days after the surrender of the German fleet aboard the repaired flagship *Queen Elizabeth*, Admiral Beatty addressed the American squadron now ready to depart for home but disappointed that it had not had a chance to engage the German fleet, whose vessels were still intact, as they finally showed themselves at the surrender. Acknowledging the disappointment of British and American seamen alike, the Admiral called upon a particularly British simile to characterize the German lack of pluck in refusing to continue the fight after Jutland.

"I do not want to keep you here any longer," Beatty told the Americans, "but want to congratulate you for having been present upon a day unsurpassed in the naval annals of the world. I know quite well that you, as well as your British comrades, were bitterly disappointed at not being able to give effect to that efficiency you have so well maintained. It was a most disappointing day. It was a pitiful day to see those great ships coming in like sheep being herded by dogs to their fold without an effort on anybody's part, but it was a day everybody could be proud of."[80]

That same pride was apparent in the reception Admiral Beatty enjoyed in Kansas City on October 31, 1921. The day of Admiral Beatty's arrival, *The Kansas City Times* printed on the front page the following tribute written by Christopher Morley:[81]

The Baron
Baron of Brooksby, and of the North Sea—
That is the kind of a baron to be!

Baron of Jutland and of Skagerrak;
Baron of gray ships that never turned back.

Baron of Fog days and crinckled gray seas;
Baron of gun smell that stings the wet breeze.

Baron of thunders, hard patience, and skill;
Baron of vigil in blackness and chill.

Baron of silence: of men and of steel;
Baron of battle from Shetland to Kiel.

Baron of Seamen wherever ships go;
Baron of drowned hulls beneath Scapa Flow.

Baron of acres of roaring and sea—
That is the kind of a baron to be!

Although not a baron nor an earl, but a French-speaking Louisiana native, "soldier of the sea," and Commandant of the U.S. Marine Corps, Major General John Archer Lejeune arrived in Kansas City on October 31, 1921, to join Admiral Beatty, Marshal Foch, and Generals Diaz, Jacques, and Pershing for the American Legion Convention and the dedication of the Liberty Memorial.

Greeted by an honor guard of four former marines as he stepped onto the platform at Union Station, the Commandant of the oldest arm of the American military saluted his fellow "Devil Dogs."

"Hello men," he said.

He then saluted each man, in turn, and shook his hand.

As the band played the National Anthem, the General and his ex-marines stood squarely at attention. Once into Union Station, General Lejeune passed through taut lines of former soldiers under the command of Capt. Gordon Letchworth and Lieutenant Ray Wilson. Matt Foster, Kansas City Police Commissioner, and Cpt J. W. Faust, Medical Corps officer and formerly attached to a marine unit, greeted Lejeune. An American Legion welcoming committee under A. E. Hutchings also greeted the General.

Out on the Union Station plaza, the General was surprised to find Corporal Victor R. Lenge, of 1320 South Paseo, at the wheel of his designated car. Corporal Lenge had been the General's chauffeur in France. Next to Cpl. Lenge, serving as orderly and relief driver, was Corporal L. L. Pittenger, of 1214 Santa Fe, who had been the General's driver before he left for France. "Hearty greetings were exchanged," *The Kansas City Star* reported, "and the party got under way to the cheers of the throng, the General at salute."[82]

"Service of Security" (a play on the S.O.S. Service of Supply that supported American troops in France), consisting of an automobile and motorcycle police escort, accompanied the General to 3757 Washington, the home of Isaac and Bessie Ryland, who hosted the General during his visit to Kansas City and whose son, Cpt. Robert K. Ryland, was a former officer of the 2nd Division of marines, a unit that had lost over twice its strength in casualties during the war.

Born in Pointe Coupee Parish, Louisiana, in 1867, General Lejuene graduated from the Naval Academy at Annapolis in 1888, and then served in Samoa as an officer on the *Vandalia*, wrecked in the great hurricane of 1889. He served in Cuba, the Philippines, and Vera Cruz. He was in command of the marine barracks at Quantico, Va., when he received orders for overseas, arriving in France in June 1918 to command a brigade in the 33rd Division. Then he took command of the marine brigade of the 2nd Division under Major General James G. Harbord.

After the Soissons offensive, he served under General Henri Gouraud's command when the 2nd Division stormed Mont Blanc Ridge in the Champagne and remained with the 2nd Division in the Meuse-Argonne. After the Armistice, Major General Lejeune took the 2nd Division to the Rhine as part of the army of occupation.

The General's 4th Brigade knew him as "Old Man Gabe," but the Marines of the 2nd Division dubbed him "Old Indian," both because he never lost his thatch of black hair and he resembled the Division insignia, the head of an Indian on a five-pointed star. The General's black hair, his dark, deep-set eyes, and heavy eyebrows so resembled the patch his men wore that he became forever identified with it, a tribute to how much his men admired him.

Officialdom admired him as well. On the morning the General arrived in Kansas City, *The Star* summed up the military honors General Lejeune had already received: "In France the General's mastery of the French language and the brilliance of his planned attack in the Champagne won him the affection and admiration of the French high command. The French government recog-

nized his valuable services and his ability as a strategist and leader with the decorations of Commander of the Legion of Honor and the *Croix de Guerre* with Palms. From General Pershing he received the Distinguished Service Medal, and the Navy Distinguished Service medal was conferred upon him on his return to the United States."[84]

Generals Lejeune, Jacques, and Pershing all spoke fluent French, but the man who more than any other represented France and the cause of the Allies was their supreme commander, Marshal Ferdinand Foch, who arrived in St. Louis with General Pershing at 9:18 on the morning of October 31, 1921.

"Now you are entering my state," General Pershing said in French to the Allied Commander as they crossed the Mississippi River into Missouri. Less than 30 minutes later, they departed from St. Louis, and for the rest of the day, the two military leaders rode the observation car through the Missouri countryside to Kansas City.

The train slowed down in small towns as children waved at the two leaders from along the tracks. Children in Kirkwood lined the tracks for blocks; a farmer came to attention and saluted. The Marshal returned the farmer's salute and waved to the children until the train was out of view. In Washington, Mo., children presented the Marshal with flowers and presents.[85]

Children in Jefferson City and Sedalia did the same, and he acknowledged them all with special attention. Even when others aboard the train had difficulty being admitted to see the Marshal, he was partial to children, perhaps part of a "sorrowful tenderness" for all of the children orphaned in France and for the loss of his own son and son-in-law. As the train pulled out of Sedalia, 13-year-old Thomas Lane, the son of train conductor B. F. Lane, who had waited all day to see the Marshal, was stopped by an officer guarding the door to the Marshall's coach.

"I'd like to see Marshal Foch," Thomas said.

"I'm sorry, sonny, but … "

Beyond the glass of the compartment a few feet away, Marshall Foch was working quietly on the speech he would give later that day at the American Legion Convention. He looked up over his glasses, spoke a few words in French, and extended his hand toward Thomas, who, once ushered in, timidly offered his hand in return. He had something important to tell the Marshall.

"I'm awful glad to meet you," the boy said. "I had a brother killed in France."

Glancing at his translator, Marshall Foch turned his sad eyes to the boy and embraced him.[86]

A similar incident occurred in Holden when Ray Stewart, Jr., not yet three years old, presented a bouquet of roses and a card to Marshal Foch.

"Greetings to Marshal Foch," the card read, "from the citizens of Holden, Mo, the home of John L. Barkley, who wears the *croix de guerre* and the *medaille militaire*; presented by Ray Stewart, Jr. whose father since the first battle of the 89th Division, sleeps in France."

Seeing the words *croix de guerre* and *medaille militaire*, Foch told the people that the *medaille militaire* was the highest honor France could confer on a soldier, pointing to a similar medal on his own uniform. Then the interpreter noticed the last part of the card and, in French, told the Marshal that the boy was born after his father had been killed. The boy had never seen his father. Foch's eyes filled with tears as the train rolled away, and looking directly at the boy in his mother's arms, threw them both a kiss.[87]

The Marshal also displayed a lighter side. Earlier that morning in Washington, Mo., the mayor presented Marshal Foch with a box of "Missouri meerschaums" – corncob pipes. Foch thanked the mayor and told the people how much he enjoyed smoking a pipe.

"How many do they make? Do they ship them out of the country? Do they employ many men?" he wanted to know. His ques-

Maj. Gen John A. Lejeune of the United States.[83]

The General's 4th Brigade knew him as "Old Man Gabe," but the Marines of the 2nd Division dubbed him "Old Indian," both because he never lost his thatch of black hair and he resembled the Division insignia, the head of an Indian on a five-pointed star. The General's black hair, his dark, deep-set eyes, and heavy eyebrows so resembled the patch his men wore that he became forever identified with it, a tribute to how much his men admired him.

tions answered, Marshal Foch passed around the pipes, along with his own tobacco, inside the railroad car, urging everyone to have a real smoke.[88] It was to the metaphor of the pipe that Foch attributed his military success.

"How, then, did I win the war?" he had asked rhetorically a year earlier in Paris.

"I did it by smoking my pipe. I mean to say, in not getting excited, in reducing everything to its essential, in avoiding useless emotions, in concentrating all my strength on the job."[89]

The job was never more critical than when the German Army advanced unimpeded through Belgium and to the Marne. In late summer 1914, General Foch was ordered to form an army from the French troops retreating before the German advance. Doing so, Foch took his position at the Marne River opposite German General Von Bulow and his crack Prussian Guard. The Germans repulsed the advance of the French center three times; the situation was rapidly deteriorating for the French.

At that point, General Foch made a daring move: He promptly withdrew his 42nd from the firing line, called on General Franchet D'Esperey to fill the gap, and marching halfway across the field behind the line, attacked the flank of the Prussian Guard, broke the German center, and drove Von Bulow into retreat.

Foch's action reinforced his reputation as a military theorist and strategist, responsible for establishing within the French army the concept of "offensive spirit": attack at all costs, under any circumstance.[90] For Foch, that spirit found its roots in the humiliation the French had suffered at the hands of the Prussians in the Franco-Prussian War.

Foch's military career began in that war at the early age of 19 when he enlisted as a private soldier in 1870. Ever since the French defeat, Foch dreamed of restoring the dignity of his country.

"I dreamed of revenge after having seen the Germans at Metz," he said, "and when a man of ordinary capacity concentrates all of his faculties and all of his abilities upon one end and works without diverting, he ought to be successful."[91]

After a brief return to civilian life, he entered artillery school and was commissioned a 2nd Lieutenant in 1874, attended the L'Ecole de Guerre, and was appointed to the staff of a division and then to the general staff in 1894. In 1895, he was appointed professor of military history, strategy, and applied tactics at L'Ecole Supérieure de Guerre. After six years of field command, where he advanced from colonel to brigadier general, he returned to the L'Ecole Supérieure as commandant. There, he devoted special attention to the training of officers and lectured on strategy and tactics. It was here that his doctrine of offensive strategy had its greatest influence. He returned to general duties in 1911 and by 1914 was commanding the 20th Army Corps at Nancy when he received command of the 9th Army in August 1914 and confronted Von Bulow at the Marne.[92]

Sixty-three years old when the war began, he served with the French army in northern France until after the 2nd battle of the Aisne, and then transferred to Flanders where he commanded the French right wing in the battle of the Somme in 1916. In April 1917, the month America entered the war, he took mandatory retirement at the age of 66. He served as an adviser of the French government and as military member of the supreme war council, coordinating allied support for Italy after its defeat at Caporetto and later coordinating Anglo-French forces in France. In April 1918, he was made Commander-in-Chief of all the allied armies. The counter-offensive he launched against the Germans in July 1918 brought them to sign the Armistice, which ended the war.[93]

On the morning of November 11, 1918, in a railroad car in the forest near Rethonde, Matthias Erzberger, head of the Catholic Centre Party in the Reichstag and a "bitter opponent of the policies that had brought Germany to rack and ruin," reluctantly agreed to lead the armistice commission across Allied lines to negotiate a cease-fire.[94]

"We have come to inquire into the terms of an armistice to be concluded on land, on sea and in the air," he said to Foch after an icy greeting.

Foch replied, "I have no terms to submit to you."

Count Oberndorf rephrased Erzberger's statement, and once more Foch replied, "I have no terms. I will let you know the Allies' conditions when you have asked for an armistice. Do you ask for an armistice?"

"Ja, ja!" Oberndorf and Erzberger exclaimed in unison.

"One act," Foch later said, "gives me satisfaction. It was the meeting at Rethondes. That was an act. That act marked the defeat of the German Empire and I saw Erzberger with rage seize his pen and sign that act. And then I was content to have willed it and to have known how to employ the means, for the business was done."[95]

But the defeats of France in 1870 and of Germany in 1918 had come at a terrible price, one war leading to the other as inevitably as the end of World War I was to lead to the beginning of World War II, but that was in the future. For Foch in the present, the personal loss had been great: his son was killed and his daughter was widowed.

"I see him going quite alone," one of his officers wrote of the general, "at the hour when the church of Cassel was deserted to meditate upon his task and to seek consolation for the immense bereavement of which

Marshal Ferdinand Foch of France.[98]

he never spoke. But what I can least of all forget is his look, which reveals his whole soul. Back of his invincible energy was a sorrowful tenderness, a great melancholy."[96]

Perhaps a touch of that "sorrowful tenderness" was in evidence when Marshal Foch rose to his feet as the delegation boarded his railroad car after its arrival in Kansas City's Union Station on the evening of October 31, 1921.[97] Reporting the event in the newspaper the next morning, *The Star* reporter noted the General's reaction to the overwhelming welcome he received:

"Recreated into a temporal giant, mad with joy, the crowd that met Foch and Pershing swirled into such immensity it had to be fought to permit them to enter Kansas City

"Through a wide stateroom window of the last coach the marshal and the general were seen. Sheer enthusiasm was only a mockery of the spirit of the crowd. It was viewing the saviors of the whole world, who took the heart of Earth and turned it back to happiness after it had almost been broken.

"Along the platform men and women, for the moment a billowing mass, mounted in a two-fold manner. Tip-toed, the outer bounds of the crowd pressed the center upward, and left many virtually in midair, supported by the buttresses of chests, arms and backs to the rear. Again, a welcoming cheer swept high, then was diffused into a welded babble—gulps, hoarse hurrahs.

"Foch and Pershing were overwhelmed. The welcomers were overwhelmed. The descent from the train was delayed fully ten

Irwin and Laura (Nelson) Kirkwood hosted Marshal Foch and General Pershing at their home, 4520 Kenwood Avenue.[101]

minutes. A secret service man from a precarious position on the coach step said, "'We must master this situation at once, or the party cannot alight.'

"Guards redoubled their efforts. Majors and captains mingled with privates to harness the whirlpool.

"Members of the official American Legion reception committee in the meantime entered the coach. Marshal Foch and General Pershing were seen through the generous window chatting and bowing while those outside swam toward the front lines

"Then—order. Suddenly, as if realizing the futility of the rush for vantage.

"Marshal Foch, his kindly face softened by the grief that only a great warrior knows, distinctly was seen to wobble slightly on his feet. The crowd darted in behind him and General Pershing, who with firm step, followed."[99]

" ... Kansas City never had given a welcome to anyone like that it presented last night."[100] Foch and Pershing then proceeded to 4520 Kenwood Avenue, the home of their hosts, Mr. and Mrs. Irwin Kirkwood, William Rockhill Nelson's son-in-law and daughter.[102] There the 70-year-old Marshal Foch rested before dinner. Irwin Kirkwood was ill during the visit and was confined to Oak Hall, the home of Nelson's widow. Major St. Clair Streett acted as site host to Marshal Foch and General Pershing during Mr. Kirkwood's illness.[103]

Meanwhile, in a departure from his announced schedule, General Pershing was able to spend a quiet hour at the Hotel Muehlebach with his sister Miss May Pershing and his 12-year-old son, Warren.[104] May had come to Kansas City from her home in Lincoln, Nebraska, where she was helping the General raise his son after the tragic deaths of the General's wife, Helen, and their three daughters, aged 6, 7, and 8, in a fire at the Presidio on August 27, 1915. The youngest child, Warren, was five years old and was sleeping in a separate room away from the main part of the blaze; when he was rescued, his mother and sisters were already dead. At the time of the tragedy, General Pershing was in El Paso, Texas, at Fort Bliss, preparing quarters for his family, who were to join him in just a week.[105] So Warren was all that remained of his immediate family, and the General cherished the little time he had with his son and the boy's aunt, Pershing's sister.[106] May, Warren, and another of the General's sisters, Mrs. D. M. Butler, joined him the next day, November 1, 1921, on the platform for the Liberty Memorial Site Dedication.[107] Later that evening at the Hotel Muehlebach, May attended a dinner for the Women's Auxiliary to the American Legion whose convention was to begin the next day.[108]

After General Pershing's visit with his son and his sister on the evening of October 31, the General returned to the Kirkwoods' home for dinner. In addition to the General and Marshal Foch, among the dinner guests that evening were General Lejeune of the U.S. Marines, Missouri Governor Hyde, Kansas Governor Allen, American Legion National Commander John G. Emery, and Bishop Thomas F. Lillis of the Catholic Diocese of Kansas City.[109]

The welcome continued the next day. At 7 a.m., General Diaz and Baron Jacques attended Mass in the chapel of Bishop Lillis' residence. Shortly after 8 a.m., Marshal Foch arrived. He greeted the other two generals for the first time on American soil and attended Mass.[110] Later that morning at the American Legion Convention in Kansas City's Convention Hall, General Pershing led the convention in a rousing three cheers for the French Marshal. Following the ovation, Pershing said,

"There was no supreme direction that would insure co-ordination or unity of effort. The dark days of the spring of 1918 forced the issue and," extending his hand toward Foch, "Marshal Foch was unanimously selected as the Allied Commander-in-Chief. Calm, confident and aggressive, this great soldier at once inspired all ranks of the allied armies by his exceptional qualities of leadership. The world knows well the story of Allied success under his direction and no words of mine can add to the glory of that achievement.

"Monsieur le Marechal," Pershing addressed the Marshal, "the American Legion is peculiarly honored by your presence here among us … Monsieur Le Marechal," he continued, "we of Missouri are especially pleased to be the first thus formally to welcome you to America."[111]

Marshal Foch responded in French, recounting the history of America's involvement in the war. "Officers, noncommissioned officers and soldiers of the great American army," he said. "My dear comrades of the American Legion, I cannot tell you how great is my satisfaction at finding myself amongst you, valiant soldiers of 1918, to live again our glorious memories. Three years ago, on the first of November 1918, the entire American Army in France took up vigorously the pursuit of the defeated enemy and did not halt until the German surrender."

Marshal Foch reminded the Legion men that in 18 months, their country had taken an army of 9,500 officers and 125,000 men to 180,000 officers and 3.5 million men. He then praised the effort of organization, effort in instruction, effort in manufacturing and transportation, effort in improving ports of embarkation in the United States and debarkation in France, and effort on the part of the entire nation's intelligence, willpower and energy – "a prodigious effort which has filled your associates with admiration and gratitude and confounded your enemy!"

Referring to the battlefields of France, Foch remembered Chateau Thierry and Belleau Wood, the Aisne and the Marne, St. Mihiel and the Argonne. "Nothing could discourage or check your Army. It threw itself with generous ardor into the immense melee. The task was a huge one, but it was carried out to a thorough finish." There followed the

99

American Legion National Commander John G. Emery, General Pershing, and Marshal Foch at the American Legion Convention In Kansas City's Convention Hall [112]

operation with the French Fourth Army in the defile of Grand Pre. Then came Buzancy and the Meuse. The war ended as the Second Army was eagerly awaiting its move on Metz.

"Your country had asked of you to lay low a redoubtable enemy," Foch concluded "You have placed him at your mercy and after having assured every guarantee for the liberty of our peoples, you have imposed upon him the peace which our governments have dictated.

"Has not your task been completely fulfilled?

"As for me, the great honor of my life will be to have guided along the road of victory the American Army of 1918, which was a grand army, beginning with its commander."[113]

At the end of his remarks, both Marshal Foch and General Pershing "stood together at the front of the platform while the storm of cheers swept over the hall in wave after wave." "It was an occasion," recalled *The Kansas City Star* reporter, "that ever will live in the memories of all who were there. Not again will this generation, and perhaps one of those to follow, witness such a memorable event."[114]

At 11:00 am at the Liberty Memorial, General Pershing introduced Marshal Foch once again. "I feel myself peculiarly honored this morning," Pershing said, "by being permitted to participate in the ceremony of dedicating to those who lost their lives from this country and city a monument which will stand as an everlasting tribute to the heroic, their heroic conduct on the battle fields of France—but it is not alone that we dedicate this monument to these 519[115] men who did not return.

"We are dedicating it to the gallantry and the patriotism and to the sacrifices, not only of the American army, but of those of our allies who fought from the beginning to the end, and with whom we finally joined in the victory. If it had not been for the unity of purpose, combined with the unity of command, it is doubtful, extremely doubtful, whether we should have been successful in the late war.

"The embodiment of that unity of purpose, and unity of command is here with us, today, in the person of our distinguished Allied Commander-in-Chief, Marshal Foch, whom I have the honor to introduce to you."

Marshal Foch responded in French: "The dead we honor here made the noble sacrifice for a cause that should not be forgotten. I congratulate Kansas City and its citizens on the erection of this monument to a memory that they must always cherish and which never shall be forgotten."[116]

Following the speech, Marshal Foch; Generals Pershing, Jacques, Diaz, and Lejeune; and Admiral Beatty moved to the stand in front of *The Kansas City Star* building on 18th and Grand to review the parade. After the parade on the way back to Corinthian Hall, Beatty was riding in R. A. Long's Pierce Arrow when it was struck by a Ford – whose driver was arrested for intoxication and careless driving – at Independence Avenue and Euclid. Quick action by the driver of the Pierce Arrow averted serious injury and property damage.[117]

That evening Marshal Foch had been scheduled to attend a reception at the Hotel Muehlebach for French-speaking guests. The American Association for the Relief of Devastated France sponsored the reception,[118] but Foch was forced to cancel because the American Legion parade had ended so late.[119]

At 11:00 p.m. that night, Admiral Beatty and General Diaz departed Kansas City on a special Santa Fe train. Admiral Beatty was on his way to Chicago, and General Diaz was bound for New York.[120]

The next day, November 2, was the anniversary of the death of Marshal Foch's son, who had been killed in action in France, and the marshall wished to spend the day in meditation. At 9:15 he attended a Mass celebrated by Bishop Lillis at Rockhurst College, breakfasted in the dinning room, and received an honorary degree from the College.[121] He then proceeded to Notre Dame de Sion School at Armour and Warwick, where he met with the 100 school children who attended there. All spoke French.

In the drawing room he faced the children dressed in white and seated in tiers. Seven small girls approached him, each prepared with a brief speech:

"Monsieur le Marechal, it was a long time ago when we first came to love France. When we were very little children we came here to learn to speak your soft beautiful language. We learned the fables of the fox, and that might does not mean right. You by your leadership of the world war, have shown us again that lesson. Here at this convent we learned to love the noble history of France, such names as Charlemagne, Bayard Dugnesclin, Jeanne d'Arc are heroes of ours, too.

"Our love for French history is again gratified when we think of our great friend, Lafayette.

"One day the horizon of France was black with war, and then you came to save France and to save us, just as the ancient heroes of France served France, so you served with your all. We sent our fathers to aid you, too, and we prayed.

"Monsieur le Marechal, this is the reason for our emotion of joy, gratitude, and admiration. One word, it is the echo of what Charles *Sept* said to Jeanne d'Arc, we say to you:

'*Ici, Marechal, tout est votre!*' 'Here, Marshal, all is yours!'"

"My little ones," Marachal Foch said, "you say much charming things about my France, now let me tell you about your country. Let me tell you how I feel about your noble country. You say you love my country, and I want to tell you that I love your country with all my heart, dear children. It was for that reason that I came all the way across the great ocean to come and see your country and see you children, too. Remember one thing: We have been united in war, and we will be united in peace. You, in the future, should remember the men must work and the women must pray."

"*Vive le Marechal. Vive la France.*"

Escorted to his car, he requested to go back in to rest. So he was escorted back into the convent where he removed his great coat and sat in a comfortable chair in the center of the reception room. The nuns, shy at first, were presented to him, then a small child entered and soon the entire school followed, all babbling in French, unafraid of the uniform and medals. He kissed four children, once on each cheek: Cathleen Green, Frances Vrooman, Maude Corrigan, and Mary Louise Phillips. The children continued to chatter. Then it was time to go, and the Marshal bade farewell once more, children waving and cheering as he left. Mother superior gave the remainder of the day off to the children saying they had something great to think about that day.[122]

Afterwards, accompanied by General Jacques and General Pershing, the Marshal made a tour of Kansas City Boulevards for the benefit of 60,000 school children in Kansas City, both public schools and private.[123] Beginning at 11:00 a.m., the tour proceeded from Penn Valley Park south to Broadway to Armour, east to Gillham, south to Westport High School, then east to Harrison, north to Armour, east to Paseo, north to Linwood, east on Benton, north to Independence Avenue, west via Independence and Admiral to the Paseo, and then to Oak Hall, where Marshal Foch called on his host and hostess, Mr. and Mrs. Irwin Kirkwood. Foch then attended a Kansas-side air show where Cpt. Eddie Rickenbacker welcomed him to the first American Legion air derby and presented him with a gold membership card in the Aero Club.[124] Later in the day, Marshal Foch traveled to Leavenworth and joined General Pershing in recognizing the quality of military instruction that had occurred there.

"'I consider that the functioning of the staff of the American Army was about as perfect as could have been expected under almost any circumstances," he said.[125] After leaving Fort Leavenworth, Marshal Foch returned to the home of his hosts, Mr. and Mrs. Irwin Kirkwood.[126]

At 10:15 that night, Marshal Foch entered Union Station and headed for the platform prior to boarding his train. Fifteen minutes later, General Pershing accompanied his son, Warren, and sister, May, to Union Station, where May and Warren boarded a train bound for Lincoln, Nebraska. General Pershing stopped briefly to talk with General Jacques who was standing on the observation platform of his train bound for Omaha and then for St. Louis and Nashville. There he would attend a reunion of the U.S. 30th Division, the unit he commanded in Belgium and France.[127]

General Pershing then joined Marshal Foch in their special Missouri Pacific car, which departed Kansas City at 11:45 p.m., November 2, bound for St. Louis. From there, Foch headed to Indianapolis and on to Chicago and Cleveland; Pershing headed for Nashville to attend to personal business.[128] Both would work their way to Washington, D.C.

■ ■ ■

Meanwhile, in Washington, Congress had just passed a resolution requesting President Harding and all state governors to declare Armistice Day, November 11, a national holiday to commemorate the burial of the Unknown Soldier and all others who had sacrificed their lives.[129]

On the morning of November 9, bearing the body of the Unknown, the cruiser *Olympia* entered the Potomac River. At anchor off the Piney Point, the battle ship North Dakota dipped her ensign and engaged a Presidential 21-gun salute as the *Olympia* passed. Each fort along the Potomac rendered the salute as the *Olympia* headed for the Capital. At 4 p.m., the *Olympia* docked in fog and rain, and the casket bearing the Unknown was escorted through the city by cavalry, troopers four abreast, a caisson, a squadron, War Secretary John W. Weeks and Navy Secretary Edwin Denby, then General Pershing and Admiral Coontz, along with other officers and officials. To the center of the Capitol rotunda they marched, crowds lining the way, and upon arrival placed the casket of the Unknown on the catafalque on which the bodies of Presidents Lincoln, Garfield, and McKinley had rested in times past.

First Lady Mrs. Florence Harding stepped forward and placed on the casket a wide white ribbon she had stitched herself. On the ribbon President Harding pinned a silver shield of the United States with 48 golden stars, symbolizing the heart of the nation. He then laid a large wreath of red roses near the head of the casket. Other dignitaries placed similar tributes. General Pershing placed a wreath of giant pink chrysanthemums on the Unknown's coffin, stood back and saluted.[130] Flowers heaped mountain high about the casket and spilled out into the rotunda chamber.[131] Later, the mountain of flowers was laid back and the flag-draped casket bore only the tribute from President and Mrs. Harding and the withering clump of roses with which Sgt. Younger had designated the Unknown three weeks earlier in the makeshift chapel at Chalons-sur-Marne.[132] During the night, five armed men guarded the Unknown.

The next day, November 10, the Unknown lay in state. East to west in the Capitol rotunda the public passed before the bier in double lines.[133] A few minutes before noon, the British party, lead by Admiral of the Fleet Earl Beatty, Arthur Balfour, and Ambassador Geddes, placed a wreath at the bier, followed by wreaths placed by other Commonwealth nations. Secretary Weeks, Assistant Secretary Wainwright, and General Harbord received foreign delegations; floral arrangements bearing the shields of each state of the Union circled the rotunda.[134]

The next day, November 11, the Unknown

was escorted to Arlington National Cemetery. General Pershing declined to ride and instead marched beside the body. At noon, two minutes of silence were observed across the nation. Following the strains of "America," master of ceremonies Secretary of War Johm W. Weeks and President Harding spoke, their voices sent through telephone wires to gatherings in New York and San Francisco.

The President then pinned, side by side at the head of the casket, the Medal of Honor and the Distinguished Service Cross. Then came the four great military leaders who had stood together for the first time in Kansas City less than two weeks before. Belgium's Lieutenant General Baron Jacques stepped forward and clutching the *Croix de Guerre* on his own breast tore it from his tunic, pinned it on the flag draping the coffin, stepped back and saluted. British Admiral of the Fleet Earl Beatty then presented the Victoria Cross to the Unknown, the first time such an honor had been bestowed on a recipient who was not a British subject. Marshal Foch presented the French *Medaille Militaire* and the *Croix de Guerre*, in French cited the Unknown for valor, and saluted. General Diaz came forward and pinned on the flag-draped coffin Italy's gold medal for bravery. Then came the Rumanian *Virtuica Militara*, the Czechoslovakain War Cross, and the *Virtuti Militari* of Poland.

Laden with the greatest honors of the Allied nations, the casket was lifted through the doorway of the crypt. Final prayers were offered, and Major General Harbord and Admiral Rodman lowered the Unknown into the crypt. Two war mothers – one American and one British – placed the last wreaths on the coffin, and Native American chief Plenty Coups removed his war bonnet and placed it and his coup stick on the tomb. The withering clump of roses Sgt. Younger had used to designate the Unknown was still there as a mark of distinction.

Three thundering blasts of artillery roared out, followed by taps and a 21-gun salute.[135] The Unknown was finally at rest, but what he represented continued to haunt those who remained. As a final reflection on the day, author H. G. Wells asked,

"What did the unknown soldier of the great war think he was doing when he died? What did we, we people who got him into the great war and who are still in possession of this world of his, what did we persuade him to think he was doing and what is the obligation we have incurred to him to atone for his death, for the life and sunlight he will know no more?"[136]

The next day, within view of Arlington, the Conference for Limitation of Armament began its deliberations in an attempt to answer those questions. Delegates from Great Britain, France, Italy, Japan, and the United States joined with the Far East interests of China, Belgium, Portugal, and the Netherlands in the intention to keep this war the "war to end all wars."[137] Not everyone was, however, at that table. Twenty years later, America was back at war, and yet another Unknown would be buried at Arlington.

At home, Kansas City would remember the Great War and those days in November when the Allied commanders came to dedicate their great memorial to the sons and one daughter who had died in the world war.

M-10 Liberty Memorial — Dedication Wall
South side of Pershing Road between
Main Street and Kessler Drive, Kansas City, Missouri

Dedication Wall depicting the five Allied commanders who dedicated the Liberty Memorial site on November 1, 1921. From left to right are bronze plaques of Admiral Beatty, Marshal Foch, General Pershing, General Diaz, and General Jacques.

This "Dedication Wall," financed by the Park Department in 1934, was designed by Walter Hancock, but the wall itself was not there when the site was dedicated on November 1, 1921.

However, the five Allied commanders, whose bas-relief busts are depicted on the wall, were present that day – standing together for the first and only time – to dedicate the place where the Liberty Memorial would be built.

The people came as well. On that Tuesday morning, November 1, 1921, huge crowds gathered where Dedication Wall now stands. In an article entitled, "A Word to the Crowd on the Liberty Memorial Dedication," which appeared on page 9 of the newspaper that morning, *The Kansas City Times* described the entire area from Union Station to the top of Liberty Memorial Hill as a "natural amphitheater. The thousands who assemble there," the article continued, "will be directed in singing patriotic and sacred songs from 10 to 11 o'clock and also in the program."[138]

Opposite Union Station, on the three acres across the top of Memorial Hill, seating was reserved for soldiers in uniform, two people from each family who suffered a death from the war, gold medal men, visiting governors, legion officers, Memorial trustees, and the Memorial's auxiliary committee.

By 11:00, the time set for the beginning of the Dedication, more than 100,000 people gathered in front of Union Station, some sitting high up on the surrounding rocky hills opposite Union Station and some even clinging on to the roof of Union Station.[139] School children had made thousands of paper flowers and families at home had contributed another 50,000 more to be dropped from airplanes during the ceremony. On the temporary stage built on the hillside, the five generals each delivered brief remarks. Without loud speakers, the crowd could not hear what they said, but that didn't stop them from cheering what the generals and the memorial itself represented. And it represented a lot to the world, the nation, and to Kansas City.

In a period of ten days, from October 27 to November 5, 1919, 83,000 Kansas Citians, about a quarter of the population, raised

Site dedication of Liberty Memorial, November 1, 1921. Union Station is in the center. Picture taken from the top of Memorial Hill.

$2,517,000 for the construction of Liberty Memorial. In 1919 dollars, that averaged about $24.10 per subscriber. In today's money, that represented $247.97 per subscriber or a total of $114,066,200.[140]

The five Allied Commanders who spoke that day each acknowledged in some way the role that Kansas City played in the war. Third from the left on Dedication Wall is the bronze bas-relief bust of General Pershing, who spoke first. A Missouri native from Laclede, Pershing led the American Expeditionary Forces that provided the final surge in the defeat of the Kaiser and his army.

At 11:00 a.m., General Pershing introduced Marshal Foch to the crowd. "I feel myself peculiarly honored this morning," Pershing said, "by being permitted to participate in the ceremony of dedicating to those who lost their lives from this country and city a monument which will stand as an everlasting tribute to the heroic, their heroic conduct on the battle fields of France – but it is not alone that we dedicate this monument to these 519 [sic 440 men and one woman] who did not return.

"We are dedicating it to the gallantry and the patriotism and to the sacrifices, not only of the American Army, but of those of our allies who fought from the beginning to the end, and with whom we finally joined in the victory. If it had not been for the unity of purpose, combined with the unity of command, it is doubtful, extremely doubtful, whether we should have been successful in the late war.

> "We are dedicating it to the gallantry and the patriotism and to the sacrifices, not only of the American Army, but of those of our allies who fought from the beginning to the end, and with whom we finally joined in the victory.
> If it had not been for the unity of purpose, combined with the unity of command, it is doubtful, extremely doubtful, whether we should have been successful in the late war."
>
> — *General Pershing*

"The embodiment of that unity of purpose, and unity of command is here with us, today, in the person of our distinguished Allied Commander-in-Chief, Marshal Foch, whom I have the honor to introduce to you."

Just to the left of Pershing's image is the

bronze bas-relief bust of Marshal Foch, the brilliant strategist who commanded all the Allied forces and orchestrated the counter-offensive that finally brought the Germans to sign the Armistice that ended the war. He spoke next, responding in French: *"Les mort qui nous ici honerons audjourd hui … "* "The dead we honor here today made the noble sacrifice for a cause that should not be forgotten. I congratulate Kansas City and its citizens on the erection of this monument to a memory that they must always cherish and which never shall be forgotten."[141]

On the Dedication Wall, the first bas-relief bust from left to right is that of First Sea Lord and Admiral of the Fleet British Earl David Beatty, hero of the Battle of Jutland, the major sea battle of the war that held the blockade of Germany and ensured that the German fleet would do nothing until the German command sunk their own ships at the end of the war. The angle of the Admiral's hat suggests something of his character. Beatty was regarded as a "jaunty" commander, and a style-setter. He regarded himself as "half American," in marriage his "better half" being Ethel Field, daughter of Chicago multi-millionaire retailer Marshall Field. In his speech on dedication day, Admiral Beatty said that the Liberty Memorial "is to be significant of the future, and those of you who came back alive, those of you whose sons came back alive, have a still greater duty to perform, of which this will be the symbol, and that is to see that unity and comradeship will enable a beneficial peace to reign in the world and to see that those who gave their lives for their country have not died in vain."

To the right of Dedication Wall's plaque of Pershing is the bas-relief bust of General Diaz. It was he who collected the remnants of the Italian Army after the defeat at Caporetto, rallied them at the Piave, and then struck through the Austrian line, creating a wedge that sent the enemy into a rout with losses in the thousands and, even before the Germans surrendered, left a defeated Austria suing for peace. Speaking in Italian on dedication day, General Diaz expressed his reason for coming to Kansas City. "Out of the fullness of heart of the Italian people, I came to America to express in person the gratitude that the whole people feel. Also I came to see the people of my native country living here, who furnished many to the battle fields that were washed in blood."

Finally is the portrait of Belgian General Jacques, the last bas-relief bust depicted on Dedication Wall and the last of the five commanders to speak on dedication day. In August 1914, as hordes of gray-coated Germans swept down into Belgium bound for Paris, Colonel Jacques threw the men of his 12th Regiment into the path of the onslaught at Vise and took the first devastating blow of the Great War. Later, he held the Germans on their assault of Dixmude, then in the last drive of the war, General Jacques assumed command of the central attack group for the offensive, re-took the Flanders ridge and held at Stadenberg and Westroosebeke. Speaking in French, he said, "I am deeply impressed by the size and grandeur of this ceremony. I am impressed further by the spirit and hearts of this vast community. It is yet almost inconceivable that these brave boys from Kansas City had to travel so far to come to the aid of our Belgium and our allies. Belgium is, indeed, proud to salute your brave living and the dead today. *"C'est magnifique,"* he said.[142]

That spirit and heart finds perhaps its greatest expression in the person and career of Missouri native and American Expeditionary Forces Commander, General John J. Pershing.

General Pershing, his wife, and three of his four children.

General John J. Pershing
"Black Jack" from Missouri: Farmhand, Teacher, Lawyer, Soldier

Missouri played a unique role in the war. Not only did it sacrifice the first medical professionals to die in the war and recruit men and women to serve in the cause of the war, but it also produced the man who would organize and lead the American Expeditionary Forces in France. General John J. Pershing knew what it meant to lose loved ones and to carry on in spite of the loss. His story touches the stories of other military heroes with ties to the region: General Leonard Wood and Colonel Theodore Roosevelt, who also served as America's 26th President.

On Friday, August 27, 1915, a week before General Pershing's family was to join him at Fort Bliss, Texas, Pershing answered the telephone at 8th Infantry Headquarters.

"Telegram for you, sir," said the orderly, hesitating. "Shall I? Shall I read it to you, sir?"

"Yes," the General replied.

The young man halted again.

"Go ahead," Pershing insisted with some annoyance.[143]

In a shaken voice the orderly read the news that early in the morning a fire had broken out in the wooden two-story Victorian house at the Presidio in San Francisco, California, where the General's wife and their four children were living. Downstairs in the house, two coal-burning fireplace grates had been allowed to burn all night. Live coals from the dining room grate had rolled out onto the highly lacquered floor, igniting it. Flames had swept up a corner of the house and burned through to the roof, causing it to collapse.

A relative of the Pershings, Mrs. Walter O. Boswell, had been staying at the house on a visit. It was Mrs. Boswell who first discovered the fire, woke her children – Philip, age 3, and James, age 6 – and called out to Mrs. Pershing. Mrs. Boswell then opened the door to the hall, but was met by a blast of smoke and flames. Unable to advance further into the hall, she called out to Mrs. Pershing again and attempted to take her own two children to the stairway. Cut off by flames once more, she turned back into the bedroom. Through a window, she and her maid emerged onto the roof of the front porch and from there, dropped the two children down to officers and men who had gathered on the lawn below. The maid then jumped from the porch roof into the hands of the men below; Mrs. Boswell followed, landing in a flower bed and wrenching her back severely enough to require hospitalization.

An aged black man, who had served the

Pershing family for years and was identified in newspaper accounts only as "Johnson," crawled into the house, leading a rescue party in search of Mrs. Pershing and the four children. Finding five-year-old Warren Pershing still alive but unconscious on the floor of his bedroom, Johnson rushed the boy to safety. Warren revived quickly and was placed in the care of nurses at the Lettermann General Hospital at the Presidio.

Finally, rescuers found the others. Suffocated by smoke and lying dead on the floor of the upstairs bedroom most severely damaged by the fire was the General's 35-year-old wife, Helen, her arms draped across the body of one of their daughters, also dead, lying on the bed. The body of another daughter lay dead in another bed, and the third daughter lay dead on the floor. All the bodies had been severely burned about the heads, hands, and feet. Mary Margaret was 6, Ann was 7, and Helen was 8.[144]

As if that were not enough, the General asked, "Is that all? Is that everything?"

"Yes sir," the orderly said.

In the three years prior to the blaze, nine people had died by fire at the Presidio. The General left Fort Bliss immediately bound for the Presidio. When he arrived and was taken to the scene, his eyes swept across the devastation.

"They never had a chance," he said.[145]

After the funeral, Pershing returned to Fort Bliss with his sister, May, who had volunteered to help care for Warren. Grief-stricken, Pershing paced through the rooms and porches of the house he had prepared for his family. Although the grief subsided in time as he threw himself into his work, the tragedy marked him for the rest of his life, and he never publicly remarried. The man who would lead thousands of young men into battle knew first-hand what the loss of family meant.

■ ■ ■

Born on September 13, 1860, in Laclede, Missouri, 20 miles east of Chillocothe, John Joseph Pershing was the son of a railroad section boss and the eldest of nine children. His grandfather, Frederick Pfoerschin, was an indentured servant, who, in 1749, had emigrated from the Alsace, a region in France which, over long periods of time, had swung back and forth between France and Germany.[146] Pershing would contribute in no small way to its remaining with France. In German, *Pförtchen* means "little door."[147]

Frederick's father, also named Frederick, wrote his son that he hoped either he or one of his descendants "would come back some day and redeem the fair lands of Alsace Lorraine from oppression."[148] In time, the hope expressed by the future general's great grandfather would be fulfilled, but Pershing had to get an education first.

He worked as a farmhand and taught at an African-American school in Laclede and later at a school in Prairie Mound, Missouri. In the summers of 1880-1882, he attended the State Normal School at Kirksville, Missouri. At the suggestion of his sister, he took the competitive examination for an appointment to West Point, not because he wanted to pursue a military career but because he could get an advanced education there. He won the appointment and graduated in 1886, president of his class, ranking 30th in a class of 77. He later returned to West Point in 1897 and served an academic year as an assistant instructor in Tactics.

Pershing also returned to teaching for four years as a Professor of Military Science and Tactics at the University of Nebraska, where he also earned a law degree in 1893. While at Nebraska, he built up a drill company, practicing for two hours in the morning and three hours in the afternoon and winning the National Competitive Drills held in Omaha in 1892. A crack shot, he also won several pistol and rifle competitions. He had developed a talent and a reputation for military discipline.

Pershing's boyhood home in Laclede, Missouri.

Photo courtesy Library of Congress.

Below, Warren Pershing.

Photo courtesy of Library of Congress.

Pershing served his first field duty with the 6th Cavalry at Fort Bayard, New Mexico. For four years he fought against the Apache Indians in the Southwest and later, in South Dakota, against the Sioux. After seeing combat at San Juan Hill in the Battle of Santiago during the Spanish-American War, he contracted malaria and was forced into confinement until he recuperated. In March 1899 he took charge of the Division of Customs and Insular Affairs newly created by the War Department to provide military administration for the newly acquired U.S. possessions of Cuba, Puerto Rico, the Philippines, and Guam. Later in 1899, he was sent to Manila in the Philippines where his service against the Moro insurrection attracted the notice of Secretary of War Elihu Root.

Then, in 1901, he was promoted to Captain and after a brief time in the United States, returned to the Philippines to serve with the 15th Cavalry. He learned the Moro language and began a series of four campaigns against the Moros, so successful that seven general officers, including Major General Leonard Wood, moved to promote Pershing to Brigadier General in recognition of his military ability and the quality of his service. Their attempt, however, was not successful because military advancement at the time was based on seniority and not on merit, even though a number of Generals, including Wood, Bliss, Funston, and Mills, had been promoted not on seniority but in the interest of Army efficiency.

For the time being, Pershing would remain a Captain stationed in Washington, D.C., but he was soon to form a connection that both helped and hindered his further promotion and that otherwise changed his personal life forever. While in Washington, Pershing attended a dinner hosted by Nebraska Republican Senator Joseph H. Millard. Also attending was fellow Spanish-American War officer, President Theodore Roosevelt, who introduced Pershing to Wyoming Senator and Chairman of the Military Affairs Committee Francis E. Warren and his daughter, Miss Helen Francis "Frankie" Warren. Twenty years younger than Pershing, Miss Warren had just graduated from Wellesley and returned to Washington, D.C., when she accompanied her father to Millard's dinner.

"We went there and met Captain Pershing for the first time," Senator Warren remembered. "My daughter was just out of school. She and Pershing were very friendly. The next evening Miss Warren attended a dance at the post at Fort Meyer and there she and Pershing danced together."[149]

"Danced every dance but one, and have lost my heart to Captain Pershing irretrievably," Miss Warren had written.[150] After a year's courtship, the couple married in Washington, D.C. President Theodore Roosevelt attended the wedding at the Church of the Epiphany and the reception at the Willard Hotel. The next day the couple left for Tokyo, where Pershing had been posted as military attaché. From there he spent a tour of duty in Manchuria as an observer of the Russo-Japanese War.

In 1906, Roosevelt promoted Pershing and four other promising officers to Brigadier General over 862 officers who were ahead of Pershing in rank. Three years earlier, Roosevelt had tried to convince Congress that the military's system of promotion was antiquated, cumbersome, and failed to reward promising officers quickly enough. He referred directly to Pershing as an example of a capable young officer whose distinguished service in the Philippines merited promotion through the ranks without having to resort to the use of presidential power. Neither the military nor Congress would listen, so Roosevelt finally used his own power to promote, and since that power was limited to appointing only general officers, he did just that. As a result, however, his action precipitated a great deal of jealousy and the accusation that Pershing's political influence and not his merit had secured the promotion. Responding to the critics, Roosevelt reasoned, "To promote him because he married a Senator's daughter would be an infamy; to refuse him promotion for the same reason would be an equal infamy."[151]

The bitterness towards Pershing was most likely responsible for rumors that he had a liaison with a native girl in Mindanao, in the Philippines, where he had been stationed as Governor of Moro Province. Helen recognized the political motivation behind the rumors and came to her husband's defense.

"If any stories about Jack come to you to his discredit," Helen wrote her father, "don't believe them. No matter how circumstantial they may be, nor how well they may seem to be substantiated, they are not true and you may be sure of it."[152]

Such testimony to the General's character was matched in another way by one who had witnessed him in combat: "He was the coolest man under fire I ever saw," Pershing's commander said, referring to the assault made by Pershing and the black Buffalo Soldiers of the 10th Cavalry during the Battle of Santiago. Lt. Col. Roosevelt, who commanded one of the other of the six regiments in that battle, noted, "The tenth Cavalry lost a greater proportion of its officers than any other regiment in battle – eleven of twenty-two."[153] Pershing was one of those officers who survived; for his gallantry in the fighting at San Juan Hill on July 1, 1898, he was awarded the Silver Star.[154] Later, after the battle, he was photographed with Roosevelt.[155]

Pershing did not forget the confidence President Roosevelt had placed in his merit and the political risk the President had taken in promoting him to brigadier general. After President Wilson's refusal of Roosevelt's offer to raise and lead a regiment to fight in the Great War, Roosevelt wrote to Pershing at the insistence of his own sons, requesting that the General allow them to fight in the front lines as enlisted men. Recognizing the merit of the training Ted and his younger brother, Archie Roosevelt, had already received with their commissions from the Officers' Training Camps of Plattsburg, Pershing responded that he would be glad to have them with him as officers.[156]

At the time, there was no Reserve Officers' Corps, and the only way to earn a reserve commission was to attend the Plattsburg camps where a man received no pay, had to buy his own uniforms, pay for his own food and incidental expenses, and provide for his own transportation.[157] Grateful for the opportunity, Ted commanded the 1st Battalion, 26th Infantry, 1st Division and his brother, Archie, served under him.[158] Their brother, Kermit, served with the Canadian forces. All three Roosevelt brothers survived the war, but Quentin, Roosevelt's youngest son, joined the 95th Aero Squadron and was killed in action.

The relationship between the Roosevelts and Pershing endured. Eighteen years after President Theodore Roosevelt died, Pershing attended a memorial service and dinner commemorating his son Quentin's life and career.[159] Another President Roosevelt, cousin Franklin, also attended.[160]

Pershing was held in high regard by many, as reflected in his nickname, "Black Jack," but at first that was not at all the case. Appointed a 1st Lieutenant with the 10th Cavalry in October 1895, he commanded black Buffalo Soldiers at Fort Assiniboine, Montana, where he and his men captured a group of renegade Creek Indians and deported them to Canada.[161] A year and a half later, in June 1897, Pershing was assigned to West Point to instruct cadets in military tactics. A West Point graduate himself, his unflinching military demeanor and strict discipline made him less than popular among his students, and the West Point cadets referred to him with the derogatory term, "Nigger Jack," for his service with the Buffalo Soldiers.

Pershing had praised the fighting spirit of the Buffalo Soldiers with whom he served. "We officers of the Tenth Cavalry could have taken our black heroes into our arms," Pershing said. "They had again fought their way into our affections, as they had fought their way into the hearts of the American people."[162]

As time went on, and respect for Pershing grew, he became known as "Black Jack," in the words of the National Park Service, "both a subtle accolade and derogation to the Buffalo Soldiers he fought with and praised." "General Pershing's time spent leading black soldiers significantly affected him throughout his military career. He remained deeply concerned with their well being and was instrumental in getting the black organizations into combat rather than being relegated to support operations in the rear."[163]

Not everyone completely agrees with that National Park Service assessment, however. In the First World War, the 92nd and 93rd Divisions were comprised of black soldiers, with some few exceptions under the command of white officers. "Although Pershing was known as 'Black Jack,' a nickname earned for his service with black troops in Cuba and Mexico, he displayed no confidence in the newly arrived black regiments. Despite his insistence that American troops fight under his command, he first tried to send the 93rd to the British for training, but they refused to accept the division. So in April 1917, he loaned them to the French, who were happy to receive them. As Colonel William Hayward, the white commander of the 369th put it, 'Our great American general simply put the black orphan in a basket, set it on the doorstep of the French, pulled the bell, and went away.'[164]

That was certainly not the case in 1916 when black troops figured prominently in the attempt to capture Pancho Villa. In a continuing effort to provoke a war between Mexico and the United States,[165] Pancho Villa attacked Columbus, New Mexico, in March, 1916, killing 23 civilians and military personnel.[166] Pershing was ordered to conduct an armed intervention, known as the Mexican Punitive Expedition and consisting of a force of 15,000 men who penetrated 350 miles into Mexican territory in pursuit of Villa, much to the consternation of the Mexican government.[167] The Buffalo Soldiers of the 10th Cavalry, then under the command of Major Charles Young, "led the attempt to locate Villa."[168] However, after ten months, President Wilson and Mexican President Carranza reached an agreement that ended the punitive expedition; Pershing withdrew, the raids across the border stopped, and Villa himself was wounded, although never captured.

Two months after Pershing returned from the Mexican Punitive Expedition, the United States declared war on Germany, and Secretary of War Newton D. Baker reviewed the files of all existing general officers. Chief of Staff General Hugh L. Scott was already 64 years old and faced mandatory retirement. General Frederick Funston, a native of Iola,

General "Fred" Funston.[169]

Kansas, had commanded General Pershing throughout the Mexican Punitive Expedition and had died suddenly while dining with friends at the St. Anthony Hotel in San Antonio.[170] After General Funston's death, Pershing was made Major General and given command of the Army's Southern Department.[171]

The decision of who would command American forces in the field came down to two men: Major General Leonard Wood and Major General John J. Pershing. Baker claimed that Wilson left the decision to him;[172] however, when Senator John Parker, the 1916 Progressive Party vice-presidential candidate was sent by Roosevelt to Wilson with the request that General Wood lead a volunteer regiment with Roosevelt as the junior brigadier general, Wilson told Parker that Roosevelt was too old and "Wood was not going to France in command of any kind of division under any circumstances whatever."[173]

Both Wood and Roosevelt had been vocal about the lack of preparedness, and the President was not about to concede to General Wood and ex-President Roosevelt the command of American forces. Baker had thought Wood, though younger than Pershing, was not as physically fit for the job, whereas Pershing most definitely was.

In the final analysis, the decision came down to the ability to demonstrate loyalty to a political superior. Wilson wrote to Baker: "Personally, I have no confidence in General Wood's discretion nor in his loyalty to his superiors."[174] Baker called Pershing to Washington and on May 10, 1917, made him commander of the American Expeditionary Forces. On May 19, President Wilson ordered General Pershing to "proceed to France at as early a date as practicable,"[175] and on May 28, Pershing sailed aboard the White Star liner *Baltic*, arriving in Liverpool on June 8. After two years and three months, he returned to the United States, landing at Hoboken, New Jersey, on September 8, 1919, aboard the liner *U. S. A. T. Leviathan*.[176]

Soon after his arrival in the United States, Congress created the rank of General of the Armies and conferred that status on Pershing, keeping him on the active duty rolls even after his mandatory retirement on September 13, 1924, when he reached the age of 64. He served at Chief of Staff up to his retirement and continued to work actively with the American Battle Monuments Commission to honor those comrades who had died in the war. Returning to France in 1937, he attended the opening of the Meuse-Argonne Monument at Montfaucon. He made his last visit to the cemeteries and memorials in France in 1939, just a few months before the beginning of yet another world war against Germany and even more loss of life.[177]

In 1920, pressure was brought on Pershing to have his name placed in nomination for the Presidency of the United States on the Republican ticket. He himself was a Republican. If nominated, he would serve, he said, but he would not agree to campaign actively. Because many other Republicans considered him as too closely allied with the Democratic Party policies of the Wilson administration, the nomination went instead to Warren G. Harding. Otherwise, Pershing kept out of politics, wrote his memoirs (1931), and continued his interest in military affairs. He spent the last few years of his life in a small suite at Walter Reed Army Hospital in Washington and died there on July 15, 1948. He was 87 years old.

For two days, Pershing's body lay in state on the Lincoln catafalque under the nation's Capitol Rotunda. Then he was laid to final

Photo courtesy Library of Congress.
General John J. Pershing.

rest in Lot 34, Arlington National Cemetery, on a slight rise of ground overlooking the graves of the men who had served with him. Buried next to him are his grandsons, Col. John Warren Pershing, III (1941-1999) and 1st Lt. Richard Warren Pershing (1942-1968), 502nd Infantry, 101st Airborne Division, killed by enemy rocket and small arms fire while searching for the body of a soldier missing in Vietnam. Richard Pershing was 25 and engaged to be married at the time he was killed.

Both John and Richard were the sons of Warren, who is remembered at Arlington in the middle name of his sons. Warren was Pershing's only son and the only one of Pershing's immediate family to survive the 1915 fire. The women, Pershing's wife and three daughters, had been dead for more than 30 years and are buried together in Laramie County, Wyoming. Of the fire that killed them, Pershing had said that they had never had a chance. Now apart from them in Arlington, it seems not at all by chance that Pershing lies with only the legacy of war beside him.

■ ■ ■

General Pershing's wife and daughters had died before he assumed command of the AEF, but he knew how important the mothers of his 488,224 boys were to their morale. That is why he approved of the "Mother's Letter of 1918," and one particular officer of his staff, the second Kansas City officer to die in the war, made a special effort to put the General's order into effect before he himself died in an attack on the General's headquarters at Chaumont and became the namesake of American Legion Post 373 in Kansas City.

Captain Rufus Montgall and the Mother's Letter of 1918 (Montgall-Richards American Legion Post No. 373)[178]

Ever attentive to the morale of his soldiers, General Pershing approved the publication of The Stars and Stripes *and recognized it as the greatest factor in sustaining the morale of the AEF. The newspaper, in turn, initiated a campaign to have every soldier send a letter home to his mother or to the one who had done the most to take her place. "The Mother's Letter of 1918" served to boost morale at home as well as at the front. Kansas City businessman-turned-soldier, Captain Rufus Ford Montgall, dutifully passed through the censorship the letters the men of his unit wrote to their mothers, and his own letter and his mother's reception of it offer poignant evidence of the personal cost of war.*

It was Mother's Day, Sunday, May 12, 1918, and tens of thousands of American boys were thousands of miles from the comforts of home: thousands of men thousands of miles away for the first time, sleeping on straw if they were lucky, on cold hard ground if they were not. Gone was the home cooking, the boys' favorite dishes that appeared without asking, the warm blankets at night or woolen gloves in the morning, the mended socks. In their places were the slop from rolling kitchens, cold by the time it reached you; a thin tarp for cover if you could find one; your skin chapped raw from the cold rain; gaping holes in your socks and, in your tunic, wide exposures where buttons used to be. And sometimes, in the night, you could hear the moans of boys tangled in the wires of no-man's land, bleeding from wounds from the previous night's raid, delirious, thirsty, calling out piteously – desperate for their mothers.

Some miles back from the front, at AEF Headquarters in Chaumont, General Pershing contemplated the numbers: by the count on Friday, two days earlier, 488,224 American boys were in France and England. To be exact, and General Pershing always was, there were "in service … a total of 283,667; in training, 176,067; en route, 21,812; and sick and detached, 6,678."[179]

In his diary on Tuesday, two days later, Pershing wrote the following: "Report from Washington indicates that we have only limited number of trained men left. Spent three days last week inspecting units of the 2nd Division, then under Major General Bundy. As Division was just out of the trenches, the salvage dumps of this unit of about 25,000 men amounted to forty carloads of clothing and unserviceable equipment.

"French and British Ambassadors are again asking the President for additional infantry and machine gun units. Washington cables that cavalry organized for A. E. F. now needed on border," the General concluded.[180]

The amount of clothing and equipment needed to sustain men at the front created enormous demands in supply; the number of men themselves was in even shorter supply.

It was clear to the General that he had to make that much more from the little he had. Morale was always an issue, and General Pershing became increasingly aware of the importance of public relations, not only with the allies but with the people on the home front as well.

The troops on the battlefront were, however, his immediate concern. A few months earlier he had approved the publication of a newspaper, *The Stars and Stripes*, "entirely by and for the soldier," with no official control by General Headquarters. Its first number appeared on February 8, 1918, and before the Armistice, its circulation reached as high as 500,000. "I do not believe," the General later said, "that any one factor could have done more to sustain the morale of the A.E.F. than *The Stars and Stripes*."[181]

The Stars and Stripes had gone to work immediately to accomplish that task, and between the battlefront and the home front, made one of the strongest connections the Great War had known. Under the management of Lt. G. T. Viskniski, the writers and illustrators on the newspaper staff spoke directly to the boys themselves in the language of good advice a buddy might use, and in the issue of May 3, 1918, began a campaign to have "every man in the A.E.F." send home a letter to his mother, or if she was not living, to the one who had done the most to take her place.

"You know what Mother's letters mean to you," the appeal in the paper read. "You know how much she puts into them, how much you can read between the lines of her longing for you, of her prayers for you, of her hopes for your safety and uprightness and well-being. But you've no idea what your letter means to Mother. You've no idea

Photo courtesy Library of Congress.
Cpt. Rufus Ford Montgall.

how many times she reads them over, how much she treasures them, how much she gets out of them—how much they buoy her up when times seem dark and work seems hard and you seem Oh! so far away. For every time that you re-read one letter of hers, she re-reads one of yours three times, easily."[182]

To drive home the point even more graphically, the paper published in the top center of page 1 a drawing of a mother emerging along the walk from the side of her front porch, right arm extended towards the postman who has stopped in the street, his right arm extended up towards her, ready to present her with the "Mother's Letter." Sister watches from the window, and the U.S. flag extends itself protectively over the front porch while the single star service flag is suspended beneath, under the eaves.

General Pershing approved the paper's request and ordered that every company censor work overtime if necessary to pass the letters. Any letter marked with the words "Mother's Letter," where a stamp would normally appear, would be treated as if a "special delivery" stamp had been affixed right there, and the "Mother's Letters" received the highest priority of any mail stateside and within the A.E.F. The YMCA was to supply plenty of paper in its huts or special postcards with which the boys could complete the task. The special card was described in the words of the time: "a gray-haired mother, with knitting on lap, looking down over her glasses at a strapping big boy, who knelt by her side and looked up into her eyes. His was the uniform of an American officer and his expression that of an American hero that can learn to fight without losing his finer instincts, most important of all, his mother's love."[183]

In compliance with the General's order, Cpt. Rufus Ford Montgall sat at a table in his billet processing the letters his troops had written home to their mothers that day. As the chief executive officer for the Quartermaster Corps Motor Truck Group in Bonviliers, northern France,[184] Cpt. Montgall had the responsibility of reading the letters of the men under his command and excising any references to information that might aid the enemy should the letters be captured en route. Raising the gavel of his censor's stamp in exclamation, he affirmed his approval of each envelope, entered his initials in pen on the stamp, sealed the envelope, and fired the letter off into the stack to be sent home.

Cpt. Montgall was used to duty. Before he entered the service, he had worked at the American Sash and Door Company in Kansas City, rising from an entry-level job at $10 a week to the ranks of director and later vice-president of the company. The same story described his experience in uniform. He had entered the service with the old Third Regiment and was with it in Mexico under General Pershing in 1916. Along with Col. R. Bryson Jones, Montgall had organized the "Business Men's Battalion," the core of what later became the Seventh Regiment and still later the 140th Infantry of Kansas City boys that went to France under Col. Albert A. Linxwiler.[185]

"In the spring of 1917 he had attended night school classes taught by Colonel Dravo of the US Quartermaster Corps, and in the summer took an examination before a board of army officers that secured the rank of a captain and qualified him to elect to serve in the United States or in France."[186] Inducted into the service on September 5, 1917, he shipped overseas on December 19 of that year.[187]

"He might have gone as quartermaster to any of the big army cantonments, or to service in Washington or any of the big cities where division quartermasters are stationed," *The Kansas City Star* reported. "But Rufus Montgall chose the munitions transportation service and asked to be sent to the front.

"He told his mother and friends that when he arrived in France, he would have command of a train of fifty-three army trucks. Upon his arrival, however, because of his superior qualifications, he at once was assigned to Col. Bertram. T. Clayton, Division Quartermaster, American Expeditionary Forces. He was made Colonel Clayton's chief executive officer and became thereby a member of General Pershing's staff," *The Kansas City Star* noted.[188]

In civilian life, the son of William H. Montgall (1850-1890), Rufus Ford Montgall carried both the first name of his paternal grandfather, Rufus Montgall, and the maiden name of his mother, Sarah Ford. His father had died eight days before his 40th birthday, leaving Sarah alone to raise their three-year-old son. The family was not, however, without means. Grandfather Rufus Montgall (1817-1888) had been one of the pioneer families of Kansas City, clearing a farm along Brush Creek north to 43rd Street between Paseo and Troost, prime real estate for residential development. Montgall Avenue passes through what was once the old farm and was named after its former owner, who himself saw military service before and during the Civil War as the commander of a militia company charged with protecting area homes. Born on the Brush Creek farm, William Montgall farmed for several years in nearby Blue Springs, Missouri, until his health began to fail and he moved back to Kansas City, where he invested in real estate and bought stock in the Bank of Kansas City.[189]

Devoted to his mother for raising him alone throughout the 28 years since his father's death, Rufus Ford Montgall happily took up his own pen that Mother's Day to honor his mother and to fulfill the duty entrusted to him by the General of the AEF. In addition to carrying his own sincere sentiments, however, his words undoubtedly reflect those of the many letters he had read that day. Its sentimental style is reminiscent of the phrasing on postal card greetings being peddled at the time by the enterprising Kansas Citian, Joyce C. Hall.[190]

IN FRANCE, Sunday, May 12.

Mother o' Mine:[191] Men never get so hardened by circumstances of their surroundings never to become so toughened by their environment, never become so mired in the muck and mire of their existence that the mention of "Mother" does not bring forth memories that are sometimes stored in a hidden cell of their innermost heart, and a certain remembrance of kinder days that have passed in their lives.

Today, therefore, is a day of days with the men of the American Army in France—Mother's Day—and General Pershing has published an order requesting every man in his command to recognize it by taking his own mother into his confidence by the only means at hand, a Mother's Letter.

As I have sat here today, censoring the letters of men pouring out a mother-love which is beyond their power to express, I am proud of the fact that I can turn from my daily stand of being a "man's man" and come back to you, Mother of Mine, as "Mother's Boy."

I had boasted to myself that as a soldier far from home and in a strange land, among strange peoples, I was a man, no longer held by apron strings. And now I find it true, for those strings have become chains and I am proud of my shackles. Who would have known from knowing me that Mother sits enthroned in my heart. But there you are, mother dear, the one who knows me best, the one who counts on me most, and by your very expectations make me such a man as I had not expected, or ever dreamed to be. Surely God did a good thing when he gave

me you. For tenderness and patience, for long suffering and understanding, for sure remembrance or, if need be, for quick forgetfulness, there is only one, mother, the world o'er. Every good woman reminds me of you. The last thoughts in my day are of your gentle deeds kind thoughts, and the silence of the great cathedrals that abound in France are all messengers of God whispering, "Mother, mother—"

Seemingly a long time ago I said good-bye to you, but you would not be left behind, for you are always with me. I cannot help thinking today of what Kipling said: "'God could not be everywhere, so he gave us mothers." And that thought particularly re-occurs to me on this day.

When I come home—home to you, mother—life will have a new incentive for me, and that will be to be the man my mother thinks I am. With that thought in view I am looking to the strong arm of never failing Providence and thoughts of you, and I'll come back the same boy you gave to your country.

So, mother of mine, with these thoughts I leave you on Mother's Day, knowing that nobody in the world loves you like I do.

RUFE.[192]

Rufus Montgall's letter and the letters of his men were among the 1,630,000 Mother's Letters that had arrived in the United States by May 31, 1918.[193]

Sarah E. Montgall, Rockhill Manor, 43rd and Locust Streets, Kansas City, Missouri, USA, received her 31 year-old son's Mother's Day Letter on June 7, 1918, three weeks after he wrote it. Just a few hours later, she received the following telegram from Adjutant General McCain in Washington:

"DEEPLY REGRET TO INFORM YOU THAT CAPT. RUFUS MONTGALL, QUARTERMASTER CORPS, IS OFFICIALLY REPORTED KILLED IN AIR RAID, MAY 30."[194]

Just three days earlier, Sarah Montgall had

had a premonition of her son's death. That day she read in *The Kansas City Star's* casualty list that Col. Bertram T. Clayton, whom she recognized from previous letters from Rufe to be his commanding officer, had been killed in an airplane raid, but the date of his death was not given in the report. Nor had the casualty list made any mention of Cpt. Montgall. Later, however, friends speculated that both Col. Clayton and Cpt. Montgall had been mortally wounded together in the same attack but did not die of their wounds until several days after.[195]

In actuality, although not known by many at the time, Rufus Montgall was not with his unit at the time of his death. Instead, he was at AEF Headquarters in Chaumont and was killed in an air raid, most likely targeted to disrupt the command function in the rapidly expanding American deployment of troops. "With American troops finally beginning to pour into France, the German high command had evidently chosen that moment to try to disorganize and dispirit the Americans by harassing—and if they were extraordinarily lucky, killing—the AEF commander."[196]

Cpt. Rufus Ford Montgall was the second officer from Kansas City to be killed in the war. The first officer, Cpt. William T. Fitzsimons, an Army physician, had lost his life a few months earlier, on September 7, 1917, ironically, in a similar attack, from the air and behind the lines. Cpt. Fitzsimons was the first American officer killed in France. Like Sarah Montgall, Cpt. Fitzsimons' mother, Catherine, was also a widow at the time of her son's death.

Other letters from Rufe had arrived on June 7 with his Mother's Day letter – five letters in all – the last written a week later, but when Sarah Montgall opened and read them one-by-one, none but the Mother's Day letter contained a card. It pictured a "gray-haired mother, with knitting on lap, looking down over her glasses at a strapping big boy, who knelt by her side and looked up into her eyes." As Sarah stretched open her son's

Mother's Day letter, her eyes were forced down to the card as it fell, fluttering like a brittle leaf to the floor.

■ ■ ■

Cpt. Rufus Ford. Montgall is buried in the U.S. Military Cemetery, Somme American, Bony, Aisne, France. But he was not forgotten. Fifty friends of Cpt. Montgall and of Lt. John F. Richards, also of Kansas City and killed in action in France, formed American Legion Post No. 373, chartered as the Montgall-Richards Post in mid-October 1921.[197] Cpt. Montgall's name also appears in the list of 441 Kansas City war dead on the west wall of Memory Hall at Liberty Memorial and on the Meyer Circle Gateway Avenue of Trees Memorial at Meyer Circle and Ward Parkway in Kansas City. Also commemorating him is a memorial plaque fixed to the headstone for his grandparents Rufus and Nancy Montgall's grave in Elmwood Cemetery in Kansas City.[198]

Endnotes

1   Richard J. Loosebrock, *The History of the Kansas Department of the American Legion.* (Topeka, KS: Kansas Department of the American Legion, 1968), p. 2.

2   Ibid, p 8.

3   Ibid, p.8.

4   Ibid, p. 5.

5   Ibid, p. 7.

6   Walter Barlow Stevens, *The Centennial History of Missouri (The Center State): One Hundred Years in the Union 1820-1921.* (St. Louis: S. J. Clarke, 1921), pp. 483-485.

7   Loosebrock, p. 10.

8   Ibid.

9   *Stars and Stripes,* March 7, 1919.

10 Loosebrock, p. 12.

11 Ibid.

12 Ibid.

13 Ibid, p. 13.

14 Ibid, p. 23.

15 Ibid, p. 26.

16 Ibid, p. 30.

17 Derek Donovan, *Lest the Ages Forget: Kansas City's Liberty Memorial.* (Kansas City, MO: Kansas City Star Books, 2001), p. 23.

18 Loosebrock, p. 31.

19 Ibid, p. 36.

20 Ibid, p. 49.

21 Ibid, p. 50.

22 Ibid, pp. 49-53.

23 Ibid, p. 50.

24 Lillie F. Kelsay, *Historic & Dedicatory Monuments of Kansas City.* (Kansas City, MO: Board of Parks & Recreation Commissioners, 1987), p. 2. Also see Sherry Piland and Ellen J. Uguccioni. *Fountains of Kansas City: A History and Love Affair.* (Kansas City, MO: City of Fountains Foundation, 1985), p. 127.

25 Sherry Piland and Ellen J. Uguccioni. *Fountains of Kansas City: A History and Love Affair*, op. cit., 123-130.

26 "A Fountain is Dedicated." *The Kansas City Star*, November 2, 1921, p. 2A. Also see the sketch titled, "A Memorial Gift from the City to Legion Posts Dedicated Today." *The Kansas City Star.* November 2, 1921, p. 2A.

27 Stacy A. Cordery. *Alice: Alice Roosevelt Longworth, from White House Princess to Washington Power Broker.* (New York: Viking, 2007), pp. 266-267.

28 Evan A. Edwards. *From Doniphan to Verdun: The Official History of the 140th Infantry.* (Lawrence, KS: The World Company, 1920), p. 148.

29 Kelsay, p. 1.

30 Michael Bushnell. *Northeast News.* March 28, 2012. http://northeastnews.net/pages/?=11750 accessed by author, January 18, 2013.

31 "A Fountain Service Today." *The Kansas City Star*, October 30, 1921, p. 11A.

32 *Quartermaster Review*, Sep-Oct 1963.

33 Associated Press. "To Get Nation's Homage." *The Kansas City Star*, October 24, 1921, p. 2.

34 Reynolds, Quentin. *Known But to God.* (New York: John Day Company, 1969), p. 28.

35 "Chalons Honors Our Hero." *The Kansas City Times*, October 25, 1921, p. 2.

36 "Select U.S. Hero Today." *The Kansas City Times*, October 24, 1921, p. 2.

37 See www.arlingtoncemetery.net/eyounger.htm

38   "Corporal Edward F. Younger, Who Selected the Body of the Unknown Soldier." Caption with photo from "The 'Unknown Soldier' and His Escort of Heroes." *The Kansas City Star*, November 9, 1921, p. 24.

39   "When the Body of America's Unnamed Hero was Chosen and One of the Medals Bestowed by Foreign Nations." Picture from *The Kansas City Star*, November 9, 1921, p. 2, © Keystone View 10, New York.

40   "Unknown on Way Home." *The Kansas City Times*, October 26, 1921, p. 10.

41   "Hero Leaves France Today." *The Kansas City Times*, October 25, 1921, p. 2.

42   Lady Fiona Carnarvon. *Lady Almina and the Real Downton Abbey.* (New York: Random House Broadway Paperbacks, 2011), p. 239.

43   "A Pledge of Comradeship in Honors to Unknown Dead." *The Kansas City Star*, October 25, 1921, p. 24. See also "London Greets Pershing." *The Kansas City Times,* October 17, 1921, p. 1.

44   "America's Highest Tribute to France's Unknown Soldier." Photograph from *L'Illustration Paris*. *The Kansas City Star*, October 29, 1921, p. 14.

45   "World at His Bier." *The Kansas City Star*, November 10, 1921, p. 1.

46   "Foch's Ship Slows Down." *The Kansas City Star*, October 27, 1921, p. A1.

47   "Nation Greets Foch." *The Kansas City Star,* October 28, 1921, p. 1.

48   "Diaz" is pronounced "*Deatz*." See "Italy's Sons Here Ready." *The Kansas City Star*, October 30, 1921, p. 7A.

49   "Three of the Legion's Distinguished Guests Enjoying a Chat in Washington." *The Kansas City Star*, October 26, 1921, p. 1.

50   "Medalion Sale Tomorrow." *The Kansas City Star*, October 23, 1921, p. 2A.

51   "Stolen Posters Being Sold." *The Kansas City Star*, October 28, 1921, p. A1.

52   "Where the Distinguished Visitors Will Live While in Kansas City for the Legion Convention." *The Kansas City Star*. (Pictures of homes of Kirkwood, Dickey, Loose, Long, Braley, and Perry). October 30, 1921, p. 6A.

53   "Jacob Leander Loose." Biographical sketch in Katherine Baxter, *Notable Kansas Citians of 1915˙1916˙1917˙1918.* (Kansas City, MO: Kellogg-Baxter Printing Co, 1925), p. 190.

54   "Robert Alexander Long." Biographical sketch in *Notable Kansas Citians of 1915˙1916˙1917˙1918*, op. cit., p. 170.

55   "Robert Ryland." Biographical sketch in Sara Mullin Baldwin, Ed., *Who's Who in Kansas City 1930.* (Kansas City, MO: Veterans of Foreign Wars), p. 167.

56   Picture from *The Kansas City Star*, October 30, 1921, p. 1C.

57   Katherine Dickey died Sep 19, 1920. See *Who's Who in Kansas City*, op. cit. pp. 57-58. Also see "Honor Guests Assigned." *The Kansas City Star*, October 23, 1921, p. A1.
     Host homes were pictured in *The Kansas City Star*, October 30, 1921 p. 6A. See also "Routes of the Visitors." *The Kansas City Star*, October 26, 1921, p. 1.

58   "A Real Legion Rush." *The Kansas City Times,* October 31, 1921, pp. 1-2.

59   "Gen. Jacques, First Guest." *The Kansas City Star*, October 29, 1921, p. A1.

60   "Jacques A True Soldier." *The Kansas City Times*, October 31, 1921, p. 3.

61   "Jacques, Who Helped to Hold the Germans Until France Was Ready." *The Kansas City Star,* October 30, 1921, p. 1C.

62   Ibid.

63   "General Armando Diaz." Picture from *The Kansas City Star,* October 30,1921 p 1C.

64   Ibid.

65   "Italy's Sons Here Ready." *The Kansas City Star*, October 30, 1921, p. 7A.

66   "Gen. Jacques, First Guest," op cit. See also "Routes of the Visitors." *The Kansas City Star*, October 26, 1921, p. 1A.

67   "Jeweled Sword to Diaz." *The Kansas City Times,* October 31, 1921, p. 1.

68   "Italy's Sons Here Ready," op. cit.

69   "Diaz, Who Stepped out of Obscurity to Become the Savior of Italy." *The Kansas City Star*, October 30, 1921, p. IC.

70   Ibid.

71   "Diaz Talks to Students." *The Kansas City Star*, October 31, 1921, p. 3.

72   "Admiral Earl David Beatty." Picture from *The Kansas City Times*, October 31, 1921, p. 1.

73   "Greet a Real Man." *The Kansas City Star,* October 31, 1921, pp. 1-2. See also "Admiral Sees Horses Race." *The Kansas City Times*, November 1, 1921, p. 4.

74   "Admiral Sees Horse Race," op. cit.

75   "Entertain Noted Guests." *The Kansas City Times,* November 1, 1921, p. 4.

76   "Corinthian Hall." Picture from *The Kansas City Star,* October 30, 1921, *p. 6A.*

77   "Beatty, the Fighting Idol of the British Navy." *The Kansas City Times,* October 31, 1921, p. 9.

78   Ibid.

79   Ibid.

80   Ibid.

81   Morley, Christopher. "The Baron." Reprinted in *The Kansas City Times*, October 31, 1921, p.1 from *The New York Evening Post.*

82   "Big Greeting for Lejeune." *The Kansas City Star*, October 31, 1921, p. 1.

83   "He Commanded the 'Devil-Dogs,' Who Fought So Valiantly in France." Picture and cutline from *The Kansas City Star,* October 31, 1921, p. 2.

84   "Soldier and Sailor, too, is Lejeune of the Marines." *The Kansas City Times,* October 31, 1921, p. 14.

85   "All Towns Turned Out." *The Kansas City Times*, November 1, 1921, p. 8.

86   Ibid.

87   "A Bouquet From a Hero's Son." *The Kansas City Star*, November 1, 1921, p. 6A.

88   "Foch on the Last Lap." *The Kansas City Star*, October 321, 1921, p. A1.

89   "Foch, Who Twice Turned Defeats into Victories." *The Kansas City Star,* October 31, 1921, p. 18.

90   Stephen Pope & Elizabeth-Anne Wheal. *Dictionary of the First World War.* (Barnsley, S. Yorkshire, England: Pen & Sword Books Ltd., 2003), p. 164.

91   "Foch Who Twice Turned Defeats into Victories," op.cit.

92   Hogg, Ian V. *Dictionary of World War I.* (Lincolnwood, Illinois: NTC Publishing Group, 1997), p. 78.

93   Ibid, p. 79.

94   Nicholas Best. *The Greatest Day in History.* (New York: Public Affairs, 2008), p. 54.

95   "Foch Who Twice Turned Defeats into Victories," op.cit.

96   Ibid.

97   "Foch, Pershing In." *The Kansas City Times*, November 1, 1921, p. 1.

98   "Marshal Ferdinand Foch." Picture from *The Kansas City Star*, October 31, 1921, p. 1.

99   "Effect on the Big Crowd." *The Kansas City Times*, November 1, 1921, p. A1.

100   Ibid.

101   "Irwin and Laura Nelson Kirkwood Home." Picture from *The Kansas City Star*, October 30, 1921, p. 6A.

102   "Foch, Pershing In," op. cit. Also "A School Captures Foch." *The Kansas City Star*, November 2, 1921, p. 1.

103   "A School Captures Foch," op. cit.

104   "Not on Pershing's Program." *The Kansas City Times*, November 1, 1921, p. 8. See also Herbert Corey. "Find Pershing Is Human." *The Kansas City Times*, November 2, 1921, p. 1.

105   Eileen Welsome. *The General & the Jaguar: Pershing's Hunt for Pancho Villa.* (New York: Little, Brown, & Co., 2006), p. 166.

106   "Not on Pershing's Program," op. cit.

107   "Guests View Ceremonies." *The Kansas City Star,* November 1, 1921, p. 3A.

108   "A Dinner for the Women." *The Kansas City Times*, November 2, 1921, p. 10.

109   "Entertain Noted Guests." *The Kansas City Times*, November 1, 1921, p. 4.

110   "Army Leaders at Mass." *The Kansas City Star*, November 1, 1921, p. 6A. See also "Three Generals Meet at Mass." *The Kansas City Star*, November 1, 1921, p. 9A.

111   "Roar a Welcome." *The Kansas City Star,* November 1, 1921, p. 2A.

112   "General Pershing Greeting Marshal Foch on the Platform at the Legion Convention Today." Picture from *The Kansas City Star,* November 1, 1921, p. 3A.

113   "Roar a Welcome," op. cit.

114   Ibid.

115   The actual count of names listed on the plaques on the west wall of Liberty Memorial's Memory Hall is 441. The source for General Pershing's count of 519 is not clear. The earliest publicized list of "Kansas City's Heroic Dead" this author uncovered appeared in *The Kansas City Times,* on May 3, 1919, p. 13, for memorial services held in Convention Hall Sunday afternoon, May 4, 1919, at 3:00 p.m. *The Star* reported that the list "was compiled by the Missouri Valley Historical Society and is believed to be as nearly correct as it is possible to make it." That list, which also appeared the next

day in the printed program for the memorial service, contained 507 names. As records of war dead were vetted, revisions in the count continued to be made, until by the 1926 dedication of Liberty Memorial, the count stabilized at 441. See the "Honor Roll" in Derek Donovan, *Lest the Ages Forget: Kansas City's Liberty Memorial* (Kansas City, MO: Kansas City Star Books, 2001), pages 96-97. For more detailed information on how the Missouri Valley Historical Society resolved issues in the count, see Nettie Thompson Grove, "Selection of Names," *World War Soldier Dead Memorial: Annals of Kansas City, Missouri* Vol II, No. 1 (Kansas City: Missouri Valley Historical Society, 1926), pp. 93-97. See also *Memorial Service for the Men of Greater Kansas City and Jackson Co. Who Gave Their Lives in the World War.* (Kansas City: War Camp Community Service and Mayor's Welcome Home Committee, May 4, 1919.)
I am indebted to Dr. James J. O'Bryan, M.D., for the loan of an original program from the memorial service.

116 "Flame Alight!" *The Kansas City Star*, November 1, 1921, p. 3A.

117 "Beatty's Car in Collision." *The Kansas City Times*, November 2, 1921, p. 2.

118 "A Reception for Foch." *The Kansas City Times*, November 1, 1921, p. 8.

119 "Had to Cancel an Engagement." *The Kansas City Times,* November 2, 1921, p. 2.

120 "Beatty's Car in Collision," op. cit.

121 "Confer Degree on Foch." *The Kansas City Star*, November 2, 1921, p. 1.

122 "A School Captures Foch," op. cit.

123 "School Children See Marshal Foch and General Pershing." *The Kansas City Times*, Thursday, November 3, 1921, p. 2 (illustration).

124 Rickenbacker, Capt. Eddie. "Foch is Now a 'Birdman.'" *The Kansas City Times,* November 3, 1921, p. 10. (Copyright 1921, by Christy Walsh Syndicate).

125 "Children to See Heroes," op. cit. See also "Veterans Met a Veteran." *The Kansas City Times*, November 3, 1921, p. 9.

126 "Honor Guests Leave." *The Kansas City Times*, November 3, 1921, p. 1.

127 "Jacques to Leave Tonight." *The Kansas City Times,* November 2, 1921, p. 10.

128 "Honor Guests Leave," op. cit. See also "Foch Captures St. Louis." *The Kansas City Times*, November 3, 1921, p. 4.

129 "A National Holiday Nov. 11." *The Kansas City Star*, November 2, 1921, p. 1.

130 "Nation in Homage." *The Kansas City Star*, November 10, 1921, p. 1.

131 Associated Press. "World at His Bier." *The Kansas City Star*, November 10, 1921, p. 1.

132 "Nation in Homage," op. cit.

133 "Unknown Hero Is Home." *The Kansas City Star*, November 9, 1921, p. 1.

134 "World at His Bier," op. cit.

135 "To the Hero Dead." *The Kansas City Star*, November 11, 1921, pp. 1-2.

136 H. G. Wells. "Was a War to End War." *The Kansas City Times*, November 12, 1921, p. 6.
(Copyright 1921, by Chicago *Tribune* and the Press Publishing Company, The New York *World.*)

137 "Begin Parley Today." *The Kansas City Times*, November 12, 1921, p. 1.

138 "A Word to the Crowd on the Liberty Memorial Dedication." *The Kansas City Times*, November 1, 1921, p. 9.

139 Derek Donovan. *Lest the Ages Forget*, op. cit. p. 52.

140 Derek Donovan. *Lest the Ages Forget,* op. cit., pp. 22-23. For monetary conversions, see Federal Reserve Bank of Minneapolis, Consumer Price Index calculator.

141 "Flame Alight!," op. cit. pp. 1, 3.

142 Ibid.

143 Eileen Welsome. *The General and the Jaguar*, op. cit., p. 166. See also http://www.knowsouthernhistory.net/Biographies/Jack_Pershing/. Accessed by the author on April 2, 2012.

144 "Fire Kills Family of Gen. Pershing." *The New York Times*, August 28, 1915. http://query.nytimes.com/gst/abstract.html?res=FB0E16FB3A5C13738DDDA10A94D. Accessed April 1, 2012.

145 "John Pershing – Success and Tragedy." National Park Service. http: www.nps.gov/prsf/historyculturejohn-pershing.htm. Accessed April 2, 2012.

146 Eileen Welsome. *The General and the Jaguar,* op. cit. p., 164. See also "John J. Pershing – Career Fact Sheet." (Doughboy Center: The Story of the American Expeditionary Forces.) http://wwww.worldwar1.com/dbc/pershing.htm. Accessed by the author on April 2, 2012.

147 Christoph Fr. Grieb. *Dictionary of the German and English Languages, Vol II: German and English.* (Stuttgart: Paul Neff, Publisher, 1873), p. 669.

148   Floyd C. Shoemaker. *Missouri and the War.* (Columbia, MO: The State Historical Society of Missouri, 1919), p. 40. For many years the president of the State Historical Society of Missouri, Shoemaker is quoting from an article that had appeared in the St. Louis *Post-Dispatch*, "Gen Pershing Fulfilled His Ancestor's Hope." At the time, the letter was in the possession of General Pershing's cousin, Rev. Justus N. Pershing.

149   "Wife Was Senator Warren's Daughter." *The New York Times*, August 28, 1915. http://query.nytimes.com/gst/abstract.html?res=FB0E16FB3A5C13738DDDA10A94D. Accessed April 1, 2012.

150   National Park Service. "Presidio of San Francisco: John Pershing – Success and Tragedy." http://www.nps.gov/prsf/historyculture/john-pershing.htm. Accessed April 2, 2012.

151   Eillen Welsome. *The Jaguar and the General*, op. cit., p. 165.

152   "Wife was Senator Warren's Daughter," op. cit.

153   Theodore Roosevelt. *The Rough Riders.* (New York: Charles Scribner's Sons, 1925), p. 129.

154   Michael Robert Patterson. "John Joseph 'Black Jack' Pershing: General of the Armies of the United States." Arlington National Cemetery Website. http://www.arlingtoncemetery.net/johnjose.htm, p. 4. Accessed April 2, 2012.

155   "John J. Pershing – Career fact Sheet," op. cit. p. 4.

156   Hermann Hagedorn. *The Roosevelt Family of Sagamore Hill.* (New York: Macmillan, 1954), p. 367.

157   Michael Robert Patterson. "John Joseph 'Black Jack' Pershing," op. cit., p. 6. Accessed April 2, 2012.

158   Stacy A. Cordery. *Alice: Alice Roosevelt Longworth, from White House Princess to Washington Power Broker.* (New York: Viking, 2007), p. 266.

159   Ibid, p. 395. See also "Obituary: John J. Pershing." *The New York Times*, July 16, 1948. http://www.prq8alumni.com/pershing.html. Accessed April 8, 2012. Also see "Services Here Honor Quentin Roosevelt." *The New York Times*, July 15, 1936, p. 21.

160   Linda Donn. *The Roosevelt Cousins: Growing Up Together 1882-1924.* (New York: Alfred A. Knopf, 2001), p.45.

161   Michael Robert Patterson. "John Joseph 'Black Jack' Pershing," op. cit., p. 5.

162   Robert D. Edgerton. *Hidden Heroism: Black Soldiers in America's Wars.* (New York: Barnes & Noble, 2009), p.53

163   National Park Service. "Buffalo Soldier Cavalry Commander: General John J. Pershing, General of the Armies 1919, Commander 10th U.S. Cavalry 1895-1898." http://www.nps.gov/pwso/honor/pershing.htm, p. 1. Accessed by the author on April 2, 2012.

164   Robert D. Edgerton. *Hidden Heroism: Black Soldiers in America's Wars,* op. cit., p. 85. Even the word "doughboy" may have originally been derogatory. The popular designation by which World War I soldiers came to be known during World War I, the term was first associated with troops Pershing commanded in the Mexican Punitive Expedition. Although some sources attribute the term to the dough-like buttons of Civil War U.S. infantry, the term may be derived from the word "adobe," "a derisory description of dust-caked infantry applied by US cavalry stationed along the Rio Grande." (See Stephen Pope and Elizabeth-Anne Wheal. *Dictionary of the First World War.* (Barnsley S. Yorkshire: Pen & Sword Military Classics, 2003), p. 136.) The 10th Cavalry Buffalo Soldiers saw service there in 1916-1917. (See James A. Sawicki. *Cavalry Regiments of the US Army.* (Dumfries, VA: Wyvern Publications, 1985), p. 171.) It was early in 1914 that Pershing and the 8th Brigade were ordered to patrol along the Mexican Border.

165   Robert D. Edgerton. *Hidden Heroism: Black Soldiers in America's Wars,* op. cit., p. 66.

166   Eileen Welsome. *The General and the Jaguar*, op. cit., pp. 338-339.

167   C. H. Cramer. *Newton D. Baker: A Biography.* (Cleveland: The World Publishing Co., 1961), p. 83.

168   Robert D. Edgerton. *Hidden Heroism: Black Soldiers in America's Wars,* op. cit., p. 6.

169   Joseph L. Stickney. *Life and Glorious Deeds of Admiral Dewey.* (Chicago: Joseph L. Stickney, 1899), p. 426.

170   Eileen Welsome. *The General and the Jaguar*, op. cit., p. 309.

171   Ibid.

172   Jack McCallum. *Leonard Wood: Rough Rider, Surgeon, Architect of American Imperialism.* (New York: New York University Press, 2006), p. 267.

173   Ibid.

174   C. H. Cramer. *Newton D. Baker: A Biography*, op. cit., p. 115.

175   "John J. Pershing – Career fact Sheet," op. cit. p. 6.

176   "John J. Pershing – Career fact Sheet," op. cit. p. 7.

177   "John J. Pershing – Career fact Sheet," op. cit. p. 8.

178   "Montgall-Richards" was among the earliest of American Legion Posts in Kansas City. See *World War Soldier Dead Memorial: Annals of Kansas City, Missouri,* Vol II, No 1. (Kansas City: Missouri Valley Historical Society, 1926), p. 10.

179   John J. Pershing. *My Experiences in the World War, Vol. II.* (New York: Frederick A. Stokes Company, 1931), p. 47.

180   Ibid.

181   Ibid, p. 318.

182   "'Mother's Letter.'" *The Stars and Stripes*, May 3, 1918, p. 1.

183   "Death Beat Son's Letter." *The Kansas City Star*, June 8, 1918, p. 2.

184   Bruce Mathews. *Elmwood Cemetery: Stories of Kansas City.* (Kansas City, MO: Kansas City Star Books, 2010), p. 208.

185   "Rufus Montgall is Dead." *The Kansas City Times*, June 8, 1918, p. 2. See also "Kansas City Troops and Where They Are." *The Kansas City Star*, December 2, 1917, p. 2B.

186   Ibid.

187   Missouri State Archives. "Soldiers' Records: War of 1812-World War I," Rufus Montgall service record. http://www.sos. mo.gov/archives/soldiers/details.asp. Accessed by author on October 4, 2011.

188   "Rufus Montgall is Dead," op. cit.

189   Bruce Mathews. *Elmwood Cemetery: Stories of Kansas City*, op. cit., p. 59.

190   Joyce C. Hall. *When You Care Enough.* (Kansas City, MO: Hallmark Cards, Inc., 1979), pp. 30-31, 67.

191   Rudyard Kipling. *The Light That Fails.* (New York: Macmillan & Co, 1891). The poem "Mother o' Mine," by Rudyard Kipling, appears as the dedication to this book, Kipling's first novel. The phrase "Mother o' Mine" is both the title and the refrain that echoes ten times through the three-stanza poem. It is the mother's love that follows the speaker if he were to be "hanged on the highest hill." It is the mother whose tears come down on him if he were "drowned in the deepest sea," and it is the mother whose prayers would make him whole if he were "damned of body and soul." As Cpt. Montgall's later reference to Kipling suggests, Montgall was familiar with Kipling's work. Montgall likely knew this particular poem and used the title in a tribute to his own mother, the way Kipling did for his mother, Alice Kipling, who had suggested a happy ending to *The Light That Fails.* When Kipling decided on a sad ending, he reportedly dedicated his book to mother, seeking forgiveness for not having followed her preference. Cpt. Montgall, on the other hand, certainly had no apologies to make, but he did use the phrase three times through his letter – in the beginning, middle and end – much like Kipling's use of the phrase as a refrain in his poem to his mother. Adding to the irony of mothers and sons is Kipling's loss of his own son, Jack, in the war.

192   "Death Beat Son's Letter," op. cit.

193   "Mother's Day in Congress." *The Stars and Stripes*, July 12, 1918, p. 4.

194   "Rufus Montgall is Dead," op. cit.

195   Ibid.

196   D. M. Giangreco. *The Soldier from Independence: A Military Biography of Harry Truman.* (Minneapolis, MN: Zenith Press, 2009), p. 90.

197   "It's the 'Baby' of Missouri." *The Kansas City Times,* October 26, 1921, p. 3.

198   Bruce Mathews. *Elmwood Cemetery: Stories of Kansas City*, op. cit., p. 208.

"Letters are always welcome!"

Seaman 2d Class James Cummings, wearing a sweater that may well have been knitted by the Kansas City women in the Navy League branch of the DAR.

Photo courtesy of the National World War I Museum, Kansas City, Missouri.

CHAPTER 4

"We Fought at Sea and in the Air"

Seaman 2nd Class James Cummings and the *U.S.S. Jacob Jones* (James Cummings American Legion Post No. 130)

American Legion Posts were often formed by men who had either served in the same unit or branch of service. Kansas City sailors, known as "Gobs," named their American Legion Post after Seaman 2nd Class James Cummings, who served on the U.S.S. Jacob Jones, *the only American destroyer to be lost in the war. The story of its service offers insight into how the American Navy operated during the war and how a particular German U-Boat commander, Captain Hans Rose, earned the respect of American naval officers, even as his U-53 sunk the* U.S.S. Jacob Jones. *Seaman 2nd Class James Cummings lost his life in the action, and his mother, Mrs. Nellie Cummings, although eligible to make the pilgrimage to Europe and to commemorate her son's loss at sea, was too ill to make the trip.*

On April 9, 1917, just 3 days after the United States declared war on Germany, James Cummings enlisted in the United States Navy at the Recruiting Station in Kansas City, Missouri.[1] He was 21 years, 8 months old at the time of his enlistment. Prior to that, he had worked at the Parker-Washington Company and resided at 2917 Fairmont Street in Kansas City, the home of his mother, Mrs. Nellie Cummings.

From April 9 to August 26, 1917, Cummings saw service as an Apprentice Seaman at the Great Lakes, Illinois, Naval Training Station. From August 28 until September 29, 1917, he served as a Seaman 2nd Class on board the receiving ship at Philadelphia, Pennsylvania. Then on September 29, 1917, he was posted to the destroyer *U.S.S. Jacob Jones*.

By that time the American Navy was well on its way to deploying the 79 destroyers that would ultimately be based at Gibralter, Brest, and Queenstown (Ireland) – three Naval installations where 8,000 American seamen would also be based.[2] These men and the destroyers they operated were placed under the command of Vice-Admiral Sir Lewis Bayley, the British Commander-in-Chief in Queenstown. Unlike his American Army counterpart, General John J. Pershing, who argued for a separately operating American Army command, American Naval commander Rear Admiral William Snowden Sims believed that U.S. Navy personnel and warships should serve as a reinforcement pool for the

Allies. Sims had convinced his superiors in Washington that an independently operating American fleet in Europe was not the best way to prosecute the war at sea. "The result," historian Robert K. Masie said, "was a remarkable suppression of national and service pride by the U.S. Navy to further the effort of winning the war."[3]

The arrangement paid off. Not long after American destroyers arrived in Queenstown, Ireland, most of Bayly's British destroyers were sent to the Channel and the North Sea, and the British Admiral was left in command of a naval force predominantly American. Sims reported that Admiral Bayly "watched over our ships and their men with the jealous eye of a father. He always referred to 'my destroyers' and 'my Americans' and woe to anyone who attempted to interfere with them."[4]

Admiral Sims explained the mission of the American destroyers: "For the purposes of patrol, the sea was divided into areas of thirty miles square; and to each of these one destroyer, sloop, or other vessel was assigned. The ship was required to keep within its allotted area, unless the pursuit of a submarine should lead it into a neighboring one." Within its operating area, the American destroyers were "assigned to hunt for submarines, to escort single ships, to pick up survivors in boats and to go to the rescue of ships that were being attacked."[5]

For seven months, the fleet of American destroyers in the war zone went about their business and survived without the loss of a single ship to torpedoes or mines. The *U.S.S. Jacob Jones* had rescued more survivors of other disabled Allied ships than any other vessel in the fleet. On a single occasion, the *U.S.S. Jacob Jones* saved 300 crewmen of a British auxiliary cruiser. Then, in French waters, the luck of the American destroyers – and of the *U.S.S. Jacob Jones* in particular – changed.

German submarine U-53 Captain Hans Rose was not unfamiliar to Americans. He had paid the citizens of Newport, Rhode Island, an unexpected visit in October 1916.[6] He was also recognized by his Allied counterparts. Admiral Sims wrote in 1920, "We acquired a certain respect for Hans because he was a brave man, who would take chances which most of his compatriots would avoid, and, above all, because he played his desperate game with a certain decency. Sometimes, when he torpedoed a ship, Rose would wait around until all the lifeboats were filled; he would then throw out a tow line, give the victims food, and keep the survivors together until the rescuing destroyer appeared on the horizon, when he would let go and submerge. This humanity involved considerable risk to Captain Rose, for a destroyer anywhere in his neighborhood as he well knew, was a serious matter."[7]

It should not come as much of a surprise then that two years after the war, Admiral Sims would call Captain Rose "one of the few U-boat commanders with whom Allied naval officers would be willing today to shake hands. I have heard naval officers say," Sims recalled, "that they would like to meet him after the war."[8]

U.S.S. Jacob Jones Commander David Bagley got that chance a little bit early. On December 6, 1917, eight months after America had declared war on Germany and James Cummings had enlisted in the Navy, watch officers on the bridge of the *U.S.S. Jacob Jones* sighted a torpedo traveling at 40 knots breaking and diving through the water and heading directly for their vessel. Immediately, the command was given to increase speed and to swing the ship.

In his report, Commander Bagley noted that when he heard the call "Torpedo!" he "jumped at once to the bridge and on the way up saw the torpedo about eight hundred yards from the ship, approaching from about one point abaft the starboard beam, heading for a point about amidships and making a straight surface run at very high speed. No periscope was sighted."[9] That was because the shot had been fired from more than two miles away, a distance from which, as Admiral Sims himself later noted, "a hit is a pure chance."[10] Fifty to 60 feet away from the *U.S.S. Jacob Jones*, the torpedo submerged and then struck a fuel-oil tank in the ship three feet below the water line, immediately flooding the after-compartment and engine-room. The ship began settling aft until the deck was awash.

"The deck was blown clean up for a space of twenty feet," Commander Bagley reported. "The depth-charges exploded after the stern sank. Lieutenant J. K. Richards, gunnery officer, rushed aft to try to set the charges on safety, but could get no farther than the after deck-house." Commander Bagley tried to send an S.O.S., "but the mainmast had carried away and all electric power failed." The commander then ran along the deck ordering all hands to jump overboard, as he himself did when the ship began to sink.

"The ship went down by the stern and twisted slowly through nearly 180° as she swung upright vertically, bow in air," Bagley wrote. "Efforts were made to get all the survivors on rafts and the boats together. All the boats were found to be smashed but one. The motor-sailer went down with the ship," Bagley noted.[11]

Then a strange thing happened. "Fifteen or twenty minutes after the ship sank," Bagley reported, "the submarine appeared on the surface about two or three miles to the westward of the rafts and gradually approached until within a thousand yards. There it stopped and was seen to pick up one unidentified man from the water. It then submerged."[12]

At considerable risk to himself, Captain Rose sent the S.O.S. which the *U.S.S. Jacob Jones* had been unable to send to the American command at Queenstown. Rose gave the latitude and longitude of the stricken ship and informed the Americans that what was left of the crew were floating around in open boats.

By the next day, the men on the rafts had been rescued and a small patrol vessel picked up the Commander, but two officers and 64 seamen drowned or were killed in the blasts.

Seaman 2nd Class James Cummings of Kansas City was among the 64 seamen who had lost their lives, and the *U.S.S. Jacob Jones* was the only American destroyer lost in the war. The loss was felt throughout the country and especially in Kansas City, where the women in the Navy League branch of the Daughters of the American Revolution had "adopted" the crew of the *U.S.S. Jacob Jones* and outfitted them with 75 sets of knitted garments. Under the leadership of Mrs. R. E. Ball, president of the Navy League Branch, Mrs. Arthur N. Maltby, secretary, and Mrs. E. B. Wingate, treasurer, more than $4,000 worth of yarn had been

> *Seaman 2nd Class James Cummings of Kansas City was among the 64 seamen who had lost their lives, and the Jacob Jones was the only American destroyer lost in the war. The loss was felt throughout the country and especially in Kansas City, where the women in the Navy League branch of the Daughters of the American Revolution had "adopted" the crew of the U.S.S. Jacob Jones and outfitted them with 75 sets of knitted garments.*

worked up for the sailors. The women had just boxed 100 more sets of knitting and sent them to the post office when news of the tragedy reached Kansas City. The items were then re-directed and sent to the crew of the *U.S.S. O'Brien.*[13]

Seaman 2nd Class James Cummings was not forgotten. On August 1, 1918, James Cummings; William C. Blake, who died at Camp Funston, Fort Riley, Kansas; and Harry N. Miller, a messenger in the 1st Division, were honored in a flag raising at Penn Valley Park, the first general memorial of world war dead to be held in the city.[14] A year later, in September 1919, American Legion Post 130, originally comprised only of sailors, was organized and took the name of "James Cummings" as its official designation. The name "Earl W. Leeman" was added in 1933.[15]

Seaman 2nd Class Cummings is also listed among the Kansas City war dead on the plaques at the Meyer Circle Gateway at Meyer and Ward Parkway, as well as on the plaques in Memory Hall at Liberty Memorial, Kansas City. His mother, Nellie Cummings, had planned to embark on the 1931 Gold Star Mothers Pilgrimage to the American cemeteries in France with two other Kansas City mothers who had lost their boys at sea. Mrs. Carrie Chaquette and Mrs. Jennie Shuntz left New York for their pilgrimage on May 27, 1931, but Nellie was too ill to accompany them and take part in the memorial service at sea, which each pilgrimage voyage observed during the crossing to France, this one on Memorial Day itself in 1931.[16] Meanwhile, annually in Kansas City, on Memorial Day and on Armistice Day, pilgrimages to the eight Great War monuments throughout the city typically included either Troost Lake or Penn Valley Lake. There the Kansas City Chapter of the American War Mothers and the members of the Gold Star League would set a wreath adrift in the water, in memory of the boys who had lost their lives at sea.[17] Hopefully, Mrs. Nellie Cummings was well enough to take part.

Lt. John F. Richards 1918 [18]

Lieut. John Francisco Richards, II
(Montgall-Richards American Legion Post No. 373)[18]

An American Legion Post was also formed by men who had served as aviators during the war. They named their post after Kansas City airman, Lt. John F. Richards, and joined with other men who had known or served with Captain Rufus Montgall, not an airman, but the second Kansas City officer to be killed in the war. Captain Richards wrote to reassure his family that the odds of survival were in his favor. Unfortunately, that did not prove to be the case, but his memory does survive in the name for the first flying field in Kansas City and the road that encircles its successor, the old Municipal Airport.

Once overseas, John F. Richards had written home to reassure his family. "Only one in nineteen thousand shots ever gets an aviator," he wrote and then reflected that the cause for which he fought was worth whatever it cost, "even one's life."[20]

However, as good as the odds were, they did not prove to be in Lt. Richards' favor. On October 29, 1918, George B. Richards, vice-president of Richards & Conover Hardware Company, 424 Delaware, Kansas City, received a cablegram from Brigadier General William S. Scott informing Richards that his son John had been killed in combat on September 26, 1918, in the Argonne Forest, France. General Scott was the young lieutenant's uncle and a commander in the 41st Division to which Lieut. John F. Richards was assigned. No further details were available.

Then, two weeks later, on Saturday, November 16, 1918, George Richards received another message from General Scott. It was then that Richards read, for the first time, the circumstances surrounding his son's death. Accompanied by an observer, the message read, "Lieut. Richards was flying over German trenches in advance of other American aircraft. While dropping bombs on the enemy, his plane was suddenly hit by anti-aircraft fire, burst into flames, and crashed.

"Later in the day, American troops storming the maze of trenches found a wrecked airplane partially buried in the

"John F. Richards II in France" "Young Kansas City aviator sitting in his airplane at the French Aviation School. Many Americans are in training there."[21]

James J. Heiman

1st Lt. John F. Richards, II gravesite, Mt. WashingtonCemetery, Kansas City, MO.

ground.

"Beneath the twisted steel and broken wood they recovered the bodies of Lieutenant Richards and the observer who had accompanied him. The two were given a military funeral," the message concluded.[22] Adding to the poignancy of the tragic details was a report that appeared in *The Kansas City Star* three days later, on November 20: "Lieut. John F. Richards was listed as 'missing in action' in a casualty list of 627 men, four of whom were from Kansas City."[23]

A native of Kansas City, Lieut. Richards was born on July 31, 1894, and lived with his parents at 4526 Warwick Boulevard. He had been a student at Yale before his induction into the Army in Austin, Texas, on May 22, 1918. He received training in aviation and served with Headquarters, 10th Aero Squadron, Chanute Field, Illinois, until July 19, 1917. One of the first 10 students sent to France, he shipped overseas on August 25, 1917, and served with the Headquarters Detachment in Issoudun, France, until December 11, 1917,

when he received his commission as a 1st Lieutenant with the 1st Aero Squadron, serving with them until the bombing mission that took his life on the first day of the Meuse-Argonne offensive.[24] He was 24 and is buried at Mt. Washington Cemetery, Kansas City.[25]

Fifty friends of Lieutenant Richards and of Captain Rufus Montgall, another Kansas City native who lost his life in the war, combined to create American Legion Post No. 373, chartered in mid-October of 1921 as the Montgall-Richards Post.[26] Lieut. John F. Richards' name also appears on the bronze plaques of the Meyer Circle Gateway – Avenue of Trees at Meyer Circle and Ward Parkway in Kansas City.

His name was early associated with the story of aviation in Kansas City – most recognized in the designation for Richards Flying Field (1922-1952); Richards Road which encircles Charles B. Wheeler Downtown Airport (formerly Municipal Airport); and later for Richards-Gebaur Air Force Base in Grandview, Missouri.

1st. Lt. John F. Richards, II.

M-11 Richards Flying Field Historical Marker
9063 Gregory Boulevard, Kansas City, Missouri

Three different memorial dedications specifically devoted to the service and sacrifice of 1st Lt. John F. Richards, II are recorded in two different plaques closely tied to the history of aviation in Kansas City. That history began during the 1921 American Legion National Convention in Kansas City when the Kansas City Flying Club sponsored an air show at the American Legion Flying Field, a temporary field at 67th and Belinder Road on the Kansas side.[27] There on Armistice Day, November 11, 1921, Kansas City Flying Club member Major Howard Wehrle conceived the idea that eventually grew into the first permanent Kansas City airport.

Rather than renting space in a temporary field, he proposed to his fellow club members at their next meeting that they purchase their own permanent airfield. Although they voted down his proposal, the idea retained its attraction, and Wehrle soon convinced four other visionary flying enthusiasts to form a corporation to purchase 156 acres of ground southeast of Kansas City on the Missouri side, 800 yards south of Blue Ridge Boulevard at what was then 71st Street and Davenport Road.[28]

One of those aeronautic visionaries came from a family that had made its fortune on the ground, serving another form of transportation – the railroad. Frederick Henry Harvey, known as "Freddy," son of Harvey House restaurant chain owner Ford Harvey and grandson of founder Fred Harvey, was an early flying pioneer and one of the partners in Major Wehrle's flying field venture. In June 1922, he joined Major Wehrle, Rogers Crittenden, Robert R. Lester, and Simpson Yeomans to purchase for $60,000 the 156-acre tract of unbroken sod.[29]

Lt. Frederick Henry Harvey [30]

Along with the purchase, they formed an Air Terminal Association with plans to create an aviation ground school and erect eight hangars, two garages, a machine shop, and a clubhouse. In the center of the sod, they talked of creating a large "KC" logo with enough contrast against a white background to be visible from the sky.[31] They wanted to put Kansas City on the aviation map.

Not only was the new airfield the first permanent airdrome in Kansas City, but it was among the first in the nation,[32] and it would be dedicated on Armistice Day, November 11, 1922, just a year after the Kansas City Flying Club had sponsored its air show at the 1921 American Legion Flying Meet. The five men who formed the Air Terminal Association were truly aviation pioneers. They were all veterans of the war, and at least four of them had received cutting edge training in aviation theory and practice. Freddy Harvey graduated with the first class of Army Air Corps volunteers trained in Miami, Florida, at a facility owned by airplane manufacturer Glenn Curtiss. There Lt. Harvey and his classmates trained and helped Curtiss design and test the JN-4, known as the "Jenny."

Meanwhile, three of Freddy's partners in the new airfield venture were receiving so-

Photo courtesy Raytown Historical Society and Museum.

Richards Flying Field 1926.

phisticated training in aeronautics from the Navy and the Massachusetts Institute of Technology. Kansas City natives Robert Redenhour Lester, Rogers Crittenden, and Edwin Simpson Yeomans had each joined the Navy at different times and places, and each had ended up at the Naval Aviation Detachment at MIT. In addition, each was later assigned to the Naval Air Station in Key West, Florida, as Chief Quartermaster officers in Aviation.[33] Now four years after the war, the three Naval aviation officers and Army aviation officer Lt. Freddy Harvey had joined Major Wehrle to name their new airfield after another war aviator, Lt. John F. Richards, II, of the 1st Aero Squadron – the first Kansas City pilot to be killed in action on the first day of the battle of the Meuse-Argonne.

On Saturday, November 11, 1922, an American flag draped over a bronze tablet set in one of two stone pillars that marked the entrance to Richards Flying Field. As Lt. Richards' sister, Mrs. C N. Seidlitz, Jr., drew the flag away, tears streamed from her eyes, and Bishop Sidney C. Partridge of the diocese of Western Missouri, lifted his hand into the air. "As we behold the achievement of men in the air," he gestured, "as we lift our eyes to the blue skies today and the firmament at night, we exclaim with the psalmists of old: 'What is man that Thou art mindful of him so that he is now rising with the wings of the angels; that he pierces the air in flight.'" Of Lt. Richards, the bishop said, "We know his sacrifice was not in vain."[34]

The bronze plaque dedicated that day depicted the insignia of a pilot's wings and read: "To the memory of First Lieutenant John F. Richards, II, First Aero Squadron, U.S.A., shot down over the Argonne September 26, 1918, this field is dedicated as a tribute to the heroism of this Kansas City aviator."

Other speakers who had served the war effort also recognized the service of Lt. Richards. Rev. Burris Jenkins, Pastor of the Linwood Boulevard Christian Church, praised Lt. Richards as one of the pioneers of the air service. Dr. Burris's remarks held special significance for people in Kansas City because he had worked in France with the YMCA from May to October 1917 and then returned to France in July 1918 to serve as a special correspondent to *The Star*.[35] Like Lt. Richards, his son Burris, Jr. had also served in the Army Air Corps during the war.[36]

Also present that day were veterans from the American Legion post who had adopted the name of Lt. Richards and another Kansas City native who had died in the war, Captain Rufus Ford Montgall.[37] George H. Combs, Jr., a veteran representing the Montgall-Richards American Legion Post, recognized the importance of Army Air Corps service during the war and the great promise contained in naming the first airport after Lt. Richards. "It is entirely fitting," Combs said, "that the men who conceived this enterprise should see fit to name it after the man who aided in the

great victory ... Outliving him in grief, the memory of this sacrifice shall be cherished until it shall be as eternal as the skies," he added.[38] Also looking to the future, Major C. L. Tinker, commander of the 16th Aero Squadron, assigned to train at Richards Flying Field, predicted that the field would become a great center for aviation.

Completing the comments from dignitaries, Master of Ceremonies, Major Leland Hazard, read a telegram from Major General Mason M. Patrick, Chief of the U.S. Army Air Service, who was unable to attend the ceremonies but congratulated Kansas City on its success in getting the aviation center. Then at 1:30 p.m., in a demonstration of the military and commercial significance of the event, eight Army planes took off and, flying in formation, joined 12 commercial planes in a flight over downtown Kansas City. Then three 400-horsepower de Haviland military aircraft piloted by officers from Ft. Riley and Ft. Sill flew over the field, scattering blossoms over the 300 people gathered to witness the dedication.[39] The next day, despite the rain, an air show was held at the newly dedicated Richards Flying Field.[40]

Shortly after the dedication, the government built two hangars to accommodate a group of Jenny bi-planes for the Army Air Corps. The Jennies needed only 500-600 feet to land, and the Air Corps Reserve continued to use Richards Flying Field's four sod runways, the longest of which was 2,600 feet, until the fall of 1926, when the size of military aircraft had increased to the point that a larger space was needed to accommodate the planes.

When the government ordered the Army Air Corps Reserve to stop using Richards Field,[41] Kansas City Chamber of Commerce

James J. Heiman

Detail of pilot's wings from 1st Lt. John F. Richards, II, memorial plaque.

president Lou Holland formed a committee headed by Cpt. William S. Green, president of the Reserve Officers Association of Kansas City. Cpt. Green's committee developed 15 criteria for a new terminal and found seven locations meeting the criterion. After due consideration, the committee proposed a weed-filled tract of 687 acres north of the Hannibal Bridge and just north of the Kaw River. The Army Air Reserve moved there from Richards Flying Field along with National Air Transport's commercial operation. The Reserve installed the Richards Flying Field plaque on top of a hangar door and designated the airfield "New Richards Field," retaining the name even after city officials adopted another one, "Kansas City Municipal."[42] City officials did, however, remember Lt. Richards by naming the road that encircles the airport "Richards Road."

When the Army Air Reserve unit moved again in the late 1930s,[43] the unit took the plaque with them and installed it on top of a hangar door in the new location, the Fairfax Municipal Airport in Kansas City, Kansas. The marker remained there until the Army dissolved the Air Reserve unit and transported the marker, along with the unit's equipment and records, to a military warehouse at Fort Leavenworth.

Photo courtesy of Raytown Historical Society and Museum.

Dedication of Richards Flying Field, Saturday, November 11, 1922. L-R Bishop Sydney C. Partridge, (2) Mann (3) Major Wehrle, (4) British Vice-Consul Reginald Davidson, (5) Lt. Richards' sister, Mrs. C.N. Siedlitz, Jr., (6) Lt. Richards's father, George B. Richards, and (7) Major C. L. Tinker.

Meanwhile, William S. Green had become manager of the Fairfax Airport, and in the autumn of 1942 received a letter from the commanding general of Fort Leavenworth. "A bronze plaque has been found in an apple orchard near this military reservation," the general wrote. "It was discovered by a group of prisoners from the United States Disciplinary Barracks engaged in cutting grass in the orchard." Green speculated that the plaque "must have fallen from the truck on its way to Leavenworth."[44] "It might have remained in the orchard for years had it not been found," he said.

Green, a former commander in the old Army Air Reserve unit, thought the plaque "deserved a better home," so he requested the General return the plaque to him. After receiving it, Green contacted R. N. "Swede" Knowlson, *The Kansas City Star* aviation editor, who presented the plaque to the Liberty Memorial Museum. Museum curator Mark Beveridge reported that the plaque was in storage there with no plans for its display.[45]

Then on September 23, 1979, the Raytown Historical Society marked the site of old Richards Flying Field with a new plaque recognizing Lt. Richards as the namesake for the site of the first Kansas City airport, which also had served as the location for the Army

Air Reserve in 1922.[46] William A. Ong, who later purchased the field in 1943 for $37,500 and trained 7,300 World War II Army Air Corps pilots there,[47] delivered comments and unveiled the marker. The Missouri Pilots Association conducted a flyover and, like the ceremony 57 years earlier, dropped flowers on the crowd gathered to witness the event. Twenty-eight years later, on April 29, 2007, the 85th anniversary of Richards Flying Field, the Raytown Historical Society refurbished and re-dedicated the marker that currently stands at 9063 Gregory Boulevard.[48]

Sometime after 1979, the original bronze plaque dedicated in 1922 found its way back home to Raytown and is now on display at the Raytown Historical Society Museum, 9703 East 63rd Street. It had returned after making an historic journey in two different states to three historically significant Kansas City area airports – Richards Flying Field in Raytown, Municipal Airport in Kansas City, Missouri (now Charles B. Wheeler Downtown Airport), and Fairfax Airport in Kansas City, Kansas. Having made those journeys, and having been buried and resurrected from an apple orchard at Fort Leavenworth, the marker had become something of a charm; Kansas City was indeed on the aviation map, and Lt. John Francisco Richards, II, would be remembered from the skies above Kansas City for the vision his service had inspired.

Photo by James J. Heiman. Courtesy of Raytown Historical Society and Museum.

Richards Flying Field dedication plaque, November 11, 1922.

James J. Heiman

Richards Flying Field Historical Marker.

Lt. Frank L. Stauver: From Artillery to Aviation

1st Lt. Frank Stauver's name was not adopted by an American Legion Post, but his name does appear on three Kansas City Memorials, one of which is The Kansas City Bar Association Monument to men of the legal profession who had served in the war. 1st Lt. Stauver began his service as part of Battery A, 129th Field Artillery and later transferred to the Aviation Corps. He trained at Camp Talliaferro, Texas, and was then sent to Hampden Field in Langley, Virginia, where he fell victim to pneumonia and died. More World War I servicemen died of disease, especially from the Spanish Flu, than died of wounds suffered in combat.

Another Kansas City aviator and the last of the eight names to appear on the plaque of the 1921 Kansas City Bar Association memorial was 1st Lt. Frank L. Stauver.[49] Born in La Grange, Missouri, on March 27, 1895, the son of George H. and Laura E. Stauver, Frank Lawrence Stauver was just 23 when he was inducted into the Army on August 6, 1918.[50]

Mr. Elison A. Neil paid tribute to Lt. Stauver in a short address to the Kansas City Bar Association on November 16, 1918, just two weeks after the lieutenant's death.[51] Mr. Neil recalled that Lt. Stauver had enlisted in Battery B, was sent to Camp Doniphan, and was later attached to the 60th Battalion Headquarters as an instructor in War Risk Insurance. Two other sources indicate that he served with Battery A, 2nd Field Artillery Regiment, Missouri National Guard, a unit that later became part of the 129th Field Artillery.[52] Stauver was a 2nd Class Private at the time and later transferred to the Aviation Corps because he saw little opportunity in his current assignment for advancement beyond NCO.

He completed ground school at Aus-

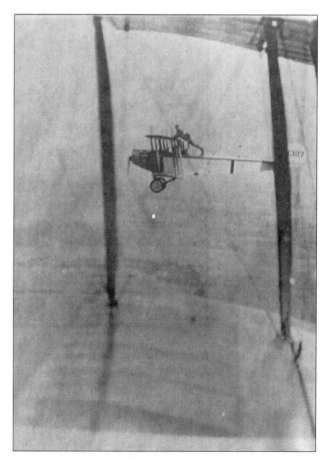

Photo from author's personal collection.

Photo taken from the cockpit of a biplane. Note the figure leaning on the top wing of the second biplane.

tin, Texas, and was sent to Carlston Field, Florida, where he was commissioned a 2nd lieutenant in aviation, then was detailed to Taliaferro Camp in Fort Worth for a course in advanced flying. In mid-October, he was sent to Hampden Field in Langley, Virginia, and was there just a few days when he was stricken with influenza so severe that it quickly developed into pneumonia. He died November 1, 1918, and a week later on November 8, 1918, was buried with full military honors at Albany, Missouri. As next-of-kin, his mother, Laura Stauver, Linden, Missouri, received official notification of his death.

Prior to his enlistment, he had worked not quite a year with O. C. Mosman's law office and before that in the office of G. W. Duval in the American Bank Building. His June 2, 1917, draft registration for Jackson County Draft Board No. 12 indicated that he was an attorney and adjudicator for the Franklin Insurance Company, paying compensation claims;[53] he also worked with the Traveller's Insurance Company.[54] He had attended Denver University, the University of Missouri, and the Kansas City School of Law. Just prior to his induction into military service, he resided at 3314 Holmes in Kansas City.

In addition to his listing on the Kansas City Bar Association Monument, his name is also included in the plaques on the Meyer Circle Gateway at Meyer Circle and Ward Parkway as well as on the list of Kansas City war dead on the west wall of the Liberty Memorial. He is also listed among the "Gold Stars" of Battery A, 129th Field Artillery, 35th Division.[55]

Photo from author's personal collection.

A training landing that proved less than successful at Camp Taliaferro, Fort Worth, Texas.

Endnotes

1   Missouri State Archives Soldiers' Records: War of 1812 – World War I, Individual Service Record of James Cummings, service number 195-45-09. www.sos.mo.gov/archives/soldiers/details.asp. Accessed by the author on February 6, 2012. See also *Officers and Enlisted Men of the United States Naval Service Who Died During the Great War From April 6, 1917 to November 11, 1918.* (Washington: Government Printing Office, 1920). James Cummings' service record at the Missouri State Archives gives the date of enlistment as April 9, 1917, but *Officers and Enlisted Men of the US Naval Service* (p. 210) indicates date of enlistment as April 4. I have preferred the Missouri Archives service record data as the more complete source.

2   Robert K. Massie. *Castles of Steel: Britain, Germany, and the Winning of the Great War at Sea.* (New York: Random House, 2003), p. 736.

3   Ibid, p. 734.

4   Ibid, p. 735.

5   Rear Admiral William Snowden Sims. *The Victory at Sea.* (Annapolis, MD: Naval Institute Press, 1984; originally published Doubleday, Page, & Co., 1920), p. 121.

6   Robert K. Massie. *Castles of Steel: Britain, Germany, and the Winning of the Great War at Sea*, op. cit., p. 736.

7   Rear Admiral William Snowden Sims. *The Victory at Sea*, op. cit., p. 128.

8   Ibid.

9   Ralph D. Paine. *The Fighting Fleets: Five Months of Active Service with the American Destroyers and Their Allies in the War Zone.* (New York: Houghton Mifflin, 1918), p. 67.

10   Rear Admiral William Snowden Sims. *The Victory at Sea*, op. cit., p. 128.

11   Ralph D. Paine. *The Fighting Fleets: Five Months of Active Service with the American Destroyers and Their Allies in the War*, op. cit., p. 68.

12   Ibid.

13   A. E. Swearingen. "When Our Sons Came Home." *World War Soldiers Dead*, Vol II, No. 1. (Kansas City, MO: Missouri Valley Historical Society, 1926), p. 88.

14   Ibid, p. 92.

15   "American Legion's First Kansas City Posts Formed Thirty-five Years Ago." *The Kansas City Times*, Thursday, August 19, 1954, p. 38.

16   "Two Sons Graves at Sea." *The Kansas City Times*, May 27, 1931. See also Mrs. Donald R. Osborne. *The Kansas City Chapter American War Mothers 1930-1931 Scrapbook #2.* (National World War I Museum Archives. Accession Number 76.268.9.)

17   "Memorial by War Mothers." *The Kansas City Star*, May 30, 1932, p. 2. See also "Gold Star League Meeting Minutes, May 17, 1924," in *Gold Star League Records, 1920-1925.* (National World War I Museum Archives. Gold Star League Box 40.4.11.)

18   "Montgall-Richards" was among the first American Legion posts in Kansas City. See *World War Soldiers Dead: Memorial Annals of Kansas City, Missouri,* Vol II. No. 1. (Kansas City: Missouri Valley Historical Society, 1926), p. 10.

19   "John F. Richards, formerly of Kansas City, Shot Down by Anti-Aircraft Guns." Picture from *The Kansas City Star,* Sunday, November 17, 1918, p. 12A.

20   *Richards Field and Ong Airport.* Raytown Historical Society Notebook. Site visit, January 26, 2013.

21   "John F. Richards II in France." *The Kansas City Star*, November 18, 1917, p. 11A.

22   "Found Kansas Citian's Body." *The Kansas City Star,* Sunday, November 17, 1918, p. 12A.

23   "A Casualty List of 627." *The Kansas City Star*, Wednesday, November 29, 1918, p. 9.

24   Missouri State Archives Soldiers' Records: War of 1812-World War I. Service record for John F. Richards. http://www.sos.mo.gov/archives/soldiers/details.asp. Accessed by author January 8, 2012.

25   *World War Soldiers Dead: Memorial Annals of Kansas City, Missouri,* Vol II. No. 1. (Kansas City: Missouri Valley Historical Society, 1926), p. 57.

26   "It's the 'Baby' of Missouri." *The Kansas City Times,* October 26, 1921, p. 3.

27   Lois T. Allen and Roberta L. Bonnewitz. *Airway Pioneers: Richards Flying Field—Ong Airport 1922-1952*

(Raytown, MO: Pilot News Press and Raytown Historical Society, 1979), p 4.

28   Ibid, pp. 2, 4 and 26.

29   "Homes on Airport." *The Kansas City Star*, June 23, 1950, p. 1.

30   "Army Airplane Settling at the Country Club Here." *The Kansas City Star*, November 18, 1917, p. 3A. See also "Fred Harvey A Captain Now." *The Kansas City Star*, March 7, 1918, p. 3.

31   Lois T. Allen and Roberta L. Bonnewitz. *Airway Pioneers: Richards Flying Field—Ong Airport 1922-1952*, op. cit., p. 26.

32   Stephen Fried. *Appetite for America: How Visionary Businessman Fred Harvey Built a Railroad Hospitality Empire That Civilized the Wild West.* (New York: Bantam Books, 2010), p. 270.

33   Missouri State Archives Soldiers Records: War of 1812 – World War I. Service records for Robert Redenhour Lester, Rogers Crittenden, and Edwin Simpson. http.//www.sos.mo.gov/archives/soldiers/details.asp. Accessed by the author on January 25, 2013.

34   "Tears at Field Ceremony." *The Kansas City Star*, November 11, 1922, p. 2.

35   "Dr. Jenkins to France." *The Kansas City Star*, June 9, 1918, p. 1.

36   Burris A. Jenkins, "Saw his 'Chick' Fly Home." *The Kansas City Star*, June 12, 1918, p. 4.

37   "Ready for Armistice Day." *The Kansas City Star*, November 10, 1922, p. 2.

38   Ibid.

39   "Flowers Shower from Air." *The Kansas City Star*, November 11, 1922, p. 2. See also "Planes Due Here Today." *The Kansas City Times*, November 10, 1922, p. 7.

40   "Weather Mars Air Meet." *The Kansas City Times*, November 13, 1922, p. 2.

41   Lois T. Allen and Roberta L. Bonnewitz. *Airway Pioneers: Richards Flying Field—Ong Airport 1922-1952*, op. cit., p. 26.

42   Ibid, p. 21.

43   Ibid, p. 24.

44   Ibid.

45   Ibid.

46   Ray Morgan, "About Town—Richards Airport Marker" The Kansas City *Times*. September 22, 1979, p. 12B.

47   "Homes on Airport," op. cit., p. 1.

48   "Former Airfield Here Set for Re-dedication." *Raytown Post*, April 11, 2007, pp. 1-2. See also Glen Reese. "Raytown to Celebrate 85th Anniversary of Richards Field." *Raytown Tribune*, April 26, 2007, p. 1.

49   Sherry Piland and Ellen J. Uguccioni. *Fountains of Kansas City: A History and Love Affair.* (Kansas City: City of Fountains Foundation, 1985), p. 130.

50   Missouri State Archives Soldiers' Records: War of 1812 – World War I. Service record for Frank L. Stauver. www.sos. mo.gov/archives/soldiers/details.asp. Accessed by the author on February 3, 2012.

51   *In Memoriam: Addresses Delivered at Memorial Meeting of Kansas City Bar Association, 1918.* (Missouri Valley Room, Kansas City, Missouri Public Library.)

52   Claire Kenamore. *From Vauquois Hill to Exermont: A History of the 35th Division.* (St. Louis, MO: Guard Publishing Co., 1919), p. 353. See also Michael Sullivan. *Boxcars and Billets: Occasional Extracts from the Diary of an Echelon Soldier.* (Kansas City, KS; John A. Shine, Printer. Undated), p. 31. *Boxcars and Billets* is a history of Battery A, 129th Field Artillery.

53   World War I Draft Registration, 8th Precinct, Ward 12, Kansas City, MO, June 2, 1917. Draft Board Registration Jackson County, MO, Roll 1683385.

54   *World War Soldier Dead Memorial: Annals of Kansas City, Missouri.* Vol. II, No. 1. (Kansas City: Missouri Valley Historical Society, 1926), p. 8.

55   Michael Sullivan. *Boxcars and Billets: Occasional Extracts from the Diary of an Echelon Soldier,* op. cit., p. 31.

"NONE BUT THE BRAVE DESERVE THE FAIR"

Major General
William M. Wright.[10]

Major General Peter E.
Traub.[11]

CHAPTER 5

"We Served on Land"

Wright and Traub: The "Santa Fe" 35th Division

Many of the original American Legion Posts in Kansas City were named for men who had served in the 35th Division, which was formed largely of men who were serving in National Guard Units in Missouri and Kansas. They trained at Camp Doniphan, Fort Sill, Oklahoma, and fought their most desperate battle in the Meuse-Argonne, where the Division nearly disintegrated. Upon their return to the States, much controversy raged over the regular Army's replacement of many of the 35th's commanding officers on the eve of the battle. Congressional reviews resulted, but no conclusion was ever reached.

Beginning in New Franklin, Missouri, and proceeding west through Arrow Rock, Fort Osage, Independence, and Kansas City, the Santa Fe Trail crosses into Kansas and stretches diagonally southwest through the state before ending 1,203 miles away in Santa Fe, New Mexico.[1] More than half of the entire trail lies in Kansas.[2] Commerce along the trail began in 1821, the year Missouri became a state, continued to thrive in 1861, when Kansas became a state, and ceased 19 years later in 1880 when the railroad took over the trade route and significantly reduced travel time.

So thoroughly does the trail bind the histories and cultures of Missouri and Kansas that it came to symbolize the journey that sons of the two states – 14,282 from Missouri and 9,781 from Kansas[3] – made together in the summer of 1918, this time to the east, across the ocean to France. Cpt. Edward P. Rankin, Jr., acting adjutant of the 110th Engineers in the Battle of the Argonne,[4] recognized the connected journeys east and west in the title of his 1933 history of the Division's road-building engineers: *The Santa Fe Trail Leads to France.* In the preface, he explained, "The title of this book connotes two facts: first, that the 110th Engineers was and is primarily a Kansas City, Missouri, and Kansas organization; and second, that in its war history the regiment vitalized the traditions of pioneer loyalty and will-to-win which made the Santa Fe Trail a glorious road."[5] In keeping with the trail's theme and in honor of the 35th Division, westbound and eastbound sections of Interstate 35 near Kansas City's Liberty Memorial have been designated as the "35th Division Memorial Highway."

James J. Heiman

35ᵗʰ Division, "Santa Fe Cross" Patch.

Translated, the words "*Santa Fe*" mean "holy faith." Earlier, in recognition of the faith and traditions the men of Missouri and Kansas brought to the journey of 1918-1919, the Santa Fe Cross became the insignia for the Missouri and Kansas National Guard units that formed the U.S. Army 35th Division at Camp Doniphan, Fort Sill, Oklahoma, on August 5, 1918.[6] The insignia's cross forms the center of two concentric circles, an inner circle and an outer circle, between which appear four quadrants equally spaced, as if a smaller Santa Fe Cross were superimposed and rotated 45° on a slightly larger one.

Maj. Gen. William M. Wright, a classmate of General Pershing's, commanded the Division from October 1, 1917, to June 16, 1918. He supervised the training of the 35th at Camp Doniphan, Fort Sill, Oklahoma. When General Wright was sent to France on a tour of inspection, Brig. Gen. Nathaniel F. McClure briefly took command from June 16, 1918, to July 20, 1918. General Wright was then assigned to temporary command of the Third Army Corps and later took command of the 89th "Midwest" Division,[7] while Major General Peter E. Traub took charge of the 35th from July 20, 1918 to December 27, 1918.[8] Brigadier General Thomas Dugan replaced Traub on December 29. Major General Wright was then returned to command on March 1, 1919, taking the 35th home and mustering it out in late spring at Camp Funston, Fort Riley, Kansas.[9]

From April 7 through April 14, 1919, while the 35th Division was on its way home from France, *The Kansas City Star* featured a series of articles called "The Log of the 35th." Written by Clair Kenamore, the war correspondent for *The St. Louis Post-Dispatch*, the log offered *The Star*'s Kansas and Missouri readers a history of the Division from its creation at Camp Doniphan to its mustering-out at Camp Funston after its return from France. A more detailed history appeared in Kenamore's 1919 book, *From Vauquois Hill to Exermont*. Also appearing the same year was another 35th Division history entitled *Heroes of the Argonne: An Authentic History of the Thirty-fifth Divison* by Charles B. Hoyt. Hoyt listed rosters of the Kansas units, while Kenamore featured rosters of both Kansas and Missouri units. A variety of small unit histories also appeared after the war, offering veterans a more detailed account of their units' engagements. Those histories, coupled with the feature stories that *The Kansas City Star* war correspondent, Otto P. Higgins, sent back from France and the stories the boys themselves told when they returned home constituted what Missouri and Kansas knew of the 35th Division in the war. Kenamore's 1919 "log articles" were important because they provided details of time and place; censorship prohibited Higgins from including these details in his articles, and the boys weren't allowed to provide specifics in their letters home.

While still "over here," the 35th Division was assembled into 20 separate commands: the 69th and 70th Infantry Brigades and the 137th, 138th, 139th, and 140th Infantry; the 128th, 129th, and 130th Machine Gun Battalions; the 60th Field Artillery Brigade with the 128th, 129th, and 130th Field Artillery; the 110th Trench Mortar Battery; the 110th Engineers; the 110th Field Signal Battalion; the 110th Train Headquarters and Military Police; the 110th Ammunition Train; the 110th Motor Supply Train; and the 110th Sanitary Train.[12]

From an organizational perspective, the Division was divided into two infantry brigades, an artillery brigade, and a number of specialized regiments, which provided administrative, police, supply, transportation, and medical support. The 70th Infantry Brigade included the 139th and 140th Infantry Regiments and the 130th Machine Gun Battery. The 69th Infantry Brigade included the 137th and 138th Infantry Regiments and the 129th Machine Gun Battery. Each of the Infantry regiments contained 12 companies.

Supporting the Infantry was the 60th Field Artillery Brigade consisting of the 128th, the

129th, and the 130th Field Artillery Regiments, with six batteries each. The 128th Machine Gun Battery was attached to the Division Headquarters, along with the military police and Division Quarter Master Corps. The 110th Field Signal, Motor Supply, Trench Mortar, and Engineer Regiments also provided specialized support in communications, transport, trench warfare, and road/bridge construction and repair, respectively. Finally, the 110th Train included an Ammunition Train of four motor companies and four horse companies as well as a Sanitary Train, which included four ambulance companies and four field hospitals.

After training at Camp Doniphan, Fort Sill, Oklahoma, the 35th entrained for Camp Mills, Hemstead, Long Island, and on April 24 and 25, 1918, boarded ships for the trip across the Atlantic. The 110th Field Signal Battalion, the 110th Trench Mortar Battery, and the 60th Field Artillery Brigade and its ammunition train did not cross with the Division but followed later.[14] The bulk of the 35th landed in Liverpool on May 7

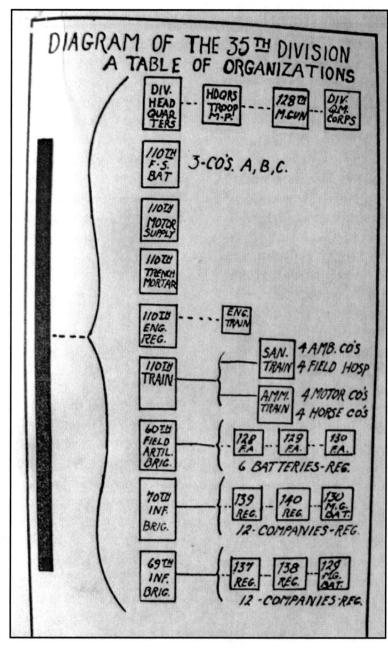

The 35th Division's Table of Organization.[13]

and boarded trains for Winchester, where the Division's first overseas casualty, Cliff Berlin, died of diphtheria.

On May 10, the 35th entrained for Southampton and during the night moved down the Solent and across the English Channel, landing in Le Harve on May 11. They moved to the vicinity of Eu, held a stretch of trench near Luneville and a quiet sector in the Vosges Mountains, and from May 14 to June 7 were held in reserve to the British Army. While there with the 35th, *St. Louis Post-Dispatch* War Correspondent Clair Kenamore commented, "it is the duty of the veracious chronicler to record that the 35th Division did not get along very well with the British. They did not like the British noncoms, or the British soldiers, or the British officers. They conspicuously disliked the British rations, and they loathed tea for breakfast. It is almost impossible," concluded Kenamore," to make Missourians and Kansans drink tea for breakfast."[15]

On June 7, French boxcars delivered the

35th to Arches, where they were issued Enfield rifles to replace the British issue they had been using. While marching along the fields to ranges where they would train with their new rifles, the Missourians and Kansans, many of whom had come from farms themselves, noticed that the women did most of the fieldwork, few French men being released from battle to help in the hayfields. When a regimental commander gave permission for men to assist in the hayfields after Sunday church services, 800 men of the 35th volunteered. Perhaps some of the men were motivated to atone for the swearing they had done within earshot of the French women – a practice for which Father Thomas D. Kennedy had severely chastised them in his Sunday sermon.[16]

Father Kennedy was not the only source of chastisement. The French women themselves were not happy when they learned that beehives they kept in the area south of Epinal had been looted and hidden away. The men responsible had not been paid in three months, and had no money with which to satisfy their craving for something sweet to eat. The practice of stealing beehives came to a halt when AEF headquarters issued a general order penalizing the offense and establishing thorough investigations of claims filed by the farm women, who also complained bitterly when a couple of doughboys cut down a dead fruit tree to build a fire to dry their clothes. After that incident, the boys learned that tree wood was precious to the French, who collected even the smallest of twigs for later use to heat their homes in the winter.

Not all claims received a favorable review. Major August R. Sauerwein, of the St. Louis 138th Infantry,[17] for example, disputed a claim that his men had stolen 100 liters of wine. The major, whose very name must have rendered some credibility in the matter, objected because "there was no singing in camp that night."[18]

However, "as a general rule," Kenamore observed, "our men were very popular with the French women of whatever age or degree of winsomeness. If a doughboy saw a girl or woman wheeling a barrow along a road, he took the handles and wheeled it for her, or if she was carrying a bundle, he carried it for her. Their own men had been away at the front for about four years, so these little attentions were a pleasant surprise and much appreciated.

"I have never been able to figure out," Kenamore continued, "how our men and the French girls, without the medium of a common language, became such good friends in so short a time, but they did, and many a homesick doughboy supplemented his ration at dusk in the generous kitchen of a French Farm."[19] Other factors may have been at play, as well.

The Vosges

Such familiarity would not last for long as the 35th moved into the Vosges Mountains. On June 17, the 2nd Battalion of the 138th Infantry became the first unit of the 35th to advance to the front. Seventy trucks carried the men through Arches and up the Valley of the Moselle through a tunnel at Bussang and into the town of Wasserling, formerly held by the Germans. From there, the men were obliged to carry a rifle and full pack of 60 pounds of equipment up a switch-back mountain road to Bussart, where they joined the line with the 19th French Regiment in the De Galbert subsector. The French had tapped into the German telephone and telegraph wires, but the Americans learned that the reverse was true, as well. Headquarters had been notified that an American soldier was killed at midnight and that the body was being brought in for burial. When headquarters responded that the funeral would be at 3:00 at the cemetery, the Germans responded by shelling the cemetery at precisely that time.

From June 20 to September 2, 1918, the

35th would continue to hold a trench sector in the Vosges Mountains.[20] On July 27, the French withdrew, leaving to the 35th the Fecht sector with the added Garibaldi subsector. Division headquarters was established at Kruth. On August 10, the south part of the Gerardmer sector was added, and Division HQ moved there.

The Vosges sectors had been considered "quiet" sectors, where the 35th was expected to profit from the more experienced French with whom they had been placed. "The real business of the Americans," Kenamore reported, "was to fit themselves for the big fight which they knew they would get into some day."[21] However, for the coming Argonne battle, "the training in the Vosges was not of great value" because the Argonne involved open field fighting, not trench warfare, and the Vosges offered few places where more than a company of men could maneuver in the open. Even if the open space were available, deploying men in it would only draw fire from entrenched and heavily bunkered German positions.

The 35th Division's Sector in the Argonne.[22]

Whatever benefits the Vosges did offer in July and August, 1918, the 35th's preparation time there was drawing to a close. The 60th Artillery Brigade, which had been left behind when the 35th left Camp Mills, reached England on about June 1 and, after crossing the Channel, proceeded to Angers on June 12 to take charge of its artillery pieces. The 60th then proceeded to Camp Coetquidan to spend two months getting acquainted with the guns and refining the skills to operate them efficiently and accurately. On August 14, the 60th joined the rest of the division then headquartered at Gerardmer. The other units that had been left behind when the 35th departed for France – the 110th Sanitary Train and the 110th Field Signal Battalion – had already joined the division at Arches on June 12.

St. Mihiel

At that point in the war, General Pershing was making preparations for a role more distinctively American. Foch had granted Pershing his request to reduce the German salient at St. Mihiel. In the order of battle, the 35th was to be held in reserve, ready to go at a moment's notice wherever it was needed. On September 2 and the nights of September 4, 5, and 6, the 35th entrained for the area around Rosieres aux Salines. The 35th moved again on the night of September 10-11 into Tomblaine at Jarville and Maron, suburbs of Nancy, and the next night through outskirts of Nancy into the Fôret de Haye, where they bivouacked, harassed by German air attacks and rain.

As it turned out, the 35th Division was not needed beyond its reserved status, but that did not diminish the unit's importance. Because General Pershing had the reserve, he "was able to order his combat battalions in whatever way he chose," Kenamore noted.[23] However, "the division would have been better prepared for the Argonne fight if it had had a place in the line of the St. Mihiel operation. The 35th's losses would have been light, and it would have then gone into the Argonne with battle experience and the assurance and confidence which the other divisions obtained at St. Mihiel."[24]

The Meuse Argonne

On the night of September 15, the 35th moved by buses into the region of Charmontois and became part of the 3rd Army Corps. On the night of September 19-20, the 69th Brigade moved to the vicinity of Auzeville, and the rest of the 35th moved to Grace le Comte Farm and into the woods east of Beauchamp in relief of the 73rd French Division.

The 69th Brigade was moving into the formation it would assume to lead the attack. Each regiment of the 69th had two battalions in the line with a machine gun company attached to each.

With the 70th Brigade in support, another machine gun company and a battalion were held in reserve for each of the battalions in the line. The 35th Division's ultimate objective was the destruction of German rail facilities at Mézières, 232 kilometers northeast of Paris.[25]

Shortly before the battle, however, significant changes were made in the leadership of the Division's units. Col. Louis Nuttman was put in command of the Division. Col. Kirby Walker replaced Brig. Gen. Charles I. Martin, who had commanded the Kansas National Guard on the Mexican Border and the 70th Brigade since its inception. Ltc. Channing E. Delaplane took command of the 140th Infantry on September 22, and Col. Frank

Rumbold was relieved of command of the 128th Artillery on September 24. Made immediately before what is often considered the major battle of the war, these last minute changes impacted communication within the units and occasioned a good deal of criticism later, after the 35th returned from France.

For four days, the men of the 35th were bivouacked in the Fôret de Hess. On the afternoon of September 25, the men received a large hot meal. Platoon leaders were briefed about the objectives and the detail of the countryside, but the noncoms did not receive maps. Each man had his rifle, bayonet, steel helmet, gas mask, and 250 rounds of rifle ammunition in a belt and two bandoliers swung over one shoulder and under the other arm. In a backpack he carried his raincoat, a mess kit, and two days' rations – usually two cans of corned beef and six boxes of hard bread. In his canteen was about a quart of water. Some men had a fresh loaf of army bread carried on the fixed bayonet. Some carried Stokes mortar ammunition – four rounds to a man, each round weighing 10 pounds, 11 ounces. "Infantry also carried ordinary explosive grenades, gas grenades, rifle grenades and incendiary grenades but the most of these were thrown away."[26]

Then at 11:30 p.m. on the night of September 25, 1918, the great artillery barrage began; nine American divisions, 400,000 men, prepared to move on German positions along a 16-mile front of the Hindenburg line.

The 35th had about two miles of front, with the 28th Division on the left and the 91st Division on the right. Ahead was Vauquois Hill, a German fortification the French had been unable to take, even with losses estimated as high of 40,000. Kenamore describes Vauquois Hill as "known to be thoroughly mined, to have excavations and tunnels of great length for quick communication and transferal of troops from one point to another. It had once been covered with trees for the most part, but these were now merely shattered stumps, so much artillery fire and been addressed to it."[27]

In the path of the 35th were Varennes,[28] Cheppy, Very, Charpentry, Baulny, Apremont, and Exermont – French villages in the valley of the Aire, whose hills and clumps of trees and brush provided excellent cover for German machine guns and whose names would forever be associated with the story of the 35th Division in the Great War.

The First Day – September 26, 1918 – Verennes and the Rossignol Wood

The Division's artillery fired more than 40,000 shells, most of them in the three hours between 2:30 and 5:30 a.m. on September 26, 1918. The noise of the shelling kept the men from getting much sleep. There was no breakfast. The order to "prepare to advance" was given, followed by, "All right, let's go." Out of the foxholes they came. The men were to advance 100 meters in four minutes to keep pace with the 75 mm "rolling barrage," which moved ahead of them for two hours until 7:40 a.m. At that point, the range for supporting artillery fire had increased to where accuracy could no longer be guaranteed. To protect the advancing men, the barrage was lifted, and the artillery pieces were ordered to move forward. The 129th Field Artillery moved toward Cheppy at 8:30 a.m., and at 8:50, one battalion of the 130th Field Artillery moved towards Varennes, followed by the other two battalions at 10:15. At 9:00, all of the 128th regiment moved east of Varennes.

Kenamore describes what happened next: "The ground over which the guns had to move had been virtually a No Man's Land for years and was soggy and full of rank weeds. At every little creek or ditch, the wheels sank in the mud and stuck. Officers' mounts and all the horses of mounted details were put

into harness to move the guns, but there was not much progress. Only one battery, which was of the 129th Regiment, got into position again that day. It took position on the north edge of the Rossignol Wood. So that virtually after 8 a.m. that day the infantry had no artillery support. The German fire never slackened."[29]

Meanwhile, the infantry was moving through a thick fog that had descended into the valley of the Aire. As a result, the advancing troops lost contact with headquarters in the rear. Signal flags and flares were useless, and the telephone wire that had been strung forward by the Signal Corps failed to connect. Confused by the fog, smoke, and roar of battle, carrier pigeons also proved useless. Runners were the only means of communication left, but they had no landmarks to guide them back through the fog.

The 69th Infantry Brigade led by Col. Nuttman led the attack with the 137th Infantry on the left, or western half, and the 138th Infantry on the right, or eastern half. The 70th Brigade was in reserve with the 140th Infantry supporting the 138th on the right flank and the 139th supporting the 137th on the left flank.

Vauquois Hill

The 138th Infantry had been ordered not to attack Vauquois Hill head on, but instead to go around to the right, attacking its eastern flank. The 137th was to attack to the left, the western flank. Not knowing that fog would settle in so heavily, artillery had been ordered to lob smoke shells towards the foot of the hill. They did so, reducing the visibility and increasing the confusion of the advance that much more. The men had to advance by compass.

Finally, as the sun began to burn away the fog, clumps of bushes and trees came into view, most likely the lairs of machine guns and sharpshooters. Two light French tanks came over a hill but could not cross the creek; not only was their fire not enough to clear out the enemy, but they had begun to draw so much German artillery fire themselves that Colonel Howland was afraid for his advancing men. He ordered the French tanks back.

Complying with the order, the French tank commander advised Colonel Howland that eight large French tanks lay to the southwest. The colonel ordered the French lieutenant to find the eight tanks and bring them up as fast as he could. The infantry waited anxiously. Then the eight tanks appeared and swung into position, ten paces abreast of one another. Squads of the 138th formed behind the tanks, the infantry firing into the brush and woods on the hillside and the tanks pounding the machine gun nests and pillboxes. Minutes later, German gunners popped out of their positions, weapons at the ready, and American rifles and machine guns then cut into them. The tanks turned to pound the right flank, and Captain Reinholdt was able to mop up the area, opening the road to Cheppy.

Behind the 138th, the 140th commanded by Ltc. C. E. Delaplane came in to mop up the eastern slope of Vauquois Hill, meeting some resistance and taking fire from the edge of the Bois de Cheppy, three kilometers south of Cheppy. "They moved on," Kenamore said, "bombing dugouts, beating clumps of woods and otherwise making the neighborhood safe for democracy as they went, and dug in for the night behind the 138th on the high ground south of Very."[30]

Meanwhile on the left flank, the 137th Infantry had been charged with attacking the western slope of Vauquois Hill. Initially the fog and smoke screen raised by the artillery caused confusion there too, but the 137th pushed through to the ruined town of Bourielles and captured two concrete machine gun emplacements. Still under fire after cleaning out the Aden strong point, the 137th pulled up before the defenses of Varennes and waited for reinforcements and for the fog to clear.

Col. Carl L. Ristine, commander of the 139th, moved up in support of the 137th but noticed that a battalion of the 137th was be-

Photo courtesy of National World War I Museum Archives.

Ltc. Channing E. "Dog Face" Delaplane commanded the 140th Infantry.

hind him. Apparently he had passed them in the fog. His own unit was still intact, and after pulling up to the other two battalions of the 137th, he requested permission from brigade to move through their lines to continue his mission. Receiving no reply and fearing that the morale of his men might suffer from another halt, he left Major William D. Stepp in charge of the rest of the regiment, took personal charge of his skirmish line, and fought through to a kilometer-and-a-half south of Charpentry, where he dug in after experiencing raking fire from machine guns and artillery. When the rest of his regiment failed to appear, he went back and found that just after he had left with his skirmish line, Major Stepp had been killed in heavy fighting. Ristine re-formed the columns, moved forward, and dug in behind the skirmish line.

Meanwhile, the roads in the rear were tangled for 20 miles, with transports trying to move supplies up to the front as ambulances struggled to evacuate wounded in the opposite direction. Kenamore describes the confusion:

"The roads were bad in the territory captured that day, and our system of traffic control was not good. Immense numbers of Negro troops, turned into labor battalions, worked constantly to repair the roads. In the tangle of traffic they plugged away. Bound northward toward the battle line were heavy guns and light guns, horse or motor drawn, and in some instances 75s were mounted on trucks that they might be carried with greater dispatch. There were automobiles of all kinds, and innumerable motor trucks carrying everything used in war. There were wagons, rolling kitchens, water carts, limbers, ambulances, ammunition wagons, machine gun carts, staff cars and, mixed in between horses feet and truck wheels, were the motor cycle orderlies shooting through every crack in the traffic jam."[31]

Attempts to separate horse-drawn from motor vehicles were not effective until later.

Most serious, however, was the effect that the traffic jam had on the wounded. Kenamore continued:

"It is a cruel necessity of war which requires, under conditions such as existed that first night, that ambulances taking wounded to the rear must be held up to let the guns and ammunition go forward. Hour after

Photo courtesy of National World War I Museum Archives.

Col. Carl L. Ristine, left facing front, commanded the 139th Infantry.

hour the long trains of ambulances lay in the congested roads, some of the wounded singing in defiance, some moaning in pain, some would become silent for a while, and some became silent forever. One of the few advantages of a regular battle is that there is no restriction on noise. You may talk, sing or shout, curse or pray and nobody cares. Occasionally a man of the Salvation Army, the YMCA, the K. of C. or some other service would work his way through, giving cigarettes to the wounded, but usually it was the ambulance drivers who supplied their passengers with smokes."[32]

Even with the loss of men, the confusion caused by weather conditions, the tangled traffic on the roads, and the mud that had mired the movement of artillery, the 35th had taken Vauquois Hill and pushed the Germans back. All nine divisions of the AEF had advanced along the 16-mile front that day, but information from German prisoners indicated that greater challenges lay ahead. The German 53rd line Division, one of the best, was in reserve.

The Second Day – September 27, 1918 – Cheppy, Very, Charpentry, and Baulny

September 27, the second day of the battle, did not go as well as the first day had, and the first day had been bad enough. All day on the 26th, the artillery attempted to move up in order to provide the same kind of support to the infantry they had supplied earlier in the morning. Based on the reports Division Headquarters had received, 35th Division command determined that artillery would not be in place before 8:30 a.m. on the 27th, so division ordered the artillery to open up at that time with a barrage that would allow the infantry to move forward.

Then at about midnight on September 26th,

Division Commander Maj. General Peter Traub received orders to attack at 5:30 a.m. the next morning. Without artillery support he knew how costly a move that would be. By 4:00 a.m. only one battalion of the 128th Field Artillery was in position near Cheppy. As it turned out, the 129th Field Artillery would not come into position until 7:00 a.m. and it wasn't until 4:30 in the afternoon of the 27th that the 130th Field Artillery would finally be in place. Orders required the 139th and the 140th Infantry of the 70th Brigade to leapfrog over the 137th and 138th Infantry regiments of the 69th Brigade that had led the attack on September 26. General Traub worried that if the new change in orders reached some units by 5:30 a.m. but did not reach others by that time, some units would move forward without the protection of the uninformed units, exposing to attack the advancing unit's flanks. So at about 1:30 a.m., he left his headquarters on Mamelon Blanc back of the line and sought out his brigade and regimental commanders in person to ensure that the new orders were received and understood.

Colonel Delaplane's 140th Infantry was to lead the attack. At 5:05 a.m., Delaplane received the change in orders and had only 25 minutes to prepare. As directed, he moved through the 138th Infantry and waited for his artillery support.

With daylight approaching, the accuracy and strength of the German artillery and machine guns grew stronger, and despite the lack of American artillery support, Delaplane decided to move his men forward rather than to continue to take the German punishment. However, German fire was so strong that American tanks could not advance, and Delaplane finally had to order his men to dig in and hold the ground they had gained.

The 138th Infantry was supposed to follow at about 1,000 meters in support of the 140th. It did so, moving out at 5:30 a.m., but the 138th was also lacking artillery support and could advance only to the ground held the previous day by the 140th. The 138th, too, was obliged to dig in and hold the ground.

Meanwhile on the other half of the field, Col. Carl L. Ristine of the 139th Infantry had orders to advance at 6:30 a.m., "probably as a sort of compromise between the first order for 8:30 and the second order for 5:30,"[34] according to Kenamore. Ristine was ready, but no artillery support had engaged, so he notified brigade that he could attack as soon as artillery opened up. Receiving no reply, he went forward anyway without the artillery support, advanced, but halted and ordered his regiment to dig in when he saw the damage enemy fire was inflicting on his men. Hearing tanks to his rear, he called them up and at noon formed his right behind them. Again he advanced, and again the enemy artillery and anti-tank fire took its toll. The tanks retired; Ristine was forced to dig in once again.

Finally in the rear, American artillery was beginning to engage, and Ristine sent word to Brigade that if he could have half an hour of artillery support in Charpentry and Baulny, he could move forward. But again receiving no reply, he pulled his right flank back in line with his left and dug in.

At 5:00 p.m., he received orders to attack at 5:30, divisional headquarters being aware that the morning attack had failed. Just as the time for the attack drew near, nine tanks emerged on Ristine's right, along the road from Very. The tanks moved in front of the 140th, which fell into the attack. Facing the fire full on, Ristine's 139th came out of their foxholes, charged the machine gun nests, and took Charpentry and Baulny. Once having broken through, Ristine moved so fast that the main part of his regiment couldn't keep up. Ristine met some resistance near the Charpentry Cemetery, overcame the resistance, and kept moving in a northwesterly direction, bombing dugouts and cutting wire.

Observing many troops moving in the dark and presuming that they were American, he called out to them and discovered that they were instead retreating Germans. When other retreating Germans came up behind him, he found cover in a large shell hole. As dawn approached and he began to lose his cover, he came across a German Officers' quarters temporarily unoccupied but with equipment ready for departure. He took an overcoat, found a German helmet, and spent the next day in the German lines disguised, gathering information on artillery positions and ammunition dumps. It wasn't until the night of the next day, however, that he found his way back to American lines and could relay his information to American artillery.

While Col. Ristine was gathering intelligence, the battalion commanders of the 139th continued to move forward, Major James E.

Brigades of the 35th Division on September 27, 1918.[33]

Rieger's 2nd Battalion advancing up to near Montrebeau Wood. In support of Ristine's 139th, the 137th's Maj. John H. O'Connor was notified at 5:30 p.m. that he was now in command of that unit. Col. Chad Hamilton, who had been in charge, was either killed, wounded, or moved – the order did not say, but it did command O'Connor to move forward immediately. Doing so, he advanced through Baulny probably as early as Ristine's 139th did, capturing 20 German prisoners. Advancing in the darkness another four kilometers, he came to the outskirts of Fleville, meeting no resistance. The Germans appeared to be withdrawing. O'Connor's scouts could find no other elements of the 35th on either side, so O'Connor decided that he had advanced too far and needed to establish contact with the rest of the Division.

As he pulled back, he heard a voice in the woods yelling in German what sounded like "Oh Gus" ("August"). O'Connor had one of his men who spoke German reply to the call, luring the German close enough for capture. Interrogation revealed that the Germans were, indeed, in retreat and that this man had left the retreat to try to find his buddy. Once O'Connor reached the line north of Baulny, he found that it was now thoroughly mixed with infantry and machine gun companies of the 137th and the 139th regiments. Several other companies were mixed in and all were crowded into a little hollow for cover, their situation proving difficult to organize for an effective defense. Since it was after midnight, he ordered the men to dig in.

Meanwhile on the right, once behind the tanks, Col. Delaplane's 140th Infantry had moved forward and cleaned out the machine guns that had held them up. They took out an artillery battery and rested on the edge of a hill until German artillery opened up on them. In support of the 140th, the 138th under Col. Harry S. Howland was dug in, taking heavy German fire during the day and on into the night.

By the end of the second day – September 27 – the 35th had advanced in a fairly distinct line, but their elements were mixed, many officers had been killed, and there was a scarcity of water. The water carts had not come up, and commanders forbade the troops to drink from water sources on the field for fear the Germans had poisoned them prior to their retreat. Men were hungry, but the iron rations were still holding out. Although the men were exhausted, Kenamore reported, "the morale was high, and it was a fine determined fighting organization that filled the foxholes which dotted the ground from Baulny eastward."[35]

At night, in the back of the line, every effort was being made to move ammunition and rations up and to evacuate the wounded from the front. The Germans, on the other hand, were regrouping and moving more machine guns up to their front. Unless the Germans could stop the American advance, the 35th would achieve its objective and cut through the four tracks of railroad lines at Mézières, leaving the German armies in Northern France and Belgium stranded without ammunition, food, or a way to escape.

The Third Day – September 28, 1918 – Montrebeau Wood and Chaudron Farm

On the morning of Saturday, September 28, the 35th Division was badly mixed before Baulny and Charpentry. The 139th had no distinct organization. Its ranks had been mixed with the 2nd and 3rd battalions of the 137th, and its commander, Colonel Ristine, was missing. Each battalion thought Ristine was with the other battalion; no one knew that the Colonel was in danger behind enemy lines. The 139th's regimental adjutant was dead and the lieutenant who replaced him was a casualty, as were the liaison, signal officers, and three officers who had charge of the Stokes mortars and one-pounder. No one from the headquarters detachment was left to establish a regimental command post. Maj. Rieger's 2nd Battalion had suffered heavy casualties, a lieutenant commanded the 3rd Battalion, and a captain commanded the 1st Battalion. Two of the four companies in the 3rd Battalion had no officers, and the 1st Battalion had but one officer to a company.

An attack had been ordered for the morning of September 28. The western half of the advance, consisting of the 137th and the 139th together on the left, was to attack first at 6:30 a.m. Cpt. D. H. Wilson led the 3rd Battalion of the 137th. The 137th's Maj. O'Connor had not received the order to advance, but was advised that the 2nd Battalion would pass through the lines. Major Rieger advanced with the 139th. As the men moved out over the open fields, they had no protection from the German machine gun fire coming from the cover of Montrebeau Wood and the strip of woods to the right or from the German artillery that was shelling them from Exermont. In spite of the German fire, they gained the lower ridge of Montrebeau Wood, where they dug in as Rieger had also done.

On the right of the advance, the 140th was ahead, with the 138th behind. At 3:30 a.m., Col. Delaplane of the 140th received orders to advance at 5:30 a.m., but by 8:00 a.m. German artillery and machine gun fire had stopped him, and he dug in. Tanks came up at 9:45 a.m., and the 140th fell in behind them, advancing slowly with little support from Division artillery and increased action from German armor-piercing anti-tank

weapons, which fired their high explosives point-blank at the tanks. In spite of heavy casualties and with assistance from the 138th, the 140th re-formed after having been driven down into a ravine from a ridge above Charpentry, re-took the hill, crossed the Chaudron Road, advanced 500 yards to the crest of the ridge to the north, and dug in. "Artillery played on them both by direct and indirect fire," Kenamore said. "Machine guns from three sides poured lead into the woods and enemy airplanes in formation flew above them and bombarded them with air bombs and machine-gunned them from the sky. At 6 p.m. a cold rain began to fall."[36]

The 139th Machine Gun Company took up a position 200 yards to the north of Chaudron Farm, holding down enemy activity to the east of Exermont and remaining with the 140th when the 138th was drawn back that night. While the 140th held the line, the 138th was to be re-formed so it could lead the attack the next day.

The forward echelon of Division Headquarters had moved up to Cheppy, and all available officers were sent into the field. Maj. Parker C. Kalloch, the Divisional Intelligence Officer, was ordered to report to Col. Hamilton, who made him his lieutenant-colonel and instructed him to gather as much as he could of the 137th, especially those who might be in the woods. Meanwhile, the 137th and 139th had been fighting all day in Montrebeau Wood. Maj. O'Connor had been out of touch with Col. Hamilton for two days and ordered the men to dig in for the night.

At 4:45 a.m. the next morning, Sunday,

35th Division Infantry Brigade positions on September 26, 27, and 28, 1918.[37]

September 29, Colonel Hamilton received a Division order to take the town of Exermont as well as the crests of the ridge on the east and west of the town. Col. Hamilton placed Maj. O'Connor in charge of the first wave of the attack; Col. Hamilton was to lead the second wave. The Division order assured Col. Hamilton that his 137th Infantry could count on an artillery barrage preceding the attack.

Another Division officer who went into the field the afternoon of September 28 was Major Clay C. MacDonald, a 25-year veteran of the National Guard and now the Divisional mail officer. In the judgment of Division command he was too old to be in combat, but that opinion was soon to change. At noon that day in Cheppy, a lieutenant had informed Maj. MacDonald that his son, Lieutenant Donald M. MacDonald, had been killed leading his company in the attack.

"Major MacDonald did not wince," Kenamore said. "I noted as I watched him, this self control. His training did not permit that while under the gaze of so many sympathetic people. His eyes seemed to be looking wistfully to the north, where the guns were pounding on the battle line three miles away. He saluted, turned and entered headquarters, explained the case briefly, and demanded of the Chief of Staff [Colonel Hamilton S. Hawkins] that he be given a command in the front line. He was at once sent forward. Major MacDonald was working through the rain in Montrebeau Wood at the same time Kalloch was assembling and organizing scattered elements of the 137th."[38]

While still in the Montrebeau Wood, MacDonald ran across Major James E. Rieger of the 139th, who had worked his way through to the northern part of the wood and was looking out to the enemy position at Exermont and especially at Hill 240, which commanded a view of the area 4 kilometers to the south. It was from this hill that the Germans had been able to correct artillery and wreck such havoc on the 35th Infantry brigades as they advanced. Desperate for

officers, Maj. Rieger placed Maj. MacDonald and the few men he had collected into the line.

Another 35th Division Headquarters officer, Chief of Staff Col. Hamilton S. Hawkins, saw little purpose to remaining in headquarters when the field was so desperate for officers. He requested and was granted from corps a replacement to sit for him at Division Headquarters while he went into the field. Once in the field, Col. Hawkins found that Col. Hamilton had been able to reorganize his regiment and had formed a line at the forward edge of Montrebeau Wood, confident that he could hold. Col. Hawkins then set out to rejoin 69th Brigade Commander Col. Louis M. Nuttman, but got lost in the darkness and was unable to locate him that night.

By the end of the day on September 28, the third day of fighting in the Argonne, the 35th had gained – at a heavy cost – another one and one-third mile. The artillery of the 35th Division was still trying to get into position to support the infantry and to counter the devastating firepower of the German artillery. The Division's three units of field artillery in the 60th Artillery Brigade had fired only 3,200 shells the third day, 2,000 rounds better than the 1,200 shells fired during the second day, but less than ten percent of the 40,000 shells hurled at the enemy on the first day of the battle.

The Fourth Day – September 29, 1918 – Exermont

All night long, the Germans shelled the line, German planes ruled the skies, and on the ground bodies of American dead began to pile up between the Aire River and Exorieux Farm. Division Headquarters had ordered the attack on Exermont to begin at 5:30 a.m. "I have heard the plan and the order criticized by officers who contended that the division should never have been sent forward on that day," Kenamore observed, "since it was already so far in advance of the division on its left that the 35th's left flank had been for two days exposed to enfilading fire."[39] The critics pointed out that the divisions on either side of the 35th should have advanced, and that the 35th should not have been ordered to create a salient into German lines on such a narrow two-mile front. Corps, however, gave assurances that the 35th's flanks would be protected.

Rain, darkness, a shortage of runners, constant shelling, and sheer exhaustion made communication of the Division orders to 69th Brigade commander Col. Nuttman doubtful, but the orders were delivered, nonetheless. Seventieth Brigade Commander Kirby Walker received the order at 12:45 a.m. and, after completing the necessary transcriptions, sent them out to the 138th and 140th Infantry Brigades at 2:55 a.m. The 138th was to pass through the 140th and lead the attack on the right, with the 140th in support. Colonel Henry W. Parker in command of the 138th said that he did not receive orders until 7 a.m. Colonel Channing E. Delaplane in command of the 140th had five minutes to prepare his attack after receiving his orders at 5:25 a.m. Nevertheless, the attack commenced.

In the 40 minutes Major Parker C. Kalloch had to prepare the 125 men of what was left of the 137th, he formed a skirmish line of 100 men with a six-man patrol on each flank. Nineteen men remained in the rear to fill in for casualties as the line advanced. He had two automatic Chauchat rifles but only two clips of ammunition per weapon, and his line was so thin that he had to space the men ten paces apart to cover the brigade front. The men knelt at the edge of the wood waiting for the artillery barrage, but it never came, so he started without it and advanced 300 yards when a machine gun opened up on them for ten minutes until it could be taken out. More and more enemy machine guns set up on both flanks, and heavy artillery pounded his

line until he could reach cover in the ravine running west from Exermont.

At 6:15 a.m., Major Kalloch saw the support line of 100 of Major O'Connor's men of the 137th come out of Montrebeau Wood, moving up to help him. Kalloch turned to look toward the front for a few minutes, and when he turned back, O'Connor and the 100 men were gone. The officers were unable to maneuver them, and when they had reached the top of the rise and met the full force of German artillery and machine gun fire, they melted. What was left of them retreated back into the woods.

Meanwhile, Major Rieger prepared his battalion of the 139th for its advance. He took them behind the Argonne Forest, intending to march through it for the protection it afforded and the opportunity to pick up any men to strengthen his force. Just as he was starting into the wood, he met 69th Brigade commander Col. Nuttman, who disregarded the explanation of Rieger's strategy and ordered him to move around the wood and attack Exermont. Rieger obeyed the direct order, but waited an hour for support on his right. He did pick up a strong party of men from the 140th, and he needed them. Once his men came over the rise, they faced intense German artillery and machine gun fire. The Germans had brought in reserves from the British and French fronts, some from hundreds of kilometers away, and put them everywhere before the 35th – behind defenses, in foxholes, and on the ground in the grass.

"In the stunning, dumbing gust of war," Kenamore wrote, "the men sensed with their physical bodies rather than their minds, that death was pouring past them in a flood. As if they were walking forward through a driving hailstorm they turned their faces to leeward and, leaning forward against the blast, pushed ahead with the point of a shoulder offered to the gale ... Across the little valley and the creek they went, through a fiendish fire, and without artillery support they charged and took the town of Exermont."[40] Once through the town and on the heights beyond, they dug in and waited for support.

On the Division's right, the 140th and 138th Infantry were also to attack at 5:30 a.m., but the orders arrived late. At 6:00, the remnants of the 140th were in position waiting for the 138th to pass through and lead the attack, but the 138th did not appear. Consequently, 69th Brigade commander Col. Nuttman ordered Col. Delaplane to lead the attack with his men, instead. Concerned about possible compromises to the battle plan he had already been handed, Delaplane asked his own 70th Brigade commander, Col. Walker, if he should advance or wait for the 138th as the original order dictated. Walker concurred with Nuttman and Hawkins that the 140th should commence with the attack, but Nuttman (or Hawkins) ordered him to move immediately.

As a result, the regiment's formations were not ordered properly, and later on Col. Walker gained the erroneous impression that the 140th had stopped completely. Delaplane faced the same devastating machine gun fire Rieger had faced, "but adroitly taking advantage of the terrain and handling his very brave men with address, he took them into Exermont despite heavy losses."[41] With his 2nd and 3rd battalions, he manned the town and connected with Rieger's 139th. After advancing 300 yards, however, the second wave of the 140th was stopped and ordered back to reform its line because Col. Walker did not realize that part of the 140th had already advanced through Exermont.

Once the part of the reformed 140th was in its former position, Col. Walker ordered it and two battalions of the 138th to lead an attack at 8:15 a.m. with one battalion of the 138th in reserve. Again German machine guns poured lead into the advancing men, mowing them down. By 10:30, it appeared to Walker that the attack had failed, and he ordered the men back to their previous positions. Many of the troops, however, had gone ahead.

At 6:00 a.m., Lieutenant William H. Leahy in command of the 2d Battalion, 138th Infantry, 70th Brigade, received orders from Col. Parker to advance to the woods north of Chaudron Farm and northeast of Montrebeau Wood and wait for the 3rd Battalion to take up a position on his right. Parker wanted to attack from the cover of the woods. However, as Leahy moved forward, Col. Nuttman, commanding the other brigade, the 69th, ordered Leahy to move through Montrebeau Wood on his left. Nuttman disregarded Leahy's explanation that he was following the orders of his regimental commander, who was depending on him to follow through on an attack already in process. Leahy followed Nuttman's direct order and took heavy fire from the machine guns to the west of Exermont, suffering extremely heavy losses over the same ground that Kalloch had been driven from. Leahy's men persisted, however, and gained ground to the north of Exermont, but at about noon, Leahy was wounded and could no longer direct operations. The only runner he had took him back for medical attention, at first leading him, then, Kenamore said, "half carrying him, and later trundling him on a wheelbarrow."

Other wounded just lay on the field because Leahy's battalion did not have enough men to fight and evacuate their wounded at the same time. Slowly they lost ground. Ltc. Henry Parker, commander of the 138th, was killed just a few minutes before Leahy was wounded. Before the battle began, Parker had orders that would have returned him to the States, but in one of the horrible ironies of war, he stayed to help his regiment instead.

Withdrawal from Exermont

It was now about 11:00 a.m. and 35th Division commander General Traub arrived on the scene to see for himself the state of the

Cpt. Harry Thompson, 138ᵗʰ Infantry, standing (right hand in pocket) next to the Red Cross nurse.

battle. Alarmed by the shortage of officers and the extent to which the units had become mixed, he ordered a withdrawal from Exermont. The Division reserve was to establish a line of resistance behind which the retreat was to regroup. After ordering the 69ᵗʰ Brigade forward a second time, Col. Walker realized that the second attack would fail and ordered the 138ᵗʰ and the 140ᵗʰ to the positions they had held the previous night.

Meanwhile, the 138ᵗʰ was trying to make sense out of a series of contradictory orders. Company A of the 138ᵗʰ had been ordered from the position held the day before to advance two kilometers and entrench before Exermont. As that order was being executed, Company A received another order directing the unit back to the position held the night before. While executing that order, the company commander saw Col. Ristine, who said he had orders countermanding all previous orders and that the company was to advance on Exermont. A half hour later, the adjutant of the 69ᵗʰ Brigade produced orders telling Company A to wait for further orders. When those orders did not appear, the Company A commander withdrew his men to a position 75 yards in front of where they had been two nights earlier.

Rieger's portion of the 139ᵗʰ northeast of Exermont was trying to hang on as the enemy massed on his front. Desperate for reinforcements and having received an order to withdraw, he fought a series of rear guard actions that enabled him to march through Exermont just as Col. Delaplane and his

Ltc. Edward M. Stayton, adjutant of The 110th Engineers.

remnant of the 140th had done shortly before. Delaplane had lost 65 percent of his men and all of his officers but one.

The 110th Engineers
Hold the Line

Now at dusk, with the exception of Cpt. Harry Thompson's battalion of the 138th, all elements of the 35th Division had fallen back to the line of resistance established by the 110th Engineers. They had earlier been assigned to prepare the roads behind the infantry for the horse-drawn vehicles, but on the night of September 28, they were designated as Division reserve, effectively transforming them from engineers to infantrymen. Then at noon on September 29, they were ordered to prepare a defensive position two kilometers across Chaudron Farm and one kilometer north of Baulny. The line, which had been chosen by the adjutant, Missourian Ltc. Edward M. Stayton, ran along behind the Chaudron Farm road. There they readied their rifles and grenades to hold the line against the pursuing Germans so that the bedraggled fragments of 35th Division American infantry regiments could find refuge behind them.

The engineers' commander, Col. Thomas C. Clark, together with his commissioned and

Photo courtesy of National World War I Museum Archives.
Col. Thomas C. Clark, commander of the 110th Engineers, at his field office.

non-commissioned officers, rounded up the retreating and leaderless infantry, faced them about, and gave them every encouragement. Now with two battalions of engineers on the left, Cpt. Thompson's remnant of a battalion of 138th Infantry on the right and various other pieces of outfits strung along the line between the two, a colonel of engineers commanded and held the entire Division front. Two machine gun companies joined in to help the line repel a German counterattack. Food and ammunition were brought up during the night, and the men slept, in spite of continuing bombardment. Kenamore reported that the men were so tired that it took six stretcher-bearers instead of four to move one man, but for all of their fatigue their spirit remained strong. Kenamore reported an especially poignant example.

Cpt. Frank Hurwitt, who commanded Ambulance Company No. 137, formerly the First Missouri Ambulance Company from Kansas City, was stationed in Charpentry.[42] Cpt. Hurwitt had been separating out the "slightly gassed" cases as they came into his station, directing them to a large barn where they could rest, while the more serious cases were sent to the back of the line for immediate treatment. A lieutenant colonel came into the aid station and asked Hurwitt if there were many slightly gassed cases there.

"'About two hundred, sir. They are in that barn,'" Hurwitt said.

Entering the barn, the lieutenant colonel stood at one end, surveyed the men lying before him and said,

"'Men, I want you to listen to me for a minute. I have just come from the first line and they are in a bad way up there. It looks very bad to me. Now you men have been gassed. I have been gassed, too. But they need us up there, and I am going back. And I want every one of you that thinks he can stand it to go back with me. There are plenty of rifles and ammunition on this salvage dump. How many of you gassed men will take another try to help out those fellows up there on the Line?'"

While the lieutenant colonel was still speaking, men had already begun to rise up, some sitting, some kneeling, some standing. When the lieutenant colonel turned to leave, every man in the barn followed him. Cpt. Hurwitt stopped three of the worst cases for which the move back to the line would have meant certain death. "But all the rest," said Kenamore, "every man of them, armed himself with the rifle of a wounded man, and went back northward and again into the fight."

The line of resistance stretched west from l'Esperance through Chaudron Farm and over to Hill 231. The 110th Engineers held the line, with badly mixed elements of infantry interspersed, the 137th generally on the left and the 138th generally on the right. Shortly after midnight on the morning of the 30th, on orders from the 69th Brigade commander, a second line of resistance was organized behind the first line and along a ridge north of Baulney. The second line consisted of some 300 to 400 men with eight or 10 machine guns. On both lines, the men settled into foxholes, dugouts, trenches, shell holes, and ditches – anywhere where they could snatch some rest. Meanwhile, the officers who remained brought up food and ammunition and readied the men for whatever they might have to face.[43]

They didn't have long to wait. At daylight on September 30, fresh German troops from the Montrebeau Wood began a counter attack against Thompson's 138th Infantry 3rd Battalion. Setting up three machine guns, the Germans emerged from the woods in a wave. By that time, 35th Division artillery was in place, coordinates were relayed, and a perfectly-directed barrage hit the German attack line. The 138th's rifles and Chauchats kept up a steady fire along the line of attack; the Germans hesitated, then fell back into the woods with heavy losses. As the day progressed, the Germans continued to advance machine gunners and launched three similar attacks but suffered the same result. The Germans continued to shell the Engineers throughout the day, and Col. Nuttman, commander of the 69th Brigade, became ill and had to be evacuated. His Chief of Staff, Col. H. S. Hawkins, took command.

The 35th Division Relieved

Meanwhile at AEF Headquarters, General Pershing had received information from German prisoners that fresh divisions of Germans were being moved in along the front. Rather than attack those fresh divisions with divisions of Americans already withered and separated from their organizations, the AEF Commander decided to relieve the 35th, 37th, and 79th divisions. After dark on September 30, Colonel Thompson received orders to withdraw his 138th Infantry Battalion, but thinking that his position was too critical to the defensive line, he waited until the 1st Division 28th Regulars came up to replace him. Sending his men back, Thompson remained for six hours longer to brief the relief on conditions.

Then at 3 a.m. on the morning of October 1, other elements of the 1st Division came up under German shellfire to replace the 35th's resistance lines. Kenamore described the men as they withdrew: "The men were unshaven, dirty and haggard. Their clothing was soiled and torn, their shoes muddy and worn out. Many had minor wounds and the white bandages were plentiful. A great deal of equipment had been lost or thrown away. They lay about their various grouping spaces, two or three together sleeping under one or two raincoats. Some had grown hoarse from cold or gas, and nearly everyone's eyes were red from gas and loss of sleep. A serious dysenteric condition had broken out throughout the entire outfit. Its cause was variously ascribed to the water, to eating canned food continuously, to the lack of hot food for five days. The epidemic greatly weakened the men and made the reassembling of units still more difficult."[44]

In the last five days, they had fought the 1st and 5th Prussian Guard, the 1st and 2nd Landwehr, and the 37th and 52nd German line divisions. The 35th had advanced eight and two-thirds miles through the Hindenburg Line. They had captured 751 men and 13 officers, 85 machine guns, 160 automatic rifles, 100 anti-tank guns, three 77-mm field pieces, five howitzers, 11 more artillery pieces, some ammunition and engineer dumps, and a variety of other accoutrements of war.

The Cost

However, the cost for the 35th was high: 232 officers and 6,688 men – more than 1,000 of whom were dead. "The heavy toll of casualties among officers," Kenamore said, "was probably the greatest factor in causing the mixing up of elements, which caused the greatest confusion."[45] For the enlisted men, Kenamore had the highest praise: "At no time in the fight were the enlisted men called upon by their officers for any action that they did not immediately try to perform. They advanced just as gallantly to the last attack as they did in the first, and they underwent the exhausting trial, privations and continuous

work with rare stamina. If the fame of the division rests upon the work of the enlisted men, it will live forever."[46]

From Charpentry to Sommedieue

After the relief by the 1st Division, the 35th regrouped around Charpentry then marched to an area south of Courupt to the eastern edge of the Les Islettes-Brizeaux road and then south to the Passavant-Beaulieu road. They rested, cleaned equipment, and then continued the march to the area around Vavincourt.[47] There they rested from October 6 to October 11, but continued to drill and serve policing details. On October 13, they arrived in the vicinity of Benoite-Baux, Courouvre, and Thillombois, and then marched in a cold rain toward Sommedieue, where they arrived later in the day.

Major General Traub set up headquarters in the village of Sommedieue. On the night of October 14-15, the 35th Division relieved the French Fifteenth C.I.C. on the Sommedieue sector amidst German shelling. The men were issued new clothing, but not quite enough to supply everyone's needs. Gradually the dysentery cleared up, but the men had to endure 7,000 rounds of German gas shells, causing 200 casualties – mostly slight.[48] They were also bombarded with German leaflets in an attempt by the Germans to secure more favorable treatment and to compromise American morale as peace negotiations continued.

"'What are you fighting for?' the leaflets proclaimed. 'Germany is tired of bloodshed and seeks peace. When the need of fighting is past, why are we fighting?'" The men joked about the propaganda and saved the leaflets as souvenirs until scouting parties were sent out to gather them up as a threat to morale.[49]

While in the Sommedieue sector, some of the men received their first seven-day furloughs. Many journeyed to Grenoble, where they were met at the train by bands and cheering crowds. "Pretty girls blew kisses from their finger tips and old women waved and wiped away the tears. There were twelve hundred men of the division who tasted again of the sweetmeats of civilization. They were given good rooms in good hotels, good meals at the best eating houses, and with no cost to themselves. They answered to no call except their own whims, went where they pleased in the city, and were treated as guests."[50]

Commercy

On November 1, the 35th came under the command of the 17th French Army Corps and on November 5, was relieved by the 81st "Wild Cat" Division. On November 6 and 7, they moved west and south into the area around Commercy. In the rain and snow they trained, drilled, and were instructed in military courtesy because some of their regular Army officers claimed a breakdown in discipline had occurred as a reaction to their five days in the Argonne. Leaves were granted, however, and men went to Paris, Nice, Monte Carlo, and the Riviera, and acted as tourists, bought postcards, and ate in restaurants in a complete and unreal contrast to what they had just endured.[51]

The moment of the Armistice, November 11, 1918, 11:00 a.m., found the 35th in haymows about Commercy, held in ready for a possible push east of Metz. Now the push was no longer necessary. At first, news of the German surrender was met with skepticism; rumors had been rampant, some proving false, but on the night of November 10, the skies lit up with flares and rockets – evidence that the war was about to end. Following the armistice were days of drills and maneuvers.[52] Men grew restless; their purpose was finished, and they wanted to go

home. Little relief was to be found in war-weary and gloomy French towns.

Gradually, the men found respite in entertainment that began to circulate through the various Army divisions. A show troupe made up of members of the 35th developed its own bill of fare for the Division and was later sent to Luxembourg and put on the entertainment circuit for other AEF units.[53] Motion picture shows were offered three times a week, and boxing matches between American and French ring champions were popular among the men. Ill-feeling against the French increased as French villagers charged high prices, eager to extract as much as they could from the Americans before they left.

Gradually, wounded officers and men began to return from the hospitals. Officers detached and assigned to other divisions returned to join their old outfits. Regular Army officers in command of the 35th were moved to other commands and the original 35th Division officers resumed their former commands.[54]

Le Mans, St. Nazaire, Brest, and Home

Originally scheduled to leave February 7, the Division was forced to wait another month until March 9, when it entrained for the Le Mans area, arriving there on March 12. Once in camp, the Division could at last relax from a strict military regimen. Inspections were held to a minimum and hikes were short. Then on April 2, the 35th moved toward St. Nazaire to wait for the ships to arrive. Major General Wright and his staff boarded the *U.S.S. De Kalb* on March 28 and sailed the next day for Newport News, Virginia. The rest of the division followed. Those who sailed from Brest landed at New York, and those who sailed from St. Nazaire arrived in Newport News. Left behind were

1,530 of the 35th's own, dead in France.[55]

Kansas City

Meanwhile, in Kansas City, a committee chaired by Charles R. Butler collected between $1,500 and $2,000 dollars to construct two arches. The first arch would greet soldiers as they emerged from Union Station, across the part of the road that stretched from Main to Grand, just 200 feet east of the station. The arch was 60-feet wide and 60-feet tall at its highest point. Constructed of lumber and canvas, it depicted the Goddess of Liberty in a chariot above a centerpiece on which the words "OUR HEORES" appeared over a victory laurel. The words "VICTORY" and "PEACE" flanked either side. On the right of the archway appeared a scene depicting "America Defiant" and on the left a scene depicting "America Victorious." The second arch was planned for Grand Avenue between 10th and 12th streets.[56]

"The Arch That Will Welcome Service Men As They Emerge from the Union Station."[57]

As the various units of the 35th Division approached Kansas City in May 1919, arrival times at Union Station were published in *The Kansas City Star*, and crowds poured down into the runways under the sheds along the tracks at the east end of the terminal yards. Arrivals occurred at all hours, rain and shine; weather and time of day made no difference to the wives and children, mothers and dads, sisters and brothers, friends and sweethearts of the men whose arms and heads hung out of the windows of the train cars, eyes scanning the crowds for the long-awaited familiar face.

Once the train had halted, the men burst forth into a crowd shouting their names, crying for joy, arms stretching out for the tight embrace of coming home. Emerging from Union Station, the men formed into their units and paraded through the victory arch on their way to Convention Hall, where hot coffee, oranges, and sandwiches awaited and the celebration continued.[58] Fed and feted, the boys boarded the trains once more, this time for Camp Funston, where they would be mustered out, paid, and re-boarded on trains for the final ride home.[59] The welcome the city boys had received in Kansas City would be repeated on a smaller scale for their buddies from small towns throughout Missouri and Kansas.[60]

For as joyous as the homecoming celebrations were, however, not everyone was welcome. Such was the case for Kansas City 129th Field Artillery commander Col. Karl D. Klemm, who was asked by the welcoming committee to "absent himself" from the arrival of the unit in Kansas City. One of the battalion majors had wired Independence,

Missouri, Mayor Christian Ott to use his influence "'to keep Klemm out of any parade of this regiment to prevent an unpleasant situation.'"[61] Many men in the Major's regiment had complained bitterly of the harsh discipline Klemm had imposed on the men, who regarded their commander as "more of a czar than a commanding officer." During the march from the Vosges, for example, Klemm appeared to derive a great deal of delight from riding along the line "snatching caps from their heads."[62] "A feeling that Colonel Klemm took advantage of his rank to gain early discharge from the army adds to their animosity," *The Star* reported.[63]

Men in Battery D, Cpt. Harry S. Truman's outfit, recalled a particularly bitter incident during the fighting in the Argonne: "Colonel Klemm rode the length of the regimental column as they were making a march," *The Star* reported the men as saying. "He found Battery D marching in more broken and weary manner than the other batteries. He ordered them to go up a hill, a distance of about a mile, in muddy roads in double quick time. It was a punishment."[64] For his part, Colonel Klemm was not at all surprised at the men's reaction, "asserting that the battery was not making a military appearance and was putting the entire regiment in the light of a poorly trained unit." Still, Klemm declared that the welcoming committee need not fear any embarrassing situations of the troops blatantly booing him in public. So when the 129th Field Artillery did arrive in Kansas City, Col. Klemm appeared in civilian clothes to acknowledge their return. He was among

Colonel Karl Daenzer Klemm.[67]

the first to greet the officers, but he did not address them nor march with them through the victory arch.[65] As for Cpt. Harry Truman, his relationship with Col. Klemm was "strained."[66]

Controversy

Col. Klemm was apparently not alone in his negative assessment of the military bearing of the 35th Division's battle-weary men. First Army Corps inspector Ltc. Robert G. Peck criticized the 35th Division as it came out of the line in the Argonne, asking the men questions often barbed with critical references to their competency as National Guard.[68] The men marched in loose ranks, were overly familiar with officers, he noted, unkempt, unpolished, lacking in the refinements of military discipline and protocol. All of this he reported in an 87-page typed single-spaced critique.[69] For their part, the men had just come out of five days of intense fighting, had no time to dress out for a parade-ground inspection by a Regular Army officer, and resented the critical tone Peck took as he questioned them – typical, they thought, of someone from headquarters who had no concept of what they had just been through and who obviously had little respect for the National Guard.

Brigadier General Hugh A. Drum, Chief of Staff of the First Army, took Peck's conclusions verbatim and sent them to 35th Division commander Major General Traub, who then distributed them to his staff, even though some of the report was critical of the General himself. "That this division was not well trained and fit for battle, was not a well-disciplined combat unit, and that many officers were not well-trained leaders are very true statements," Traub said.[70] Traub admitted that the Division had not had the opportunity to train for months, and as the 35th moved from its sector with the French to the Meuse-Argonne, it had marched at night and bivouacked during the day to avoid enemy detection.

Consequently, it was not at all well prepared for the fight in the Argonne. In addition, as a reflection of the lack of discipline in the 35th, the First Army that had replaced the 35th in the line complained that the 35th had left the sector littered with all manner of materiel, food, rifles, and ammunition – some of the equipment left by stragglers tired of lugging it around.[71]

As time went on, criticism of the 35th grew even worse, and Henry J. Allen, former editor of the Wichita *Beacon*[72] and a YMCA director with the 35th, took up their cause. While he was still with the 35th in France, Allen had been elected Governor of Kansas. He had observed first-hand the treatment of the men and, like many of them, attributed their forced withdrawal from Exermont and the casualties they had endured to the incompetence of the Regular Army and its prejudice against the National Guard.

To begin with, on the very eve of the battle, National Guard officers, who originally had formed many of the Guard units, trained with their men, and knew them well, were replaced by Regular Army officers who had no previous contact with the men at all and, in some instances, couldn't even recognize their command staff. Many of the Regular Army officers considered themselves more professional than the Guard officers whose authority, in the opinion of the Regulars, depended upon their popularity, having been elected to their positions by the men they commanded. Consequently, and partially as a result of the lack of rapport with the men, the command structure of the 35th Division broke down during the battle in the Argonne. A significant number of officers were lost, and as a result, orders were confused, contradictory, received at the last minute, or were not received at all. Units were broken apart and scattered and communications deteriorated – sometimes completely.

The breakdown in communications and command was manifested physically, as well. Roads were so clogged that supplies and food could not advance to the front, the wounded could not be moved to the rear, and artillery support could not be brought into position to support the men as they attacked a reinforced German line. Peck reported that artillery commander Brigadier General Lucien G. Berry "had failed to cooperate with and make full use of the Air Service until ordered to do so."[73] Air support could have helped direct the artillery barrages the infantry needed for its advances.

The controversy grew even more intense as the men mustered out. Once out of uniform they were freer to express themselves. The result was three separate hearings: the House Rules Committee, the Senate Committee on Military Affairs and the Senate Committee on Military Affairs for the Army Appropriation Bill of 1920.[74] The House hearings involved Henry Allen, General Traub, Secretary of War Newton D. Baker, and Army Chief of Staff General Peyton C. Marsh. Allen and Traub also appeared before the Senate committee. For the hearing on the appropriation bill, the Senate asked for testimony from Brigadier General Charles I. Martin, Adjutant General of Kansas and former commander of the 70th Brigade until Traub relieved him just prior to the Argonne.[75]

Charges and counter-charges continued to be exchanged, and the pages of *The Kansas City Star* were filled with accusations from both sides. In the end, however, nothing was really resolved. "The Regulars did not learn much," Robert Ferrell concluded.

"General Traub, supported by Secretary Baker and General March, refuted, to their satisfaction, what Governor Allen was attempting to say. The changes that the army could have instituted were never begun, as it slipped back into peacetime routines … World War II taught its lessons in cruel ways similar to World War I, with the U.S. Army surprised time after time by the tactics and weapons of Germany and Japan."[76]

For the men, it was over, over there. They had left the war and the controversy associated with it behind. Eager to return to civilian life, the 1917-1918 men of the 35th Division had better things to do. In their minds, they had accomplished a lot, advancing more than eight miles against crack German troops, taking Vauquois Hill and Exermont, and holding the line until ordered to pull back. They had done everything they had been asked to do. Once home, they returned to the cities, towns, and farms from which they had come. They helped elect one of their own, 35th Division, 129th Field Artillery, Battery D, Captain Harry S. Truman to the Vice-Presidency in 1944 and to the Presidency in 1948. While President, Truman reorganized the military and in 1962 protested when then President John F. Kennedy allowed the 35th Division to disband. It had continued as a National Guard unit and had fought with distinction in World War II, but it was to be no more.

Memory

Now all the veterans of the 35th Division who fought in the Great War are gone; 35th Division veterans of World War II are dying off, but the small green signs posted on the northbound (mile marker 0.4) and southbound (mile marker 234) lanes of Interstate 35 remain as a salute to the 35th. They commemorate its Memorial Highway, as it marches through Kansas City and for a little while, at least, steps in time abreast of the old Santa Fe Trail.

They had done everything they had been asked to do. Once home, they returned to the cities, towns, and farms from which they had come. They helped elect one of their own, 35th Division, 129th Field Artillery, Battery D, Captain Harry S. Truman to the Vice-Presidency in 1944 and to the Presidency in 1948.

M-12 **35th Division Memorial Highway**
I-35 Southbound Mile Marker 234 &
Northbound Mile Marker 0.4

Kansas law directs that "the Secretary of Transportation shall provide appropriate signs at proper intervals along the federal Interstate Highway No. 35, bearing an inscription to show the designation."[77] In 1963, this provision enabled the Kansas Department of Transportation to designate the Kansas portion of Interstate 35 as the "35th Infantry Division Memorial Highway."

During World War I, the officers and men who enlisted in the National Guard units in the Kansas City area became part of the 35th Division. They trained at Camp Doniphan on the Fort Sill Military Reservation near Lawton, Oklahoma, about six and a half hours from Kansas City via I-35 and I-44.

In 2003, Kansas chose Interstate 35 as its portion of the national Purple Heart Trail. Established by the Military Order of the Purple Heart in 1992, the Purple Heart Trail begins in Mount Vernon, Virginia, and winds through 20 states, including Hawaii. Highways in Puerto Rico and Guam also bear the designation. The Purple Heart Trail honors those men and women wounded and killed in action serving their country.[78]

35th Division Memorial Highway I-35 Southbound Mile Marker 234 & Northbound Mile Marker 0.4

Eleven men of that group hold special significance for Kansas City. Captain Sanford M. Brown, Major Murray Davis, Sergeant Joseph Dillon, Private James Arthur Maloney, Sergeant Major Roswell Barry Sayre, Captain Arly Luther Hedrick, Sergeant Fred James Shackelton, Private Robert Thomas Clements, Private William T Law, Private Grover Metzger, and Lieutenant Harry W. Herrod all served with the 35th Division in the Great War. All were remembered by having their names inscribed on various monuments or carried with the names of American Legion Posts throughout the city. Together, these men represent a variety of service, social strata, walks of life, and circumstances of death – with one thing in common: all died in the service of their country. Following are their stories and the stories of how they were remembered.

Cpt. Sanford M. Brown, Jr. and the Attack on Charpentry
(Sanford Brown, Jr., American Legion Post No. 124)

One American Legion post, in particular, reflected the close bonds shared by the brotherhood of Ivanhoe Masonic Temple and Ivanhoe Lodge No. 446. Cpt. Sanford M. Brown was a member of the lodge, whose brothers dedicated a monument to his memory near the site where he and his brother, Joseph E. Brown, also a veteran of the war, had grown up and near where the Ivanhoe Masonic Temple was located. Those bonds were so close that when the lodge moved its temple near to where many of its members were buried in Mount Moriah Cemetery, the lodge moved the memorial to Cpt. Sanford Brown there, as well.

On Tuesday, November 26, 1918, exactly two months to the day the Battle of the Meuse-Argonne began, the Reverend S. M. Brown, 3430 Euclid, Kansas City, received a letter from the officer commanding his son's detachment. Enclosed with the letter was a copy of 35th Division commander Maj. Gen. Peter E. Traub's official order citing Cpt. Sanford Brown for bravery.

The citation read:

Capt. Sanford M. Brown, Jr., while regimental adjutant, on September 26 and 27 fearlessly exposed himself to intense artillery and machine gun fire in order to assist his commanding officer by assuring the proper execution of orders. He was killed while assisting informing his regiment (the 139th Infantry) for an attack on Charpentry. At the time of his death he was wearing the insignia of first lieutenant as he had not been advised of his promotion to a captaincy, which occurred September 18, 1918.[80]

Born on March 19, 1893, Brown was employed by the Commonwealth National Bank in Kansas City and was 24 years old when he was inducted into the Army on August 15, 1917.[81] He shipped overseas on April 24, 1918 and was killed in action near Varennes, France, on the second day of the Battle of the Meuse-Argonne, September 27, 1918. He was 25 years old. His brother, Joseph, was in active service at the time.

American Legion Post No. 124 was named after Cpt. Brown, who was initiated into the Ivanhoe Masonic Lodge on March 13, 1918.[82]

Besides appearing on the American Legion Monument II at Budd Park Esplanade on Van Brunt Boulevard, north of Independence Avenue, in Kansas City. Cpt. Brown's name also appears on the bronze plaques of the Meyer Circle Gateway – Avenue of Trees at Meyer Circle and Ward Parkway and in Memory Hall at Liberty Memorial in Kansas City.

Cpt. Sanford
M. Brown, Jr.

James J. Heiman

Sanford Brown,
1918.[79]

M-13 Captain Sanford M. Brown Jr. Memorial
Mount Moriah Cemetery— 10507 Holmes, Kansas City, Missouri

The face of this Tennessee marble monument features five stars at the top. Beneath the stars in a bronze medallion is the portrait of Cpt. Sanford M. Brown, Jr., below which is the inscription:

Captain
Sanford M. Brown, Jr.
1893-1918
Meuse-Argone Offensive
World War

On the back of the 10-ton monument, under the logo for the American Legion, is the motto "For God and Country."

An eagle outstretched above four stars is carved at the top of two sides of the monument. On one side below the eagle and stars are the words "Dedicated Sept. 27, 1931, by the Sanford Brown, Jr. Post of the American Legion." The opposite side of the monument states the monument's purpose: "To inculcate a sense of individual obligation to the community, state and nation."

Originally, the monument stood on the northern portion of a 3,089-acre park, first known as Linwood Plaza. There and across the street at the ten-

James J. Heiman

Monument to Sanford M. Brown, Jr., in Mount Moriah Cemetery.

nis court, Sanford Brown had played as a boy when he and his brother, Joseph E. Brown, lived at 3430 Euclid in Kansas City, Missouri.[83] The area had been acquired for a park by condemnation in 1908 and was laid out on both sides of Linwood Boulevard between Brooklyn and Park Avenue. By 1914, paths, landscaping, and a drinking fountain had been added, and in 1931 permission was granted to Sanford M. Brown, Jr. Post 124 to erect the monument in their namesake's memory near the center of the park.

Also nearby at Linwood Boulevard and Park Avenue was the Ivanhoe Masonic Temple, which housed four Masonic lodges, among which was Ivanhoe Lodge No 446. The Ivanhoe Masonic Temple was dedicated on November 13, 1922.[84] Before he left for war, Sanford Brown, Jr. was a member of the Ivanhoe Lodge, and after the war many members of the American Legion Sanford M. Brown, Jr. Post 124 were also members of the Ivanhoe Masonic Lodge.

American Legion Post 124 dedicated the monument to Sanford Brown at 3:00 on Sunday afternoon, September 27, 1931, 13 years to the day he had been killed along the road north of Varennes by enemy artillery and machine gun fire from the Argonne Forest.[85] After a service in the lodge room of the Ivanhoe Temple, Lieutenant Colonel Ruby D. Garrett, who commanded Kansas City's 117th Field Signal Battalion addressed the 2,000 people gathered to remember Cpt. Brown. Col. Carl A. Ristine, Sanford Brown's regimental commander of the 139th Infantry joined Ltc. Garrett. Col. Ristine spoke about the battle that killed Cpt. Brown, who at the time of his death was the regiment's adjutant.[86]

On March 6, 1941, 10 years after the Sanford Brown, Jr., monument was dedicated, Kansas City Parks and Recreation granted Post 124's request to change the name of the park from "Linwood Plaza" to "Sanford Brown Plaza."[87] Then on Memorial Day 1941, American Legion Post 124 dedicated a flag pole in his honor. Joseph E. Brown,

James J. Heiman

Sanford Brown Plaza, Linwood between Brooklyn and Park.

Sanford Brown's brother, a veteran of the war and former commander of Major William J. Bland American Legion Post No. 50, spoke at the event.[88] Also active in area war remembrance was Cpt. Brown's mother, who served as chaplain of the Kansas City chapter of the American War Mothers.[89]

Twenty-two years later, in 1963, American Legion Post No. 124 moved the monument to Mount Moriah Cemetery, then a Masonic burial ground and not far from the Ivanhoe Masonic Lodge, which had relocated to 8640 Holmes Road. Sanford Brown was the first member of the Ivanhoe Masonic Lodge to be killed in the war[90] and the monument to his memory now stands in a cemetery where many of his lodge members and war comrades are buried. Artifacts from the Sanford M. Brown, Jr., American Legion Post No. 124 are housed at the Ivanhoe Masonic Lodge, which is, as it had been in 1931 in another part of the city, now in a new location and near the monument to its former lodge brother.

Major Murray Davis: "Take Care of My Men"
(Murray Davis American Legion Post No. 10)

Among the most active of the Kansas City American Legion posts and the most prominent of Kansas City World War I monuments are the post and monument named for Major Murray Davis, a Kansas City lawyer whose dedication to his profession and his men has earned him the highest respect. Major Davis commanded the 3rd Battalion of the 35th's Division 140th Infantry, which suffered heavy losses in the Battle of the Meuse-Argonne.

On Tuesday, September 24, 1918, Maj. Murray Davis spent almost the entire day taking care of his men. That was not unusual – he had been doing so for some time as lieutenant and later as captain of Company L of the old 3rd Missouri Infantry, all men from Kansas City, who had been training at their armory at 39th and Main.[91] That was before the 3rd Missouri was joined with the 6th Missouri to form the 140th Infantry Brigade, 35th Division, at Camp Doniphan. This Tuesday, though, was different from those times. Now Major Davis was in France, just southeast of the town of Exermont. It was the eve of the battle of the Meuse-Argonne, and Murray Davis was practicing law again, listening to his men, helping them make out wills or settle business that, in the words of Chaplain Evan Edwards, "should have been attended to long before."[92]

"With a brilliant mind, he had made an excellent Judge Advocate," Edwards noted.[93] A 1909 graduate of the University of Missouri, Davis had been a law partner of Judge William Thomson in the Scarritt Building in Kansas City. Then on May 13, 1913, he began his military career, joining Company K of the old Third as a private, on his own merit rising in rank to become 2nd lieutenant, then 1st lieutenant, and finally captain of Company L. Shortly before his unit deployed overseas, Davis passed a competitive examination for major and was appointed judge advocate of the general courts-martial for the 35th Division. In that capacity he was detailed in March 1918 to prosecute the commandant of the base hospital at Camp Doniphan, a case that grew out of Senator Chamberlain's Senate speech in which the Senator referred to Albert Hestwood, who had died from the unsanitary conditions at the Camp Doniphan base hospital.[94]

Major Davis also served as counsel for Brigadier General Arthur B. Donnelly in the court-martial proceedings against him. The General had been charged with participating in games of cards in which money was passed and liquor served in his tent. Clair Kenamore, a reporter with *The St. Louis Post-Dispatch*, who had served as a reporter with the 35th Division, later asserted that Donnelly, along with more than 10 other officers of the Missouri National Guard, had been subjected to an "unceasing war" to oust them from their positions in favor of replacements from the Regular Army.[95] So Murray Davis had been sucked up into the maelstrom of malpractice and political maneuvering early in his career as a military lawyer. However, all of that seemed like ages ago and required a very different kind of law than what Davis was practicing that Tuesday in the foxholes outside of Exermont.

1st. Lt. Evan A. Edwards, regimental chaplain of the 140th Infantry, remembered what Murray Davis was doing that day. "When I asked him for his help, reluctantly, as I knew how busy he was at the time, he replied, 'Chaplain, there is nothing I can do for any man in this regiment that I will not do gladly!'"[96]

Chaplain Edwards knew Davis' character, having billeted with him at Camp Marquette, and, as he put it, having "talked over a number of matters seriously."

"He had no fear of shell and felt that no bullet could harm him. But he dreaded gas, and gave great attention to his gas mask," Edwards remembered. Murray Davis' sense of security and purpose, however, went far beyond the threat of physical harm.

"I never knew a man with a keener sense of fairness and justice, and he was an admirable judge of men and character," Edwards noted. "His skill as an officer, his buoyant, virile spirit, and his care for his men made him typical of the best America had to offer."[97]

"Major Murray Davis, D.S.C., Killed Near Exermont."[98]

That care was about to be put to the ultimate test late on September 28, while the 3rd Battalion prepared to spend the night in foxholes they had dug between Chaudron Farm and Montrebeau.

"About 8 o'clock that night an enemy plane swept a terrific machine gun fire over our line," recalled Harry S. Whitthorne, formerly a 1st lieutenant and later captain of Company L.

"Major Davis was passing among his exhausted troops when a bullet from the plane tore through his helmet and nearly severed his right ear. The wound was deathly painful. I helped Murray dress the wound and begged him to go to the hospital. He refused, saying that as long as he could stand he would not leave his boys."[99]

As the night wore on, Major Davis could still hear the groans of his men dying in the mud and the rain. He lay there, too, with them, suffering from a wound nearly mortal, still refusing to remove to the rear where he could have the attention he needed.

Then morning came, still raining. Brigade Commander Lieutenant Colonel Delaplane ordered Davis' 3rd Battalion into the second assault wave to go over at 5:20 a.m.

Lt. Whitthorne recalled, "at 5 o'clock lines of combat were formed. Murray Davis couldn't get off the ground. His complexion had turned to yellow from loss of blood. I made one last effort to induce him to go to the rear. He refused.

"I placed my hands under both his arms to assist him to his feet. I held him up and staggered with him across the shell-swept battlefield. His battalion was in line, ready for the zero hour. Our barrage had commenced. Davis gained strength as we moved forward. The 1st Battalion was held up by heavy machine gun fire.

"Davis stopped to say a word to little Guy Milley, [Pvt. Guy Ora Meily] who had lain out in No Man's Land all night, with both legs blown off by shrapnel … a whole squad of M Company was wiped out by one shell."

"The major ordered his battalion toward Exermont," but his advance, too, was halted by enemy fire.

James J. Heiman
Major Murray Davis gravesite, Forest Hill Cemetery, Kansas City, Mo.

"Four of us moved forward on reconnaissance," Lt. Whitthorne recalled, "Davis; Dumas, his faithful orderly; Posh, my orderly; and myself. Machine gun bullets and artillery swept the ground over which we passed. Each step forward was a further entry into hell. Major Davis, nearly dead on his feet, moved forward like a phantom soldier … The fire got hotter. I began to wonder how we could live.

"We were forced to stop at the crest of a hill where we were in a good position to observe the enemy defenses. The sun broke through, then the clouds closed.

"A spurt of machine gun fire [came] at us.

Davis turned to say something to me. The end, a bullet crashed through his head. He turned quickly, his hands moved toward his head, and he whispered quietly, 'Take care of my men.'

"Dumas lay dead, Posh shot through the arm, and myself through the leg."[100]

Chaplain Edwards recalled that all four had been standing in the angle between the hedge and the road a few hundred yards southeast of Exermont.

Davis had turned 31 just four days earlier.[101]

Soon after the Armistice, Major Murray Davis was awarded the Distinguished Service Cross, created just two months before his death to recognize valor such as his. The citation read:

The President of the United States of America, authorized by Act of Congress, July 9, 1918, takes pride in presenting the Distinguished Service Cross (Posthumously) to Major (Infantry) Murray Davis, United States Army, for extraordinary heroism in action while serving with the 140th Infantry Regiment, 35th Division, A.E.F., near Exermont, France, September 26-29, 1918. Major Davis led his battalion brilliantly, and, when wounded, refused to go to the rear, but having his wound dressed on the spot continued in command of his battalion. Later he was killed while leading his command in an advance.

--War Department General Orders No. 59 (1919).[102]

■ ■ ■

Born in Burlingame, Kansas, September 24, 1887, Murray Davis came with his parents to Kansas City in 1899. He attended Garfield School and Kansas City Central High School, and in June 1909, graduated from the University of Missouri with a law degree. He was then admitted to the bar and began practicing law in Kansas City. He was a member of the Phi Lamda Epsilon and Sigma Epsilon Fraternities, the City Club, and the Kansas City Athletic Club.[103]

In 1912, he enlisted in the 3rd Infantry, Missouri National Guard, and was promoted to lieutenant and later captain of Company L. After war was declared in 1917, the Missouri 3rd and 6th Regiments were consolidated into the 140th Infantry, and Cpt.

Lowering the casket into the grave at Forest Hill Cemetery.[113]

Davis was promoted to the rank of major and given command of the 3rd Battalion. His unit saw service in the Vosges Mountains and the Battle of the Meuse Argonne and was in reserve at the Battle of St. Mihiel.[104]

Major Davis was buried in the National Cemetery at Romagne, France.[105] His father, William B. Davis, president of Kansas City's Gold Star League, a service organization formed in March 1920 to facilitate the return of America's war dead, arranged for his son's body to be returned to the United States and accompanied the body from the receiving facility at Hoboken, New Jersey, back to

Kansas City on October 14, 1921.[106]

A week later, on October 21, 1921, Kansas City Mayor Cowgill issued a proclamation calling upon "all citizens of this city in general to participate" in the memorial services for Major Davis.[107] In addition, the mayor ordered that all flags at public buildings be lowered to half mast during the hours of the funeral. On October 23, 1921, a military escort led by Colonel Edwin M. Stayton and comprising the entire 3rd regiment of combat engineers, members of the Murray Davis American Legion Post No. 10, as well as American Legion members from all of the other Kansas City posts, the Gold Star League, and the Veterans of Foreign Wars attended the funeral at the Second Presbyterian Church, 55th and Oak, Kansas City,[108] with interment following at Forest Hill Cemetery.[109] Kansas Governor Henry J. Allen, "who knew Major Davis when the latter was a boy in Kansas and who was one of the last to wish him godspeed before the fatal battle," spoke at the funeral.[110]

At the old armory at 39th and Main,[111] Major Murray Davis's own men gathered once more. The survivors of the 3rd Battalion, 140th Infantry, 35th Division, were taking care of their man, their commander, marching with him one last time from his home to his church and from his church to his final resting place in Forest Hill Cemetery.[112]

M-14 **Major Murray Davis Memorial**
Main at 40th Street, Kansas City, Missouri

On Memorial Day 1928, seven years after Murray Davis' burial in Kansas City and 10 years after the end of the war, members of Murray Davis American Legion Post No. 10 gathered once more at 40th and Main streets in Kansas City to unveil a monument to their namesake, Murray Davis, lawyer and soldier. Many of the men of the 35th Division, 3rd Battalion, and the remainder of the 140th Infantry Regiment came together again to witness the event at the site of their old armory.

Approved by the City Council at a cost of $10,000, the monument was designed by

James J. Heiman

Looking north at the Major Murray Davis Memorial.

Kansas City architects Wight and Wight. It is built of Tennessee marble resting on a base of granite. In height, six feet and in length 32 feet overall, the monument is 13 feet wide.[114] "The marble buttresses and graceful seats on the sides of the memorial tablet were an artistic symbol of the peace and dignity their chieftain had gained by valiance of war," *The Star* reported.[115]

In the center of the monument is a large stone at the corners of which are carved bundles of sticks modeled on the *fasces*, symbols of legal authority. In Roman times, these bundles of birch or elm rods were bound together by red thongs and carried by servants who walked in advance of state rulers. The *fasces* reminded the people of the ruler's power to punish by flogging. Often embedded in the *fasces* was an ax, whose blade projected from the top and symbolized the ruler's power to punish by death. In the city of Rome, the ax was removed because a man condemned to death had the right to appeal directly to the people.[116]

The ax is omitted from the *fasces* depicted here, too, but on the sides of the monument between the corner *fasces*, a sword pointed towards the ground suggests the ultimate price paid by Major Davis for the survival of a just country in whose defense he served as both a lawyer and an Army officer. An

outstretched eagle, whose torso is encircled by a wreath, stretches its wings above the inscription, memorializing the service and sacrifice America made at Amiens, St. Mihiel, the Vosges, and the Meuse-Argonne.

The inscription reads:
MAJOR MURRAY DAVIS   D. S. C

140TH INFANTRY 35TH DIVISION A. E. F.
KILLED IN ACTION AT EXERMONT,
FRANCE
SEPTEMBER TWENTY NINTH MXMXVIII

A KINDLY, JUST AND BELOVED OFFICER
WISE IN COUNSEL
RESOLUTE IN ACTION
COURAGEOUS UNTO DEATH

SERIOUSLY WOUNDED HE REFUSED TO RELINQUISH HIS COMMAND UNTIL MORTALLY WOUNDED HE FELL LEADING HIS COMRADES TO VICTORY. HIS LAST WORDS

"TAKE CARE OF MY MEN"

On May 30, 1928, the men of the 140th Infantry took care of their man, rendering permanent witness to the words of his own last will and testament, "Take care of my men." Major Murray Davis had spoken those words in the angle between the hedge and the road a few hundred yards southeast of Exermont, France. Now his words are set in stone in another angle of ground along a road, 40th and Main Street, Kansas City, Missouri – just a few hundred yards from the site of the old armory where he and his men had trained in the manual of arms in a quieter time, before they had known the terrible price of war.

Sgt. Joseph Dillon and the Sanitary Unit of the Old Missouri 3rd (Joseph Dillon American Legion Post No. 81)

The work of the sanitary detachment was critical to the morale and survival of men in combat. The sanitary detachment was the medical unit whose stretcher-bearers moved up under sometimes withering fire to offer immediate first-aid to the wounded, remove them from the battlefield, carry them to triage, and transport them in ambulances to field hospitals. Along with the rest of Murray Davis' battalion of which it was a part, the Sanitary Detachment of the 3rd Battalion, 140th Infantry, suffered heavily during the Battle of the Meuse-Argonne. Sgt. Joseph Dillon was hit by shrapnel and killed while carrying wounded comrades from the field.

Joseph Dillon joined the Sanitary Detachment of the old 3rd Regiment, Missouri National Guard, on November 20, 1913,[117] and saw service with the regiment on the Mexican border in the Loredo, Texas, District from July 8 until September 2, 1916. A few weeks later, on September 26, 1916, the Missouri 3rd was released from federal service, only to be mustered back in again six months later on March 26, 1917, when it went into encampment at Camp Nichols, 63rd and Ward Parkway, in Kansas City.[118]

The 3rd Missouri was assigned to guard the Missouri River Hannibal Bridge and other bridges in Kansas City. Then at the end of May 1917, a portion of the unit took up duties on the Pawnee Flats near Fort Riley, where the first bundles of lumber were being unloaded from railroad gondolas to build what would soon become Camp Funston, the largest of the U.S. Army training cantonments. Two complete companies of men at a time mounted guard over an expanse of territory so large that it took an hour to relieve the guard. Then on October 13, 1917, both the Camp Nichols and Pawnee Flats deployments of the 3rd departed for Camp

Doniphan at Fort Sill, Oklahoma, where the Regiment joined the Missouri 6th to become the 140th Infantry, 35th Division, under the command of Colonel Albert Linxwiler.[119]

After enduring wind, sand, and bitter cold, large numbers of men succumbed to an epidemic of spinal meningitis, leaving many units hardly able to function, but training continued in scouting, observation, intelligence, bayonet, grenade, machine-gun, signaling, telegraphy, gas, and musketry. An array of trenches and barbed wire was constructed to provide training in the conditions the men would soon encounter in France. In mid-April, the Sanitary Detachment entrained with the rest of the 140th for Camp Mills, Long Island, for a week in the mud and cold before they boarded the train at Mineola for Brooklyn and then to Hoboken, New Jersey, by ferry. The Sanitary Train, Supply Train, Regimental Headquarters, and the 1st Battalion then boarded the Australian freighter *Shropshire*, popularly nicknamed the "Slopjar" for the Atlantic crossing.

Through the North Channel southward, skirting the Scottish coast and the Isle of Man, the *Shropshire* worked its way up the

River Mersey to Liverpool and later down to Southampton, where the Sanitary Train landed and marched to a British rest camp. Crossing the channel, the regiment reached Le Havre, France, on May 9, 1918. On its way to British Rest Camp No. 1, the men encountered a Red Cross hospital train filled with wounded men fresh from the front, a portent of things to come.

There in the camp the men were re-outfitted with British Enfield rifles; the rifle issued to them in the States and that they had trained with and taken care of for so long was suddenly declared useless, further unnerving the men. They had to turn in their barracks bags, as well, and endured seeing them plundered before they left camp. On May 11, they entrained for Eu, where they marched ten miles to Gamasches to take up positions with the British.

Three weeks later on June 6, the regiment left the British, received a third rifle – this time, the American Enfield – and were issued steel helmets and overseas service caps[120] along with other gear and provisions. On June 23, the Sanitary Train and the rest of the 140th moved into the German-Alsace and on July 20, back over the mountains and into the front lines in the Fecht sector,[121] considered a "quiet sector," but still active with artillery and night raids.

After being held in reserve for the St. Mihiel Offensive September 12-15, the regi-

ment moved with the rest of the 35th Division into position in the Argonne Forest, where they prepared for the last great battle of the war. Cpt. Stephen Slaughter of Major Murray Davis' Company L recalled the events of September 26-29: "The men realized that at last they were to meet the acid test. Everywhere men could be seen reading over old letters from home, many being left in the Regimental Post Office to be mailed only in case they did not return. A large mail from the States arrived and greatly heartened the men."[122]

Less heartening for the men were last-minute changes in command, as Regular Army officers were ordered to replace the original National Guard officers who had trained the men and with whom the men were familiar.

After the artillery barrage in the early hours of September 26, the regiment went "over the top" to clean up Vauquois Hill, which had fallen in an hour to the 138th Infantry.[123] The next day, the 140th moved up on line with the 139th, failing in successive attacks against German machine gun nests, but towards dark finally swept over the machine guns and took Charpentry, with heavy casualties.[124]

On Saturday, September 28, the 140th was north of Charpentry and northeast of Baulny. Their flank came under heavy German artillery fire from Apremont and the woods beyond.[125] Ordered to advance and provide protection for the 69th brigade on their left, the 140th was forced to dig in under heavy

After enduring wind, sand, and bitter cold, large numbers of men succumbed to an epidemic of spinal meningitis, leaving many units hardly able to function, but training continued in scouting, observation, intelligence, bayonet, grenade, machine-gun, signaling, telegraphy, gas, and musketry. An array of trenches and barbed wire was constructed to provide training in the conditions the men would soon encounter in France.

enemy fire. With tank and cavalry support, the 140th took up the advance once again, with heavy losses from artillery and enemy aircraft. By the time the 140th reached Montrebeau Woods with the 2nd Battalion in reserve in the hedge north of Chaudron Farm, the regiment was "badly cut to pieces."[126] The 3rd Battalion had lost half of its men.

Chaplain Evans describes the work of the Sanitary Detachment that third day of the battle: "Over the field the men of Major Slusher's detachment were living up to the best traditions of the American Army. Broyles, Howell, Rothman, Schlegelmilch, Biggs—all did what men could do and more. The Dentists could not be kept back and rendered what aid they could. And the men did what might be expected with such leaders. After we came out, and Slusher had won his D.S.C., Major Broyles wrote his report for the Sanitary Detachment. Usually these reports are long and full of detail. Major Broyles wrote simply, and truly as follows: 'NOTHING SPECIAL TO REPORT. EVERY MAN DID HIS BEST.'

"McGaugh, Krenzer, Sydney Johnson, Messara, Howey, George, Krause, Lane, Lee, McDonald, Prater, Boyle, Washington, Warren, Snyder and Harry Davis and the rest of the men in the Sanitary Detachment did heroic work. Nearly all of these men mentioned were wounded, and Sgt. Dillon was killed."[127] He and Corporal Arthur P. Mahaney were killed by shrapnel while carrying wounded comrades from the field.[128]

Sgt. Joseph Dillon's service record shows that he died on September 29, 1918, having served overseas five months from April 25, 1918. As next of kin, his sister Mrya Dillon of Omaha, Nebraska, was notified of her brother's death.[129]

Sgt. Dillon's name appears on three of Kansas City's World War I memorials: The plaque in Memory Hall, Meyer Circle Gateway at Meyer Circle and Ward Parkway and the American Legion I Monument in Budd Park Esplanade, at Anderson and Van Brunt, just north of Independence Avenue. American Legion Post No. 81 was named for this sergeant, who had seen nearly five years of service with the Sanitary Train of the old Missouri 3rd Regiment, National Guard.

James Arthur Maloney: (American Legion Post 93')

American Legion Post No. 93 is named after James Arthur Maloney, who died from accidental drowning on June 13, 1917, only nine weeks after the United States entered the war. He was 19 years old.

Inducted in Kansas City a year earlier on May 15, 1916, he served in Company F of the 3rd Regiment, Missouri National Guard, the same regiment in which Sgt. Major Roswell Barry Sayre and Major Murray Davis served and that later was merged with the 6th Missouri to form the 140th Infantry, 35th Division.

James was born in Shelhart, Texas, and his family moved with his father, John Maloney, to Kansas City, where James worked at the Kansas City Power and Light Company[130] and lived at 4100 Michigan. His friend Louis Stinger, a resident of Illinois, was notified of his death as next-of-kin.[131] James Arthur Maloney is buried at Mount St. Mary's Cemetery in Kansas City[132] and is memorialized in the American Legion I monument in Budd Park Esplanade, on the Meyer Circle Gateway plaques, and in Memory Hall of the Liberty Memorial in Kansas City. American Legion Post No. 93 took his name as their official designation.

Sgt. Major Roswell Barry Sayre:
"Not the Son-in-law of President Wilson"

Another soldier in Major Davis' 3rd Battalion was, like Major Davis, a member of Kansas City's legal profession. Roswell B. Sayre became a protégé of Murray Davis and served as 3rd Battalion sergeant major. Unit Chaplain and historian 1st Lt. Evan A. Edwards describes what happened as the 3rd Battalion lost half of its men, including its major and its sergeant major. In one of the supreme ironies of war, the citizens of Ferguson, Missouri, Roswell B. Sayre's hometown, learned of his death in the evening edition of The St. Louis Post-Dispatch, the evening of the day the Armistice was signed, ending the war.

Roswell Barry Sayre attended the Kansas City School of Law at night and graduated with his law degree at the age of 27 in 1914, the first year of the war in Europe. That year, his resemblance to Woodrow Wilson prompted the editors of the law school yearbook to acknowledge that Sayre was, in fact, "Not the son-in-law of Pres. Wilson." Four years later, Roswell Sayre was the subject of a much more serious tribute.

On Saturday, November 16, 1918, Mr. Frank Hagerman rose to speak to members of the Jackson County Bar Association who had gathered at the United States Court House in Kansas City to memorialize those of their profession who, in the words of the special program printed in their tribute, "gave their lives in the service of their country in the war with Germany."[134] Frank Hagerman announced that he wanted to pay

Roswell Barry Sayre, "Not the son-in-law of Pres. Wilson."[133]

special tribute to Roswell B. Sayre, whom he knew very well and whom he regarded as the public face that Hagerman's law office had depended upon so much. Responding to an introduction from the President of the Jackson County Bar, Mr. Hagerman said, "Mr. President, you never spoke more truly than when you said there was not a human being that opened the door of my office, but was met with polite courteous treatment. Every member of the Bar who knew anything of him thought most kindly of Roswell B. Sayre."[135]

In addition to the tribute to Sgt. Major Sayre, similar tributes were also paid that day by Mr. Hagerman and others to Major Murray Davis, 1st Lt. Frank Stauver, Major William J. Bland, 2st Lt. Harry Herrod, 1st Lt Carl W. Haner, Pvt. William T. Law, and Pvt. Lawrence W. Fulton – all members of the law profession, all from Kansas City, all of whom had lost their lives in the service of their country, and all of whose names would later appear engraved for the public to see on two of the city's war monuments. The first is the 1930 Meyer Circle Gateway – Avenue of Trees at Myer Circle and Ward Parkway, close to the site of Camp Nichols where Sayre's unit had trained. The names of the eight members of the Kansas City Bar appear with another 433 names of the Kansas City men and one woman who lost their lives in the war.

The eight names also appeared in a drinking fountain that the Kansas City Bar Association had erected in the lobby of the old courthouse at Missouri and Oak at a cost of $2,000 in 1921. A panel of Tennessee marble three feet high and three-and-one-half feet wide was affixed to the lobby wall and bore the names of the eight Bar members on a bronze relief panel. A standing figure in uniform with a rifle in his right hand and a law book under his left completed the memorial. The plans to move the fountain to the new courthouse at 12th and Oak never materialized when the old courthouse was torn down, and the monument with its inoperable drinking fountain has since been lost.

Kansas City Bar Association Fountain[136]

But on that Saturday in the same federal courthouse in Kansas City, just five days after the Armistice had ended hostilities, grief was still fresh – the oral tributes, surviving memories of service to profession and country. Mr. Hagerman keenly felt the loss of his colleague, almost as if Sgt. Major Sayre were his own son.

"Here is a boy," Mr. Hagerman continued, "who was left with no mother, no sister, no brother, and a lone father down at Ferguson, Missouri. He went out at his country's call. He was a good man." Mr. Hagerman impressed upon his listeners that one point in particular. Like his professional peers, Roswell B. Sayre was dedicated to service, but unlike the rest, no one was left to mourn for him but an aging father who lived alone in Ferguson, Missouri.

There just a few weeks earlier, Thomas D. Sayre, an agent for the Wabash Railroad, had received official notice that his son, Roswell, had been killed in action six weeks prior, on September 28, 1918. Thomas was not yet 60 years old, and Roswell, his only child, half that age.

Only a year-and-a-half before, on May 16, 1917, in Kansas City, Roswell had been inducted[137] into the Missouri National Guard's Third Infantry Regiment under the command of Colonel Philip J. Kealy.[138] Their armory was at 39th and Main in Kansas City,[139] and after their unit had been mustered into federal service on March 26, 1917, they went into training at Camp Nichols, 63rd and Ward Parkway, Kansas City. On October 13, 1917, the Third Infantry departed Camp Nichols for Camp Doniphan, Fort Sill, Oklahoma, and joined with the Sixth Missouri to become the 140th Infantry, 35th Division.

"Colonel Kealy, then of the 3rd Regiment, took him under his wing," Mr. Hagerman remembered, "and later when the call came to go to war, he wanted Sayre to go with him. Afterwards in the physical examination, Colonel Kealy was incapacitated and it fell to his lot and that of Sayre, to say that this boy should associate himself with Major Davis, his close intimate friend. The boy fell in action. He was Sergeant Major, and his Major fell with him."[140]

Sayre had gone overseas with his unit on April 25, 1918. On May 19, 1918, he earned the rank of Battalion Sergeant Major, Headquarters Company, 140th Infantry.[141] Five months later, he was killed in action on the third day of the Meuse-Argonne offensive.[142]

First Lt. Evan A. Edwards, Chaplain of the 140th, was eye-witness to the action on Saturday, September 28, 1918, the day Sergeant Major Sayre died along with half of his 3rd Battalion, while its severely wounded commander and Sayer's friend and fellow lawyer, Major Murray Davis, barely hung on, joining the dead of his battalion the next day.

"The Third Day, Saturday, September 28th"

"The dawning of the third day found the 140th lying in fairly regular formation northeast of Baulny and north of Charpentry. It was cold, and a keen, biting fine rain drove in our faces.

"We had swung to the left, or west, and the 91st was not quite up with us, while there was a wide space between them and our right. The 28th was held up, and had as yet failed to cross the Aire. Enemy batteries in Apremont were able to sweep our flank, and from the woods beyond, heavy artillery played upon us.

"The 129th F.A. [Field Artillery] had moved its second battalion in front of Cheppy Friday afternoon and the first battalion entered Charpentry under fire at 10:30 Saturday morning. The 128th was in position just west of Very, while the 155s of the 130th were in position at Varennes. They gave what support they could on this day. Our front had swung to the west so far that a flanking fire might easily seem to be short fire from our own guns …

"At half past three in the morning orders were received from the Brigade Adjutant to push forward with all speed and protect the right flank of the troops on our left, the 69th brigade which was to attack at 6:30. The tired men advanced, starting at 5:30 in the following order: Mabrey's battalion with a company from the 130 M.G. [Machine Gun] Battalion, Murray Davis and the third battalion with another company from the 130 M.G. Bn., [and] the Headquarters Command Group with the second battalion …

"At about eight the line was held up, the fire becoming so heavy that the men dug in and waited. At 8:20 a patrol of Cavalry reported, and about 9:45 the tanks came up, about twenty of them, and the attack was launched under terrific fire from the enemy. Through the draws, over the hillocks, through the dense brush and woods the men lost heavily. The regiment passed Chaudron Farm, reaching Montrebeau woods. There was little support from the Artillery, while the enemy planes were very active. It was

189

a grueling hour. The enemy artillery overwhelmed us with direct, indirect, and flanking fire. Planes with machine guns and bombs cut down on us from the sky. The losses were terrible, and when the regiment rested for the night in Montrebeau Wood, with the second battalion in the hedge north of Chaudron Farm as reserve, it was badly cut to pieces. The third battalion had lost half its men.

Sgt. Major Roswell B. Sayre, 3rd Battalion, 140th Infantry, Killed in Action Sept 28th, 1918.[143]

"Murray Davis was wounded but refused to pay any attention to it. But in the driving rain the men held firm. We had won a little over a mile—a costly mile. And every yard of the way was spotted with crimson."[144]

Citizens in Ferguson, Missouri, near St. Louis, learned of Roswell Sayre's death in the Monday evening edition of *The St. Louis Post Dispatch* the day the Armistice was signed. The notice was included with the report of casualties for the 138th Infantry, the St. Louis National Guard regiment.[145]

Roswell Barry Sayre is buried in Chapel Grove Cemetery, one mile south of Clark, Missouri, where he was born on May 5, 1887.[146] He was an officer candidate at the time of his death, only 31 years old.

Sgt. Major Roswell B. Sayre, 3rd Bn. Killed in Action Sept 28th, 1918.[147]

Captain Arly Luther Hedrick: Bridge-Builder of the 110th (Hedrick / Shackleton American Legion Posts 146 and 120)

Like a number of other Kansas City professional and business men, and the namesake for another American Legion post, Arly Luther Hedrick wanted to form a unit comprised of men he knew and who practiced his same profession. He was an engineer and recruited fellow engineers to serve in the war. His regiment, the 110th Engineers, formed the resistance line largely responsible for saving the tattered and scattered units of the 35th Division as they gathered behind it for protection, regrouped, and continued the fight. Cpt. Arly Hedrick performed an extraordinary feat of courage and survived, only to succumb to disease just a few days before he was to embark for home.

Arly Luther Hedrick, an engineer, recruited men for a unit of engineers to serve in the war. He was commissioned Captain on July 30, 1917, and he and his unit were inducted into military service as Company A, Missouri Engineers, on August 5, 1917. They were stationed at Camp Doniphan, Fort Sill, Oklahoma, until September 1, 1917. There his company was joined with two other companies of Missouri engineers and consolidated with three companies from Kansas to become the 110th Engineers, 35th Division. He was made Captain of Company D, 2nd Battalion, and a month before his regiment, he was sent overseas for training, sailing for France on March 24, 1918.[148] The 110th Engineers spent two months from July 8 to September 2, 1918,[149] digging tunnels and doing road work in the Gerardmer Sector of the Vosges mountains in France before becoming engaged in more intense hostilities, the most

Insignia of the 110th Engineers.[151]

severe of which was the Battle of the Meuse-Argonne, September 26 to October 1, 1918.

During the battle, the Engineers were charged with a critical responsibility: They were "to construct and connect roads across No Man's Land," "to provide road material for the one-way-up-lanes in which to move ammunition and artillery forward," and to assist wheeled traffic and clear the roads to keep the traffic moving.[150] Their work included creating critical signage along the roads to warn other units of local conditions, especially about the safety of drinking the water from area rivers and creeks ("GOOD," "BAD," and "POISONED").

At 5:30 a.m. on September 26, the Battle of the Meuse-Argonne began with a step barrage "advancing one hundred metres each four minutes, eighty-two feet per minute, closing two hours later near the Varennes—

Cheppy road."[152] By 9:00 a.m. to the south, Captain Hedrick was less than a half kilometer from Boureuilles, expecting to complete road work to there by 10:30 a.m., but anticipating a great amount of work on the road through the village itself, "as it is all shot up," he reported.[153] By the end of the day, "the 2nd Battalion of which he was a part had cleared Boureuilles, working slowly east and north."[154]

At 6:35 the next morning, Hedrick received orders to inspect the bridge at Varennes[155] and then to liaison with 1st Battalion commander Cpt. Orlin Hudson, who was receiving bridge construction material at Cheppy. Ten minutes later, Hedrick was busy repairing the bridge near Cheppy so that it would carry the big guns needed in the fight.[156] At 9:30, Hedrick reported from the bridge that Lt. Luther Tillotson's Company A had passed his position to rejoin the rest of the 1st Battalion, which was then making slow progress. Hedrick also reported that although there was very little artillery fire, the liaison with the advance infantry was not working,[157] and the two battalions of the 110th Engineers were forced to alternate periods of roadwork with digging themselves into fox holes for protection from shell fire out of the heights of the Argonne Forrest.

The acting regimental adjutant, Cpt. Edward Rankin, reported, "On the 27th, the 2nd Battalion spread along the road toward Very, returning at night to bivouac in Cheppy. On

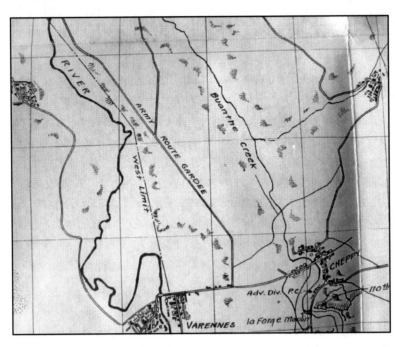
Detailed map showing Varennes and Cheppy.[158]

the 28th it resumed this work through Very toward Charpentry, touching the 1st Battalion early in the evening. Mud was removed from the rock road-base, and shell holes filled in as they bubbled up. The battalions attracted fire, which made more work, which drew more fire, in a round that ceased only at dark. Corps engineers reached Cheppy, but none advanced beyond until we moved up again."[159]

During their advance, while reconnoitering for mined bridges with a small detail of men not far from Baulny, Cpt. Hedrick learned that a masonry bridge some distance ahead was covered by enemy machine gun fire. The Germans had mined the bridge with heavy explosives ready to be detonated as soon as the Americans attempted to cross. Someone had to remove the detonators.

Cpt. Hedrick placed his detail under cover and said that he would disarm the detonators himself. Immediately, five sergeants volunteered to accompany him. Reaching for his binoculars, he surveyed the 300 yards from their position to the bridge. A fellow officer of Company D later recalled, "The Germans were so close that even their heavy artillery was 'sniping.' It seemed as if shells were dropping on every square yard of the area. Geysers of earth shot up in every part of the surface."[160] Lowering the binoculars, Cpt. Hedrick turned to the sergeants and said,

"'No. One man might get through. A half dozen of us would be too good a target.'"[161]

So he went it alone, under constant exposure to enemy fire. He reached the bridge, disconnected every detonator, and returned over open ground – unharmed. For his unselfish bravery he was awarded the Distinguished Service Cross.[162]

Now other units could safely cross the bridge, but at that particular point in the battle, the infantry units of the 35th Division had taken severe losses, and on the night of September 28, the 110th Engineers were called upon to act as reserve infantry while the Division regrouped.[163] The First Army Chief of Staff later reported, "after September 27th the [35th] Division was one in name only, as maneuvering power with intact units, except the Engineers, ceased to exist," although the Chief of Staff Brig. Gen. Hugh A. Drum added, "the fighting spirit and bravery of officers and men was excellent."[164]

By 9 a.m. the next morning, Cpt. Hedrick's front platoons had reached the south edge of Montrebeau Wood near Chaudron Farm and extended to the main highway opposite Apremont.[165] Hedrick reported, "I supervised the organization and protection of the extreme left flank, which I found unprotected, with about one and one-half platoons under my direct command, the balance of the men being on my right under Lieutenant Frank E. Lewis with the exception of one platoon which was ordered to report to Captain Rouse."[166]

At noon, the Engineers were ordered to

Detailed map showing Charpentry, Baulny, Apremont, L'Esperance, and Chaudron Farm.[170]

prepare a defensive position two kilometers behind the Chaudron Farm Road, one kilometer north of Baulny.[167] There, equipped with rifles and grenades, the two battalions of the 110th Engineers suddenly became infantry. The battalions joined what was left of Cpt. Harry Thompson's 138th Infantry. Together they held the line as remnants of various other infantry regiments of the 35th Division retired across the Chaudron Farm road[168] and back through the 110th's and the 138th's defensive position.

The 110th's "Col. Edward M. Stayton and his officers and non-commissioned officers rounded up and faced-about tired, leaderless groups, put them in place and encouraged them in every way possible."[169] The 110th Engineers and the 138th Infantry had established protection and restored order, but the 110th took its greatest number of casualties during those hours around noon.[170]

The next day, September 30, at about 8:30, the Germans came out of Montrebeau Wood on the attack: Shell-fire opened up with great force on the forward slope and machine gun fire 1,000 yards from the 110th. Captain Rankin described what happened next: "Our own artillery barrage broke at once on the south edge of Montrebeau and in the open adjacent to the wood. It was comprehensive in disposition and gratifying in severity. It seemed to me to be much heavier than we were encountering."[172] The Germans were repulsed.

At 1:00 p.m., Cpt. Hedrick sent a comprehensive report from his position on the extreme left flank down by the Aire River:

"'Everything O.K. on left flank. Machine guns and personnel intact. Only slight shelling. Think from information on hand that Captain Schrantz [C.O. of 128th Machine Gun Battalion] received rumor infantry had withdrawn, leaving machine guns in front line unprotected. A detail from my company was relieved at 11:00 a.m. by another detail from my company their duty being to guard the most advanced machine guns. They report everything O.K. On their sector I have now 25 men guarding 3 machine guns on my flank. Will make every effort to increase this from those missing from their organization. Will notify you at once in writing if conditions change."[173]

Finally, early on the morning of October 1, the 2nd Engineer Battalion was relieved, filtering back one man at a time to Baulny, marching to Charpentry, and arriving in Cheppy by early morning.[174] The Engineers then deployed to a rest area four days to the south, and there received replacements, equipment, and transport animals. Two weeks later, the Division Commander wrote to Major General W. C. Langfitt, Chief Engineer, A.E.F., praising the work of the 110th: "The 110th Engineers has done fine work, not only as Engineers but as Infantry as well. When on September 29th I had everything in the line, I had to use the 110th Engineers as Reserve, and finally had to establish them in line to enable disorganized troops to fall back behind them, thus causing the Engineers to occupy what became my advanced line, which they held for two days and during which they repelled two determined counter-attacks of the enemy."[175]

From October 15 to November 7, the 110th was assigned engineer duties in the Sommedieue east of the Meuse. Then came the Armistice. "Withdrawn from this position several days before November 11th," Cpt. Rankin recalled, "we passed the first Armistice Day in secluded villages where *vin ordinaire* and a bit of talk to the accompaniment of church bells sufficed for the great moment. We were close enough to the front to *hear the silence* of 11:00 o'clock, to be quite unaware of the revelry which followed the news across the world."[176]

The Engineers spent the next five months salvaging German materiel from the St. Mihiel salient, policing the 35th Divisional area in the Meuse Valley, and engaging in drill and classes. They took part in entertainment and athletic programs as a respite from their work with construction and maintenance at the embarkation Camp Pontenezen near Brest, France. Finally, in February 1919, they entrained for the port of Brest. Then on February 10, just prior to the unit's arrival in Brest, Captain Arly Hedrick contracted what first appeared to be a slight cold. His lungs had, perhaps, been weakened by exposure to gas during the Argonne.[177] Then he entered the hospital on February 19 with what proved to be a case of spinal meningitis.[178] There at Camp Pontenezen on March 5, 1919, he died of cerebro-spinal meningitis. He was 29 years old.[179]

Captain Rankin concludes his recollections of the part the 110th Engineers played in the Battle of the Meuse-Argonne by attempting to express – with the precision typical of an engineer – the severity of fire the regiment took that noontime on Chaudron Farm: "There were surely not many guns trained upon us at any one time, perhaps not over two batteries, but the fire was steady in its application and vicious in its accuracy. The enemy had full observation on us from several sides: from the Argonne Forest crest and from Montrefagne, each two and a half miles distant and about one hundred twenty-five feet higher than our hilltop on the farm; from Hill 269, three miles directly north of us and two hundred twenty feet higher than our position.

"Our division lost most heavily, during the first four days of battle, of all nine divisions engaged in the initial attack, ours being the fourth division to be relieved. Our 110th Engineer losses were very much greater, proportional to the time we were engaged, than our divisional infantry losses."[180] Ironically, Captain Hedrick survived those losses only to fall to disease just a few days before his regiment embarked to come home. He had been recommended to receive his commission as Major, but died before he could accept the promotion. He left his wife, Geraldine Olive, and 5-year-old daughter, Mary Adeline, in mourning.

On April 6, 1919, a month after Cpt. Hedrick's death and exactly two years from the date America entered the war, during a presentation of battle and sector ribbons conducted in a fenced field near where Cpt. Hedrick died at Camp Pontenezen, Cpt. Arly L. Hedrick received a posthumous award of the Distinguished Service Cross.[181]

Photo courtesy National World War I Museum Archives.

Cpt. Arly L. Hedrick.

In Memory Hall at the Kansas City Liberty Memorial in 1926 and also at the Meyer Circle Gateway Avenue of Trees in Kansas City in 1930, Cpt. Hedrick's name appears on plaques commemorating the 441 dead Kansas City lost in the war.

But it was in 1927 that Cpt. Hedrick received an especially unique tribute. On June 30, the Kansas City Park Board accepted a proposal from H. E. Barker and Son to erect – for $160.00 at their expense – a bronze tablet on the 542-foot concrete bridge carrying 27th Street over Vine. The bridge had been designed by Arly Hedrick, who had entered Yale University at the age of 14, graduating from there in 1908, the youngest of anyone graduating from Yale. He embarked on an engineering career that included a B.S. degree in Civil Engineering in 1912 and later the degree of Civil Engineer – both from the University of Wisconsin.

Hedrick had served as assistant resident engineer on a reinforced concrete bridge in

Cedar Rapids, Iowa, and had conducted surveys for the Dallas-Oak Cliff Viaduct in Dallas, Texas. He also assisted in the design of a reinforced concrete bridge across the Kaw River in Lawrence, Kansas, and served as resident engineer during the foundation work.[182] "He resigned from this position to assume a partnership with his father under the firm name of Hedrick & Hedrick, Consulting Engineers."[183] It was at that time that he designed the bridge at 27th and Vine.

The memorial plaque affixed to it read:

"CAPTAIN ARLEY LUTHER HEDRICK
110TH ENGINEERS

Designer of this structure, which was his last important work before going overseas. He died in Brest, France, on the sixth day of March 1919 and was posthumously awarded the distinguished service cross for extraordinary bravery in the battle of the Argonne Forest."[184]

The plaque remained on the bridge until the bridge was dismantled in 2005. Now the whereabouts of the plaque is unknown, but Captain Arly Luther Hedrick's service is not forgotten. His name appears with another casualty of the 110th Engineers, Sgt. Fred J. Shackleton, in the hyphenated form of "Hedrick-Shackleton," as one of 12 American Legion posts listed on the American Legion I Monument at Van Brunt and Anderson. He is buried in Mt. Washington Cemetery, Kansas City.[185]

1st Sgt. Frederick James Shackelton: Holding the Line (Hedrick / Shackleton American Legion Posts No. 146 and 120)

Frederick J. Shackelton was born in Cornell, Livingston County, Illinois, in June 1889, the son of Fred W. Shackelton and Lucy A. Gates. He moved to Kansas City with his family and worked for the Daley Motor Company.[186]

Inducted into the Army in Kansas City, Kansas, on June 3, 1918,[187] he was assigned to the Kansas Engineers Battalion, which was joined with engineer companies from Missouri to form the 110th Engineers, 35th Division. Shackelton served in Company C, 1st Battalion, under Cpt. Orlin Hudson.[188] On May 3, 1917, he married Lottie K. Noel, age 23, in Jackson County, Missouri.

He went overseas with his unit on May 2, 1918, and was made a sergeant on September 15, 1918. On the night of September 28, the 110th Engineers were called upon to act as reserve infantry while the 35th Division, which had taken heavy casualties during the first two days of the Meuse-Argonne offensive, regrouped.[189] At noon on September 29, the Engineers took up a defensive position two kilometers behind the Chaudron Farm Road, one kilometer north of Baulny.[190] There, equipped with rifles and grenades, the two battalions of the 110th Engineers joined the remnants of Cpt. Thompson's 138th Infantry. Together they held the line as remnants of various other infantry regiments of the 35th Division retired across the Chaudron Farm Road and back through the 110th's and the 138th's defensive position.[191]

The 110th's "Col. Stayton and his officers and non-commissioned officers rounded up and faced-about tired, leaderless groups, put them in place and encouraged them in every way possible."[192] The 110th Engineers and the 138th Infantry had established protection and restored order, but the 110th took its greatest number of casualties during those hours around noon.[193] Among those casualties was 1st Sgt. Fred James Shackelton. Just two weeks after his promotion, he died in combat in the Battle of the Meuse-Argonne near Baulny, France.

At the time of his death, his wife, Lottie K. Shackelton, resided at 3622 Chestnut in Kansas City, Missouri. Three years later, on September 30, 1921, she married another veteran of the Great War, Kansas City University medical student Earl T. Shepley, age 37.

First Sgt. Fred James Shackleton is buried in the Meuse-Argonne American Cemetery, Plot A, Row 3, Grave 37, Romagne, France.[194] He is also memorialized in Cornell Cemetery, Livingston County, Illinois, along with two of his children, Eula (1900) and Lola (1906), both of whom died in infancy.

American Legion Post 146 was named for 1st Sgt. Shackelton.[195] Later, American Legion Post 120 was created and named Hedrick/Shackelton Post 120 for Cpt. Arly L. Hedrick and Sgt. Fred J. Shackelton, both of the 110th Engineers.

Photos courtesy Library of Congress

Details of 27th Street bridge over Vine Street designed by Arly Hedrick.

Pvt. Robert Thomas Clements:
"He Wanted to Get Back There Again"
(Robert Clements American Legion Post)[196]

The importance of the bonds men formed before, during, and after the war is emphasized yet again by the story of Private Robert T. Clements, a member of Battery F, 2nd Regiment, Missouri Field Artillery, comprised of Kansas City men and commanded by Harry S. Truman, who served as 1st Lieutenant. Its St. Louis complement, the 1st Regiment of Missouri Field Artillery, was understaffed. So a number of men from Truman's Battery F, including Private Clements, were transferred to the St. Louis unit and became known as the "Orphan Battery." Private Clements suffered the breaking of bonds with his old unit but gradually adapted, as did his mother, Mary B. Clements, whose poetic tribute to her son reflects th-bond she had with him.

As recruitment gained momentum during the spring and fall of 1917, many Kansas City men enlisted together to continue in military service the strong attachments that they had formed during civilian life. Such attachments were essential to the morale of the units and sustained the men as they left behind their families, their work, and all else that was familiar to them. Cpt. Leslie L. Bucklew, commander of Battery E. of the 128th Field Artillery, 35th Division recalled this attachment some 50 years later. The 128th Field Artillery was comprised of the old 1st Regiment of Missouri National Guard, almost all from St. Louis. Its complement, the 129th Field Artillery, was comprised of men from the other side of the state, the old 2nd Regiment of Missouri National Guard from Kansas City and Independence.

Because recruitment for the field artillery had slowed in St. Louis, Cpt. Bucklew had been asked by Col. Frank Rumbold, who commanded the St. Louis men of the 1st Regiment, to raise a battery of men from Kansas

City that would be joined with other batteries of the 1st to fill out its strength. Cpt. Bucklew did so, and his battery became known as the "Orphan Battery" because it was the only unit of the 1st Regiment that was *not* made up of boys from St. Louis.[197]

"The [standard] battery strength was something over 200," Cpt. Bucklew remembered, "but we had organized and come down [to Camp Doniphan, Ft. Sill, Oklahoma] quickly, and we had only about 165."[198] "The others were still back recruiting. When they came, they had full strength, and there were some that were transferred to my battery. I remember some of them that didn't want to come. They had their friends in there."

To bring the 128th up to field strength, higher command had ordered transfers from another Kansas City field artillery unit in a whole other regiment, Battery F of the 1st Missouri Field Artillery, where Harry S. Truman served as 1st Lieutenant. On one occasion, Cpt. Bucklew mentioned to Lt. Truman "a small incident in the handling of the troops" during the transfer of men from Battery F to Bucklew's Battery E. The forced change of regiments sometimes created a good deal of stress for the individual man.

"There was one young fellow," said Bucklew, "that felt just so bad about it [the transfer] because he didn't want to leave Truman and he wanted to get back there again, but I couldn't do it, because this all came through from up above."[199] The young fellow's name was Robert Clements.

He was inducted in Kansas City on July 26, 1917,[200] and his transfer from Battery F of the 2nd Regiment into Battery E of the 1st Regiment was made official that same day. From that point on, Robert T. Clements was a part of the 128th Field Artillery. Although reluctant to make the change, Clements did so and eventually "fitted in very well with these fellows," Bucklew observed.

Clements was made a private in September 1917. He went overseas with his unit on March 30, 1918, and was with it for seven months when the Battle of the Argonne began on September 26, 1918. On the second day of battle, September 27, 1918, working as a courier delivering messages along the line, Robert T. Clements was wounded and died.

As next-of-kin, Robert's mother, Mrs. Mary B. Clements, 2805 Gillham Road, was notified of her son's death. His body was returned to Kansas City and brought to its final resting place at Mount Washington Cemetery.[201] He was 24 years old.[202]

In tribute to her son, Mary Clements wrote:

God gave my son in trust to me.
Christ died for him and he should be
A man for Christ. He was his own,
And God's and man's; not mine alone;
He was not mine to give. He gave
Himself that he might help to save
All that a Christian should revere,
All that enlightened men hold dear.

"He did not come!" you say
Oh well! My sky is just more gray,
But thru clouds the sun will shine
And vital memories [will] be mine.
God's test of manhood is, I know,
Not "Will he come?" but "Did he go?"

My son well knew that he might die,
And yet he went with purpose high,
To fight for peace and overthrow
The plans of Christ's relentless foe.
He dreaded not the battle field;
He went to make fierce vandals yield.
(barbarians)

And when the war was over, when
His gallant comrades came home,
I cheered them as they marched by
Rejoicing that they did not die.
And when his vacant place I see
My heart bounds with joy that he
*Was mine so long—my fair young
Son, and cheer for him whose
Work is done.*

*--A Gold Star Mother
M. B. C [Mary B. Clements]*[203]

Robert T. Clements was also remembered by the men with whom he served. In further tribute to him, an American Legion post took his name for its official designation.[204] The post was one of 13 functioning in Kansas City when the reburials from France occurred during 1920-1921. Clements' name is listed on the plaques on the west wall of Memory Hall at the Liberty Memorial and on the Meyer Circle Gateway plaques at Ward Parkway and Meyer Boulevard. His name also remained in the memory of his Captain, Leslie L. Bucklew, who, after 53 years, had never forgotten the loyalty his Private Robert T. Clements had to Lieutenant Harry S. Truman and to the old outfit of Battery F, 2nd Regiment, Missouri National Guard.

Pvt. William T. Law: Legal Aspirant, Officer Candidate, and Bridegroom

One of three enlisted men whose name appeared on the bronze plaque of the 1921 Kansas City Bar Association Fountain,[205] William T. Law, appropriately enough, wanted to study law. To that end, he worked for John G. Paxton for four or five years. But instead of going into law, he was inducted into the service in Kansas City on October 31, 1918.[206] He joined the 16th Observation Battery, Field Artillery, just 11 days before the Armistice brought the war to a close, and he died the day after the Armistice, November 12, 1918, a victim of lubar pneumonia.

"He was as much a sacrifice to the call of his country as if he had died in battle," Paxton said in a memorial tribute addressed to the Kansas City Bar Association just four days later on November 16, 1918. "He had toiled through poverty and difficulties, now happy in his marriage and prospects, in sight of the celestial city, and surrounded by the delectable mountains, he was stricken. It is sad, indeed, to contemplate a tragedy and the dedication of so young a life with so much that was sweet and beautiful before it," Paxton concluded.[207]

Born on August 28, 1885, in Virginia, William Law was just 33 years old, newly married only 10 days, when he was stricken and died at Camp Taylor, Kentucky. He was an officer candidate.[208] His wife, Mary H. Law, 3552 Broadway, Kansas City, was notified as next-of-kin.

Pvt. Grover Metzger: Stockman, Officer Candidate, and Bridegroom (Grover Metzger American Legion Post No. 224)

By the time the war ended in November, 1918, influenza had taken more lives than the conflict itself had taken. Private Grover Metzger was one of those casualties. He was an officer candidate at the time of his death.[209]

Born on February 10, 1889, and inducted into the Army at the age of 29 in Kansas City on July 22, 1918,[210] Grover Metzger served in the Supply Company of the 29th Field Artillery until he died of pneumonia at Camp Funston, Fort Riley, Kansas, on October 7, 1918.

Notified as next-of-kin was his 25-year old bride, Ruth A. Metzger, neé Christopher, a native of Milford, Kansas, just west of Fort Riley. She and Grover had been married in Kansas City on July 13, 1918, only nine days before he entered military service. The couple made their home at 2915 East 28th Street in Kansas City.

Before he entered the service, Grover worked as a livestock trader. He was part owner of Metzger Brothers, located in 602 of the Live Stock Exchange building in the city's west bottoms. His father, 66-year old Simon Metzger (1851-1923), who had emigrated from France in 1872[211] was a butcher who also owned his own shop. Grover and his brother Lester, five years older, had grown up in the livestock business.

Besides his wife, his father, and his brother, Grover left his mother, Fannie Wolf Metzger (1858-1929), 58 years old, also a native of France, and his sister Sylvia, who was three years older than Grover. He is buried along with his parents at Elmwood Cemetery in Kansas City,[212] and his name appears both on the American Legion I Monument at Budd Park Esplanade and on the Meyer Circle Gateway Plaques as well as in Memory Hall at Liberty Memorial in Kansas City. Thirteen months after Grover Metzger's death, in December, 1919, American Legion Post No. 224 was named after him.[213]

2nd Lt. Harry W. Herrod: Lawyer and Infantryman

Another former member of the Jackson County Bar and former practicing lawyer in Kansas City was Harry W. Herrod, a 2st lieutenant, who was mustered out of the service with 100 percent disability on October 5, 1920. Two months later, in December 1920, Lt. Herrod died of tuberculosis. His next-of-kin was his mother, Mrs. Pearl Herrod, 1729 Pearl, Joplin, Missouri.[214]

Born in Webb City, Missouri, on October 17, 1895, Harry Herrod was inducted into the Army on November 27, 1917, and served as a 2nd lieutenant with the 11th Infantry. He served overseas from January 4, 1918 to July 14, 1918.[215]

Prior to his service, Lieutenant Herrod was a lawyer with the firm of Nourse and Bell in the Gloyd Building. His name is not included on the plaques at the Meyer Circle Gateway Avenue of Trees or at Memory Hall, Liberty Memorial, most likely because he died after having been mustered out of service. However, the 100 percent disability recognizes that his death was service-related, a fact recognized by the Jackson County Bar Association, who placed his name on their memorial fountain.[216]

Victory and Democracy, *Kansas City Star.* **Christmas, 1918.**

Endnotes

1   National Park Service, U.S. Department of the Interior. "Santa Fe National Historic Trail," in *National Trails System Map and Guide* brochure. (Washington, D.C.: Government Printing Office, 1993.)

2   Mark Simmons. *Following the Santa Fe Trail: A Guide for Modern Travelers.* (Santa Fe, NM: Ancient City Press, 1986), p. 59.

3   Clair Kenamore. *From Vauquois Hill to Exermont: A History of the 35th Division.* (St. Louis, MO: Guard Publishing, Co., 1919), p. 20.

4   Clair Kenamore. "Took Exermont!" *The Kansas City Star*, April 13, 1919, p. 16 A. Copyright 1919, Pulitzer Publishing Company, *The St. Louis Post-Dispatch.*

5   Edward P. Rankin, Jr.. *The Santa Fe Trail Leads to France.* (Kansas City, MO: Dick Richardson Company, 1933), p. vii.

6   "Arm Mark Tells Division." *The Kansas City Star*, February 10, 1919, p. 16.

7   Charles B. Hoyt. *Heroes of the Argonne: An Authentic History of the Thirty-fifth Division.* (Kansas City, MO: Franklin Hudson Publishing Company, 1919), p. 10. See also William M. Wright. *Meuse-Argonne Diary: A Division Commander in World War I.* (Robert H. Ferrell, ed. Columbia, MO: University of Missouri Press, 2004.)

8   "Changes in the Commands of Thirty-fifth Divison." *The Kansas City Star*, April 13, 1919, p. 16A.

9   Clair Kenamore. *From Vauquois Hill to Exermont*, op. cit., p. 263.

10   Charles B. Hoyt. *Heroes of the Argonne: An Authentic History of the Thirty-fifth Division*, op. cit, p. 11.

11   Ibid, p. 13.

12   "Changes in the Commands of Thirty-fifth Division," op. cit.

13   Charles B. Hoyt. *Heroes of the Argonne: An Authentic History of the Thirty-fifth Division*, op. cit., p. 13.

14   Clair Kenamore. "Log of the 35th." *The Kansas City Star*, April 7, 1919, p. 2. Copyright 1919, Pulitzer Publishing Company, *The St. Louis Post-Dispatch.*

15   Ibid.

16   Ibid.

17   Clair Kenamore. *From Vauquois Hill to Exermont,* op. cit., p. 333.

18   Clair Kenamore. "Log of the 35th," op. cit.

19   Ibid.

20   "Where the 35th Division Was in Service in France." *The Kansas City Star,* April 7, 1919, p. 2.

21   Clair Kenamore. "Hike Days of the 35th." *The Kansas City Star*, April 8, 1919, p. 8. Copyright 1919, Pulitzer Publishing Company, *The St. Louis Post-Dispatch.*

22   Clair Kenamore. *From Vauquois Hill to Exermont*, op. cit., map facing p. 176.

23   Ibid.

24   Ibid.

25   Pierre Gioan. *Dictionnaire Usuel Quillet Flammarion par le Texte et par L'image.* (Paris: Libraires Quillet-Flammarion, 1957), p. 888. See also Clair Kenamore. "Attack Led by 140th." *The Kansas City Star*, April 10, 1919, pp. 14-15. Copyright 1919, Pulitzer Publishing Company, *The St. Louis Post-Dispatch.*

26   Clair Kenamore. "The 35th Into Battle." *The Kansas City Star*, April 9, 1919, p. 15. Copyright 1919, Pulitzer Publishing Company, *The St. Louis Post-Dispatch.*

27   Clair Kenamore. "Hike Days of the 35th," op. cit.

28   Varennes holds a special place in French history. On June 21, 1791, Louis XVI and Marie Antoinette were stopped by a postmaster's son who recognized the king from his likeness on a coin. The royals were trying to escape the French Revolution, but the King's carriage was turned back towards Paris, where 19 months later the guillotine awaited. See Pierre Gioan. *Dictionnaire Usuel Quillet Flammarion*, op. cit., p. 1405.

29   Clair Kenamore. "The 35th Into Battle," op. cit.

30   Ibid.

31   Ibid.

32   Ibid.

33   Drawing from *The Kansas City Star*, April 10, 1919, p. 14-15.

34   Clair Kenamore. "Attack Led by the 140th," op. cit.

35   Ibid.

36   Clair Kenamore. "A Bloody Third Day." *The Kansas City Star*, April 11, 1919, p. 4. Copyright 1919, Pulitzer Publishing Company, *The St. Louis Post-Dispatch*.

37   Drawing from Clair Kenamore. *From Vauquois Hill to Exermont*, op. cit., p. 197.

38   Clair Kenamore. "A Bloody Third Day," op. cit.

39   Clair Kenamore. "Took Exermont!" op. cit.

40   Ibid.

41   Ibid.

42   Clair Kenamore. *From Vauquois Hill to Exermont*, op. cit., p. 366.

43   Clair Kenamore. "Relief for the 35th." *The Kansas City Star*, April 14, 1919, p. 13. Copyright 1919, Pulitzer Publishing Company, *The St. Louis Post-Dispatch*.

44   Ibid.

45   Ibid.

46   Ibid.

47   Charles B. Hoyt. *Heroes of the Argonne: An Authentic History of the Thirty-fifth*, op. cit., p. 123.

48   Clair Kenamore. *From Vauquois Hill to Exermont*, op. cit., p. 246.

49   Charles B. Hoyt. *Heroes of the Argonne: An Authentic History of the Thirty-fifth*, op. cit., p. 127.

50   Ibid.

51   Clair Kenamore. *From Vauquois Hill to Exermont*, op. cit., p. 247.

52   Charles B. Hoyt. *Heroes of the Argonne: An Authentic History of the Thirty-fifth*, op. cit., p. 135.

53   Ibid, p.136.

54   Clair Kenamore. *From Vauquois Hill to Exermont*, op. cit., p. 248.

55   Charles B. Hoyt. *Heroes of the Argonne: An Authentic History of the Thirty-fifth*, op. cit., p. 139.

56   "Start a Welcome Arch." *The Kansas City Star*, April 8, 1919, p. 2.

57   "The Arch That Will Welcome Service Men As They Emerge from the Union Station." Picture from *The Kansas City Star*, Tuesday, April 8, 1919, p. 2.

58   "Into the Arms of Home." *The Kansas City Star*, Saturday, May 3, 1919, p. 1-2.

59   "The 129th Off for Funston." *The Kansas City Star*, Saturday, May 3, 1919, p. 1.

60   "When the Old Home Town Shouted 'Welcome Boys!'" *The Kansas City Star*, Sunday, May 18, 1919, Editorial Section, page 1C.

61   "Klemm Out of the Parade." *The Kansas City Star*, Sunday, April 27, 1919, p. 3A.

62   D. M. Giangreco. *The Soldier from Independence: A Military Biography of Harry Truman*. (Minneapolis, MN: Zenith Press, 2009), p. 250.

63   "Klemm Out of the Parade," op. cit.

64   Ibid.

65   "The 129th Off for Funston," op. cit.

66   D. M. Giangreco. *The Soldier from Independence: A Military Biography of Harry Truman*, op. cit. p. 106, 121-122.

67   Katherine Baxter, Ed. *Notable Kansas Citians of 1915·1916·1917·1918*. (Kansas City, MO: Kellogg-Baxter Printing, Co, 1925), p. 201.

68   Robert H. Ferrell. *Collapse at Meuse-Argonne: The Failure of the Missouri-Kansas Division*. (Columbia, MO: University of Missouri Press, 2004), p. 109.

69   Ibid, p. 121-122.

70   Robert H. Ferrell. *Collapse at Meuse-Argonne: The Failure of the Missouri-Kansas Division*, op. cit., p. 113.

71   Ibid, p. 109.

72   William Allen White. *The Martial Adventures of Henry and Me*. (New York: Macmillan, 1918), p. 1.

73   Robert H. Ferrell. *Collapse at Meuse-Argonne: The Failure of the Missouri-Kansas Division*, op. cit., p. 112.

74   Ibid, p. 117.

75   Ibid, p. 22, 107.

76   Ibid, p. 129.

77   "Powers and Duties of Secretary of Transportation." Article 10: Naming and Marking of Roads and Bridges, Chapter 68, Roads and Bridges, Part I—Roads. *2009 Kansas Statutes 68-1015. http://kansasstatuteslesterama.org. chapter_68/Article-10/68-1015.html.* Accessed by the author on January 18, 2013.

78   "The Purple Heart Trail." Miami County, Kansas Economic Development Website, Janet M. Rae, Director. http://www.miamicountyks.org/tourism/historic.html. Accessed by the author on January 18, 2013.

79   "Sanford Brown." Picture from *The Kansas City Star*, Tuesday, November 26, 1918, p. 2.

80   "G. P. Whitsett in Hospital, Wife Hears Kansas Citian Gassed and Wounded is Recovering, Mother says Letters Show Frank R. Jeffords Was Not Killed, as Casualty List Says; Capt Sanford Brown Cited for Heroism." *The Kansas City Star*, Tuesday, November 26, 1918, p. 2.

81   "Missouri State Archives Soldiers' Records: War of 1812 – World War I." Service record for Sanford M. Brown. http://www.sos.mo.gov/archives/soldiers/details.asp. Accessed by the author on January 8, 2012.

82   Date of lodge induction from on-site visit and examination of Ivanhoe Masonic Lodge ledger.

83   "A Memorial To Capt. Sanford M. Brown, Jr., Will Be Dedicated Sunday." *The Kansas City Times*, September 25, 1931, p. 8.

84   "Ivanhoe Temple is Ready." *The Kansas City Star,* November 12, 1922, p. 11A.

85   "The memorial to Capt Sanford M. Brown, Jr., and His Regimental Commander." Pictures of Col. Carl Ristine and of Cpt. Brown's parents, Reverend and Mrs. Sanford M. Brown, from *The Kansas City Times*, September 28, 1931, p. 12.

86   "A Memorial to Capt. Sanford M. Brown, Jr., Will Be Dedicated Sunday," op. cit.

87   "Add to City's Beauty." *The Kansas City Times*, March 7, 1941, p. 2.

88   "Pay Homage to a World War Hero." *The Kansas City Star*, May 30, 1941, p. 2.

89   "A Ceremony in Memory of the World War Dead." *The Kansas City Star*, May 30, 1932, p. 8. See also "Wreaths for the Heroes." *The Kansas City Star,* May 30, 1932, p. 2

90   Ann McFerin. "Sanford Brown." Unpublished manuscript in Kansas City, MO Parks and Recreation Archives, undated.

91   Evan Alexander Edwards. *From Doniphan to Verdun: The Official History of the 140th Infantry.* (Lawrence, KS: The World Company, 1920), p. 249.

92   Ibid, p. 83.

93   Ibid.

94   Otto P. Higgins. "The Blame on the People." *The Kansas City Times*, January 28, 1918, p. 1.

95   Clair Kenamore. *From Vauquois Hill to Exermont.* (St. Louis, MO: Guard Publishing Co., 1919), p. 23. See also "To Try Gen. Donnelly." *The New York Times*, April 26, 1918, http://query.nytimes.com/gst/abstract.html. See also "A Division's 'Lawyer' Overseas." *The Kansas City Star*, June 12, 1918, p. 5.

96   Ibid.

97   Ibid.

98   Photo from Evan Alexander Edwards. *From Doniphan to Verdun: The Official History of the 140th Infantry*, op. cit., p. 80.

99   "Drama in a Hero's Death." *The Kansas City Star*, May 30, 1928, p. 2.

100   Ibid.

101   Suzanne P. Cole. "War Hero's Last Words: 'Take Care of My Men.'" *The Kansas City Star Magazine*, September 26, 2010, p. 3.

102   War Department General Orders No. 59 (1919). http://militarytimes.com/citations-medals-awards/recipient.php?recipientid=11503. Accessed by author on May 14, 2011.

103   "Body of Hero Home." *The Kansas City Times*, October 18, 1921, p. 2. See also Katherine Baxter. *Notable Kansas Citians of 1915·1916·1917·1918*, op. cit., "Major Murray Davis," p. 207-208.

104   Ibid. See also "A Division's 'Lawyer' Overseas." *The Kansas City Star*, June 12, 1918, p. 5.

105   Katherine Baxter, Ed. *Notable Kansas Citians of 1915, 1916, 1917, 1918.* (Kansas City, MO: Kellogg-Baxter Printing Co., 1925), p. 208.

106   "Body of Hero Home." *The Kansas City Times*, op. cit.

107   "Calls All to Honor Hero." *The Kansas City Star,* October 21, 1921, p. 10.

108   Ibid.

109   "Scenes at the Funeral Yesterday of Maj. Murray Davis, Ranking Missouri Casualty in the World War, Buried in Kansas City." *The Kansas City Times,* October 24, 1921, p. 2. See also Missouri Valley Historical Society, *World War Soldiers Dead: Memorial Annals of Kansas City, Missouri.* (Kansas City, MO: Missouri Valley Historical Society, 1926), p. 57.

110   "Davis Escort Entire 3D." *The Kansas City Star,* October 20, 1921, p. 11. See also "Allen to the Davis Funeral." *The Kansas City Times,* October 21, 1921, p. 2.

111   "Calls All to Honor Hero," op. cit.

112   "Final Tribute for Hero." *The Kansas City Times,* October 24, 1921, p. 1. See also "Maj. Davis Funeral Today." *The Kansas City Star,* October 23, 1921, p. 14A. See also "Throngs at the Church." *The Kansas City Times,* October 24, 1921, p. 1-2.

113   "Scenes at the Funeral Yesterday of Maj. Murray Davis, Ranking Missouri Casualty in the World War, Buried in Kansas City," op. cit.

114   Lillie F. Kelsay. *Historic & Dedicatory Monuments of Kansas City.* (Kansas City, MO: Kansas City, Missouri Board of Parks and Recreation Commissioners, 1987), p. 13.

115   "His Heroism to Inspire." *The Kansas City Star,* May 30, 1928, p. 1.

116   *The World Book Encyclopedia,* Vol. 6 (F). (New York: Field Enterprises, Inc., 1954), p. 2493. See also William Rose Benét. *The Reader's Encyclopedia,* Vol. I, 2nd ed. (New York: Thomas Y Crowell Company, 1965), p. 340.

117   Missouri State Archives Soldiers' Records: War of 1812 – World War I. Service record for Joseph Dillon, service number 1,459,481. www.sos.mo.gov/archives/soldiers/details.asp. Accessed by author on February 3, 2012.

118   Evan A. Edwards. *From Doniphan to Verdun: The Official History of the 140th Infantry,* op. cit., p. 250.

119   Military Council, Missouri National Guard. *History of the Missouri National Guard.* (Military Council, Missouri National Guard, November, 1934), p. 54-57.

120   Ibid, p. 60.

121   Ibid, p. 61.

122   Ibid, p. 64.

123   Ibid, p. 65.

124   Ibid, p. 66.

125   Ibid.

126   Ibid, p. 67.

127   Evan A. Edwards. *From Doniphan to Verdun: The Official History of the 140th Infantry,* op. cit., p. 73.

128   Missouri Valley Historical Society. *World War Soldiers Dead,* Vol II, No. 1, op. cit., p. 89.

129   Missouri State Archives Soldiers' Records: War of 1812 – World War I. Service record for Joseph Dillon, Service Number 1,459,481. http://www.sos.mo.gov/archives/soldiers/details.asp. Accessed by the author on February 3, 2012.

130   Missouri Valley Historical Society. *World War Soldiers Dead: Memorial Annals of Kansas City, Missouri,* op. cit., p. 25.

131   Missouri State Archives Soldiers' Records: War of 1812 – World War I. Service record for James A. Maloney. www.sos.mo.gov/archives/soldiers/details.asp. Accessed by author on February 6, 2012.

132   Ibid, p. 57 and 61.

133   *The Pandex: Nineteen Hundred and Fourteen, Volume X.* (Kansas City, MO: Kansas City School of Law Senior Class, 1914), p. 51.

134   *In Memoriam: Addresses Delivered at Memorial Meeting of Kansas City Bar Association,* 1918. (Kansas City, MO: Missouri Valley Room, Kansas City, Missouri Public Library.)

135   Ibid, pp. 25-26.

136   Sherry Piland and Ellen J. Uguccioni. *Fountains of Kansas City: A History and Love Affair.* (Kansas City: City of Fountains Foundation, 1985), p. 130.

137   Missouri State Archives Soldiers' Records: War of 1812 – World War I. Service record for Roswell B. Sayre, Service number 1,458,808. www.sos.mo.gov/archives/soldiers/details.asp. Accessed by the author on January 27, 2012.

138   Military Council Missouri National Guard. *History of the Missouri National Guard,* op. cit., p. 54.

139   Ibid, p 55.

140   *In Memoriam: Addresses Delivered at Memorial Meeting of Kansas City Bar Association*, op. cit., p. 25.

141   Evan A. Edwards. *From Doniphan to Verdun: The Official History of the 140th Infantry.* (Lawrence, KS: The World Company, 1920), p. 233, 237.

142   Missouri State Archives Soldiers' Records: War of 1812 – World War I. Service record for Roswell B. Sayre, op. cit.

143   Evan A. Edwards. *From Doniphan to Verdun: The Official History of the 140th Infantry*, op. cit., p. 74. See also photo in W. M. Haulsee, F. G. Howe, A. C. Doyle. *Soldiers of the Great War: Memorial Edition.* (Washington, D.C.: Soldiers Record Publishing Association, 1920), p. 164.

144   Ibid, p. 67, 68, 77.

145   "3 More Men of the 138th Among Today's List of Dead." *St. Louis Post-Dispatch*, November 11, 1918, p. 2.

146   *Randolph County, Mo. Cemetery Records*, Vol. 3.

147   Evan A. Edwards. *From Doniphan to Verdun: The Official History of the 140th Infantry*, op. cit., p. 74.

148   *Resumé of the Professional Experience of Arly L. Hedrick.* (Kansas City, MO: Kansas City Parks and Recreation Archives, undated.)

149   Edward P. Rankin, Jr. *The Santa Fe Trail Leads to France: A Narrative of Battle Service of the 110th Engineers 35th Division in the Meuse-Argonne Offensive.* (Kansas City, MO: Dick Richardson Company, 1933), p. 1, 37.

150   Ibid, p. 2.

151   Ibid, p. 43.

152   Ibid, p. 7.

153   Ibid, p. 9.

154   Ibid, p. 14.

155   Ibid, p. 17.

156   Ibid.

157   Ibid, p. 18.

158   Map tipped into the inside back cover of Edward P. Rankin, Jr. *The Santa Fe Trail Leads to France*, op. cit.

159   Ibid, p. 20.

160   George Henry Nettleton. *Yale in the World War: Part I.* (New Haven, CT: Yale University Press, 1925), p. 77.

161   Ibid.

162   War Department General Orders No. 59. (1919). Distinguished Service Cross Citation for Arly L. Hedrick. http://militarytimes.com/citations-medals-awards/citation.php?citation=793.

163   Clair Kenamore. *From Vauquois Hill to Exermont*, op. cit., p. 226.

164   Edward P. Rankin, Jr. *The Santa Fe Trail Leads to France: A Narrative of Battle Service of the 110th Engineers 35th Division in the Meuse-Argonne Offensive*, op. cit., p. 21.

165   Ibid, p. 25.

166   Ibid, p. 27.

167   Clair Kenamore. *From Vauquois Hill to Exermont*, op. cit., p. 226.

168   Ibid.

169   Ibid, p. 227.

170   Edward P. Rankin, Jr. *The Santa Fe Trail Leads to France: A Narrative of Battle Service of the 110th Engineers 35th Division in the Meuse-Argonne Offensive*, op. cit., p. 39.

171   Map tipped into the inside back cover of Edward P. Rankin, Jr. *The Santa Fe Trail Leads to France*, op. cit.

172   Ibid, p. 31.

173   Ibid, pp. 31-32.

174   Ibid, p. 35.

175   Ibid, p. 36.

176   Ibid.

177   John Henry Nettleton. *Yale in the World War, Part I*, op. cit., p. 77.

178   *Resumé of the Professional Experience of Arly L. Hedrick*, op. cit.

179   Edward P. Rankin, Jr. *The Santa Fe Trail Leads to France*, op. cit., p. 42. See also Missouri State Archives Soldiers'

Records: War of 1812 – World War I. Service record for Arly Hedrick. www.sos.mo.gov/archives/soldiers/details.asp. Accessed by author on January 15, 2012.

180   Ibid, p. 39.

181   Ibid, p. 38.

182   "Kaw Bridge Builder Dead." *Lawrence Journal-World,* Tuesday, March 25, 1919, p. 6.

183   *Resumé of the Professional Experience of Arly L. Hedrick,* op. cit.

184   "Postcards of Historic Northeast.: Arly L. Hedrick Bridge and Troost Lake Marker (Troost Lake) in 1921." *Northeast News,* Vol 75, No. 2, January 11, 2006, p. 10. See also "The Arly L. Hedrick Bridge." *The Kansas City Star,* May 13, 1972. See also "Troost Park Bridge." Kansas City Public Library. http://www.kclibrary.org/sc/post/parks/200000204.htm

185   Missouri Valley Historical Society. *World War Soldiers Dead: Memorial Annals of Kansas City, Missouri,* op. cit., p. 57.

186   Missouri Valley Historical Society. *World War Soldiers Dead,* Vol II, No. 1, op. cit., p. 10.

187   Missouri State Archives: Soldiers' Records: War of 1812 – World War I. Service record for Frederick J. Shackelton, Service number 1,468,026. www.sos.mo.gov/archives/soldiers/details.asp. Accessed by author on January 15, 2012.

188   Frederick Shackleton is listed as a corporal in Charles B. Hoyt, *Heroes of the Argonne,* op. cit., p. 237 and in Clair Kenamore, *From Vauquois Hill to Exermont: A History of the 35th Division,* op. cit., p. 416.

189   Clair Kenamore. *From Vauquois Hill to Exermont: A History of the 35th Division,* op. cit., p. 226.

190   Ibid.

191   Ibid.

192   Ibid, p. 227.

193   Edward P. Rankin, Jr. *The Santa Fe Trail Leads to France,* op. cit., p. 39.

194   Amercian Battle Monuments Commission. *World War I, World War II, Korean War Casualty Listings.*

195   Walter Barlow Stevens. *Centennial History of Missouri: The Center State, One Hundred Years in the Union, 1820-1921.* (St. Louis, Missouri: Walter S. J. Clarke Publishing Company, 1921), p. 594.

196   Missouri Valley Historical Society. *World War Soldiers Dead: Memorial Annals of Kansas City, Missouri,* op. cit., p. 56. This source indicates that an American Legion post was named for Pvt. Robert T. Clements, but the post number was not given, and the post is no longer in existence.

197   J. R. Fuchs. "Oral History with L. L. Bucklew, Associate of Harry S. Truman in World War I as an Artillery Officer in the 35th Division and Friend of His Since that Time." Interview conducted in Encinitas, CA, on March 10, 1971. Truman Library. www.trumanlibrary.org/oralhist/bucklew.htm#25. Accessed by the author on February 18, 2012.

198   Ibid, p. 25.

199   Ibid.

200   Missouri State Archives: Soldiers' Records: War of 1812 – World War I. Service record for Robert T. Clements, Service number 1,463,331. www.sos.mo.gov/archives/soldiers/details.asp. Accessed by author on February 18, 2012.

201   Missouri Valley Historical Society. *World War Soldiers Dead: Memorial Annals of Kansas City, Missouri,* op. cit., p. 57.

202   Robert T. Clements was born on March 25, 1894. At the time of his death, he was 24 years, 6 months, 2 days old. See date of birth in service record, Missouri State Archives: Soldiers' Records: War of 1812 – World War I, op. cit.

203   Mary B Clements. "God Gave Me My Son in Trust to Me." Mary Clements prefaced her tribute with a note that her son, Private First Class R. T. Clements, had been killed in the Argonne, September 27, 1918. Her handwritten poem was attached with a straight pin to the October 21, 1922, meeting minutes of Kansas City's Gold Star League. The minutes acknowledged, "Mrs. [Nettie Thompson] Grove read a poem by Mrs. Clements. The poem was received and incorporated with these minutes, same attached hereto." National World War I Museum Archives, Gold Star League archival box.

204   Missouri Valley Historical Society. *World War Soldiers Dead: Memorial Annals of Kansas City, Missouri,* op. cit., p. 56.

205   Sherry Piland and Ellen J. Uguccioni. *Fountains of Kansas City: A History and Love Affair,* op. cit., p. 130.

206   Missouri State Archives Soldiers' Records: War of 1812 – World War I. Service record of William T. Law, Service number 4,744,911. www.sos.mo.gov/archives/soldiers/details.asp. Accessed by the author on February 3, 2012.

207   *In Memoriam: Addresses Delivered at Memorial Meeting of Kansas City Bar Association,* op. cit., p. 29.

208   List of Kansas City War Dead by category. National World War Museum. http://www.theworldwar.org/s/110/new/index.aspx.

209 Missouri Valley Historical Society. *World War Soldiers Dead: Memorial Annals of Kansas City, Missouri,* op. cit., p. 9.

210 Missouri State Archives Soldiers' Records: War of 1812 – World War I. Service record of Grover Metzger, Service number 3,791,687. http://www.sos.mo.gov/archives/soldiers/details.asp. Accessed by the author on February 6, 2012.

211 *Twelfth Census of the United States 1900.* Ward 9 Jackson County, Missouri, SD 5, ED 90, Sheet 7, June 5, 1900. For additional biographical information on the Metzger family, see *Thirteenth Census of the United States 1910.* Ward 9 Jackson County, Missouri, Roll T, 624_787, p. 4b, SD 5, ED 115, Sheet 4, April 18, 1910.

212 Missouri Valley Historical Society. *World War Soldiers Dead: Memorial Annals of Kansas City, Missouri,* op. cit., p. 61.

213 "American Legion's First Kansas City Posts Formed Thirty-five Years Ago." *The Kansas City Times,* August 19, 1954, p. 38.

214 Missouri Valley Historical Society. *World War Soldiers Dead: Memorial Annals of Kansas City, Missouri,* op. cit., p. 41.

215 Missouri State Archives Soldiers' Records: War of 1812 – World War I. Service record of Harry W. Herod. www.sos.mo.gov/archives/soldiers/details.asp. Accessed by the author on February 18, 2012.

216 Sherry Piland and Ellen J. Uguccioni. *Fountains of Kansas City: A History and Love Affair,* op. cit., p. 130.

French bank note, 50 Centimes, reverse and obverse, 1917

1 Franc note, 1917

General Douglas MacArthur.[3]

CHAPTER 6

"We Saw the Rainbow"

Over There, Over the Rainbow: Kansas and Missouri in the 42nd Division

The first Kansas and Missouri units to land in Europe were a field signal battalion from Missouri and an ammunition train from Kansas, both labeled the "117th" and both part of the 42nd Division, constituted with National Guard units from 26 different states and named the "Rainbow Division" by one of its commanders, General Douglas MacArthur. The Missouri 117th Field Signal Battalion was commanded by then Major Ruby D. Garrett, one of the field grade officers who met to advise the AEF on how to transition the men back home after the Armistice and who proved to be instrumental in the formation of the American Legion in Kansas City. The Kansas 117th Ammunition Train was commanded by Lieutenant Colonel Travis, whose story of the appearance of the rainbow explains why that symbol became so important for the ammunition train men, for Rosedale, Kansas, and for the landmark known as the great "Rainbow Arch."

At the outset of the war, a number of states already had National Guard units large enough to constitute full divisions of 27,500 men each. However, instead of immediately federalizing those guard units into their own separate divisions, the government devised a plan to have the first guard units in France represent as many states as possible, rather than just a few. As a result, 26 states and the District of Columbia were assigned roles in what was to become the 42nd Division. Upon seeing the plan, Secretary of War, Newton D. Baker, said that there were as many states represented as there were colors in the rainbow.[1] Then Douglas MacArthur, one of the officers assigned to lead the division, is said to have designated the unit the "Rainbow Division."[2] From that time on, the rainbow was to hold special significance for the men of the 42nd – the Missouri 117th Field Signal Battalion and especially the Kansas 117th Ammunition Train.

Within the rainbow, Missouri was assigned the role of signal corps – men whose primary responsibility it would be to provide phone lines and to secure communications during combat. These men were also responsible for keeping a photographic record of the war. They were the nerve system of the 42nd Division.

Three detachments of Missouri National

Guard Corps had been organized since 1908 as "Company A." To their number were added Companies B and C in April and May of 1917, shortly after war had been declared and just a couple of months after Company A returned from service on the Mexican Border.[4] The expanded companies were known as the 1st Battalion, Signal Corps[5] and were based in Kansas City, Missouri, under the command of then Major Ruby D. Garrett, a Kansas City lawyer. When the unit left Kansas City for Camp Clark on August 13, 1917, its strength was 367 men.[6] "These officers and men," Major Garrett said, "knew that they were to constitute the nerve system of a combat division, and each one seemed eager to train every nerve to function at its best."[7]

On September 26, 1917, the Field Signal Battalion arrived at Camp Mills, Hemstead, New York, where its numbers were doubled from New York recruits and men from other units of the 42nd. On October 18, the Field Signal Battalion set out for France, joining other units of the 42nd aboard the *President Grant*, an impounded and renamed German vessel which, before its surrender, had been sabotaged by the Germans so thoroughly that after five days out to sea, the ship was forced to turn back for repairs to its four boilers.

Meanwhile, the Signal Corps Battalion voluntarily installed a telephone in every observation post on the ship so that the bridge was in constant communication with the lookouts. Out to sea once more, the Field Signal Battalion landed in Liverpool on November 18, 1917, and after a brief stay outside of Winchester, set out from Southampton for Le Harve and from there across France to Vaucouleurs.

Major Ruby D. Garrett.[8]

Major Garrett recalled the accommodations: "In Challannes the Battalion was introduced to French billets of the cow stable variety, and to French villages decorated with towering manure piles. In cow stables and hay lofts these men from comfortable American dwellings, began to make their homes, singing 'My Country 'Tis For Thee,' and wading through mud, fog and ceaseless rains, the men paid their compliments to 'Sunny France.'"[9]

From Vaucoleurs, the Battalion moved with the 42nd Division to the St. Blin area and spent Christmas at Orquevaux. From there, they proceeded to the Rolampont Training Area, marching through snow and wind in sub-zero temperatures with only their summer clothing issue for protection. Major Garrett credited the endurance of the men to the hard physical training through which they had already been put.

On January 7, 1918, Major Garrett was promoted to Lieutenant Colonel and was made 42nd Division Signal Officer. He observed British and French front line divisions to gain an understanding of the signal corps challenges the 42ⁿᵈ would face once in combat. Returning to his battalion, Garrett used battalion equipment and personnel to create signal schools for 42ⁿᵈ Division infantry regiments. As a teaching model, he and his men created a miniature trench system in which every unit of the Division was represented to demonstrate how signal equipment and personnel could operate in trench, semi-open, and fully-open warfare.[10]

On February 19, 1918, the Signal Corps Battalion went into the line with four French divisions, setting up communications among all the various division elements. A month later on March 15, the Signal Battalion took its first casualty, Private Wilbur Wilkerson, who was posthumously awarded the *Croix de Guerre* and was buried at Croismare, just back of the front lines, in the presence of Secretary of War Baker, General Bliss, and other high-ranking French and American officers.

At Luneville, the men were exposed to active trench warfare, at night repairing telephone lines under shellfire and gas. At Baccarat on March 31, the Signal Corps built new communication lines, salvaged old lines, installed miles of buried cable, and took on the instruction of signal officers from other units. Then signal platoons from regiments of infantry and artillery as well as machine gun battalions gathered at St. Germain on

> *"In Challannes the Battalion was introduced to French billets of the cow stable variety, and to French villages decorated with towering manure piles. In cow stables and hay lofts these men from comfortable American dwellings, began to make their homes, singing 'My Country 'Tis For Thee,' and wading through mud, fog and ceaseless rains, the men paid their compliments to 'Sunny France.'"*
>
> — *Major Ruby D. Garrett.*

June 29 for special instruction in signal before marching to the front through the streets of Chalons.

Standing on the curb in Chalons was General Henri Joseph Eugene Gourard, commander of the 4ᵗʰ French Army, under which the 42ⁿᵈ Division had been placed. Silently, with no light permitted, the men passed in review. Five years later on July 20, 1923, Ltc. Garrett of the Missouri 117ᵗʰ Field Signal Battalion and Ltc. Travis of the Kansas 117ᵗʰ Ammunition Train joined with other civilian and military personnel to accompany General Gourard in a parade from the old Grund Hotel at 6ᵗʰ and Ann in Kansas City, Kansas, east across the Intercity (Lewis and Clark) Viaduct to Grand Avenue on the Missouri side, south to Pershing Road, west to Broadway, south through Penn Valley Park, and west on 39ᵗʰ Street to State Line Road. General Gourard was on hand to witness the ground breaking for the Rosedale Arch. Under a temporary welcome arch that read "Champagne – 1918 Rosedale – 1923," 200 Rosedale service veterans joined the parade following the French general before whom many of them had passed that night in Chalons five years earlier.[11]

By daylight on June 30, 1918, the Field Signal Battalion had reached the village of Vadenay, 13 kilometers north of Chalons. The signal officers and men from the infantry, artillery, and machine gun units quickly returned to their commands. Preparations were underway to attack a salient north of Chatillon sur Marne, and trucks with wire and signal equipment had been sent with a detachment to begin installing communications for the advance.

Suddenly the orders were reversed; the 42nd was sent up to support three French divisions in the sector from Souain to Esperance, where a German attack was in progress. A command post was designated in a 36-foot deep solid chalk dugout two kilometers north and west of Vadanay Farm. Before midnight, four trunk lines were extended from the P.C. dugout to the existing divisional exchange, and two lines were hooked up to each brigade with two additional lines connected to the French Corps to which the 42nd had been sent. During the bombardment of July 14-16, the lines to Corps were shot out repeatedly, and the signalmen strung field wire to replace the broken lines. For five days, the signalmen worked without rest until July 18, when they hiked 32 kilometers to board a train for La Ferte-sous-Jouarre.

From there, the 42nd Division moved to the vicinity of Epieds, north of Chateau Thierry, and then to an objective north of Ourcq, where it forced the Germans to withdraw. After being relieved and returning to Ferte-sous-Jouarre, the 42nd moved by rail to the Bourmot area and underwent intensive training. Night marches beginning on August 30 moved the 42nd to the Foret de la Reine, and from September 12-13, 1918, the 42nd took part in the St. Mihiel Offensive as the center division of the 4th Army Corps, advancing 19 kilometers in two days.

During the first two weeks of October, the 42nd Division moved to Benoit-Vaux, Couvent, and to Recicourt, and then to Bois de Montfaucon, all the while ensuring that the advance Division command post was connected to the old P.C. and at all times to regimental and even to battalion levels.

On the Argonne-Meusse front, the 42nd Division relieved the 1st Division on October 13 with Division headquarters established at Cheppy, and then 2 kilometers south of Exermont, where it was shelled nightly and attacked from the air with bombs and gas. Two days later on October 15, the 42nd took Hill 288 and on October 16, Cote de Chatillon, breaking through the German Kriemhilde-Stellung in spite of constant and heavy artillery and machine gun fire. "The lines were blown out repeatedly," Ltc. Garrett remembered, "the valleys were continually flooded with gas, a deadly spray of machine gun bullets covered most of the area, but no unit of the Division was ever without communication longer than thirty minutes."[12]

Relieved by the 2nd Division on October 31, the 42nd passed through the 78th Division as part of the 1st Army Corps and advanced 19 kilometers in two days to the Meuse, where it captured the heights over Sedan. Ltc. Garrett recalled the scene: "The weather had been wet, the roads were slick and muddy, and all bridges had been blown out, irrigation dams had been destroyed and the lands flooded. There had been little or no food for men or animals. The horses fell from exhaustion, or mired in the lowlands and were abandoned or killed. The tired men carried telephone equipment and wire on their backs. Continuously marching and fighting in the rain and mud caused the men to suffer indescribable hardships. But not once did the communication fail and not one man complained."[13]

During it all was the unaccountable loss of life. On November 6, just below Sedan, 1st Lt. Ralph Estep, Signal Corps Photographic Officer, was taking pictures of the 167th Infantry when he was killed, according to Pathe Laboratories in Paris, the only Photographic Officer in the American Army killed in action during the war. And, as Ltc. Garrett noted, there were also really marvelous escapes. One night, two Marines visited one of the signalmen operating a station. After working, they retired to a room to sleep, the signalman in the center and the two Marines on either side. Suddenly a shell crashed through the roof, bored through a stone wall, and exploded in the room where the men slept. The two Marines were killed instantly; the signalman escaped injury entirely.[14]

The 42nd was finally withdrawn from the fighting on November 10, and that same day alerted that it would be part of the Army of Occupation. At 7 a.m. the next morning, four hours before the Armistice was to go into effect, the Signal Battalion radio picked up the message from the Germans that they would accept the conditions for an armistice. Still the firing continued until it ceased completely at 11:00 a.m. "That night for the first time," Ltc. Garrett said, "lights shone through unscreened windows, and after more than four years the old lamps were lit in the streets. The men were too tired and too happy to make much of a demonstration. All believed it was the end of the war, but none fully realized it."[15]

On November 20, the 42nd began its march through Belgium toward the Rhine to take up its part in the occupation of Germany, reaching Adenau, Germany, on December 9, 1918. The Signal Battalion marched the entire distance from France, 380 kilometers, using German circuits to maintain communication with Brigades and Corps. On December 13, the Signal Battalion moved to Ahrweiler, the site of 42nd Division Headquarters. Finally, in April 1919, the 42nd Division left Germany and departed from the port of Brest, France, for home. Meanwhile, back in Paris, the Pathe Laboratories assembled the war pictures made by the Signal Corps. "The Battalion had made a grand collection," Ltc. Garrett said. "Six of the best movie reels taken of the 42nd Division were brought back and shown before all organizations."[16]

Summing up the experience, Ltc. Garrett observed, "From the first, our men realized fully the arduous nature of their work and the vital importance of the communication they were required to furnish. They were taught to treat their work not only as a high duty but as a sacred privilege, and they were eager to give in service the very best that was in them. Sufficient tribute cannot be paid to their unselfish devotion and their heroic conduct. By their industry and efficiency Missouri's signal men made a vital contribution to the success of our armies and played a proud part in the glorious achievement of America in this war."[17]

■ ■ ■

Across the Missouri state line into Kansas, another element of the 42nd Division had been formed, also designated the 117th, but not a field signal unit. Instead, for its share in the rainbow, Kansas was assigned the role of an ammunition train, a unit responsible for stockpiling and delivering the ammunition necessary for artillery and infantry units engaged in combat. They were the lifeline for the fight. Capt. Frank L. Travis of Iola, Kansas, was promoted to Lieutenant Colonel and assigned the task of organizing the train. He had been captain of a Kansas supply train on the Mexican border the summer before and decided that the first six of the 12 companies of 55 men would be raised in Wyandotte County, Kansas.[18]

In June 1917,[19] he opened a recruiting office, inserted a "Men Wanted" ad in a Tuesday edition of the local paper, and by Saturday of the succeeding week had assembled 375 men on top of Mount Marty on the bluffs of the Kaw River. There he swore them into the service. Recruits had signed up from Rosedale, Kansas; Kansas City, Missouri; and surrounding communities. Also known as "high school hill" after Rosedale High School, which was located there, Mount Marty received yet another designation when the recruits set up camp on the side of the hill. It became known as "Camp Rushton," after Rosedale resident George Rushton, who had devoted much time and effort to the formation of the unit.[20]

The remaining six companies of the ammunition train came from cities across Kansas. Companies 7 and 8 were from Chanute, Company 9 hailed from Dodge City, Company 10 from Parsons, Company 11 from Manhattan, and Company 12 from Pratt.[21] In all, the 117th Ammunition Train numbered 1,100 men.[22]

After striking their tents at Camp Rushton, the 117th Ammunition Train left for Topeka on August 19, 1917, and from there on September 3, entrained for Camp Mills, Hemstead, New York, where the unit arrived three days later. The advance guard detachment of 61 men left for France in October 1917.[23] The rest of the train departed Camp Mills later on a ship that had been confiscated from the Germans. On board was a large oil painting of Kaiser Wilhelm II said to have cost $10,000. In a letter describing the trip across the ocean, Corporal Clarence H. Lavery took pride in reporting to his parents that the painting "had been ruined by our soldiers," as he put it.[24]

As part of the 42nd Division, the Kansas 117th Ammunition Train was engaged in the same battles the Missouri 117th Field Signal Battalion fought, although the two units played different roles. At the end of the war, the service of the 117th Ammunition Train was recognized in Major General Flagler's General Orders No. 21-K issued by Chief-of-Staff Colonel William N. Hughes:

Ltc. Frank L. Travis.[25]

Throughout the battles in which the Division has been engaged never once has the steady flow of ammunition toward the front been stopped. In spite of the long, dangerous hauls and almost insurmountable difficulties, the 117th Ammunition Train maintained the supply necessary for the guns. The 117th Ammunition Train worked as an integral part of the artillery brigade. It ever functioned with the ease of a well oiled machine. Its trucks were always in splendid working order; its caisson and wagon companies were ready for all emergencies.

Undergoing its preliminary training at Camp De Coetquidan, France, it served with the French in the Luneville sector. In the Baccarat sector it perfected its technique. In the Champaign sector it worked feverishly, during the dark days before the final German offensive, to pile up that reserve of ammunition that made the German defeat possible. During the battle it continued to serve.

It has been the fate of this organization to undergo dangers equally as great as those of the troops in the front line and to suffer these dangers without being able to strike back.

At Chateau Thierry it worked day and night, feeding the guns. Going forward over unknown and badly charted territory, it always found the batteries. It was to be depended on.

It went to Bourmont, then St. Mibiel, by

night marches. Working in the mud and slime and almost completely destroyed roads, in the rear of the Forest de la Reine, it again laid the foundations for the attack. In the Argonne Meuse, night and day it toiled; heartrending, muscle-breaking toil. Men were in the saddle for days at a time. Trucks went where trucks were not expected to go. A measure of endurance was demanded that would have been thought impossible before. Aeroplane bombs and enemy shells did not stop it. The reserve of ammunition was built up.

Throughout, one is struck by the silent efficiency of this command. The work was done. By its service, by the devotion and loyalty of all ranks, it has won the gratitude of the division and the thanks of the division commander.

The 117th Ammunition Train has a magnificent record, and Kansas may well be proud of her representation in the Rainbow Division.[26]

After 18 months of service, the 117th Ammunition Train arrived in Newport News, Virginia, on May 1, 1919, aboard the transport *U.S.A.C.T. Koningen der Nederlanden*.[27] The 117th Ammunition Train had been the first Kansas unit into the battle line, and the 42nd Division of which it was a part was the first American unit to hold an all-American sector in France. Governor Henry J. Allen, former editor of the Wichita *Beacon*[28] and Red Cross Home Communications Service Director in France,[29] had been elected governor of Kansas while he was still in France.[30] After he returned and assumed office, Allen traveled to Newport News to greet the 117th when it disembarked.

While also still in France, Ltc. Travis was elected Kansas State Insurance Commissioner. He had suffered "a physical breakdown caused by the strain of the war." After he returned to Kansas, he gave an interview to *The Kansas City Star* and confirmed the stories of what many of his troops had reported. "The rainbow appeared to us," he said, "before virtually every engagement in which we participated."[31]

"At first the men looked upon it as a rather remarkable coincidence, then they began to attach a more serious importance to it. Finally at the close of the war it had become sort of superstition, yes, something more than that, a spiritual augury of victory."

Ltc. Travis recounted the instances of the rainbow's appearance. "It was early in the spring when we first noticed it," he said. "The division had received a hard pounding up in the Baccarat sector and was awaiting an attack. The rainbow appeared and the attack failed."

Then there was the especially strange appearance of a rainbow at the battle of Chauteau Thierry. "It was a wonderful sight," Tra-

> *Then there was the especially strange appearance of a rainbow at the battle of Chauteau Thierry. "It was a wonderful sight, a great rainbow of extraordinary beauty and one end of it touched the earth not more than two hundred yards away from us, fairly bathing the spot in a vari-colored light. It was the first time I ever had seen the fabled end of the rainbow. Well, everybody knows the outcome of the Chauteau Thierry operations."*
>
> — *Ltc. Frank L. Travis*

vis said, "—a great rainbow of extraordinary beauty and one end of it touched the earth not more than two hundred yards away from us, fairly bathing the spot in a vari-colored light. It was the first time I ever had seen the fabled end of the rainbow. Well, everybody knows the outcome of the Chauteau Thierry operations.

"Again before St. Mihiel," Travis continued, "that first operation carried out solely by American troops, we saw a magnificent rainbow. By that time all the men of the division had become imbued with the feeling that the rainbow was the sign by which we, like Constantine, were to conquer. There could be no stopping the men of the 42nd.

"When we went into the Argonne the rainbow again heralded victory for us. And we saw it over the Meuse and on the advance toward Sedan. Why, you could not have persuaded a lot of the men that it was not a supernatural omen of success. They say that a fine rainbow dipped into the Rhine the day the boys went across into Germany. I know they came to look for the rainbow every time that we were due to go into battle. And when the rainbow would appear, there would be remarks go up from the fellows that we were going to win sure."

Ltc. Travis concluded by weighing the significance of the rainbow's appearances.

The men, he said, "were a bit reverent toward it, too, near the last, though some joked about it at first. A soldier gets to feel a sort of spiritual dependence when in battle. I don't know what it is or particularly what causes it, but I know that men feel a little more inclined to look for signs and portents that are not earthly in character. Perhaps it is the strain and hardship, the pain and loss of sleep that makes the imagination rather feverish so that men see unusual meanings in things that otherwise would pass as mere coincidences. And maybe there is something deeper, something supernatural to such things. I don't profess to know. But a lot of those men who fought in the Rainbow Divi-sion are convinced that we were guided to victory by something greater than man."[32]

Rosedale Mayor Shelby H. Rennick and the Rosedale City Council officially recognized the significance that the rainbow held for the 117th Ammunition Train. The mayor and council changed the name of what was then known as "Hudson Road" to "Rainbow Boulevard." "Said name," they asserted, "to remain Rainbow Boulevard forever in honor of the Rosedale boys who gave their lives in France and those who saw service there."[33] Nearby, on top of Rushton Hill, Mount Marty, where the 375 men of the 117th Ammunition Train first camped and took their oath of service, the Rosedale Arch now stands, a tribute in stone to the rainbows those same Rosedale boys saw "Over There."

M-15 Rosedale Arch
Booth Street & Memorial Drive, North of Rosedale Middle School, Kansas City, Kansas

As one of 26 states contributing military units to the 42nd "Rainbow Division," Kansas was assigned the 117th Ammunition Train and the role of delivering ammunition to the front during combat. Iola native Captain Frank L. Travis was promoted to Lieutenant Colonel and charged with organizing the unit. It would consist of 12 companies of 55 men each, and Travis decided to raise half of them, 6 companies, in Wyandotte County. In less than a week after advertising in the local newspaper, he assembled 375 men on top of Mount Marty in Rosedale, and there he swore them into the service of the United States. They went off to war and returned to march through Rosedale on May 12, 1919, when Rainbow Boulevard came into being.

Less than two years later, on March 21, 1921, the citizens of Rosedale, Kansas, held a special election approving $25,000 in bonds to purchase land for

The Rosedale Arch.

James J. Heiman

an athletic field and memorial park and to build there an arch "to commemorate the valorous achievements" of those men from Rosedale who served in the Great War.[34] The arch was to serve as the entrance to the athletic field, which would be 150 feet by 290 feet, the remaining ground serving as a park.

On the same spot of ground where Travis had sworn 375 men into service as the 117th Ammunition Train, the planning committee spent $10,000 of the bond money for the equivalent of 21 lots, 5.2 acres just north of 36th and Springfield, overlooking Turkey Creek. There on July 20, 1923, ground was broken for a memorial arch designed by J. LeRoy Marshall, a Rosedale member of the American Legion. He modeled his design on sketches he had made of the *Arc de Triomphe* in Paris. The proportions of his design are classical: 34½ feet high, 25 feet 5 inches wide, with an archway 20 feet high and 10 feet wide. The pillars are 7 feet square at the base, tapering through 6 feet square as the arch grows in height.[35]

That date, July 20, 1923, was selected because General Henri Gouraud, the French 4th Army commander under whom the 117th had served in France, was touring the United States and agreed to help dedicate the project. John B. Smith and Rosedale American Legion Post 346 made the arrangements, and the General arrived at Union Station at 7:30 a.m. on July 20. From there, the General and his reception committee motored to the Grund Hotel at 6th and Ann in Kansas City, Kansas, for a breakfast with the veterans of the 42nd Division. Ltc. Frank Travis, commander of the 117th Ammunition Train; Ltc. Ruby D. Garrett, commander of the 117th Field Signal Battalion; Brigadier General H. A. Smith, the Commandant of Fort Leavenworth; other military figures; and the mayors of Kansas City, Missouri, and

Kansas City, Kansas, attended. Then the General and his party crossed back into Missouri on the Lewis and Clark Viaduct (the old Intercity Viaduct) to Grand Avenue, then south to Pershing Road through Penn Valley Park to 39th Street, where they headed west into Kansas. In those days, the 7th Street Trafficway did not exist, so to get from downtown Kansas City, Kansas, to Rosedale, one had to cross back into Kansas City, Missouri, go south, then west.

The parade that formed at 39th and State Line consisted of the infantry band and infantry and artillery details from Fort Leavenworth, a detachment of Marines from the recruiting station, 200 Rosedale ex-servicemen, Rosedale American Legion Post 346, and standard bearers from American Legion Posts representing Rufus J. Montgall, William F. Fitzsimons, William R. Nelson, Hewitt Swearingen, James Cummings, Tank Corp 381, Joseph Liebman, Arthur Maloney, Peter Smith, Overland Park, Wyandotte, and Olathe. Six thousand

The parade that formed at 39th and State Line consisted of the infantry band and infantry and artillery details from Fort Leavenworth, a detachment of Marines from the recruiting station, 200 Rosedale ex-servicemen, Rosedale American Legion Post 346, and standard bearers from American Legion Posts representing Rufus J. Montgall, William F. Fitzsimons, William R. Nelson, Hewitt Swearingen, James Cummings, Tank Corp 381, Joseph Liebman, Arthur Maloney, Peter Smith, Overland Park, Wyandotte, and Olathe. Six thousand spectators watched them march through an arch inscribed "Champagne – 1918" and "Rosedale – 1923."

spectators watched them march through an arch inscribed "Champagne – 1918" and "Rosedale – 1923."[36] There on the crest of Mount Marty, the notes of the "Marseillaise" and "America" followed a 21-gun salute. Father Anthony Dornseifer, pastor of Holy Name Church, delivered the invocation and General B. H. Duncan, commander of the 17th Army Corps, presented the Distinguished Service Cross to H. D. Heitz as medal-draped veterans of the Civil War, the Spanish-American War, and the Great War looked on. Senator Arthur Capper, Governor Davis, State Legion Commander W. P. Mc Lean, and Committee Chair John B. Smith spoke before General Gouraud, who delivered his address to an enthusiastic crowd through an interpreter. The General and his party then left for a brief visit with the French sisters of Notre Dame de Sion before returning to Union Station and their train departing to Denver.[37]

After a "Notice to Contractors" was published in *The Kansas City Kansan*, the contract for the construction of the arch was awarded to H. C. Raedecker, a resident of Rosedale and a contractor and stonemason. In April, a committee from the Rosedale American Legion Post 346 met with Park Department Engineer George K. Grindrod to determine the location of the arch at the north end of the park. The construction of the arch itself was completed during the summer of 1924 at a cost of $12,179.[38] Work on the stadium was started five years later in 1929, and the retaining wall, 14 feet wide at its base, close to 22 feet high in places, was built with rock quarried on the hill next to the athletic field. The retaining wall allowed the field to be widened another 50 feet.

Through the years, the arch suffered from neglect as brush and weeds took over and the rock deteriorated. Some people even questioned whether the cost of maintenance was worth it, but in June 1962, R. E. Jameson, a Rosedale barber and member of the city planning commission, met with 14 representatives of business and civic organizations to rehabilitate the arch. After spotlights were added, the road re-graveled, and the site cleaned up, the arch was re-dedicated to all veterans of all wars on Sunday, November 11, 1962. The University-Rosedale Urban Renewal Project that followed during the years from 1962 to 1968 proposed to move the Arch to the Recreation Center at 36th and Rainbow Boulevard, but that move was rejected, and in June 1968, the Rosedale Business Association and the KCK Street and Park Department cleaned the area, sand-blasted the arch, and built a new gravel access road. On November 11, 1968, the high intensity floodlights were added and a lighting ceremony proclaimed new life for the arch. The city park department added a concrete road in 1972 and new walkways and rest areas in 1974.

And now one can look out over the valley, through the arch, and read the words inscribed above:

Erected by the People of Rosedale
In Honor of Their Sons Who
Answered Their Country's Call
Served Under Arms for the Triumph
Of Right Over Might in the Great War.

Pvt. Hewitt Jordan Swearingen:
Delivering Ammunition to the Front
(Hewitt Swearingen American Legion Post 201)

American Legion Post No. 201 was named for Private Hewitt J. Swearingen, whose father, Armstead E. Swearingen, served as chairman of the Jackson County Gold Star League Committee of Service, which assisted in the reburials of nearly 70 Kansas City boys returned from the American cemeteries in France. A private in the 42nd Division's 117th Ammunition Train, Private Swearingen was killed in the line of duty. At the time of his death, he was only 20 years old, had been in the service a little more than a year, and was newly married. He was reburied at Mt. Washington Cemetery.

On June 5, 1917, two months after the United Stated declared war on Germany, 19-year-old Hewitt J. Swearingen enlisted in the 117th Ammunition Train, 42nd Division.[39] He was inducted in Rosedale, Kansas, on June 11, 1917,[40] and served with Motor Company 5 of the Kansas National Guard until August 23, 1918, when that unit officially became Company D of the 117th Ammunition Train.

Throughout Kansas that June, 12 truck companies were being raised for the ammunition train, the first six of which were recruited in Rosedale, Kansas, just over the state line from Kansas City, Missouri. The Ammunition Train became part of the famous 42nd "Rainbow Division," whose Chief of Staff was Brigadier General Douglas MacArthur. Banty E. Hackney of Chanute, Kansas,[41] commanded Hewitt's Company D. Colonel Frank L. Travis was the overall commander of the Ammunition Train's 1200 men.[42] Also in the service at the same time was Hewitt's broth-

Hewitt served with the 117th Ammunition Train until he was killed in action on July 1, 1918, in Beauvardeau, France. He and three of his companions were returning after having delivered ammunition to the front lines when they were killed by bombs in an air raid on the night of July 31. The following day he was buried with his companions. He was 20 years old.

er, Ernest, who had joined the Navy and was stationed at the Great Lakes Naval Training Station.

Prior to his enlistment in the Ammunition Train, Hewitt had been working in insurance at Policy Holder's Adjustment Company and, just the year before, graduated from Northeast High School in Kansas City, Missouri, where from 1914, he had been a right guard on the school's first basketball team. By the time he graduated in 1916, he was team captain.

On November 8, 1917, Hewitt took leave to marry Mecca Duffield, daughter of Mr. and Mrs. Charles O. Duffield of 3337 Montgall in Kansas City, Missouri.

Private Hewitt Swearingen deployed overseas with his unit on January 4, 1918. On the way over, Hewitt, also known by his friends as "Hugie," and his buddy Earnest Cassing from the 117th Ammunition Train, met Kansas City friends who happened to be in the Navy and aboard the same transport – Eddie and Jack Beebe and "Biff" Evans. A picture of the five friends appeared in *The Kansas City Star* on March 8, 1918.[44]

Hewitt served with the 117th Ammunition Train until he was killed in action on July 1, 1918, in Beauvardeau, France.[45] He and three of his companions were returning after

Private Hewitt J. Swearingen.[43]

having delivered ammunition to the front lines when they were killed by bombs in an air raid on the night of July 31. The following day he was buried with his companions. He was 20 years old.[46]

In addition to his wife, Mecca, he was survived by his brother, Ernest T. Swearingen, and his parents, Mr. and Mrs. Armstead Ernest Swearingen, 318 North Lawndale, who received a telegram on August 15, 1918, notifying them of their son's death six weeks earlier. Hewitt's father, Armstead Swearingen, served as chairman of the Committee of Service for the Gold Star League of Jackson County. In that capacity, he and his committee assisted at the reburials of almost 70 Kansas City boys who had been returned from cemeteries in France. Pvt. Hewitt Swearingen was among those to be reburied in Mt. Washington Cemetery, Kansas City.[47] His name appears on the plaques of the Gateway Avenue of Trees at Ward Parkway and Meyer Circle, on the bronze tablets in Memory Hall at Liberty Memorial, and on American Legion I at Van Brunt and Anderson, where American Legion Post No. 201 is named for him.

Endnotes

1   Grant W. Harrington. "Historic Spots Number Forty." *Historic Spots or Mile-Stones in the Progress of Wyandotte County, Kansas.* (Merriam, KS: The Mission Press, 1935), p. 307.

2   "Named the Rainbow Division." *The Kansas City Star*, April 2, 1919, p. 26.

3   "General Douglas MacArthur, Credited with Naming the Rainbow Division." Picture from *The Kansas City Star*, April 2, 1919, p. 26. See also MacArthur picture with "Staff Officer is Wounded." *The Kansas City Times*, March 26, 1918, p. 10.

4   LTC Ruby D. Garrett. "The 117th Field Signal Battalion" in *History of the Missouri National Guard.* (Military Council, Missouri National Guard, November 1934), p. 241-241.

5   "The 42nd Home in April." *The Kansas City Star*, March 10, 1919, p.1.

6   Ibid.

7   LTC Ruby D.Garrett. "The 117th Field Signal Battalion" in *History of the Missouri National Guard*, op. cit., p. 243.

8   "Maj. Ruby D. Garrett, Who Leads the One Hundred Seventeenth Field Signal Battalion, (Missouri Signal Corps) in Foreign Service." Photo from *The Kansas City Star*, November 16, 1917, p. 1.

9   Ibid, p. 245.

10   Ibid, p. 246.

11   Margaret Landis. *The Winding Valley and the Craggy Hillside: A History of the City of Rosedale, Kansas.* (Kansas City, KS: Arrowhead Instant Printing, 1976), p. 79-80.

12   LTC Ruby D.Garrett. "The 117th Field Signal Battalion" in *History of the Missouri National Guard*, op. cit., p. 249.

13   Ibid.

14   Ibid, p. 250.

15   Ibid.

16   Ibid, p. 251.

17   Ibid.

18   "Commanding the Kansas Ammunition Train." *The Kansas City Star*, September 6, 1917, p. 9.

19   Margaret Landis. *The Winding Valley and the Craggy Hillside: A History of the City of Rosedale, Kansas*, op. cit., p. 71.

20   "Rosedale is Proud." *The Kansas City Star*, March 17, 1918, p. 24C.

21   Margaret Landis. *The Winding Valley and the Craggy Hillside: A History of the City of Rosedale, Kansas*, op. cit., p. 71.

22   "Our Own Boys Over." *The Kansas City Star*, November 16, 1917, p. 1.

23   Ibid.

24   "Ruined 'Old Kaiser Bill.'" *The Kansas City Star*, December 18, 1917, p. 8.

25   "Colonel Frank. L. Travis, Commanding the One Hundred Seventeenth Ammunition Train." Photo from *The Kansas City Star*, November 16, 1917, p.1. See also photo with "Commanding the Kansas Ammunition Train." *The Kansas City Star*, September 6, 1917, p. 9.

26   Grant W. Harrington. "Historic Spots Number Forty." *Historic Spots or Mile-Stones in the Progress of Wyandotte County, Kansas*, op. cit., p. 308-309.

27   "The 117th Train Docks." *The Kansas City Star*, May 1, 1919, p. 1.

28   William Allen White. *The Martial Adventures of Henry and Me.* (New York: Macmillan, 1918), p. 1.

29   "Allen Pays His Own Way." *The Kansas City Times*, May 15, 1918, p. 1.

30   "Allen Back to Kansas." *The Weekly Kansas City Star*, December 11, 1918, p. 3.

31   "A Rainbow Led the Yanks to Victory." *The Kansas City Star*, March 16, 1919, Editorial Section (p. 1C).

32   Ibid.

33   Margaret Landis. *The Winding Valley and the Craggy Hillside: A History of the City of Rosedale, Kansas*, op. cit., p. 72.

34   Ibid, p. 73.

35   Ibid, p. 74.

36   Ibid, p. 80. See also Grant W. Harrington. "Historic Spots Number Forty." *Historic Spots or Mile-Stones in the*

Progress of Wyandotte County, Kansas, op. cit., p. 310-312.

37   Margaret Landis. *The Winding Valley and the Craggy Hillside: A History of the City of Rosedale, Kansas,* op. cit., p. 82.

38   Grant W. Harrington. "Historic Spots Number Forty." *Historic Spots or Mile-Stones in the Progress of Wyandotte County, Kansas,* op. cit., p. 312.

39   "A Kansas City Soldier Fell." *The Kansas City Times*, Friday, August 16, 1918, p. 2.

40   Missouri State Archives Soldiers Records: War of 1812 – World War I. Service record of Hewitt J. Swearingen. Service number 207143. http.//www.sos.mo.gov/archives/soldiers/details.asp. Accessed by author on January 27, 2012.

41   Johnson, Harold Stanley. *Roster of the Rainbow Division (42nd), Major General William A. Mann, Commanding*, 1917, p. 42. www.ebooksread.com/authors-eng/Harold-Stanley.Johnson/roster. Accessed by the author on January 27, 2012.

42   "Kansas City Troops and Where They Are." *The Kansas City Star*, Sunday, December 2, 1917, p. 2B.

43   Photo from *The Kansas City Star*. See also picture in W. M. Haulsee, F. G. Howe, and A. C. Doyle. *Soldiers of the Great War*. (Washington, DC: Soldiers Record Publishing Association, 1920), p. 172.

44   "On a Transport to the War Zone." *The Kansas City Star*, March 8, 1918, p. 5B with photo.

45   *World War Soldiers Dead, Vol. II, No. 1*. (Kansas City, MO: Missouri Valley Historical Society 1926), p. 29.

46   Ibid, p. 88.

47   Ibid, p. 57.

At Camp Funston, workmen were building barracks to house the troops even as the men themselves began to arrive for training.[6]

CHAPTER 7

"We Occupied Germany"

Wood, Winn, and Wright: The Midwest 89th Division

Unlike the 35th and 42nd Divisions, the 89th Division was comprised largely of draftees, men who had not served in the National Guard and who had been drafted from civilian life directly into the service. The men were trained at Camp Funston, Ft. Riley, Kansas, by Major General Leonard Wood, who tried unsuccessfully to accompany his men to France and lead them in battle. Instead, his place would be taken by Major General William Wright and later by Major General Frank Winn, who, respectively, led the division during the fight and later in the occupation of Germany. The last names of the generals combined to form the moniker of the 89th ("Right Would Win") and, in the imagination of some, when the Midwest Division was on the move, the "W" (for "West") rotating upside down into an "M" (for "Mid") became known as the Midwest "Rolling 'W.'"

First to command and organize the 89th Division was Major General Leonard Wood, then Major General Frank L. Winn assumed command during training, and finally Major General William Wright led the Division in combat. Because the last names of these three commanders began with the letter "W," some have said that is why the insignia for the 89th Division resembles the letter "W." Yet another explanation for the divisional insignia can be found in the division history written by George H. English. "The happy combination of names also served sometimes as a kind of slogan, 'Wright, Wood, Winn,' – 'Right would win.'"[1]

Another explanation for the divisional insignia is more dynamic. When rotated half a turn from its upright position, the "W" becomes an "M." And when rotated continuously in the imagination, the "M" "W,"

James J. Heiman

The "Rolling 'W'" shoulder patch of the 89th Division.

or "Rolling 'W'" as it was known, forms the initial letters for "Mid-West," the name for the 89th Division. In the Great War, the "Midwest Division" was comprised of troops from the midwestern states of Kansas, Missouri, Colorado, Arizona, New Mexico, Nebraska, and South Dakota.[2]

As part of the new "National Army" made up mostly of men drafted into the service, the 89th Division contained infantry regiments, engineer units, field artillery batteries, ammunition trains, and machine gun battalions – at full strength, 28,000 men[3] all drawn from the seven Midwestern states, each unit more or less localized from within a particular state. The unit known as the "All Kansas," for example, was the 353rd Infantry; each of the 105 counties in the state was at some time represented in its ranks. Missouri contributed the largest number of men of any of the seven states to the 89th, with southeastern and eastern parts of the state comprising the 354th Infantry and 314th Engineers. Men from northwest Missouri made up the 356th Infantry – sometimes called the "All Missouri" – and men from southeast Missouri filled the 342nd Field Artillery. Nebraska provided men for the 355th Infantry and the 314th Ammunition Train, with the city of Omaha supplying all the men for the 341st Machine Gun Battalion. Men from several of the other states made up the other units. South Dakota furnished men for the 340th Machine Gun Battalion, and South Dakota, Arizona, and New Mexico supplied men for the 342nd Machine Gun Battalion. Arizona and Colorado men made up the 340th as well as the 341st Field Artillery. The 164th Depot Brigade included men drafted form all seven states, while the men of the 314th Field Signal Battalion were not draftees at all, being almost entirely composed of men from the Signal Enlisted Reserve Corps.[4]

The enlisted reserves already had military training, but the draftees needed immediate training in the very basics of military life, and even that training had to be modified. Shel-

ter, clothing, rifles, horses, and instruction in sanitation and military protocol had to be adapted to the circumstances created by a federal government and civilian draftees not at all prepared for war. The Camp Funston grounds themselves proved as inadequate as the preparation, and the effects proved as lethal as the war itself. The camp was located within the Fort Riley reservation "on a flood plane that turned into a black, gummy morass that swallowed cars to their axles and horses to their bellies when it rained." General Wood called it "a death trap of infectious diseases." In October 1917, meningitis swept through the camp.[5] A year later to the month, in October 1918, 800 cases of the Spanish flu appeared for the first time anywhere in the world. It may have originated in Haskell County, Kansas,[7] and then carried by recruits to Camp Funston, where, within 48 hours of the outbreak, men began dying by the hundreds. Within a few weeks, the number of new cases at the camp reached 1,000 a day.[8]

Major General Leonard Wood

A former surgeon, camp commandant General Leonard Wood immediately set out to combat the illness that had attacked his troops. He eliminated mass assemblies, spread the men out to minimize contact, and hung cotton screens to separate mess tables. Then suddenly, within one week, the number of new flu cases dropped as dramatically as they had started. By that time, however, the disease had already spread east to military camps in America and then early in April overseas to the port of Brest, France.[9] Before the virus abated, it had "circled the globe three times and left 20 million dead."[10] In the words of one biographer, "Wood had unknowingly presided over the most lethal pandemic in history."[11] Ironically, the microbes that had mustered out in force at Camp Funston and marched three times around the

Outfitted in bib overalls and campaign hats, newly arrived recruits at Camp Funston, queue up for blankets. The state of readiness is reflected in the signs posted to reassure the men.[15]

Above, Major General Leonard Wood.[12]

Left, A new recruit at Camp Funston puts the finishing touches on his hand-made rifle.[13]

world killed twice as many men as the human combatants did themselves.[14]

Disease wasn't the only issue confronting General Wood. To outfit the units of the 89th, Wood was forced to improvise; the lack of preparedness for war had left the military with hardly any equipment, weaponry, or soldier gear. So when uniforms failed to arrive, General Wood ordered blue denim overalls, and when rifles were not available, he had the men make wooden replicas so the troops could at least drill in the manual of arms. The distinctive campaign hats were available, however, and the combination of khaki hats, blue denim overalls, and wooden rifles tested the credulity of all but the most casual military observer. Thousands of men wearing bib overalls and wide-brimmed hats and carrying wooden rifles appeared less than seriously military.

Their training appeared equally unreal. Saddles were strapped to barrels mounted on wooden legs to teach cavalry men correct positions while mounted for various maneuvers. White woolen balls were dropped to simulate artillery bursts so forward observers using field glasses could practice locating and relaying positions for artillery calculations. When trucks were needed for the 314th Motor Supply Train, a detail was sent to the Velie Plant in Moline, Illinois, to drive a convoy back to Camp Funston. Discovering upon their arrival that the trucks had not yet been assembled, the detail was put to work on the assembly line, in the process becoming completely familiar with the construction and the operation of the trucks which, after assembly, the men then drove back to camp, deployed, maintained, and repaired.[16]

In training, however, proverbial American ingenuity received its greatest opportunity, taking advantage of every resource to meet unprecedented challenges. The introduction of the machine gun into modern combat had contributed to a virtual stalemate of the war in Europe. There, combined with barbed wire, the machine gun had confined war to the trenches rather than to the open field. With the rest of the Army, the 89th Division had to train for both trench warfare and for war in the open. Consequently, the 89th welcomed French, British, and Canadian officers assigned to Camp Funston to offer their firsthand experience with the trench war that had at that point locked the Western Front into a stalemate.

To train for trench warfare, the men covered 1,000 square yards of Camp Funston's Carpenter Hill with an elaborate system of trenches. Three parallel rows of trenches joined by communicating trenches were completed with dugouts, barbed wire, and machine gun emplacements. Through the winter of 1917 and the spring of 1918, the men trained there, practiced relief rotations, and under a variety of conditions attacked, defended, and attacked again. The men trained with gas masks in a specially built "gas house" where they remained exposed to deadly gas for prolonged periods.

General Pershing, however, did not accept the position that the war had to be fought only in trenches. He favored, in addition, training in open-field tactics where the enemy would have to confront a much more mobile and versatile strategy defined by the dexterity of individual riflemen. On the Smoky Hill Flats near the Smoky Hill River, five miles from Camp Funston, the men dug an even more elaborate system of trenches and participated in more complex scenarios training with bayonet, rifle, and grenade. Once they were issued Enfield rifles, the men practiced sharp shooting on a 300-target range on the Republican Flats, near the Republican River.

By Christmastime 1917, the men were ready to spend the holidays at home, but a last-minute order from the War Department kept the men at camp because the nation's transportation system was so unprepared and so severely stressed by the production needs of the war that it could not handle the additional burden of large numbers of troops on leave. In an effort to provide some entertainment and to lift the morale of the troops, the command staff staged a huge rodeo featuring riding, roping, and Wild West sports and later a staged attack of Indians and bandits on a wagon train. Soldier spectators acted the part of the bandits who robbed the wagon train of Christmas delicacies.

Besides the rodeo, soldiers could also enjoy leisure time in an area known as "The Zone," a collection of stores, restaurants, theaters, and canteens, which men could patronize without leaving camp. The YMCA, Knights of Columbus, and Jewish Welfare Board had buildings specially constructed and staffed to serve the recreational needs of the boys.

Two months earlier in October, General Wood, along with all other division commanders of stateside training camps, was ordered to spend a month in France observing combat conditions. On the way over, General Wood stopped in England to confer with a number of officials eager to have American forces assigned as reinforcements under British and French commanders. Both General Pershing and President Wilson were opposed to such a move, preferring instead that American units function on their own, under their own commanders in their own sectors. General Wood, however,

To train for trench warfare, the men covered 1,000 square yards of Camp Funston's Carpenter Hill with an elaborate system of trenches. Three parallel rows of trenches joined by communicating trenches were completed with dugouts, barbed wire, and machine gun emplacements. Through the winter of 1917 and the spring of 1918, the men trained there, practiced relief rotations, and under a variety of conditions attacked, defended, and attacked again. The men trained with gas masks in a specially built "gas house" where they remained exposed to deadly gas for prolonged periods.

suggested that perhaps American units the size of intact battalions could be rotated into British and French units, where they could serve as reinforcements and receive valuable training at the same time.[17] General Pershing grew increasingly more irritated at the publicity Wood was generating, and when Pershing discovered that the British were about to confer a medal on Wood, ordered a moratorium on American soldiers receiving a decoration from a foreign power.

Once in France, Wood continued to express the opinion that smaller-sized American units could possibly serve under the command of British and French commanders. Wood's Chief of Staff, Colonel Charles Kilbourne, who had accompanied Wood to Europe, noted that wherever the General went he seemed to draw "everyone who had a grouch against Pershing or the Administration," sometimes attracting as many as 70 men who gathered around him in a "great camp fire circle of complaint."[18] Pershing's irritation with Wood only increased.

Then an event occurred that threatened Wood's life and necessitated his remaining in France longer than the originally intended one month. On January 27, 1918, Wood and Kilbourne visited the Sixth Army School of Automatic Arms at Fere en Tardenoise to observe a trench mortar demonstration. The French wanted to demonstrate how the range of 3-inch mortars could be increased by adding rings of cordite, a stringy explosive containing nitroglycerin, to the base of the mortar rounds. The French artillery officer added one, then two, then three rings separately in succession to three different mortar rounds, each time increasing the new round's range. After he added the fourth ring and lit the fuse, however, the round stuck and the mortar casing exploded, sending chunks of shrapnel into the observers 10 feet behind.

The commandant of the camp was decapitated, his assistant was killed instantly with a wound to the heart, and Kilbourne lost his right eye before a piece of shrapnel stuck in the front of his brain. Six other French men and officers were killed and others were seriously injured. Six pieces of shrapnel ripped through Wood's tunic and a seventh severed a vessel in his right arm, stopping just short of the median nerve. After being fitted with a tourniquet, Wood refused further treatment until the others could receive attention. He walked a mile to the nearest road, from which he was transported to the hospital at Fere en Tardenois. There, French surgeons cleaned the wound and removed the metal from the nerve.[19]

Wood spent three weeks recuperating at the American hospital in the Hotel Ritz in Paris. Then General Pershing invited him to AEF headquarters in Chaumont to complete his recuperation. There, surprisingly, Wood continued his criticism of Pershing, this time before the General's face at a dinner party hosted by the AEF Commander. Although Pershing exercised restraint, he later ordered Wood to proceed directly to the port of Bordeaux and from there, back to Camp Funston, clear of any further interference.

General Pershing wrote Secretary of War Newton D. Baker that Wood, now 58 years old, was permanently disabled by the shrapnel wound, totally unfit for command, had a disloyal attitude, was only a "political general" with little knowledge of military tactics, and had no combat command experience. "It would settle his pernicious activities," Pershing wrote, "if he could be retired."[20]

Undaunted but piqued by being ordered back to the states, Wood maneuvered to pass a mandatory physical examination and departed on May 22, 1918, from Camp Funston with the 89th Division on its way to France. Meanwhile, an order relieving Wood of his command of the 89th caught up with him at the Waldorf Hotel in New York, and he immediately proceeded to Washington where Baker bluntly told him he would never go to France because Pershing didn't want him interfering there.[21]

Finally, granted a meeting with President Wilson, Wood reminded the President that as the Army's senior officer and now certified as fit for combat, he deserved to go to war. Instead, Wood was assigned to train the newly formed 10th Division, a concession to his being sent completely out of the way to the Army's Western Department in San Francisco. After a public outcry against Wood's treatment, Wilson suggested to Baker that, after all, perhaps Wood could be given command of an American division in Italy, away from the Western Front, but Baker was adamantly opposed and Wood was returned to Camp Funston in June 1918. There he remained until the end of the war.

After a brief but serious run at becoming the 1920 Republican candidate for the presidency, Wood was appointed Governor General of the Philippines. His health continued to decline from partial paralysis and seizures until he met his death on August 6, 1927, two months short of his 67th birthday.

Brigadier General Frank L. Winn

During the four-and-a-half months of General Wood's absence from Camp Funston (December 26, 1917 to April 12, 1918) his Chief of Staff, Brigadier General Frank L. Winn, a native of Winchester, Kentucky, took over the training of the 89th Division.[22]

At the same time, however, morale within the division suffered from constant re-assignments of men to fill vacancies in other divisions, some in the United States and others already deployed in France. The re-assignments most often occurred in specialty occupations where expertise depended upon prior civilian experience and was more acutely felt when it was in short supply. *Collier's Weekly* reporter William Slavens McNutt visited Camp Funston in January 1918 and described the situation from the point of view of the troops themselves:

The company is just at the top of its stride when along comes a requisition for fifty men from the organization to go toward filling up a National Guard unit perhaps. Then the top sergeant of whom the captain brags is taken for some special construction work abroad. This, that, and the other noncommissioned officer and private are taken from the skilled tradesmen, numbering among the best men in the organization, are picked for special service according to their occupation, and sent away a few at a time.[24]

The re-assignments had a great impact on morale, as McNutt went on to illustrate:

"Visit that same orderly room, say four or

Major General Frank L. Winn.[23]

five months from the time the company was first organized in September last. You find the captain blue and tired.

'We had one of the best outfits in the division,' he tells you regretfully. 'Wish you could have seen it when we were at our best. Course there's no use your sticking around now; we're all shot to pieces. They've bled us of all our best men. They've got all my noncoms and so many carpenters and blacksmiths and chauffeurs and the Lord knows what all, that we've got only the skeleton of an organization left. Now we'll have to take new men to fill up the company and go through the training all over again. What's the use of breaking your heart to build up an organization only to have them tear it to pieces!'"[25]

The situation began to change after General Wood returned to Camp Funston in April 1918 and replacements into the 89th began to arrive, many from Camp Grant, Illinois. Vacancies were filled, and training efforts redoubled before the first units of the 89th, now under the command of General Winn once again, began to entrain for Camp Mills, Long Island, and on June 4, into nine camouflaged British ships[26] for the voyage to Liverpool, where the convoy arrived on June 16, having spent 12 days at sea. After spending a few days at Winchester, the 89th moved by rail to Southampton and then across the channel to Le Havre and Cherbourg, France, between June 20 and June 29, 1918.

After two days on freight cars, the division stopped between Chaumont and Neufchateau in an area in the Haute-Marne known as the "Fourth Training Area," or more commonly as the "Reynel Training Area."[27] There, the troops trained in the tactics of open warfare with live grenade and rifle fire.[28] The overseas cap now replaced the wide-brimmed campaign hat, field shoes displaced russet shoes, and wrap leggings succeeded canvas. Steel helmets were issued along with gas masks, and rifle units became familiar with the French Chauchat automatic rifle.[29]

On August 3 and 4, 1918, the 89th boarded trucks and headed through Neufchateau for the front lines north of Toul to relieve the 82nd Division between the towns of Remenauville and Bouconville.[30] The 89th was the first American unit to be deployed into the line as a unit without having first been sent in with French or British troops, but the Division was still under the command of General Passaga of the 32nd French Army Corps, which was, in turn, part of the Eighth French Army commanded by General Gerard.[31]

On August 7-8, the front line 1st battalions of the 354th and 355th Infantry regiments in Bois de Jury, Bois de la Hazelle, and to the south and west of Fliery were bombarded with between 9,000 and 10,000 mustard and phosgene gas shells interspersed with high explosives,[32] killing 42 officers and men. The 89th subsequently repelled a series of German raids and encountered enemy resistance as patrols penetrated more deeply into German lines to establish the extent and condition of German trenches and wire.

On August 10, the First American Army formed, and the 89th became part of it,[33] holding a front line from before the western edge of Limey to about a kilometer west and north of Flirey. Directly in front of them was the forest of Mort Mare, the key to German positions between St. Mihiel and Pont-a-Mousson.

Major General William M. Wright

On September 6, 1918, during the planning for the St. Mihiel Offensive, General William Wright assumed command of the 89th, and General Winn took command of the 177th Infantry Brigade, one of two infantry brigades that made up the 89th.[34]

Preparations were under way for the St. Mihiel Offensive, September 12-16, 1918. For the first time in the war, American units under American commanders would stand the test of combat. Four hours of artillery bombardment in which more than a million rounds were fired became the "most intense concentration of artillery fire known in history" to that point.[36] The 177th and 178th Brigades worked their ways through the forest of Mort Mare before meeting

Major General William M. Wright.[35]

up with each other and allowing the Division to advance to the heights north of Euvezin, where the advance halted and the lines reorganized before moving on to Xammes, the final objective. (See map of the St. Mihiel Offensive, p.235) The 89th now confronted the German Hindenburg Line and was under fire from the fortifications of Metz.

Meanwhile, on the heights south of Bouillonville, Sergeant Harry Adams of Company K, 353rd Infantry accomplished an incredible feat. Pursuing a German soldier through a house and into an opening in the hillside behind the house, Sgt. Adams fired the last two shots left in his pistol into the door of the opening and called for the occupants to show themselves. To the sergeant's amazement, approximately 300 prisoners emerged with their hands in the air, including seven officers, one of whom was a Lieutenant Colonel. Brandishing his empty pistol, Sergeant Adams escorted the group back to his platoon commander, Lieutenant Chase, who upon their approach thought that a German counterattack was in the works, until Adams was able to assure him otherwise.

All in all, the 89th had succeeded beyond all expectations, but had experienced severe problems in the process. These included deficiencies in liaison – troops with Division, and in other cases, brigade with troops. Roads were so seriously congested at Flirey that food and supply lines were tied up for two days and the evacuation of the wounded was nearly impossible. Worst of all was that failure to manage road traffic kept artillery from advancing in necessary support. In addition was the confusion caused by disorientation. Plenty of maps were available, but they were never distributed to most platoon and company commanders, who were thus placed at a severe disadvantage as they attempted to advance under fire. It was necessary to address these deficiencies before the next offensive, the Battle of the Meuse-Argonne.

After a series of raids and relief of various units, the 37th Division took over from the 89th on the nights of October 7-8 and 8-9, 1918. According to the unit history, the 89th had been in battle for two months and a day, "perhaps the longest period of uninterrupted conflict which any American division was called upon to endure."[38] The 89th moved from Commercy through the towns of Gironville, Boncourt, Erize, and St. Dizier enroute to a rear area on the Argonne as part of the reserve of the First American Army. Leaving the road at Erize la Petite, troops followed the valley of the River Aire through Fleury, Rarecourt and Auzeville to Recicourt. The division was immediately east of the central part of the Argonne and south of the road from Verdun to Ste. Menhould.

On October 12, the 89th became part of the Second Army, commanded by Lieutenant General Robert L. Bullard; the Division was transferred from Third Corps to Fifth Corps and ordered to move to the vicinity of Eclisfontaine and Epinonville to support the 32nd and 42nd Divisions. On October 13, the 89th left the Recicourt area, went past Avocourt and Cheppy Wood, and arrived outside

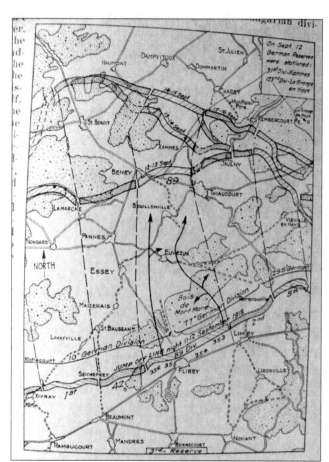

The St. Mihiel Offensive, September 12-15, 1918.[37]

of Montfaucon.[40] The next morning, the Division bivouacked around Epinonville and Eclisfontaine, and on October 18-19, relieved the 32nd Division

Prior to the final attack of the war, the 89th was assigned the critical task of cleaning up the Bois de Bantheville. These woods were vital to the German position, and the 89th advanced foot by foot for two days enduring gas and shell until the woods were finally cleared. On November 1, the division took the heights of Barricourt, and on November 2, again endured

The area of the 89th's operation in northeast France relative to the English Channel, Belgium, an the Alsace-Lorraine.[39d]

heavy artillery, gas, and shrapnel on the reverse slopes of Barricourt. The next day, the 178th Brigade passed through the 177th's lines and continued to advance. The infantry took Halles, Beauclair, Maucourt Farm, and the woods northeast of Champy. On November 4, the 356th Infantry reached the Forest of Dieulet, and the right of the 89th forced its way into Laneuville.

By November 5, the 89th Division had advanced 25 kilometers in 15 days against heavy resistance, and Corps Commander General Summerall ordered the 1st Division to its relief. However, General Wright objected; he wanted the 89th to finish the job. The Division's boundary was extended westward, and the 178th Brigade pushed on to the Meuse River and had patrols in the town of Pouilly. The Division then brought up bridge material to cross the Meuse; the 90th Division on the right was to take Stenay by the river's east bank.

Stenay had been the headquarters of the German Crown Prince for two-and-a-half years.[42] Behind the town were the German fortifications positioned in the hills above the river, with the advantage of machine gun, artillery, and gas constantly raking the Americans entrenched on the other side. On November 8, a general order was issued on the American side: "'Call for volunteers to cross the Meuse River and obtain information upon the enemy's position,' it read."[43] Six men from the 356th, the "All-Missouri" Regiment[44] immediately stepped forward to cross the chilling 150-200 feet to the other side.

"'It is certain death to go across,' the commanding officer told them.

'You will have to leave everything behind you. You will have to swim the river. You probably will be shot at by machine guns and artillery, for the boche are guarding it carefully. The river is wide, swift, and deep. If you cross, the chances are that you will be killed, captured or drowned on the way back. I want you to know just what chances you are taking. You will be expected to locate the enemy strong points. Learn how strong the town of Pouilly is garrisoned, just where the machine guns are located and what is going on within the German lines.'"

Undaunted, the men set out in pairs to different points along the river. They laid aside their rifles, shed their boots, heavy clothing, and gas masks, then slid into the icy November water. Sergeant Waldo M. Hatler, Company B, and Corporal John W. McAfee, Company D, entered the water together, but before reaching the opposite bank, McAfee drowned.

Lieutenant St. George S. Creaghe of Company A and Lieutenant Francis E. A. Hayes of Company D entered the water together at the mouth of Wame Creek, but encountering a German patrol boat, they waited in the freezing water until the boat passed. Going further downstream for another attempt, they were surprised by the voice of a German watch on the opposite shore, but heard him in enough time to avoid detection. Increasingly aware of the approaching morning light and exhausted by their efforts, they abandoned any further attempts at crossing.

Private First Class Harold I. Johnston and Private David B. Barkley, both of Company A, entered the water together near Pouilly. Both successfully swam across the river, and Johnston crawled 150 yards to inspect the condition of the banks and their suitability for a crossing. During their return Barkley was drowned.[45]

The Kansas City Star war correspondent, Otto P. Higgins, who was on the scene, de-

Map of the Meuse-Argonne offensive.[41]

scribed what happened next: "It was almost dawn when two lone sentries doing outpost duty were surprised into sudden wakefulness by two cold, shivering, dripping men climbing out of the water near them. The sharp command to 'halt' was given, and the men explained who they were. Whereupon they were hustled to headquarters wrapped in warm blankets and given hot food and drink.

"The two were Sergt. Harold Johnston of Denver, Col., and Sergt M. Waldo Hatler of Neosho, Mo., and they had completed the trip across the river into the woods on the other side, up and down the bank and up to the edge of the town. The information they obtained that night resulted in the plans being made for the eventual crossing of the river the night of November 10 and the morning of November 11 by the 89th Division, the capture of the towns of Pouilly and Stenay and the capture of the heights on the east bank of the Meuse, the principal thing in the great Meuse-Argonne offensive.

"Sergeant Johnstone received the Congressional Medal of Honor for the feat. Sergeant Hatler received the Distinguished Service Cross, the *Croix de Guerre* and had been recommended for the Congressional Medal of Honor, the highest honor that can be bestowed upon a soldier by the United States of America for bravery and sacrifice."[46]

Later, Hatler did receive the Medal of Honor, and Private Barkeley, the man who had risked his life with Johnston that night, received the same distinction posthumously.[47]

The Division history describes in detail what happened next during the final two days of fighting: "10-11 November. The 353rd Infantry was to clear the east heights as soon as the 90th Division would take Stenay. When the 90th stopped south of Stenay our engineers and 1st Battalion, 353rd, pushed across from Laneuville and seized Stenay. Our operations to the north made this possible. By 6 p.m. of the 10th the 356th Infantry advanced down Wame Creek where the engineers had prepared a catamaran ferry. Under cover of brisk shelling, two battalions each of the 356th and 355th Infantry put over. Pouilly was passed and Autreville taken. Patrols entered Moulins and the objective on the heights gained before 11 o'clock. On the right we seized Stenay. Word as to the Armistice was received late, so that 11 hours 11 November found the 89th pushing forward beyond the Meuse. At Letanne a battalion of 356th Infantry crossing in joint operation with the 2nd Division suffered heavy losses."[49]

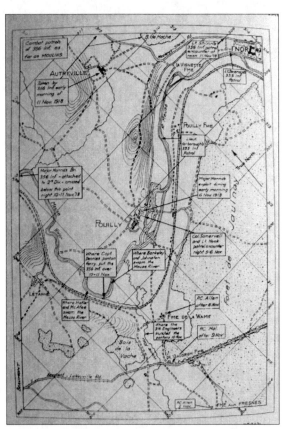

"Scene of operations by the 355th and 356th Infantry in the vicinity of Pouilly and Letanne, Nov. 5-11, 1918."[48]

Some controversy ensued when the 90th Division introduced a formal claim to be accorded sole credit for the capture of Stenay. Colonel John C. H. Lee, Chief of Staff of the 89th Division, investigated the 90th's claim and concluded that "'there is no question in my mind but that the 89th Division at least shared in the taking of Stenay, and this fact was apparently recognized at the time by the Corps and Army drawing the boundary in the town, giving the northern and larger part of the town to the 89th Division. There is no attempt on the part of this division to steal glory from the 90th Division. Our troops took a chance and entered the town to clinch it, while the 90th Division apparently set still and waited for the cessation of hostilities.'"[50]

Some controversy also attended General Wright, who was criticized for continuing the advance into Stenay at the cost of American lives when he knew that the Armistice was just a matter of hours away. In his defense, Robert Ferrell, who edited General Wright's diary of the Meuse-Argonne battle, pointed out that Wright did not want any more casualties at the Meuse than was necessary but, with other senior officers, believed that American bridgeheads were necessary to keep German defenses from hardening and requiring even more loss of life should these defenses need to be overcome in case the Armistice did not hold.

"In later years the cost of crossing the Meuse was often remarked," Ferrell said, "usually in criticism, and as the achievements of Allied victory gradually lost favor with broad masses of the American People (all that is subject in itself) there often was a finger pointing at undue casualties taken by the Americans, with the critics citing the Meuse crossings: the soldiers, it was said, were driven like cattle to the slaughter, just as the war was ending. All this was nonsense."[51]

The Army of Occupation: General Winn Resumes Command

On November 12, the day after the Armistice, General Wright was transferred to command of the 1st Corps, and Major General Frank L. Winn resumed command of the Division until it was mustered out. He was then returned to his rank of Colonel in the regular service and was assigned command of Camp Custer, Michigan.[52] In 1919, General Winn was awarded the Distinguished Service Medal. His citation read in part: "In the St. Mihiel and Meuse-Argonne offensives he accompanied the assaulting battalions and placed them on their objectives, inspiring all by his personal courage and gaining their confidence by his exceptional tactical skill and ability as a leader. At all times he was tireless in energy, showing keen judgment and initiative in handling difficult situations."[53]

Now came the occupation of Germany. The march into Germany began on the morning of November 24, as the Division advanced from the Meuse to Virton in Belgium. Headquarters was established at Dampicourt. The Division then moved to Echternach, Luxembourg, from which it entered into Germany on December 5. The area that the 89th occupied surrounded the German city of Trier and was 50 miles long from north to south and 30 miles wide, with a population of just more than 200,000.[54] The area included the German *kreisen*, or counties, of Prüm, occupied by the 177th Infantry Brigade; Bittburg, occupied by the 164th Artillery Brigade; Trier (land), occupied by the 178th Infantry Brigade; and Saarburg, occupied by the 355th Infantry. The city of Trier itself was not included in the 89th's area of occupation because it had been reserved as advance headquarters for the General Headquarters of the AEF. Eighty-ninth Division headquarters were located in the village of Kyllburg.

The troops spent a good deal of time in training and athletics that included football, basketball, indoor baseball, and soccer. The YMCA donated athletic equipment, and in the spring of 1919, General Winn established a league of regimental teams. Otherwise, General Winn spent his time attending to the establishment of a civil administration that had been allotted for German territory by the provisions of the Armistice.

Besides military training and athletics, troops took part in the Army's educational program, which set out as a first priority to eliminate within its ranks the incidence of illiteracy, estimated at that time to be about three percent of the troops. At the conclusion of their operation, the Post Schools could boast of a rate of 80 percent satisfactory completion for the attendees.

Opportunities for higher education were also available to the troops. Approximately 150 men of the 89th attended some of the leading universities of England and France, with a large number attending the AEF University organized at Beaune, France. Many of the teachers were recruited through the educational branch of the YMCA, but even more came from the military forces themselves. In April 1919, the YMCA educational program was taken over by the U.S. Army, and the teachers became non-military government employees. Approximately 250 students and teachers in the AEF University came from the 89th Division.[55]

In addition to literacy and higher education opportunities, the Division also established an educational center under the direction of a Divisional Educational Officer, Lt. Col. George H. England, who later wrote the divisional history. Three Divisional schools operated from March 17 to early May, 1919, and included a Technical School attended by 250 students and located in the large German munitions plant at Kehr, near Halschlag, in the northern portion of the area of occupation. At the German Convent at Prüm, in a facility formerly used as a *gymnasium* (a secondary school for boys), a program of studies similar to those offered during the first two years of college was established and pursued by about 125 men of the 89th. Finally, a School of Agriculture was opened at Hermeskail in the southeastern part of the occupation area and was attended by about 150 students, who took courses in animal husbandry, agronomy, and English.[56]

Those military personnel not attending the schools took on duties as guards at bridge crossings, tunnels, culverts, water points, switches, railroad stations, ferries, and the border between Luxembourg and Germany. In addition, weekly patrols were ordered for all towns with a population of more than 200. These patrols met with the burgomaster and inspected sanitation, liquor regulations, and the regulations pertaining to discharged German soldiers.[57] Troops also took charge of repair and maintenance of German roads, which were found considerably inferior to roads in France and had seen hardly any maintenance since the start of the war. For the most

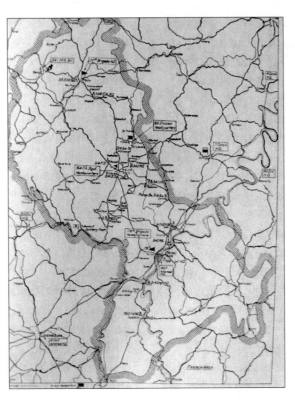

"The area in Germany occupied by the 89th Division."[61]

part, German civilian labor was requisitioned for this work, but American engineer troops sometimes took the labor on themselves, especially where military transportation needs took precedence. The American engineers also supervised public utilities within the occupied area.[58]

Finally, it was time to come home. Prior to the departure of American divisions for the States, General Pershing made a personal review. His review of the 89th took place on April 23, 1919, at the airplane station in Trier. Service decorations of regimental colors, as well as individual decorations for gallantry, were a highlight of the review. Both General Pershing and Secretary of War Newton D. Baker, who had accompanied the Commander-in-Chief for the occasion, addressed the troops, commending them for their service.

That service had indeed been impressive. Nine men of the 89th had been awarded the Medal of Honor, four Medals of Honor were awarded to soldiers of the 356th Infantry, and three members of the 354th Infantry won medals.[59] The Division had captured 5,061 prisoners, more than eight percent of all prisoners captured by the 29 combat divisions of the AEF and surpassed only by the 2nd and 1st Divisions. The 89th was first in a number of other respects:

A larger percentage of time in contact with the enemy than any other division after its first contact,

First to move from the training area to the front by American trucks under American command,

First to enter the line without previously being brigaded with French or British troops,

First to be continuously in the front line for more than eight weeks, and The fist National Army Division to enter Germany.[60]

As for casualties, the 89th suffered 3,424 in the St. Mihiel Sector from August 7 to October 9. In the Meuse-Argonne, the Division suffered 3,578 casualties for a grand total of 7,002. Further analysis of the casualties revealed that in the St. Mihiel Offensive, "it cost fifty per cent more to hold than to take," and in the mopping up operation in the Bois de Bantheville Offensive, "getting ready for that advance cost about two-thirds as many casualties as the advance itself." Holding the line on the Meuse River from November 6-10, "involved more than a third as many losses as those suffered during the advance which preceded."[62] Finally, "the last twenty hours of the war cost more than a fifth as many casualties as occurred during the Meuse-Argonne advance, most of them falling, moreover, on a single battalion."[63]

Its work finished, the 89th began its departure for home from the port of Brest, France, at 10:30 a.m. on May 15, 1919, in the steamship *Leviathan*, with the 355th Infantry, the 353rd Infantry, and the 340th and 341st Machine Gun Battalions on board. Later at 8:30 p.m. that night, the 354th Infantry and the 177th Infantry Brigade HQ sailed on the *S.S. Imperator*. Other units sailed on May 16, 18, and 19, aboard the *U.S.A.T. Agamemnon*, the *U.S.A.T. America*, the *S.S. Montana*, and the *Prinz Frederic Wilhelm*. On May 19, the Division HQ and HQ Troop, the 178th Infantry Brigade HQ, and the 314th Supply Train sailed on the *S.S. Rotterdam*, the last elements of the 89th to leave France.[64]

As the various ships arrived in New York, officers and men were sent to nearby Camp Upton, and from there to various demobilization camps closest to the men's homes, chiefly to Camp Funston, Fort Riley, Kansas, where the men had received their first training. The U.S.A.T. *Leviathan* was the first to arrive in New York on May 22, beating the *S.S. Imperator* into the Hudson River by ten minutes. Both ships were greeted with huge yells.

"Someone on the pier let out a yell," wrote *The Kansas City Star* war correspondent Otto P. Higgins, who had reported on the 89th in France. "This seemed to be the signal for everybody to yell, and the men on board did yell to their heart's content. I have seen many transports leaving France and many of them land in this country, but never before did I hear so much noise among them. Maybe it was because they came from the Rhine, and therefore doubly glad to get home, or maybe it was the spirit that goes with the monster boat. I don't know, but there was something different in it. The men on the *S.S. Imperator* that passed a few minutes later, didn't yell like those on the *U.S.A.T. Leviathan*; I doubt if the men on any more of the transports do. But the 11,958 on the big liner sure opened their lungs."[65]

Once on shore, the officers and men of the "All Kansas" 353rd Infantry were taken to a large dining room on the docks where they were met by Kansas Governor Henry J. Allen, who had himself served with the Red Cross in France and was elected governor while still overseas in service.

Photo from author's collection.

Coming home on the *U.S.A.T. Leviathan*.

"'Kansas is certainly glad to welcome home her heroes,'" the Governor told the regiment. "'We are all proud of you. You made a wonderful record in your fight for democracy, one that will go down into history and live forevermore. You will find that there isn't anything that you will not get when you get home. They have been fattening up the calves and the chickens for some time now, in preparation for your return, and when you get there all will be in readiness for you.'"

Besides Governor Allen, Major General Wood was also there to meet his former command. "He circulated among the officers," Higgins wrote, "renewing old acquaintances and congratulating them on the excellent record of the Kansas regiment."[66]

Eight days later, on May 30, 1919, the 353rd Infantry arrived in Topeka to be greeted by thousands of visitors from every county in Kansas. So great was the joy of the home folks to see their men that the engine was forced to stop several hundred yards from the Union Pacific depot as the crowds broke through the barricades, surged out onto the tracks, and pulled the soldiers out of the car windows, down into the arms of eager relatives.[67]

The 89th was finally home, and its service would be commemorated on both sides of the state line – in Kansas City, Missouri, as well as in Kansas City, Kansas.

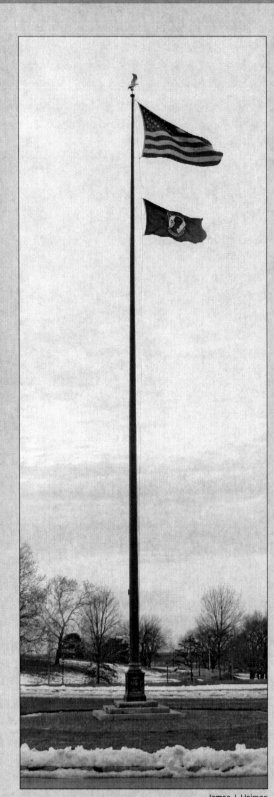

The 89th Division Memorial Flagpole at the entrance to Liberty Memorial Mall.

M-16 89th Division Flagpole
Entrance to Liberty Memorial Mall,
100 West 26th Street, Kansas City, Missouri

In Kansas City, Missouri, the flagpole at the entrance of the Liberty Memorial Mall was erected to commemorate the men of the 89th Division and its commanders. The idea for the memorial began even before the 89th Division returned to the States after the war. With the formation of the 89th Division Society in Bitburg, Germany, on May 4, 1919, while the unit was still serving as an occupying army, the Society stated as one of its first objectives "the erection of a suitable memorial to those 89th Division men who gave their lives during the war."[68]

The idea, however, was not acted upon until 1935, when the William Bland American Legion Post sent a delegation to the society's annual meeting in St. Louis, urging the society to revive the idea of a memorial. Still no action was taken until, at the annual meeting in Los Angeles in 1938, General Winn made a moving appeal for a memorial. To reinforce his plea, he brought sketches of other monuments and urged that a fund be raised. As a result, the 89th Society began a subscription drive for the $6,000 needed to erect a flagpole 70 feet high from a concrete base to be faced with four plaques, three of which would recognize the three generals who commanded the 89th and the fourth which would depict the unit insignia, its years of service in the American Expeditionary Force, and the countries where it served. General Winn died before he could see the memorial, but in his will, as an assertion of his commitment, he left $1,000 in war bonds for its construction.

The formal dedication happened 10 years later on Saturday, November 6, 1948, when Inghram D. Hook, a veteran of the 89th Division's 356th Infantry and vice president of the 89th Division Society, presented the flagpole to the Kansas City Parks Department.[69] Several hundred people stood their ground as a chill wind rippled the flag into action. Also in attendance were retired Lt. Gen. John C. H. Lee, formerly the Chief of Staff of the 89th, and Col. Adrian H. Lindsey, a former battery officer of the 342nd Field Artillery and the current commander of the 89th, which was at the time on reserve status. Kansas City WWI heroes included Maj. Gen. Edward M. Stayton, who commanded Kansas City's 35th Division 110th Engineers during the war and Maj. Gen. Ralph Truman, first cousin of then current President Harry S. Truman and during the war an infantry officer in the 35th Division.[70]

Lt. Gen. Lee highlighted the history of the 89th, Col. Lindsey told of its current status, and prominent Kansas City businessman Charles S. Stevenson, Chair of the Military Affairs Committee of the Chamber of Commerce and former top sergeant of the 314th Engineers and keeper of the records of the 89th, delivered a history of the memorial itself.

Three other attendees were especially significant to the memory of the 89th: Mrs. Mary T. Bland, widow of Major William J. Bland, who commanded the 1st Battalion, 356th Infantry, and Colonel William M. Wright, Jr. and Admiral

Photo by James J. Heiman

Left, Major General William Wright and Major General Frank Winn plaques at the base of the 89th Division Flagpole.

Jerauld Wright, sons of deceased General William Mason Wright, a former commander of the 89th.[71]

Col. Lindsey remembered Mary Bland's husband in an especially poignant way. An artillery officer during the intense barrage in the early days of the St. Mihiel offensive, Lt. Lindsey was exhausted by the action of the battle and the incessant rain. After working all night positioning the Howitzers along a ridge running from Xammes to Boullionville, he crawled into a wagon to get some rest out of the drizzle. Later, he was awakened by a ration cart

coming up the road. He jumped out of the wagon and landed next to four or five freshly dug graves. Looking up at the identification tag on one of the wooden crosses, he read Major Bland's name and was struck by the force of recognition. He knew Major Bland well, and knew that he had led a charge against the enemy on the very ridge where Lindsey now stood staring at the identification tag on the major's grave. "That was the first time that I realized war was not all romance and that you might get hurt," he said. "It made a lasting impression on me."[72]

Not quite as poignant, but certainly powerful in its symbolism, was the gesture made by Charles S. Stevenson. During his brief speech on the story of the memorial, Stevenson turned to Colonel Wright and Admiral Wright and presented them with a replica of the bas relief of their father, General William Mason Wright, depicted on the east side of the base of the memorial flagpole. He asked them to present the image to their mother, who was unable to attend the ceremony. Also unable to attend was the widow of General Winn, the man who had advocated so strongly for the memorial. Stevenson told the audience that the 89th Society had a similar memento for his widow, a replica of General Winn's image on the west side of the base of the monument.

By 1948, the third general commemorated by the 89th memorial, Maj. Gen. Leonard Wood, was dead, and so was his widow, so a similar presentation could not be made to her.

At the flagpole are original images of those three generals who commanded the boys from the Midwest – the 7 states of Kansas, Missouri, Nebraska, Colorado, South Dakota, New Mexico, and Arizona. The boys were mostly draftees who trained at Camp Funston, Fort Riley, Kansas, and Gen. Leonard Wood, after whom the Missouri Fort Leonard Wood is named, trained them there. For political reasons, Gen. Wood was denied the opportunity to lead them in combat, so Gen. William Mason Wright took command of the Division during the battles of St. Mihiel and the Meuse-Argonne, capturing the stronghold of Stenay just before the Armistice. Brig. Gen. Frank L. Winn commanded the 89th at Funston while Gen. Wood was in France, becoming familiar with the conditions the troops would face when they arrived. Gen. Winn also took the boys "over there" when Gen. Wood was denied the opportunity to do so. Gen. Winn then resumed command during the occupation, when Gen. Wright was assigned command of the 1st Army Corps, and it was Gen. Winn, who brought the boys back home.

Three generals whose names began with the letter "W" were in command of a division whose insignia was a "Rolling W." That is, the division patch looked like an "M" in one position and a "W" when rotated 180 degrees to form the initial letters for "Mid-West," which is what the Division was called. Another rather fortuitous piece of luck is that the names of the generals spells out the phrase "Right Would Win," the destiny of one of the most successful of the AEF divisions.

James J. Heiman

A "demonstration" of the "Rolling W" of the 89th Midwest Division.

M-17 Soldiers and Sailors Memorial
7th Street between Tauromee and Barnett, Kansas City, Kansas

Besides being honored by the 89th Division Flagpole at Liberty Memorial Mall in Kansas City, Missouri, the World War I service of a number of 89th Division Kansas veterans is also commemorated in the Soldiers and Sailors Memorial across the state line in Kansas City, Kansas. These soldiers were part of the approximately 6,482 men from Wyandotte County, Kansas, who served in the Army, Navy, and Marine Corps during the Great War.[73] Throughout Kansas, a total of 69,051 served.[74] To recognize their sacrifice, the Kansas Legislature enacted a law permitting local governments to erect memorials as long as 25 percent of the registered voters approved. The result was a handsome building and prominent flagpole – and a controversial attempt to house a national veterans association.

Shortly after the Kansas law passed, Harry Darby, with the backing of World War I veterans, petitioned the Kansas City, Kansas, commissioners to hold an election for the approval of $500,000 in bonds for the purchase of a site and the construction of a building. Nearly 61 percent of the 3,553 votes cast approved, and the present site was purchased for $96,046.01.

The site along 7th Street between Barnett and Tauromee was dedicated on May 14, 1923, with Kansas Governor Jonathan M. Davis and American Legion Commander-in-Chief Alvin M. Owsley officiating. The plans developed by Rose and Patterson were accepted on July 19, 1923, and the Baer Engineering Company of Leavenworth contracted to complete the work. The cornerstone was laid on May 26, 1924, with the then current American Legion Commander in Chief John R. Quinn in attendance.

The structure is 45 by 73 feet, with 12 Corinthian columns supporting the entrances. The civic auditorium itself consists of an arena and balcony capable of seating 3,532. Smaller halls to the left and right of the large hall provide meeting space for military organizations and their auxiliaries, and a chapel over the "Memorial Hall" can accommodate 800. The basement houses kitchen and other facilities. Pictures and mementoes of the 114 Wyandotte County men who died in the war are housed in a "Room of Silence" on the south side of the hall room. Their names are inscribed on bronze tablets fixed to the walls in the "Memorial Hall" at the front of the building.

Although the American Legion figured prominently in the dedication of the site and the building, the Soldiers and Sailors Memorial Hall has the distinction of being, for eight months, the national home of the Veterans of Foreign Wars before that organization relocated to Missouri. In August 1922, the Kansas City, Kansas, commissioners invited the national encampment of VFW in Seattle to move their national headquarters from Union Square in lower Manhattan, New York, to the 20,000 square foot top floor of the Kansas City, Kansas, memorial building as soon as it was completed. After the legality of the offer was questioned, the city addressed the legal technicalities and renewed their offer at the next VFW encampment, this time in Norfolk, Virginia.

At the center of the nation, Kansas City's location could offer many advantages: a

Soldiers and Sailors Memorial, Kansas City, Kansas.

maximum mail service delivery time of three days to anywhere in the nation, 400 passenger and freight trains arriving daily, and a growing airline industry. Those advantages – along with free utilities, free custodial services, and free rent – made Kansas City's offer much more enticing than the offers from Detroit and Minneapolis.[75] So the VFW accepted the offer, signed a long-term lease for the nominal charge of $1.00 a year, and proceeded to move their national headquarters from the edge of Greenwich Village, New York, to Kansas City, Kansas, housing temporarily at 616 N. 7th until Memorial Hall was ready in October 1924.

Then the trouble began. In June 1925, the Soldiers and Sailors Memorial was placed under a board of three trustees. "Its first move was to demand that the VFW pay for part of building maintenance and give up office space—contradicting the original agreement. Insult was added to injury when trustees ordered the VFW symbol removed from the base of the flagpole in front of the building."[76]

Trustee Harry Darby filed a petition against his fellow trustees, James L. Otterman and Frank Strickland, alleging that Kansas City, Kansas, had unlawfully and wrongfully entered into a conspiracy and agreement with the VFW to provide necessary rooms and accommodations for the national headquarters of the organization at the expense of the taxpayers."[77] Darby thought a reasonable rental would be $25,000. Judge Fischer held a hearing and agreed that furnishing occupancy, light, water, fuel, and janitorial service to the VFW without compensation constituted taxation for private purposes and was therefore unlawful.

On appeal, the Kansas Supreme Court held in February 1927, "a city has no power to lease to a private corporation any part of a building erected under the provisions of the statute under which the Memorial was built."[78] "This unseemly confrontation ended when the VFW struck a deal with the city council in Missouri."[79] As a result, the national headquarters of the VFW packed up once again and this time moved on January 1, 1930, across the state line to a 12-story building at 34th and Broadway, the previous site for the Jackson County Medical Society, where the VFW Headquarters has remained ever since. Just a few months later, in November 1930, a joint committee of the Kansas City Chamber of Commerce and the VFW named Jackson County, Missouri, Judge Harry S. Truman as chair of the national convention committee to bring some 10,000 delegates, members, and guests to Kansas City for the national encampment in the fall of 1931.[80]

■ ■ ■

Both the Veterans of Foreign Wars and the American Legion have figured prominently in Kansas City, not only representing the interests of veterans of the Great War but also providing them with the opportunity to keep close the ties they had forged with their comrades during the war. Those bonds are demonstrated with special poignancy in the stories of three 89th Division Kansas City men, two of whose names, Private Joseph Liebman and Private Thomas J. Kiely, were adopted by American Legion posts and one of whom, Major Mark Hanna, is remembered by his orderly in an especially moving way.

James J. Heiman

Confederate monument in Forest Hill Cemetery, Kansas City, Missouri.

Joseph Liebman: Still in a Field of Battle
(American Legion Post No. 148)

American Legion Post No. 148 is named for Private Joseph Liebman, the son of a German immigrant, who came to the United States in 1883. Private Liebman holds the distinction of being the first burial and having the only grave stone upright in Rose Hill Cemetery. In another one of the ironies of war, Joseph Liebman's gravestone lies where a stone fence once served as temporary protection for General Sterling Price's Confederate Army as it retreated from the Battle of Westport. Across the street in Forest Hill Cemetery, a tall stone monument rises to mark the graves of many of the Confederates who fought that battle and are now buried under stone markers.

On October 23, 1864, a line of stacked stone fences two to three feet high extended west to State Line Road from what is now the 6901 Troost Avenue entrance to Kansas City's Forest Hill Cemetery. That day, along this line, an estimated 20,000 men engaged in what later became known as "Shelby's Last Stand." Behind the stone fences, Confederate General Jo Shelby's men crouched in defense after being driven back from Westport by Federal troops under the command of General Samuel R. Curtis. Union General Alfred Pleasonton flanked Shelby on the east. Later that day, after 1 p.m., Confederate Colonel Sidney D. Jackman's brigade arrived to defend Shelby's right flank, while Shelby's redoubtable "Iron Brigade" under General M. Jeff Thompson's command took up a position farther west.[81]

The Confederates, however, could not hold; after a bloody fight, Generals Curtis and Pleasonton drove them from their position into a southerly retreat that eventually ended up in Arkansas.[82] Shelby's action, however, is credited with saving General Price's army from complete annihilation after the defeat it had suffered just days earlier at Westport, known by some as the "Gettysburg of the West."[83] A Confederate monument now stands in Forest Hill Cemetery at the east end of where the stone fences once stood, and scattered about it are the graves of General Shelby and many of the men who had fought for and against him that October day, 1864.

Fifty-four years later on September 12, 1918, in a 16-mile salient before the town of St. Mihiel, 150 miles east of Paris, a continent away in France, the American Expeditionary Forces under the command of Missouri native General John J. "Black Jack" Pershing engaged in its first action as a separate American entity in the Great War. Nine divisions of 550,000 Americans constituted the largest collective force of Americans up to that time, rivaling the combined Confederate and Union forces at Gettysburg, Pennsylvania, in 1863.[84] The Americans were victorious that day in 1918, proving their worth as a fighting unit, but victory came at a price – 7,000 killed and wounded in a 48-hour period.[85] Among those casualties was Private Joseph Liebman.

West of the Confederate monument in Forest Hill Cemetery, across Troost Avenue, along the old fence line whose stones are now scattered over the years, are ten acres of ground purchased by the Bnai Jehudah Congregation in 1919. There in 1921, the body of Private Joseph Liebman, removed from his burial in France, became the first burial in the newly formed Rose Hill Cemetery.[86]

Photo courtesy of National World War I Museum Archives.

Pvt. Joseph Liebman.

Of the some 3,200 burials in the cemetery since then, his is the only monument of its kind,[87] a single stone standing upright where hundreds of other smaller stones had once stood stacked in a line. The other cemetery markers are bronze, level with the ground, and all of a uniform design.

Inducted into the U.S. Army in Kansas City, Missouri, on April 25, 1918,[88] Pvt. Liebman first served with the 35th Company, 164 Depot Brigade, Detention Camp 2, from April 25, 1918, until May 13, 1918, when he joined Company G, 354th Infantry, 89th Division. He served with that unit from June 15, 1918, when he went overseas, to September 13, 1918, when he was killed in action during the battle of St. Mihiel. As next of kin, his brother Sam was officially notified of his death.

Prior to his induction, Joseph had worked as a buyer for the Adler Millinery Company at 1212 Main in Kansas City. He lived at 3308 Prospect Avenue in the home of his parents, Rose and Siegmund Liebman, a saloon keeper and dealer in wholesale liquors, who had immigrated to the United States from Germany in 1883.[89] The fourth of six children, Joseph was born in July 23, 1894[90], and lived in Rosedale, Kansas City, Kansas,

250

James J. Heiman

Joseph Liebman gravesite, Rose Hill Cemetery, Kansas City, Missouri.

during his early years. He was 23 ¾ years of age at the time of his death.

Joseph Liebman's name is inscribed with those of 410 other Kansas City war dead in the Meyer Circle Gateway Memorial and also on the plaque in Memory Hall of the Liberty Memorial. Because his name was taken by American Legion Post No. 148, which received its charter in 1919, he is included in the list of names on the 1921 American Legion I Monument in Budd Park Esplanade. After World War II, the Post added the name of Jay R. Rosenbloom to its official designation.[91]

Although Joseph Liebman fought and died in a different war and was buried for three years in foreign soil, he came home to lie un-der a single stone in unique commemoration where other stones had once marked the battlefield of a civil war. Joseph Liebman, too, in one sense, had fought a civil war: In combat he had given his life against the very country from which his father had immigrated some 35 years earlier. Once fallen in France and now home, he lies still in a field of battle.

Pvt. Thomas J. Kiely:
Company E's Liaison to the 356th
(Thomas J. Kiely Post of the American Legion)

An American Legion post was also named for Private Thomas J. Kiely, and the little park that features The Fitzsimons-Battenfeld monument at Paseo and Cleaver II Boulevard also bears his name. During the battle of St. Mihiel, Pvt. Kiely served as a liaison between the 354th and the 356th Infantry regiments of the 89th Division, to help coordinate their movement through the heavily wooded area of the Bois de Mort Mare ("the woods of the dead sea"), a name that proved prophetic. He was killed while away with the 356th Infantry and never returned alive to his buddies in the 354th. The Americans won the battle of St. Mihiel, but for Private Thomas J. Kiely, the war was over.

A half-acre triangle of ground along Cleaver II Boulevard and the southbound lanes of the Paseo in Kansas City is known as Kiely Park. To the delight of many children who visited the little park years ago, a French 75 mm cannon had been placed there – a relic of the Great War. Although the cannon was no longer operational and certainly posed no military threat to the children, its use by them as a teeter-totter did, and so on May 18, 1941, it was removed, and a week later, on May 25, 1941, the Thomas J. Kiely Post of the American Legion dedicated the site to the memory of Pvt. Thomas J. Kiely, who was killed on the third day of the Battle of St. Mihiel, September 14, 1918.[92] Later, as if to emphasize the concern for the safety and well-being of visitors to the little park, in place of the canon, the Fitzsimons-Battenfeld Post No. 8 of the American Legion erected a granite monument to the memory of two physicians: World War I Army doctor William T. Fitzsimons and World War II U.S.

Navy flight surgeon Lieutenant Senior Grade Jesse R. Battenfeld, Jr.[93]

Thomas J. Kiely, for whom the park was originally named, was not a physician but a worker in the mailroom of *The Kansas City Journal* on 8th and McGee. He was born in Kansas City, Kansas, on January 28, 1896, and his father, John Kiely, worked in the Kansas City stockyards.[94] When Thomas registered for the draft on June 5, 1917, he was 21 years old, and his registration card described him as "short, medium build, gray eyes, with black hair."[95] At the time of his registration, he lived at 3927 Chestnut Ave. until he was inducted in Kansas City on April 24, 1918.[96] At that point, he became part of the 35th Company of the 164th Depot Brigade at Camp Funston, where he had been sent for training. He then joined Company E, 354th Infantry, 89th Division, which had been organized on September 5, 1917, with just five men.[97] Exactly two weeks after Kiely joined Company E, the unit entrained from

Camp Funston for Camp Mills, New Jersey, where the men received their equipment. From there, Thomas J. Kiely and the rest of Company E were to experience a variety of modes of transportation in three foreign countries until they reached their destination in the trenches of France. First, they boarded a train for Montreal, Canada, on the night of June 3.

Two days later, on June 5, they sailed down the St. Lawrence River on board the *S.S. Ascanius* and headed out over the Atlantic, finally landing in Tilbury Docks, England. They spent June 21-25 at a rest camp near Winchester, England, and on June 25, crossed the English Channel. Detraining on June 28 at Rimaucourt, France, they marched 12 kilometers to a training area at Morrionvillers, and on August 5, set out for the Toul Sector in trucks. The next day in barns around Bruley, they had their first encounter with "cooties."

Still scratching from the body lice, they took a narrow gauge railroad to Minorville, and on August 8, advanced to Noviant in the support line of the Fliery element of the Toul Sector. Five days later, one of the platoons moved forward to rescue 1st Battalion victims of a German gas attack. Then the company relieved Company C in the Bois de Hazelle.

On August 19, the Germans lobbed 12,000 shells at their position. Relieved by Company M, Company E withdrew to Noviant before marching to Rehanne Woods for eight days of rest. On August 24, they took their first casualties from 155 mm shells that hit Company F's mess line near where Company E was positioned.

One of their number was killed; two were wounded. After taking over front line trenches before Fliery and enduring an enemy raid on September 7, E Company's Captain Wendell Hay[98] was hit by fragments from an enemy grenade. Turning to his men he said, "Go get them boys. Never mind me." He died as the words left his mouth.

More deaths were to come for Company E.

The next day, the Company moved 200 yards to the right to cover a gap in the line, but the Germans detected the movement and leveled a heavy bombardment on their position, killing Private Samuel DeWitt and medics Sergeant Bernard Reuter and Private Homer J. Butler. From September 9 to 12, Company E dug in, preparing for the big attack of the Battle of San Mihiel.

Early in the morning of September 12, American artillery opened up what was, up to that time, the largest bombardment Americans had ever launched – four solid hours of artillery shelling at the German fortifications around St. Mihiel.

"Artillery was massed everywhere behind our lines," a unit history recalled, "and during the preparatory bombardment its fire was concentrated on the German trenches and roads in rear areas. The effect of this fire was especially noticeable around Bouillonville and on the road thence to Thiacourt, where a German supply train was practically annihilated. Just before the jump off, a heavy barrage was laid on all the front line consisting of gas and H.E. [high explosive] shells from the artillery division. At H hour the barrage crept forward; the infantry followed close behind it."[99]

The St. Mihiel salient had posed a threat to Paris, and the French had attempted to take the salient's German fortifications but had failed in the attempt. General Pershing wanted to eliminate that threat and at the same time, for the first time in the war, engage the American Army as an independent fighting unit, demonstrating to the Germans, the Allies, and to the Americans themselves, that the American Army was a force with which to be reckoned.

The attack on St. Mihiel had been months in planning, and the boys of the 89th Division were to have a key role in it. Known as the "Midwest Division" because its soldiers came from Missouri, Kansas, Nebraska, Colorado, Minnesota, Wisconsin, Arizona, and Illinois, the 89th was assigned to support the 42nd

Division on its left and the 2nd Division on its right[100] in an advance in the general direction of Dampvitoux. A heavily wooded area, the Bois de Mort Mare was directly in its path. To enter the woods directly would cost many lives, so the 89th divided itself into two parts, attacking the woods on both its flanks, but in the process of the attack risking an "interruption of liaison between the two brigades of the Division, the 178th Infantry Brigade on the left and the 177th Infantry Brigade on the right."[101] It was just such an interruption in communication that would later concern Pvt. Thomas J. Kiely. His unit, the 354th Infantry Regiment, was joined with the 353rd Infantry Regiment to form the 177th Infantry Brigade. Meanwhile, the 178th Brigade was made up of the 355th Infantry Regiment and the 356th Infantry Regiment.

"On 12 Sept at 5:30 am, the 356th, the 355th & 353rd advanced … The 354th remained in position before Mort Mare acting as division reserve. The 353rd Infantry passed around east of Mort Mare, mopping up the eastern portion. The 355th Infantry and 356th Infantry advanced through the woods connecting with [the] 353rd Infantry north of Mort Mare, the brigades thereafter moving abreast. By early afternoon the troops had advanced to the high ground between Euvezin and Bouillonville and had sent patrols into Bouillonville and beyond. Hundreds of prisoners had been taken. Resuming the advance, the line of Xammes to the center of Bouillonville, Dampvitoux was reached [on the] night of [the] 12th – 13th. Early on [the] 13th [the] 354th took [its] position on this line between [the] 353rd and 355th.

"Between September 13 and 16th the line was gradually advanced to one extending from about a kilometer south of Charey to the northern edge of the Bois de Dampvitoux. The front line troops dug little fox holes wherever they halted. In the nights they, with the engineers, strung wire in front of the line of fox holes and connected the holes to form continuous trenches. In the day they lay in the fox holes while the enemy's artillery, machine guns and air planes rained fire upon them."[102] It was during this time that Pvt. Thomas J. Keily was killed while on liaison duty with the 356th Infantry.[103]

The 89th had paid a price, but it had achieved its objective and more. It had reached Dampvitoux and had supported the advance of the 42nd and the 2nd Divisions, keeping up with both in the advance. It had held an infantry regiment in reserve, outflanked the Germans in the Bois Mort Mare woods, and had rejoined to withstand continuing enemy air and ground fire. General Pershing could have confidence in these farm boys from the Midwest.[104]

For Thomas J. Kiely, though, the war was over. The casualty reports of May 2, 1918, officially announced his death, and his mother, Julia, was notified as next of kin. His was among the reburials from France to Mount St. Mary's Cemetery in Kansas City.[105] Also removed from France but placed on the angle of ground across from Paseo High School in Kansas City, the French 75mm would remain for a while as a visible reminder of the physical apparatus of the war Thomas J. Kiely had fought.

Later, the children who had found for the canon a much more imaginative purpose would now find the park named for him much less interesting, once their play piece had been removed. But the Thomas J. Kiely Post of the American Legion and the tablets in the Meyer Circle Gateway and on the west wall of Liberty Memorial's Memory Hall would continue to keep his memory alive, and the little park on the Paseo bears his name still.

Major Mark Hanna: To Cross the River

Although no American Legion post bears Major Mark Hanna's name, his exploits behind the German lines in the town of Pouilly proved that he was a man of courage and character. With his orderly, he crossed the River Meuse, and alone walked boldly into the occupied town, stood smoking cigarettes on a busy street, and there observed the activities of the Germans, before returning to his lines once more with valuable information on strength and disposition of forces. Five days later, on the last day of the war, he returned to the Meuse again, leading groups of his men across, until a German shell exploded near him, killing him and wounding his orderly. Major Hanna was awarded the Distinguished Service Cross for his bravery, and his loyal orderly, Private Rudolph Rietsche, wrote to Mrs. Corine Hanna from the hospital in Jefferson Barracks, Missouri, where he was recuperating, to fulfill a promise he had made to the Major while they served together with the 356th Infantry, 89th Division in France.

It was Wednesday, November 5, 1918, just six days before the Armistice would silence the guns along the western front. The 356th Infantry, 89th Division, had reached the Meuse River near Poully, France. German machine guns and artillery held the opposite bank, ready to rain death on any attempt to cross. The need for reconnaissance was critical, so Major Mark Hanna went across a damaged bridge and, for two hours, gathered information on the German position. He returned in broad daylight, pursued by enemy fire, but safe. "The very audacity of this exploit seemed to have rendered him immune," the Division historian wrote.[106] Major Hanna had just two weeks earlier returned from the hospital. He had already been wounded three times.[107]

Otto P. Higgins, *The Kansas City Star's* correspondent who was on the scene, described what happened in detail: "The river was at flood stage and all bridges were destroyed, so no effort was made to cross with troops.

Patrols, however, spent much time on the east bank of the river investigating the enemy's strength and systems of defense.

"Major Mark Hanna, a Kansas City man commanding a battalion of Western Missouri troops, made a bold patrol visit into Pouilly in the fourth day of the drive. Pouilly is on the east bank of the Meuse and was not captured. Major Hanna's troops were on the west bank of the river, across from Pouilly. Bridges had been destroyed, but girders were left standing.

"Major Hanna, accompanied by his orderly, crawled across the girders, a distance of a hundred yards. He stationed the orderly at the east end of the bridge to cover a retreat and walked boldly into the town. Major Hanna stood on a busy street corner in Pouilly, smoking cigarettes, while French civilians and boche soldiers passed by in great numbers. By the audacity of his performance he was not suspected and made a safe return, bringing with him valuable information as to the enemy's strength and activities."[108]

Five days later, close to midnight on November 10, Major Hanna went back to the river again, this time leading small groups of his own men across, but on the third attempt a German shell exploded near him, killing him and wounding his orderly along with others of his command. "Company G, which was designated an assault company, was reduced to 19 men and 2 non-commissioned officers; all officers were killed or wounded. That remnant attached itself to Company F. By 06:00, 300 men of the battalion were consolidated and began to move on the east bank."[109] They went on to Stenay.

Later, mechanic Phil S. Little had occasion to write about his commander the night of the crossing. "Major Hanna was a man to the core and I was afraid that none might sing his praises," Little wrote. "If it were not for him with his cool way, I have my doubts whether I would be here to write you tonight. He went through Hell twice that night of November 10th and met his death after accomplishing the job he was assigned to do. I hope God has mercy on his soul, for without a doubt, <u>he was a man</u>."

Photo courtesy National World War I Museum Archives.

Major Mark Hanna.

Almost three weeks later, on the evening of November 30, 1918, Mark's wife, Corine, 2954 East 28th Street, Kansas City, received a telegram from the War Department informing her of her husband's death.[110] Just the day before, Corine had received a letter from her husband telling her of his promotion to Major.[111] Ironically, he had taken over command of the 2nd Battalion after its commander, Kansas City's Major William J. Bland, and been killed by shell fragments on September 12 at Euvazin, in the Battle of St. Mihiel.

Then on February 10, 1919, Corine Hanna received another letter from the War Department:

To Mrs. Corine Esther Hanna:

This office has been informed by cablegram by the Commanding General, American Expeditionary Forces that he has awarded the Distinguished Service Cross posthumously to your husband, Major Mark Hanna, 356th Infantry.

The citation read:

The Distinguished Service Cross is presented to Mark Hanna, Major, U.S. Army, for extraordinary heroism in action near Stenay, France, November 6 - 11, 1918. Major Hanna

256

displayed extreme courage on November 6 by making a daring reconnaissance of the town of Pouilly, near Stenay. This town was held in strength by the enemy, with evident indication of determination to prevent a crossing of the River Meuse at this point. He remained in this town over two hours, returning with information of great value. On the night of November 10 - 11 he was in command of the second battalion of the 356th Infantry, and while waiting to cross the River Meuse Major Hanna's battalion was subject to terrific shell fire. During this period he walked up and down the line encouraging and steadying his men. Major Hanna was killed at the head of his command.[112]

Born in Chillicothe, Pike County, Ohio, on December 23, 1889,[113] the namesake and nephew of the famous Senator Mark Hanna of Ohio, young Mark Robert Hanna grew up and graduated high school in Ruthven, Iowa, before attending Iowa University in Iowa City to study law. Later he moved to Kansas City and worked in real estate and insurance.

Hanna was 26 years old when he enlisted in Kansas City on June 19, 1916, joined Company G of the 3rd Regiment, Missouri National Guards, and served in the Mexican Border conflict. He advanced to the rank of corporal, and re-enlisted on August 15, 1917. After attending Officer Training School at Fort Riley, he received his commission and on September 3, 1917, took command of Company B, 356th Infantry. He went overseas with the 356th Infantry, 89th Division, on June 4, 1918, and soon became the 356th Infantry Operations Officer.

Five months after receiving notice of her husband's DSC, Corine received another letter remembering the early morning of November 11 – this one from her husband's orderly, Private Rudolph Rietsche:

April 15th, 1919
Mrs. Corine Esther Hanna

My Dear Madam:

I thought the Major's wife would like to know about his life in France. I had the honour of being the brave Major's orderly and I am in a position to give you any information that you may desire, for as his orderly it was my duty to be by his side at all times. I ate, slept and fought with the Major and was also wounded by the shell that killed the Major early on the morning of November the Eleventh, Nineteen-Eighteen only a few hours before the Armistice was signed. The Major often told me to write to his wife in case anything happened to him. I am a patient in the Post hospital at the Jefferson Barracks, MO and will gladly render any service as to information or anything else that is in my power.

Pvt. Rudolph Rietsche[114]

No doubt Private Rietsche had much more to tell her.

Endnotes

1   George H. English. *History of the 89ᵗʰ Division, U.S.A.* (Denver: The War Society of the 89ᵗʰ Division, 1920), p. 50.

2   Ibid, p. 2.

3   Ibid, p. 290.

4   Ibid, p. 22.

5   Jack McCallum. *Leonard Wood: Rough Rider, Surgeon, Architect of American Imperialism.* (New York, 2006), p. 269.

6   Photo by *The Kansas City Star* war correspondent Otto P. Higgins. Sheila Scott Collection.

7   Anthony Kovac, Nancy Hulston, Grace Holmes & Frederick Holmes. "'A Brave and Gallant Company': A Kansas City Hospital in France during the First World War." *Kansas History*, Vol. 32, No. 3, Autumn 2009, p. 169-185.

8   Jack McCallum. *Leonard Wood: Rough Rider, Surgeon, Architect of American Imperialism*, op. cit., p. 274.

9   Anthony Kovac, Nancy Hulston, Grace Holmes & Frederick Holmes. "'A Brave and Gallant Company': A Kansas City Hospital in France during the First World War," op. cit., p. 183.

10   Jack McCallum. *Leonard Wood: Rough Rider, Surgeon, Architect of American Imperialism*, op. cit., p. 274.

11   Ibid.

12   George H. English. *History of the 89ᵗʰ Division, U.S.A.*, op. cit. Photo in frontispiece.

13   Photo by *The Kansas City Star* war correspondent Otto P. Higgins. Sheila Scott Collection.

14   H. P. Wilmott. *World War I.* (New York, DK Publishing, 2007), p. 307.

15   Photo by *The Kansas City Star* war correspondent, Otto P. Higgins. Sheila Scott Collection.

16   George H. English. *History of the 89ᵗʰ Division, U.S.A.*, op. cit., p. 29-30.

17   Jack McCallum. *Leonard Wood: Rough Rider, Surgeon, Architect of American Imperialism*, op. cit., p. 270.

18   Ibid, p. 271.

19   Ibid, p. 271-272.

20   Ibid, p. 272-273.

21   Hermann Haggedorn. *Leonard Wood: A Biography.* (New York: Harper & Brothers, 1931), p. 285-286.

22   George H. English. *History of the 89ᵗʰ Division, U.S.A.*, op. cit., p. 37.

23   George H. English. *History of the 89ᵗʰ Division, U.S.A.* op. cit. Photo in frontispiece.

24   William Slavens McNutt. "R'arin to Go! The Middle West Wants to Be Off for France." *Colliers Weekly.* March 30, 1918, p. 8, 9, 27-29.

25   Ibid.

26   George H. English. *History of the 89ᵗʰ Division, U.S.A.*, op. cit., p. 39.

27   Ibid, p. 44.

28   Ibid, p. 48.

29   Ibid, p. 49.

30   Ibid, p. 55.

31   Ibid, p. 56.

32   Ibid, p. 71.

33   Ibid, p. 89.

34   Ibid, p. 96, 291, 292.

35   George H. English. *History of the 89ᵗʰ Division, U.S.A.* op. cit. Photo in frontispiece.

36   Ibid, p. 97.

37   George H. English. *History of the 89ᵗʰ Division, U.S.A.*, op. cit. Photo from p. 133.

38   Ibid, p. 135.

39   "Routes of 89ᵗʰ Division in the A.E.F." From C. J. Massek, *Official Brief History 89ᵗʰ Division U.S.A.* (G-2, 89ᵗʰ Division, undated).

40   George H. English. *History of the 89ᵗʰ Division, U.S.A.*, op. cit., p. 148.

41   George H. English. *History of the 89ᵗʰ Division, U.S.A.*, op. cit. Photo from p. 245.

42   Ibid, p. 228.

43   Otto P. Higgins. "Unsung Heroes of 356ᵗʰ." *The Kansas City Times*, May 29, 1919, p. 2.

44   "Boys From Home Land." The Kansas City *Star*, May 28, 1919, p. 6,

45   George H. English. *History of the 89th Division, U.S.A.,* op. cit., p. 215-216.

46   Otto P. Higgins. "Unsung Heroes of 356th," op. cit.

47   George H. English. *History of the 89th Division, U.S.A.,* op. cit., p. 216.

48   Map of the Meuse showing the points where elements from the 356th Infantry attempted to swim across the river. Photo from George H. English. *History of the 89th Division, U.S.A.,* op. cit., p. 216.

49   George H. English. *History of the 89th Division, U.S.A.,* op. cit., information from map facing p. 240, "Advance of the 89th Division in the Meuse Argonne, October 18th November 11th 1918."

50   Ibid, p. 242.

51   William M. Wright. *Meuse-Argonne Diary: A Division Commander in World War I.* Robert H. Ferrell, Ed. (Columbia, MO: University of Missouri Press, 2004), p. 155.

52   George H. English. *History of the 89th Division, U.S.A.,* op. cit., p. 329.

53   Frank L. Winn. Distinguished Service Medal Citation. War Department. General Orders No. 62 (1919). http://www. homeofheroes.com/members/03_DSM/army/citations/04_WWI-armyAt.html. Accessed by author on April 7, 2012.

54   George H. English. *History of the 89th Division, U.S.A.,* op. cit., p. 264.

55   Ibid, p. 277.

56   Ibid, p. 278.

57   Ibid, p. 282.

58   Ibid, p. 283-285.

59   Ibid, p. 323-324.

60   Ibid, p. 324.

61   George H. English. *History of the 89th Division, U.S.A.,* op. cit. Photo from p. 265.

62   Ibid, p. 325.

63   Ibid, p. 326.

64   Ibid, p. 329.

65   Otto P. Higgins. "Home for the 89th." *The Kansas City Times,* May 23, 1919, p. 1.

66   Ibid.

67   "An All-Kansas Greeting: Thousands of People Welcomed the 353rd at Topeka." *The Kansas City Times,* May 31, 1919, p. 3. See also, "Boys from Home Land." *The Kansas City Star,* May 28, 1919, p 6.

68   Charles E. Stevenson in 89th Division Society. *Dedication Services 89th Division Memorial.* (Englewood, CO: 89th Division Society, 1948), p. 18.

69   "A Memorial Flag Pole to 89th Division War Dead." Picture from *The Kansas City Star,* November 7, 1948, p. 1A.

70   "Honor to Men of 89th." *The Kansas City Star,* November 7, 1948, p. 3A.

71   Ibid.

72   Col. Adrian H. Lindsey in 89th Division Society. *Dedication Services 89th Division* Memorial, op. cit., p. 17.

73   Grant W. Harrington. *Historic Spots or Mile-Stones in the Progress of Wyandotte County, Kansas.* (Merriam, KS: The Mission Press, 1935), p. 299.

74   Adjutant General. Kansas Casualties in the World War, Regular Army, National Guard, National Army, Enlisted Reserve Corps. Supplement 1. Topeka, KS: Kansas Adjutant General's Office, March 1921.

75   Herbert Molloy Mason, Jr. *VFW: Our First Century 1899-1999.* (Lenexa, KS: Addax Publishing Company, 1999), p. 67.

76   Ibid.

77   Grant W. Harrington. *Historic Spots or Mile-Stones in the Progress of Wyandotte County, Kansas,* op. cit., p. 306.

78   Ibid.

79   Herbert Molloy Mason, Jr. *VFW: Our First Century 1899-1999,* op .cit., p. 67.

80   "Truman to V.F.W. Body." *The Kansas City Star,* November 11, 1930, p. 3.

81   Fred L. Lee. *Gettysburg of the West: The Battle of Westport, October 21-23, 1864.* (Shawnee Mission, KS: Two Trails Genealogy Shop, 1996), p. 133.

82   Jay Monaghan. *Civil War on the Western Border.* (New York: Bonanza Books, 1955), p. 353.

83   "Gettysburg of the West" is the title of Fred L. Lee's book, op. cit. See also, Howard N. Monett. *Action Before Westport 1864.* Revised. (Niwot, CO: University Press of Colorado, 1964), p. 20.

84   James H. Hallas, ed. *Doughboy War: The American Expeditionary Force in WWI.* (Mechanicsburg, PA:

Stackpole Books, 2000), p. 223.

85   Ibid, p. 237.

86   *World War Soldiers Dead: Memorial Annals of Kansas City, Missouri*, Vol. II, No. 1. (Kansas City, MO: Missouri Valley Historical Society, 1926), p. 57. See also, *History of Rose Hill*. www.bnaijehudah.org/worship/cemetery. Accessed by the author on February 12, 2012.

87   *History of Rose Hill*, op. cit.

88   Missouri State Archives Soldiers' Records: War of 1812 – World War I. Service record of Joseph Liebman, service number 2,200,587, www.sos.mo.gov/archives/soldiers/details.asp. Accessed by author on February 6, 2012. See also, *World War I Draft Registration Cards 1917-1918. Jackson County, Missouri.* Roll Number 118338. [database on-line]. Ancestry.com. Provo Utah. Accessed by the author on February 9, 2012.

89   Twelfth United States Census (1900), SD 5, ED 40, Sheet 13 (T623_861), June 8, 1900. See also, Thirteenth United States Census (1910), SD 5 Ed 159, Page 3A (T624_788), April 16, 1910.

90   Granite grave marker, Rose Hill Cemetery, site visit by author on February 1, 2013.

91   "American Legion's First Kansas City Posts Formed Thirty-five Years Ago." *The Kansas City Times*, Thursday, August 19, 1954, p. 38.

92   McGrath, Lt. John F. McGrath, Sgt W. B. Carson, Cpl E. G. Geissert, Pvt. F. G. Morfeld. *War Diary 354th Infantry, 89th Division*. (Trier, Germany: J. Lintz, undated), p. 68 and 75.

93   Lillie F. Kelsay. *Historic & Dedicatory Monuments of Kansas City*. (Kansas City, MO: Board of Parks & Recreation Commissioners, 1987), p. 21.

94   United States Census 1910, Ward 10, Jackson County, MO, SD 5, ED 146, Sheet 1A. T624-788. Ancestry.com. Accessed by the author on March 5, 2012.

95   Draft Registration Card #51, Jackson County, Kansas City, MO, Draft Board 13, Precinct 8, Ward 13, June 5, 1917 (Roll 1683386). Ancestry.com, Accessed by the author on March 5, 2012.

96   Missouri State Archives. Soldiers Records: War of 1812 – World War I. Service record for Thomas J. Kiely, service number 2,200,731. http.//www.sos.mo.gov/archives/soldiers/details.asp. Accessed by the author on March 3, 2012.

97   McGrath, Lt. John F. McGrath, Sgt W. B. Carson, Cpl E. G. Geissert, Pvt. F. G. Morfeld. *War Diary 354th Infantry, 89th Division*, op. cit., p. 67.

98   Ibid, p. 70.

99   George H. English. *History of the 89th Division, U.S.A.*, op. cit. Information from map facing p. 144.

100   George H. English. *History of the 89th Division, U.S.A.*, op. cit., p. 95.

101   Ibid.

102   See map, "St. Mihiel Offensive, Advance of the 89th Division in the St. Mihiel offensive Sept 12th to 16th and Sector held after the advance Sept 17th Oct 9th 1918," tipped in between p. 144-145 of George H. English. *History of the 89th Division, U.S.A.*, op. cit.

103   McGrath, Lt. John F. McGrath, Sgt W. B. Carson, Cpl E. G. Geissert, Pvt. F. G. Morfeld. *War Diary 354th Infantry, 89th Division*, op. cit., p. 68, 75.

104   George H. English. *History of the 89th Division, U.S.A.*, op. cit., p. 95, 112-115.

105   *World War Soldiers Dead: Memorial Annals of Kansas City, Missouri*, Vol. II, No. 1, op. cit., p. 57.

106   Col. Rolfe L. Hillman. "Crossing The Meuse." Originally Published in the *Marine Corps Gazette* November 1988, http://www.mca-marines.org/gazette/crossing-meuse. Accessed by the author on February 20, 2012.

107   "Maj. Mark Hanna Killed." *The Kansas City Star,* December 1, 1918, p. 1.

108   Otto P. Higgins. "The 89th Hit 7 Divisions." *The Kansas City Star*, November 13, 1918, p. 2.

109   Col. Rolfe L. Hillman. "Crossing The Meuse," op. cit.

110   "Maj. Mark Hanna Killed." *The Kansas City Star*, op. cit. See also, "On a Casualty List of 1,768." *The Kansas City Star*, December 9, 1918, p. 4.

111   "Maj. Mark Hanna Killed," op. cit.

112   General Orders No. 20, W.D., 1919.

113   Soldiers' Records: War of 1812 – World War I. Service record for Mark Hanna, Missouri State Archives. http//www.sos.mo.gov/archives/soldiers/details.asp. Accessed by the author on January 8, 2012.

114   "Vignettes from those Alive During the War." National World War I Museum, Liberty Memorial www.theworldwar.org/s/110/.../East%20Museum%20new%20exhibits.doc. Accessed by the author on February 20, 2012.

German 50 Pfennig note, Bitburg, c. 1918

German 2 Mark note, 1914

Major William J. Bland.

CHAPTER 8

"We Came to Rest"

Major William J. Bland and His Wife, Mary T. Johnson Bland: In the Service of Their Country
(William J. Bland American Legion Post No. 50)

Major Mark Hanna replaced Major William J. Bland as commander of the 356th Infantry when Bland was killed by a shell that exploded between him and his orderly, who was 20 feet away fixing his pack. Major Bland was killed instantly, and his orderly, Messick E. Toalson, remained with the body until it could be buried near where he fell. Eleven months later, Major Bland's wife, Mary, went to France to find his body, and after locating it, waited two years to bring it home for burial in Arlington National Cemetery. While in France, she assisted others unable to come to Europe to find the bodies of their loved ones, and during World War II she returned to France once again, this time as assistant director of club operations for the Red Cross.

On September 8, 1918, the 356th Infantry, along with the rest of the 89th Division, received orders for the first fully-American engagement of the war, the St. Mihiel offensive. Departing from Newton Cross-Roads, the regiment had hiked to Ansauville for two days before taking a position on September 9 with the rest of the 1st Battalion in the Hazel Woods.

Three days later, at 1 a.m., September 12, American artillery laid in one of the greatest barrages of the war. The 356th's unit history recorded, "thousands of guns from the marvelous French 75s to the 12-inch American navel guns belched forth a stream of iron upon the well-prepared positions of the enemy. For miles the sky was lighted up by the exploding shells and the flash of guns, and it was a wonderful and terrible sight."[1]

The barrage lasted four-and-a-half hours until 5:30 a.m., when the Americans went "over the top" fully confident that, in the words of the unit history, nothing could stop them. Major Bland's orderly, Messick E. Toalson, a young boy from Osceola, Missouri, described what happened next near the village of Euvezin.[2]

"We went over with the Major at the appointed time before daybreak and the sky was brilliantly lighted by the flashes from the guns," he said. "It had been raining about three days, and it was lots of fun to slide down the side of a trench, when it was too wide to jump, and do the 'mud turtle wallow' up the other side.

"The major had finished his lunch, and I was fixing my pack just about twenty feet away, when a shell struck almost between us, a piece striking him near the left temple, killing him instantly. Lieutenant [Erskine R.]

Myers was seated within three feet of him and several others were near, but he was the only man hit, save a scratch on a runner nearby. I was with the body the rest of that day and night. Next day I got the chaplain, and we buried him near where he fell, in a pretty little valley between two villages[,] which the Americans had taken on General Pershing's birthday,"[3] Toalson said.

Eleven months later, in August 1919, Major Bland's 27-year-old wife, Mary, left her home at 3659 Harrison in Kansas City and set sail for France to find her husband's grave. She finally located it in a cemetery in the Lorraine near Thiaucourt and "remained there two years waiting for the slow details of war burial transfers to be completed by the government." She then accompanied her husband's body back to America.[4] They had been married for only a year when he was killed; she never remarried. While in France, she assisted others unable to travel to Europe to locate their relatives lost in the war.

Once home, she saw to it that her husband would be buried in Arlington with full military honors. On June 10, 1921, Mary had her wish. Attended by her father and mother, Judge and Mrs. William T. Johnson of Kansas City; her husband's father, Meigs Bland; and Attorney J. L. L. Harvey; and E. R. Morrison of Kansas City, representing the Jackson County Bar Association, Mary Bland buried her husband at Arlington, Section 1, Site 412-A-WS.[5] Next to him, she was laid to rest on June 9, 1977, at the age of 85.[6]

During her long life, she continued the spirit of service to which her husband had also been dedicated. In 1917, even before the United States entered the war, she was making surgical dressings for the French in the old Red Cross room of the Lathrop building in Kansas City. While her husband was

Mary T. Johnson Bland.[10]

in training at Camp Funston, she worked with the Red Cross in Manhattan, Kansas, and continued to volunteer there after he left Camp Funston on May 23, 1918, arriving overseas on June 4.[7]

Then, when World War II broke out in 1939, she took up Red Cross work again, eventually serving full time with the Kansas City-Jackson County Chapter, volunteering in the canteen, first aid, knitting, and surgical dressing branches. This time, however, it was she who went into the war. When Red Cross workers began arriving overseas, she paid for her own passage aboard the *Queen Mary*, departing New York on December 7, 1942, one year to the day Japan had attacked Pearl Harbor. During the remainder of the war, she worked in England, France, and Germany, finally serving as assistant director of club operations on the continent before she departed Le Havre in December 1945, to return to the States.[8]

But before she left the war zone, and while she was still at her station in Nancy, France, Mary Bland slipped away one day in March 1945, to visit again the cemetery where her husband had been buried and where, in nearby Thiaucourt, she had waited two years to bring him back home. The Germans had occupied the town for almost four years, but had not damaged it or the cemetery – with one exception, she noted. "Seven American grave stones marked by the Star of David, had been knocked down by the Nazis. These were later repaired," she said,[9] and in less than two months, the hatred that had desecrated those graves lay in defeat. The cause in which her husband had died 27 years earlier was finally over, and the ground where he had lain was finally at peace.

M-18 Major William J. Bland Memorial
East Side of Gilham Road at 42nd Street, Kansas City, Missouri

This red granite monument 4 feet high by 2 feet square rests on a base 1 foot wide and 3 feet square. The attached bronze plaque measures 18 by 24 inches and reads:

To the memory of Major William J. Bland, 1st Battalion, 356th Infantry, 89th Division. Killed in action September 12, 1918 during the St. Mihiel offensive in France. "A nobler man, a braver warrior, lives not this day within the City Walls."

Three hundred people huddled together against a raw wind sweeping cross the open field along Gillham Road at 42nd Street in Kansas City on Saturday afternoon, November 7, 1936. They were there to dedicate a red granite stone to the memory of Major William J. Bland, who had commanded the 1st Battalion, 356th Infantry, 89th Division, in the Great War.

When Major Bland's widow, Mary Bland,

James J. Heiman

William J. Bland Memorial East Side of Gilham Road at 42nd Street, Kansas City, Missouri

arrived at this spot where the marker honoring her dead husband would soon be dedicated, she may have wondered if the cause for which he had died was about to be threatened again in the very same place where he had fallen in France 18 years earlier. The Holocaust had already begun in Germany, and in March 1936, in defiance of the Treaty of Versailles, the German Army had re-occupied the Rhineland, Italy had annexed Ethiopia, and Civil War had broken out in Spain – the League of Nations had lost its ability to keep the world safe for democracy. It was only a matter of time – the world would be again at war.

For now, 300 people gathered along the east side of Gillham Road in the very field where Major William J. Bland had conducted military drills. Here, they remembered the life of the Army major and of the more than 400 Kansas City men and women whose deaths he came to represent. A week earlier on November 1, *The Kansas*

City Star noted the importance that Major Bland's death held for Kansas City: "In the fall of 1919, a year after Major Bland's death, patriotic Kansas Citians were working for a memorial suitable to the memory of the 400 Kansas City war dead. This tribute, which took form in the Liberty Memorial, was identified with Major Bland, whose career and death symbolized heroic sacrifice. During the campaign to raise funds for the memorial, Bland's record was emphasized, illustrating as it did the necessity of a permanent reminder of the promising lives cut short by the war. 'Lest the ages forget' was the motto, Major Bland the symbol."[11]

The Star article continued its reminder of the importance Major Bland had to the city's efforts to remember its war dead. Quoting from its own newspaper files from 15 years earlier, *The Star* observed, "His death blighted a career which might have been one of the most brilliant of any young man ever reared in Kansas City, the public was reminded when funds for the Liberty Memorial were sought.

"In college he made such a record that he was admitted to competitive examination for appointment to one of the four scholarships which Cecil Rhodes had established for American youths. The young student won that competition. At Oxford he was one of the most popular students of the entire body,

and in his senior year was elected president of the Oxford Union Society—the first time an American ever had won that honor.

"When the young men of Great Britain began to fall by thousands, Bland enlisted. Knowing so many of the young heroes who were giving up their lives for humanity, he felt more intensely than the average American what the war really meant. Unselfishly he gave up his career, and that he could apply his ability to army as well as to civil affairs is proved by his record. Commissioned a captain at Ft. Riley, he was made a major shortly thereafter.

"Major Bland would have meant much to Kansas City. He was of the type most needed here—a brilliant, clean-living, high-minded young man, possessing and executing the best ideals for the political and social welfare of his fellow citizens. It will be strange, indeed," *The Star* concluded in 1921, "if we who are so greatly in his debt do not try partially to repay that obligation by adequately subscribing to the Liberty War Memorial."[12]

The Liberty Memorial was opened to the public in 1926, but, for the 10 years following, an individual marker honoring Major Bland had not been erected. In the words of *The Star*, "A symbol in the erection of the city's memorial, Bland deserved individual honor. To this end his friends have worked

> "Major Bland would have meant much to Kansas City. He was of the type most needed here—a brilliant, clean-living, high-minded young man, possessing and executing the best ideals for the political and social welfare of his fellow citizens. It will be strange, indeed," The Star concluded in 1921, "if we who are so greatly in his debt do not try partially to repay that obligation by adequately subscribing to the Liberty War Memorial."[12]

almost from the inception of the American Legion here and, it is with a feeling of pride at the discharge of an overdue debt that they await the dedication of the Bland memorial Saturday."[13]

And so on that Saturday, November 7, 1936, at 4:00 p.m., the drum and bugle corps and a company of cadets from Westport High School's R.O.T.C. marched across the cold, windy field at 42nd and Gillham Road. The crowd stood at attention while three youths clad in khaki raised the colors and Joseph E. Brown, former commander of the Major William J. Bland American Legion Post No. 50, read the invocation. A veteran of the war, Joseph Brown was the brother of Sanford Brown for whom Kansas City American Legion Post 124 was named.

Current post commander Dick Richardson then rose to speak. Along with the Park Board, he formally presented the memorial to the city, pointing out as he did so that Major Bland had drilled many times on the same field where they were all now standing and where his memorial would now permanently remain. President of the Parks Board Frank C. Cromwell accepted the memorial on behalf of Mayor Smith and pledged that the Parks Board would cooperate with all veterans' groups to preserve it.

Then the youngest bishop in the United States, 45-year old Henry W. Hobson of the Episcopal Diocese of Southern Ohio, delivered the dedicatory speech. A major in command of the 3rd Battalion, 356th Infantry, Bishop Hobson was wounded twice and received the D.S.O. A close friend of Major Bland, he recalled that the Major's last words to him were filled with help and encouragement. The Bishop noted his friend's sense of justice, honesty, unselfishness, and courage. Then he read the inscription on the plaque: "A nobler man, a braver warrior, lives not this day within the city walls," a quote from Shakespeare's 1593-94 tragedy, *Titus Andronicus* (Act I, sc i, lines 25-26).[14]

"'May we think of these words,' the Bishop suggested, 'Not as referring to some dead hero, but as referring to one who lives today in the city of our lives.'"[15] After Monsignor John W. Keyes pronounced the benediction, the Bishop's words continued to ring in the ears of the 300 gathered there.

Some remembered fallen relatives, and some who had served under Major Bland heard again what another fellow officer had observed years earlier: On the day following Major Bland's death, he said, members of the battalion seemed still to hear in the depth of the Hazel Woods the Major's voice urging them onward.[16] Although she was not physically present in the Hazel Woods that day, in the years to come, Mary Johnson Bland had certainly heard that same voice.

It was a voice that called out to the strength within one's character to serve a greater cause, a voice not unlike that which Private Wayne Miner heard on the very last day of the war.

Private Wayman "Wayne" Miner:
A Hero Should Be Recognized at Last
(Wayne Miner American Legion Post No. 149)

American Legion Post No. 149 is named for Private Wayne Miner, who, like Major Mark Hanna, was killed on the last day of the war. Pvt. Miner was one of 21 African-American soldiers from Kansas City killed in the war and, by some accounts, was the last Kansas City man and perhaps the last American to die in the conflict. In another irony of war, his memorial paver is located in the central walkway in the Black Veterans Memorial in the median of the Paseo, just above the Fitzsimons fountain, so that the first American officer killed in the war and the last African-American soldier killed in the war are commemorated in the same place. Like Lt. Fitzsimons, Private Wayne Miner was killed in action during the performance of a necessary mission for which he had volunteered his service.

I was commanding the foremost advancing units of Company A, 1st Battalion of the 366th Infantry," 1st Lieutenant William H. Clark noted 47 years after the unit's attack on the village of Caney in the Marbache Sector. It was Armistice Day, November 11, 1918, at 7:30 in the morning; only three-and-a-half hours remained before the guns would fall silent and the armistice ending the Great War would take affect. Five hours earlier, Lt. Clark had received his orders from company commander Cpt. George A. Holland. The first and fourth platoons under Clark's command were to move from the high ground around the village of Montfaucon overlooking the Bois Vivrotte and, as their first objective, take the German outposts about a mile away.[17]

"To the east of us were the Vosges mountains and a network of rivers that in all wars between France and Germany, no army had ever attempted to cross," Lt. Clark continued.

"On our left were units of Company F led by First Lieutenant Mallileau W. Rush and to his left was First Lieutenant Oscar Brown, commanding the 351st Machine Gun company supporting both of us.

"One-half hour before jumping off time, Lieutenant Brown sent through an appeal relayed by our companies for four men from each company to assist in carrying machine gun ammunition. This was an unwanted assignment and I called for volunteers. I made a strong appeal, but for a minute or two, no one stepped forward to accept. I told the boys they were letting me down, and I would use the lottery system. As I was about to execute that method of selection, Private Wayne Miner stepped forward as the first volunteer; then another, and others until the four had responded.

"When Wayne Miner stepped out, a lump-like feeling accumulated in my throat. He was a highly cultured and courageous soldier, respected by the entire company of 250 men. I had used him on every patrol I had made, including one on October 16 the same year, when the members of the patrol were so pleasing to Division Headquarters that Brigadier General Malvere H. Barnum came to the company and assembled the seven of us who had carried it out, praised us highly and had our company clerk to type out a personal eulogy [commendation] that he gladly signed. It was my most-prized possession until I lost it going through a delousing plant.

"An ammunition carrier slings his rifle, his main defense, across his back and becomes a pack-horse. The terrain was of such a rough nature that Lieutenant Brown had to use this method as mules and ammunition vehicles could not be used.

"I never saw Wayne Miner again. From my hospital bed at Tours, France, where I was carried after we occupied our first objective[,] I learned he was killed by bursting shrapnel. I recommended him for the Distinguished Service Cross. Somehow, my captain through whom it was sent, never received it and a brave, sacrificing, and deserving soldier did not receive his just reward—even posthumously," Lieutenant Clark concluded.[18]

Three weeks later, on December 6, 1918, the War Department confirmed that Wayne Miner was among 870 casualties, five of whom were from greater Kansas City.[19] Private Miner was buried in Plot B, Row 14, Grave 17 of the World War I St. Mihiel American Cemetery and Memorial at the west edge of Thiaucourt, France.[20] He was 24 years old. Miner's wife, 23-year-old Belle Miner of 571 Troost Avenue, was notified as next of kin. Belle later moved back to live with her brother Archie Carter in Appanoose County, Iowa, where she had likely first met her husband.

Pvt. Wayne Miner.[21]

Born August 17, 1894, the son of former Missouri slaves, Ned and Emily Miner, Wayne Miner had lived for a time with his family on a farm in Henry County, Missouri. Later he moved with them to a 10-acre farm three miles east of Plano, Iowa, Johns Township, Appanoose County, Iowa, where he and his older brother, Joseph, worked in the coal mines. There in Iowa it is likely that he met and married Belle Carter.

Wayne enlisted in the Army in Kansas City on October 26, 1917, and completed basic training at Camp Dodge, Iowa. On January 1, 1918, he was promoted to the rank of Private First Class and on June 15, 1918, shipped for France with Company A, 366th Regiment, 92nd Division, an all-black Division under the command of Major General Charles C. Ballou.[22] The 92nd Division saw combat for 17 days, occupied the Marbache Sector from October 9 to November 11, and participated in the attack of the 2nd Army November 10-11, 1918.

The Division suffered 1,570 battle casualties.[23]

Wayne Miner was the last soldier from Kansas City to die in the Great War, and by some accounts, the last of all the American soldiers to die in the final hours before the armistice.[24] He was one of 21 African-American soldiers from Kansas City killed in the war. His name appears not only on the American Legion I Monument in Budd Park Esplanade along Van Brunt Blvd at Anderson but also on the bronze plaques in Memory Hall, Liberty Memorial and at the Meyer Circle Gateway – Avenue of Trees at Meyer Circle and Ward Parkway in Kansas City.

He is also honored by a flagstone in the Black Veterans Memorial along the Paseo just north of 12th Street, where the first Kansas City casualty of the war and the first American officer to be killed in the war, 1st Lt. William T. Fitzsimons, is also commemorated. His is a separate memorial with a fountain placed in the retaining wall in 1922.

Nearby at 11th and Woodland is the site of Wayne Miner Court, an apartment complex built in 1962 comprising 738 apartments for low-income residents. In 1987, the local Housing Authority ordered the demolition of the high-rise apartments, but the Wayne Miner Community Center still stands as a living tribute to the life and service that this young African-American soldier voluntarily sacrificed for his fellow soldiers and his country.

James J. Heiman

Black Veterans Memorial, at the Paseo and 12th Street, Kansas City, Missouri, above and behind the Fitzsimons Memorial Fountain.

M-19 **Wayne Miner Commemorative Plaque At Black Veterans Memorial**
The Paseo at 12th Street, Kansas City, Missouri
[Above and Behind the Fitzsimons Memorial Fountain]
Kansas City, Missouri

Private Wayne Miner was one of eight Kansas City soldiers killed in action on November 11, 1918, the last day of the war. He is one of 21 African-American soldiers from Kansas City whose names are listed on the bronze plaque in Memory Hall at the Liberty Memorial and on the tablets at the Meyer Circle Gateway Avenue of Trees.[25]

The granite paver dedicated to his memory at the Black Veterans Memorial is one of 2,500 pavers in a central walkway through the median of the Paseo, from the Fitzsimons Memorial Fountain in the terrace at 12th and Paseo north to 11th and Paseo. The pavers honor the service of black veterans in all of the nation's wars and are available for purchase to build an endowment for the memorial.

At the 11th Street entrance to the memorial is a polished black granite plaque with the following inscription:

Wayne Miner Commemorative Plaque, Black Veterans Memorial, the Paseo at 12th Street, Kansas City, Missouri, above and Behind the Fitzsimons Memorial Fountain.

Black Veterans Memorial
This Plaza is Dedicated
To Honor Black Americans
Who Have Served & Are Serving
America
With Unsung Distinction

In Our Quest
For Freedom and
Peace
Around the World

Listed on the bottom left are the names of 17 "Enshriners," a civic organization responsible for raising the $250,000[26] required to build the monument and to repair the Fitzsimons fountain: Ollie Gates, Jack Bush, George Oliver, John F. Myers, Henry Riojas, Otis Taylor, Leon Stapleton, Bill Washington, Bill Grigsby, Mark McHenry, Elbert Anderson, Ralph Caro, Steve Lampone, Curtis McLinton, Eddie Penrice, Chuck Byrd, and Jimmie Woodley.

Between the two columns listing the names of the Enshriners is the logo for Gates Bar-B-

Q, whose founder, Ollie Gates, is a veteran of the Korean War and a leader of the Enshriners' efforts to build the monument. "Heretofore, we've had nothing to honor the services of black veterans of Kansas City," he said. "I think it is high time that we do that."[27]

The logo for Kansas City Missouri Parks and Recreation appears to the right along with a list of the Parks and Recreation Commissioners. Between the names of the Enshriners and the Park Commissioners is the dedication date, September 2010, and below that the name of Kansas City Mayor, Mark Funkhouser.

At the south end of the median is a 50-foot flagpole, at the foot of which in the sides of an octagon are replicas of eight seals: the Great Seal of the United States and the seals of all the branches of military service, including National Guard, Army Reserve, Coast Guard, Air Force, Navy, Navy Marine Corps, and Army.

A crowd of 200 to 300 people gathered at 5:00 p.m. on Sunday, September 12, 2010, to witness the dedication, which featured a band from Ft. Leonard Wood and addresses from Congressman Emmanuel Cleaver and Representative Sharon Saunders Brooks. Kansas City Councilwoman Deb Hermann and Chair of the Parks Board, John Fierro, offered remarks and Chuck Moore, whose 90-year-old father-in-law was reportedly the oldest veteran in attendance, served as master of ceremonies. Mayor Funkhouser read a proclamation from the city as uniformed Buffalo Soldiers and the Enshriners, dressed in their own distinctive green and white, looked on.[28]

■ ■ ■

Not all of those who lost their lives in the war died in combat as Major William Bland did or as a result of volunteering to carry out an especially dangerous mission, as was the case for Private Wayne Miner. Some, like 1st Lieutenant Carl Haner, died from disease, while others, like Private Lawrence Fulton, felt so strongly about the cause that they joined the fight even before the United States entered the war.

1st Lt. Carl W. Haner: Died from Disease

As one of the Kansas City law professionals who lost their lives in the Great War, 1st Lieutenant Carl W. Haner's name appeared on the Kansas City Bar Association drinking fountain plaque in the old courthouse on Missouri and Oak.[29]

He is also remembered as one of 411 names on the bronze tablets in Memorial Hall and of the Soldier's and Sailor's Memorial at 7th and Barnett in Kansas City, Kansas: "Carl W. Haner, 1st Lt. AS. Sig. Co. died December 12, 1918."[30] The March 1921 Kansas Adjutant General Office's report of Kansas war casualties indicated that Lt. Haner had died of disease as a member of the Signal Corps of the Army Air Service. Next of kin was not indicated.[31]

Pvt. Lawrence Fulton:
To "Die Like a Martyr"

"If I had to die," Lawrence Fulton said when he learned that the Lusitania was sunk on May 7, 1915, "I hope I will die like those martyrs." So Mr. Carl H. Adams remembered his law school classmate at the memorial meeting of the Kansas City Bar Association held at the U.S. Court House in Kansas City on November 16, 1918.[32] .

Even before America entered the war, Fulton thought it was his duty to become part of the fight, so he paid his own expenses to Toronto to enlist in the Canadian cavalry in December 1917.[33] He was in the thickest of the fighting for more than a year before he was killed in action on October 1, 1918. He is buried in Flanders Field.[34]

Born in Canada, Fulton was brought up in Missouri and received his early education in the state. Later, he graduated from the Kansas City School of Law and the Law Department of Yale University. Following graduation, he resided at the Broadlands Hotel in Kansas City and worked for the law firm of Lathrop, Morrow, Fox and Moore as well as for the law firm of L. C. Boyle.

"He was noted among his friends for his sincerity, and was one of the most loyal men I have ever met," said Mr. M. Stanford Lyon, speaking of Fulton at the Kansas City Bar Association memorial meeting.

His is the third name to appear on the 1921 plaque of the Kansas City Bar Association monument. His name is also listed on the plaques of the Meyer Circle Gateway Memorial and those on the west wall of Memory Hall at Kansas City's Liberty Memorial.

■ ■ ■

Major Bland, Private Miner, Lieutenant Haner, and Private Fulton all died under completely different circumstances, but their sacrifices were recognized by fellow citizens in special tributes that personified the contributions of many others of their profession or of their race, who have otherwise remained unnamed and unrecognized.

Endnotes

1. *The World War with Company A, 356ᵗʰ Infantry, 89ᵗʰ Division, National Army: From Camp Funston, Kansas to Schweich, Germany via Canada, England, France, Belgium, Luxembourg, Treves, 1919.* (National World War I Museum Archives.)

2. Frank Hagerman. "In Memoriam: Addresses Delivered at Memorial Meeting of Kansas City Bar Association, US Court Room at Kansas City, Saturday, November 16, 1918," p. 25. Missouri Valley Room, Kansas City, Missouri Public Library.

3. "War Comrades Join in Tribute to Maj. William J. Bland." *The Kansas City Star*, Sunday, November 1, 1936, p. 1C.

4. Erma Young. "Mrs. William J. Bland, Red Cross Worker in England." *The Kansas City Star,* May 5, 1946, 3C.

5. "Bury a Kansas City Hero." *The Kansas City Times*, June 11, 1921, p. 1.

6. "William J. Bland, Major, United States Army." Arlington National Cemetery Website. http://www.arlingtocemetery.net/wjbland.htm. Accessed by the author on December 29, 2011.

7. See http://www.usgennet.org/usa/mo/county/stlouis/89thdivision/1bat89-coa. Accessed by the author on December 29, 2011.

8. "Red Cross Worker Relates Story of Three Years' Service Overseas." *The Kansas City Star*, Sunday, January 20, 1946, p. 15 C.

9. Erma Young. "She Lit Cigarettes for the Boys at Cherbourg." *The Kansas City Star,* Sunday, May 5, 1946, p. 3C.

10. Erma Young. "Mrs. William J. Bland, Red Cross Worker in England," op. cit., photo accompanying article.

11. "War Comrades Join in Tribute to Maj. William J. Bland." *The Kansas City Star,* Sunday, November 1, 1936, p. 1C.

12. Ibid.

13. Ibid.

14. Craig Hardin, ed. "Titus Andronicus." *The Complete Works of Shakespeare.* (Chicago: Scott Foresman, 1961), p. 370.

15. "In Memory of a Hero." *The Kansas City Star,* November 8, 1936, p. 3A.

16. Frank Hagerman. "In Memoriam: Addresses Delivered at Memorial Meeting of Kansas City Bar Association, US Court Room at Kansas City, Saturday, November 16, 1918," op. cit.

17. "They Came to Fight: Kansas City's Role in the Years Leading Up To and After World War I." Interview of William H. Clark, of Kansas City, Kansas, by Marie Ross, Kansas City *Call.* http://www.theycametofight.org/Kansas city.html. Accessed by author on January 7, 2012.

18. Joe Louis Mattox. "Raising Private Miner: Elevating the Rank of the Great War's Last Fallen." *The Jackson County Historical Society Journal,* Vol. 48, No. 2, Autumn 2007, p. 7.

19. "An Oversea List of 870: Five Greater Kansas City Men are Included." *The Kansas City Times*, December 6, 1918, p. 6.

20. World War I Honor Roll database posted at http://www.abme.gov, viewed November 8, 2007 by Joe Louis Mattox. "Raising Private Miner: Elevating the Rank of the Great War's Last Fallen." *The Jackson County Historical Society Journal,* Vol. 48, No. 2, Autumn 2007, p. 8-9.

21. "They Came to Fight: Kansas City's Role in the Years Leading Up to and After World War I." Portrait of Wayne Miner at http://www.theycametofight.org/kansascity.html. Accessed by the author on January 7, 2012.

22. Robert B. Edgerton. *Hidden Heroism: Black Soldiers in America's Wars.* (New York: Barnes and Noble, 2001), p. 80.

23. Joe Louis Mattox. "Raising Private Miner: Elevating the Rank of the Great War's Last Fallen," op. cit. pp. 5-6.

24. Ibid, p. 4.

25. *World War Soldiers Dead: Memorial Annals of Kansas City, Missouri.* (Kansas City: Missouri Valley Historical Society, 1926), p. 38. Note on spelling: "Minor" is the spelling on the American Legion I Monument. "Miner" is the spelling son the other Kansas City World War I monuments and is the preferred spelling.

26. Matt Campbell. "Memorial to Black Vets to be Unveiled Sunday Along the Paseo." *The Kansas City Star*, September 7, 2010, p. A5. See also, Matt Campbell. "Veterans Memorial Along Paseo Gets Go-Ahead." *The Kansas City Star*, February 3, 2010, p. A4.

27. Ibid, p. A4.

28. "Black Veterans Memorial Dedication." http://hyperblogal.blogspot.com/2010-09-black-veterans-memorial-dedication.html.

Accessed by the author on January 20, 2013. See also, Emily Randall. "Memorial to Honor Black Veterans on Paseo." *Northeast News*, Vol. 80, Issue 4, January 19, 2011. http://stjdesign.net/paseomemorial.html. Accessed by the author on January 20, 2013.

29   Sherry Piland and Elen J. Uguccioni. *Fountains of Kansas City: A History and Love Affair.* (Kansas City, MO: City of Fountains Foundation, 1985), p. 130.

30   Grant W. Harrington. "Historic Spots Number Thirty-nine." *Historic Spots or Mile-Stones in the Progress of Wyandotte County, Kansas.* (Merriam, KS: The Mission Press, 1935), p. 302.

31   *Kansas Casualties in the World War, Regular Army, National Guard, National Army, Enlisted Reserve Corps.* (Topeka, KS: Adjutant General's Office, March 1921), p. 60-69, Number 698. Transcribed at skyways.lib.ks.us/genweb/archives/statewide/military/wwl. Accessed by the author on December 31, 2012.

32   "In Memoriam: Addresses Delivered at Memorial Meeting of Kansas City Bar Association, 1918." (Missouri Valley Room, Kansas City, Missouri Public Library.)

33   *World War Soldiers Dead: Memorial Annals of Kansas City, Missouri.* (Kansas City: Missouri Valley Historical Society, 1926), p. 2, 40.

34   "In Memoriam: Addresses Delivered at Memorial Meeting of Kansas City Bar Association, 1918," op. cit., p. 43.

"Paul Sunderland, 22, son of Mr. and Mrs. L.T. Sunderland, 3711 Harrison Boulevard, a first class musician on the U.S.S. Charleston, a graduate of the Westport High School." [5]

CHAPTER 9

"Will We Be Remembered?"

The Last Chapter: Back to the Beginning
Navy Musician 1st Class Paul Sunderland
"Kansas City's Last Man Standing"

The last World War I veteran from Kansas City to survive the war was Navy Musician 1st Class Paul Sunderland, who died at the age of 107 and is buried at Mt. Washington Cemetery. Paul Sunderland had seen the Kaiser as a boy, went to fight him as a man, and outlived all of the other men from Kansas City who served in the Great War. With his death, the war had come full circle for Kansas City: He had served on cruiser escorts to protect American boys as they headed across the North Atlantic to the war zone, and he was the last to join the Kansas City boys as they were returned for eternal rest to their native soil. Now that all who fought in the Great War are dead, how will they continue to be remembered?

From October 24, 1917, until his discharge at Kittery, Maine,[1] December 13, 1918, Paul Sunderland served aboard the cruiser *U.S.S. Charleston* as a Musician 1st Class.[2] Seven times during that period, the *U.S.S. Charleston* crossed the North Atlantic, escorting American supply vessels, troop ships, and battleships in what amounted to a trans-Atlantic ferry service. To fulfill its roll in that service, the *U.S.S. Charleston* was rated at 12 knots per hour and was staffed by 151 officers and 1,389 enlisted men.[3] At first, the *U.S.S. Charleston* was one of four cruisers the Navy employed in its Cruiser and Transport Force. Later, that number expanded to 28 cruisers in six divisions divided between two squadrons. The *U.S.S. Charleston* was part of Division 4, the Newport News Squadron II, with the *U.S.S. Salia* as the flagship of Rear Admiral H. P. Jones, the Division 4 commander.[4]

In one of the ironies of war, the cruisers escorted former German transport vessels that had been impounded after war was declared. Those re-fitted and "de-sabotaged" German vessels came into United States service beginning in September 1917[6] and became the core of the American troop transport convoys on their way to fight the Germans in France.[7] Each U.S. Navy convoy averaged 14 days at sea and together carried nearly one million men to France.[8] To speed up the deployment of men so critical to the war-weary Allies, who had been fighting for three years already, British and French ships assisted in the transport of American troops to the war zone. It was the U.S. Navy, however, that brought all two million men and women of the AEF back to the states at the end of the war.

Under the command of Rear Admiral Robert Gleaves in his flagship, the cruiser *U.S.S.*

Seattle, the *U.S.S. Charleston* departed on its first convoy voyage from New York at 10:00 a.m. on June 14, 1917, four months before Musician 1st Class Paul Sunderland joined the crew. At that time, the *U.S.S. Charleston* was part of the third of four groups constituting the very first American troop convoy to France and was one of four cruisers, each assigned to escort one of the transport groups within the first convoy.[9] Each of the convoy's four groups had been assigned a set speed, the *U.S.S. Charleston's* group, including the troop transports *S.S. Mallory, U.S.A.C.T. Finland*, and *U.S.A.C.T. San Jacinto,* proceeding at 13 knots, while groups 1, 2, and 4 moved at 15, 14, and 11 knots, respectively. The various speeds were determined by the slowest vessel within the particular group, the last group including the slow cargo ships so that spaced apart, the entire convoy could move with maximum speed, at the same time affording the greatest protection of its elements. Three destroyers accompanied each of the four groups in that first convoy.

The first convoy's 36 ships constituted "the most strongly protected troop convoy sent across the Atlantic during the War"[10] and served to test a carefully-designed strategy for safe transport of troops and supplies. The strategy was designed by Admiral Gleaves and was known as "Orders for Ships in Convoy." In the opinion of Benedict Crowell, the Assistant Secretary of War and Director of Munitions, 1917-1920, the orders were "enough to explain why the Germans were never able to sink one of our troopships."[11] The convoy groups maintained their maximum assigned speeds; lookout watches included efficient communication systems to the deck officer and the fire control watch; the fire control officer, in turn, was in continuous communication with the lookouts and gun watches; zigzagging was practiced when deemed necessary; and the deck officer was ready to use helm and engines to dodge torpedoes. All troop

transports and their escorts were armed with depth charges and followed set procedures for communicating a submarine sighting and maneuvering to avoid the menace. Reducing the use of the radio, keeping smoke to a minimum, completely darkening the ship at night, and carefully avoiding discharge of floating objects into the sea helped to secure the ship's presence from the enemy.

During the trip across, the ships in the first convoy conducted battle station drills, put into operation the "Orders for Ships in Convoy" and encountered no submarines, but once the first two groups had entered the war zone, submarines picked them up and pursued them during the day, waiting for the dark night of June 22 to attack. The careful preparation, however, paid off. Early detection, strategic maneuvers, and careful positioning of depth charges enabled the ships to escape danger. Group 3, of which the *U.S.S. Charleston* was a part, had encountered no submarines and neither had group 4. Group 3 safely reached St. Nazaire, France, on June 26, 1917.[12] After the convoy had unloaded the first AEF troops, their "provisions, ammunition, baled hay, automobile trucks, horses, locomotives and other military freight,"[13] the ships were accompanied by destroyers through the war zone, and from there the four cruisers took over responsibility for protection of their respective groups until, by July 14, all the ships had arrived safely back in New York.

From that time on, for the duration of the war, Admiral Gleaves managed the troop convoys from the port of Hoboken, New Jersey,[14] and later from New York.[15] The number of officers and men under his command alone was larger than the entire American Naval force prior to 1917.[16] His command grew so large with the work of transport that, early in 1918, Admiral Gleaves split the cruiser fleet into two squadrons, with the *U.S.S. Charleston* assigned to the second squadron, which was headquartered in Newport News under the command of Rear Admiral Mar-

The cruiser *U.S.S. Charleston* at port.

bury Johnston.[17] When the German drive of 1918 opened and the Port of Embarkation at Newport News began to send large numbers of troops to meet the demand in France, the four cruisers of Division 4, including the *U.S.S. Charleston,* were detached from the work of cargo transport and assigned to escort the Newport News troop convoys.[18]

After that first convoy had reached France, destroyers were no longer needed to accompany convoys from the United States and back again because there was no submarine activity in the mid-Atlantic, and the destroyers were needed only in the war zone where the submarine threat existed. The cruisers could adequately manage the job of protecting the convoys from chance surface raids on the voyage from America to the edge of

the war zone and back again,[19] but that did not mean that the cruisers or the transports were free from danger, especially when the Germans harassed the edges of the European war zone and, later on in the war, actually established a war zone off the coast of the United States.[20] As a cruiser, the *U.S.S. Charleston* served the mission to protect the cargo and troop transports from the United States to the European war zone. It returned sometimes on its own and sometimes with the empty transports and cargo ships. Of the seven trans-Atlantic trips Musician 1st Class Paul Sunderland made aboard the *U.S.S. Charleston,* three included troop convoys: November 26, 1917, with six transports (*U.S.A.C.T. Æolus, U.S.A.C.T. Calamares, U.S.A.C.T. Tenadores, U.S.S. Mallory,*

U.S.A.C.T. San Jacinto, and *U.S.S. Julia Luckenbach*),[21] July 31, 1918 with one transport (*U.S.A.C.T. Maui*), and October 21, 1918, with one transport (*U.S.A.C.T. Sobral*).[22]

On board the *U.S.S. Charleston*, Sunderland worked as a mechanic below deck and above deck as a saxophone player in the ship's band – duties requiring him to help keep the ship and the spirits of the men on it in good repair. The Navy didn't supply him with a saxophone, though. He brought his own sax and, while at port in New York, took it in for refurbishing. What the Navy did supply, however, was a lot of work.

"Time went fast because a lot was going on," he said during an interview about his war experience.[23] Every morning at sunrise while in dock, the band played during the raising of the flag, and sometimes the captain would ask for music during dinner. Sunderland on the saxophone, a violin player, and a piano man played for the captain when he requested. Sunderland kept his sax until the 1950s, when he "traded it in for a more modern instrument," he said. Life-long, he remained a "first-class" musician.

A lot was going on below deck as well, Assistant Secretary of War Benedict Crowell reported. "A spirit of competition arose among the crews of the transports; the average turn-arounds" from the United States to the war zone and return "grew shorter and shorter, until by the spring of 1918 the pinnacle of efficiency had been attained; and when the German drive started, the Cruiser and Transport Force, sparing neither ships nor crews, was able to drive all of them at top speed in order that America's men might not be too late. Major repairs, which meant shipyards and dry-docks, were neglected; it was anything to keep the ships going. The crew repair parties worked overtime, day and night, at sea and in port, in order to keep the transports everlastingly at their task of ferrying back and forth across the Atlantic. It was necessary abuse, but not one vessel broke down under the punishment."[24]

Crowell also described the work of sailors and the prohibitive conditions onboard the cruisers: "The duties of the service kept all the cruisers at work, winter and summer, through fair weather and foul. American warships never before experienced such continuous operations over such a long period of time. The winter of 1917-1918 descended upon the North Atlantic with a severity which sailors will never forget; but the cruisers kept at it without a break, often heavily sheathed in ice, but maintaining a watch and a vigilance that did not falter. Death was not an uncommon visitor to the cruisers. Cold, wet, exposure, and the strain of responsibility all claimed their toll; but they could not stop the ships.

"Not one of the cruisers had normally a steaming radius that would take her almost across the ocean and then back again to a home port, and in heavy weather the normal radius was materially reduced; so that every one of them which started out with a convoy had to load great piles of coal on her decks—sometimes as much as 600 tons. This extra fuel further cramped the quarters aboard ship and added to the discomfort of life."[25] During its subsequent Atlantic crossings, the *U.S.S. Charleston* never docked at British or French ports, but instead, Paul Sunderland later recalled, carried enough sacks of coal on its deck to fuel the trip back across the ocean because no coal was available for refueling either in France or England and stopping at a port would have taken extra days that could be spent in heading back to Newport News for escort duty with the next troop embarkation.[26]

As for the business of protection, the *U.S.S. Charleston* "had eight 6-inch guns and some '3-pounders,'" Sunderland remembered. "Also depth charges piled up at the end of the ship." He didn't remember sighting any submarines, but did recall the crew pushing depth charges overboard on one occasion. He thought that the ship might have detected the presence of submarines and had therefore taken the defensive action, but he wasn't sure. Serving two decks below the main deck, he and the men with him didn't know much of what transpired above deck, and didn't question it either.

"We weren't informed on lots of stuff, you know. We were just there. I felt good about my service, though, and I did the best I could." One thing of which he was aware were the number of sick from the flu epidemic, so bad that some had to be put on deck, and some of them died, but again, Sunderland said, "the men below deck didn't know much about it."

On board the transports, though, the flu epidemic was even worse. In order to fulfill the need for a rapid build-up of American forces in France, Admiral Gleaves had devised measures to increase troop carrying capacity by as much as 50 percent by installing additional collapsible sleeping accommodations along available walls, assigning the men to sleep in shifts, and feeding the men standing up in shifts so that sleeping and eating became almost continuous, day and night. This overload plan worked successfully until, by the end of August 1918, the troop transports had landed an extra 100,000 troops in France,[27] "the equivalent of twenty new transports of average size without the expenditure of a dollar in money or a day in time for new floating equipment."[28] However, the increased troop capacity did come at price. The close quarters promoted the spread of disease, with the result that "the influenza epidemic at sea put a stop to overloading."[29]

The conditions of cruiser service were probably not on Paul Sunderland's mind when he considered the part he would play

Paul Sunderland, Kansas City's "Last Man Standing" from World War I.

in the war. He did know that he preferred service in the Navy to being drafted into the Army, and having had a good experience at Culver Navy School, Indiana, in the summer of 1916, he enlisted at the Navy Recruiting Station in Kansas City, Missouri, on September 4, 1917, at the age of 21 years, 4 months.[30] He trained at Norfolk, "8 or 10 to a tent," and at Cape Hatteras Navy Yard, North Carolina, before joining the crew of the *U.S.S. Charleston*. Altogether, he served 15 months of active duty. "There was a war," he said, "and we had to do something about it."

He was born in Omaha on April 24, 1896, the second son of Lester T. and Georgianna Boulter Sunderland. In 1905-1906, he spent a year in Charlottenburg, Germany, near Berlin, where his mother and her sister went to study music. While there, he remembered "seeing the old Kaiser" at public ceremonies, but later recalled that he didn't bear the Kaiser any particular ill will during the war. He added, however, that the Germans were "awfully funny people—awfully dangerous people."

He came to Kansas City in 1910 when his father joined the Ash Grove Cement Company as Vice President and General Manager. He began playing the saxophone in 1912 at the age of 16, graduated from Westport High School in Kansas City, and went on to attend the University of Wisconsin, where he returned after the war. In 1920, he married Avis Peters of Madison, Wisconsin, and together they raised two sons, Robert and James Paul.

From 1922 to 1946, the family lived in Springfield, Missouri, after Paul, too, joined the Ash Grove Cement Company. They moved back to Kansas City when Paul took the job as Ash Grove Cement's Chairman of the Board, a position his father had also held and that Paul's grandson would later hold. Paul's wife, Avis, died in 1962 and, in 1967, he married Thelma V. Crick. He retired from Ash Grove Cement 20 years later in 1987.

In May 2002, at the age of 105, he attended the re-dedication of the Liberty Memorial. Eighty years earlier, he had watched it being built, and now at the re-dedication, he was being recognized as the Kansas City area's oldest living veteran of the war. As Kansas City's "last man standing,"[31] Paul Sunderland saw the Kaiser as a boy, went to war against him as a man, lived through the whole of the 20th century, and is now buried at Mount Washington Cemetery in Kansas City.

In some ways, with his death,[32] the war had come full circle for Kansas City: Paul Sunderland had served to protect the boys at the very beginning of their overseas service as they went across to fight in France. Now he was the last to join them after they were returned to their native soil, both in the cemeteries here and in the American cemeteries abroad.

Another native Missourian, Cpl. Frank Buckles, was the very last American veteran of World War I. He was born on a farm in northwest Missouri near Bethany, and was

James J. Heiman

Paul Sunderland's grave stone (1896-2004) at Mt. Washington Cemetery.

back in Missouri to be honored at the Liberty Memorial on Memorial Day, 2008.[33] Less than three years later, he died of natural causes in Charles Town, West Virginia, on February 26, 2011, at the age of 110. Both Missouri men are now recognized as "last men standing" – one for the city and the other for the country – but it was a woman, Florence Green, who was the very last of all the known World War I veterans. She served in Great Britain's Women's Royal Air Force as a mess steward at Royal Air Force bases in Marham and Narborough, England, and died on February 4, 2012, at the age of 110.[34]

For almost a century now, the war has been over. All of its combatants are dead, their stories are history, and their monuments and memorials gradually erode from the elements of time. How will they be remembered now?

Oh, Dolly, Dolly, I'll be with you, Dolly dear.

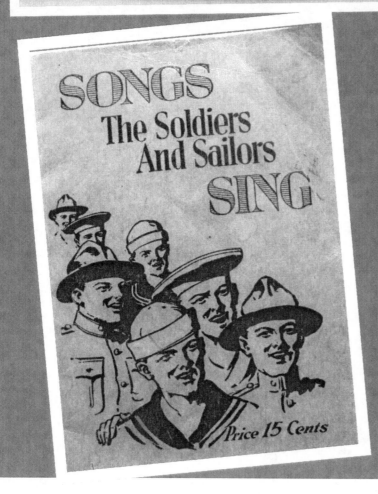

Top, Postcard of popular song title, c.1918

Bottom, Songbook for soldiers and sailors c.1918

GUIDE TO THE MONUMENTS TOUR MAP

Tour 1

1 **M8 American Legion I**
Budd Park Esplanade – Van Brunt & Anderson (north on Van Brunt from Independence Ave)

2 **M9 American Legion II**
Swope Park West Entrance

3 **M5 Jackson County American War Mothers**
Blue Ridge Blvd & 47th Street

4 **M6 Inter-City American War Mothers**
Winner Road (US 24) & Brookside

5 **M7 Kansas City American War Mothers**
Meyer Blvd & Paseo

Tour 2

6 **M3 Lt. William T. Fitzsimons Memorial Fountain**
12th & Paseo

7 **M19 Black Veterans Memorial**
12th & Paseo

8 **M4 Fitzsimons-Battenfeld Memorial at Kiely Park**
Paseo & Cleaver II Blvd

9 **M2 Meyer Circle Gateway**
Avenue of Trees, Ward Parkway at Meyer Circle

Tour 3

10 **M18 Maj. William J. Bland Memorial**
Gilham Road & 42nd Street

11 **M14 Maj. Murray Davis Memorial**
Main & 40th Street

12 **M16 89th Division Flagpole**
Liberty Memorial Mall Entrance
(100 W. 26th St.)

13 **M1 Memory Hall at Liberty Memorial**
Liberty Memorial, 100 West 26th St., KCMO

14 **M10 Dedication Wall at Liberty Memorial**
Liberty Memorial, 100 West 26th St., KCMO

Tour 4

15 **M12 35th Division Memorial Highway**
I-35 Southbound Mile Marker 234 and I-35 Northbound Mile Marker 0.4

16 **M15 Rosedale Arch**
Booth Street & Memorial Drive, KCK (1 block west of Rainbow Blvd & Southwest Blvd)

17 **M17 Soldiers and Sailors Memorial**
7th Street Between Tauromee & Barnett, KCK (3 blocks south of 7th & Minnesota)

Tour 5

18 **M13 Cpt Sanford Brown—Mount Moriah Cemetery**
10507 Holmes Road, KCMO

19 **M11 Lt. John F. Richards Marker**
9063 Gregory Blvd KCMO

MAP OF THE MONUMENTS

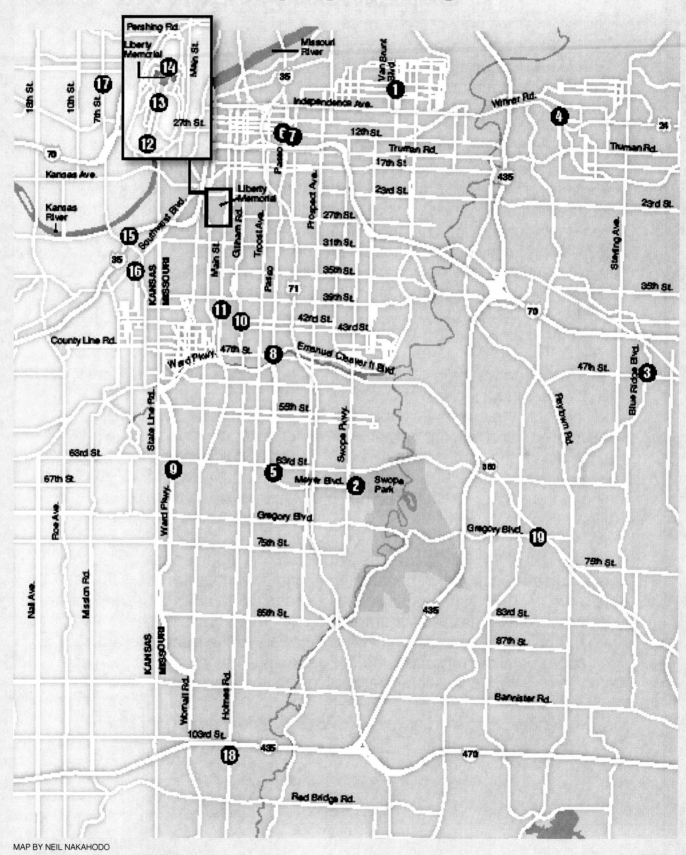

MAP BY NEIL NAKAHODO

MONUMENTAL CONVERSATIONS

The following questions are included to enhance the experience of visiting the 19 existing monuments featured in this book through the stories of the men and the women who served in the Great War.

The questions can, of course, be used by anyone, but they are specifically designed to invite young people in the elementary (grades 4-5), middle school (grades 6-8), and high school grades (9-12) to read the stories and then, on their visits to the monuments, focus attention on and share their observations of particular aspects the monuments present: their design features, their location, the inscriptions they contain, the physical imagery they depict, the similarities and contrasts they offer, the context in which they were created, the stories they tell, and what may be left out in the telling. The condition of the monuments may also be of particular interest.

Students can first be invited to read the selections ("RELATED READINGS") pertaining to the monuments they are to visit. During the visit, they can use the questions to observe, reflect, and then journal their observations and reflections much the way a war correspondent might do on-site. Later, after some revision, sharing and publishing what they have written can provide opportunities for students to experience something of the social impact the monuments have as students express their different points of view.

At the end of this list of tours are additional questions whose aim is to create a sense of the experience of memorialization as a whole. Teachers, parents, guardians, grandparents, leaders of youth groups, and the students themselves are encouraged to explore the possibilities for engagement that these questions invite. Answers to the questions are not so important as the reflection, the conversations, the inquiries, the interactions, and the applications the questions stimulate.

The monuments are organized by proximity and themed into five "tours."

TOUR ONE

AMERICAN LEGION I FOUNTAIN– Budd Park Esplanade – Van Brunt north of Independence Avenue at Anderson

Elementary School:

Three soldiers appear on one side of the monument. In what ways are the soldiers alike?

Two of these men have their mouths closed, but one man has his mouth partially open. Why do you suppose the sculptor made them that way?

Middle School:

One side of the monument shows men without helmets. What are these men doing? Another side of the monument shows men with helmets. What are these men doing? What branches of service do the two sets of men represent? How are the expressions on their faces different?

This monument was built as a fountain. Why is water an important element to include here?

High School and Adult:

What contrasting messages are conveyed on the "Dedication Side" of this monument?

Read the quotation from Theodore Roosevelt. How are "daring and courage" displayed by the figures on the monument? How are the "ideals of honor and the glory of the flag" displayed on the monument?

RELATED READINGS

M-8 American Legion I Fountain, pp. 77-79

"Soldiers Known and Unknown: Marshal Foch, Admiral Beatty, and Generals Diaz, Jacques, and Pershing at the Liberty Memorial" (Liberty Memorial 1921 Site Dedication) pp. 81-104

"General John J. Pershing—'Black Jack' from Missouri: Farmhand, Teacher, Lawyer,

Soldier" pp. 109-115

"The American Legion: To Continue the Fight for Democracy" pp. 69-76

The American Legion Posts and the stories of the men for whom they are named are listed below;

No. 8 William T. Fitzsimons

"William T. Fitzsimons: That Americans Might Not Forget" pp.13-19.

No. 10 Murray Davis

Major Murray Davis: " 'Take Care of My Men' '" pp. 178-181

No. 50 William J. Bland

"Major William J. Bland and His Wife Mary T. Johnson Bland in the Service of Their Country"

pp. 263-264

No. 81 Joseph Dillon

"Sgt. Joseph Dillon and the Sanitary Unit of the Old Missouri 3rd" pp. 184-186

No. 93 Arthur Maloney

"James Arthur Maloney: American Legion Post 93" pp. 186

No. 124 Sanford Brown, Jr.

"Capt. Sanford Miller Brown, Jr. and the Attack on Charpentry" pp. 174

No. 130 James Cummings

"Seaman 2nd Class James Cummings and the *U.S.S. Jacob Jones*" pp. 129-132

No. 148 Joseph Liebman

"Joseph Liebman: Still in a Field of Battle" pp. 248-251

No. 224 Grover Metzger

"Pvt Grover Metzger: Stockman, Officer Candidate, and Bridegroom" pp. 200-201

No. 201 Hewitt Swearingen

"Private Hewitt Jordan Swearingen: Delivering Ammunition to the Front" pp. 222-223

No. 120 Hedrick / Shackelton

"Captain Arly Luther Hedrick: Bridge-Builder of the 110th" pp. 191-196

"1st Sgt. Fred James Shackelton: Holding the Line" pp. 196-197

No. 149 Wayne Miner

"Private Wayman 'Wayne' Miner: A Hero Should be Recognized at Last" pp. 268-270

AMERICAN LEGION II FOUNTAIN
Swope Park West Entrance – Loose Memorial Flagpole.

Elementary School:

1. Some of the figures shown here might seem scary to some people. Which one is most scary to you? What is it about that figure that creates a scary effect?

2. Find the two children in the picture. Why do you suppose they are there?

Middle School:

1. There are really two sides to the scene. Point out the dividing point between the two sides. How would you describe each side? How are they different? Why do you think the artist decided to show these two parts?

2. Step back a little from the face of the monument and look at its setting. Why was this an especially good place to set the monument?

High School and Adult:

1. As you face the monument you notice that the soldiers on the right do not face the same direction. One soldier in particular stands out. How is he different from the rest? Why do you think the artist made him this way?

2. What differences do you observe about the heads of these figures? Why do you think the artist showed them this way?

RELATED READINGS

M-9 American Legion II Fountain, p. 80

"Soldiers Known and Unknown: Marshal Foch, Admiral Beatty, and Generals Diaz, Jacques, and Pershing at the Liberty Memorial" (Liberty Memorial 1921 Site Dedication) pp. 81-104

"General John J. Pershing—'Black Jack' from Missouri: Farmhand, Teacher, Lawyer, Soldier" pp. 109-115

"The American Legion: To Continue the Fight for Democracy" pp. 69-76

JACKSON COUNTY AMERICAN WAR MOTHERS AND GOLD STAR LEAGUE MEMORIAL
Blue Ridge Boulevard, at 47th Street, Kansas City, Missouri.

Elementary School:

Most war memorials are made of cut stone that is finished to a flat, polished surface. This War Mothers monument is not at all like that.

1. In what other ways is it different from most other war memorials?

2. Why do you suppose Mrs. Howard C. Boone, the president of the War Mothers at the time, selected this kind of stone rather than the usual finished kind?

Middle School:

The two verses on the monument say, "there is no death." According to the poem, the evidence to support that claim comes from what we do not see, both near and far.

1. How are the two verses evidence for the claim that "there is no death?"

2. Explain why or why not you think that evidence is strong enough to prove the poet's point that "there is no death."

High School and Adult:

Only the first and last stanzas of the poem are given on the bronze plaque. Read the rest of the poem printed in the sidebar on page 291.

1. How does the evidence of "leaves," "dust," "mists," "robes of clay," and the insight of our own "spirit" support the poet's claim that "there is no death?"

2. What is the poet's final argument that "there is no death?"

3. Do you agree? Why or why not?

RELATED READINGS

M-5 Jackson County American War Mothers and Gold Star League Memorial, pp. 58-60

"American War Mothers: The Pilgrimage to France" pp. 45-51

"Agnes Dora Fraas: The Journal of a Mount Washington Chapter War Mother's Voyage to France" pp. 52-57

"Suffrage and Service: Needles Are Guns, Wool is Ammunition, the Soldiers are Kansas City Women" pp. 37-44

"Kansas City Women at War: The Nurses of Base Hospital No. 28: Kansas City and the Red Cross Nursing Service" pp. 25-30

"There Is No Death"

There is no death! The stars go down
 To rise upon some other shore,
And bright in heaven's jeweled crown
 They shine forevermore.

There is no death! The forest leaves
 Convert to life the viewless air;
The rocks disorganize to feed
 The hungry moss they bear.

There is no death! The dust we tread
 Shall change beneath the summer showers
To golden grain or mellow fruit,
 Or rainbow tinted flowers.

There is no death! The leaves may fall,
 The flowers may fade and pass away—
They only wait through wintry hours
 The warm, sweet breath of May.

There is no death! Although we grieve
 When beautiful familiar forms
That we have learned to love are torn
 From our embracing arms.

Although with bowed and breaking heart.
 With sable garb and silent tread,
We bear their senseless dust to rest,
 And say that they are dead—

They are not dead. They have but passed
 Beyond the mists that blind us here,
Into the new and larger life
 Of that serener sphere.

They have but dropped their robe of clay
 To put a shining raiment on;
They have not wandered far away,
 They are not "lost" or "gone."

Though unseen to the mortal eye,
 They still are here and love us yet;
The dear ones they have left behind
 They never do forget.

Sometimes upon our fevered brow
 We feel their touch, a breath of balm:
Our spirit sees them, and our hearts
 Grow comforted and calm.

Yes, ever near us, though unseen,
 Our dear, immortal spirits tread—
For all God's boundless Universe
 Is Life—there are no dead.

—John McCreery (1863)

291

INTER-CITY AMERICAN WAR MOTHERS MEMORIAL
US Highway 24 (Winner Road) at Brookside
(Across from the entrance to Mt. Washington)

Elementary School:

This War Mothers memorial is called the "Inter-City" memorial. How does that term make this memorial different from an "inner-city" war memorial?

Middle School:

Stand in front of the memorial and look directly across the street at the sign that says "Mount Washington." Now turn around and look directly at the marble plaque on the face of the memorial. Think about what the plaque would look like if it were sitting by itself standing up from the ground. Why do you think the War Mothers decided to place the marble plaque and their memorial directly across from Mount Washington?

High School and Adult:

Read the story about the trip Agnes Fraas made to see her son Frank's grave in France pages 52-57.) At one time Agnes was the president of the Mt. Washington Chapter of the American War Mothers. What discrepancy do you notice between what is written on the monument and what we know about Agnes' son, Frank? (See detail page 62 and caption, p. 63.)

RELATED READINGS

M-6 Inter-city American War Mothrs Memorial, pp. 61-62.

"War Mothers: The Pilgrimage to France" pp. 45-51

"Agnes Dora Fraas: The Journal of a Mount Washington Chapter War Mother's Voyage to France"

"Kansas City Women at War: The Nurses of Base Hospital No. 28: Kansas City and the Red Cross Nursing Service" pp. 25-30

KANSAS CITY AMERICAN WAR MOTHERS MEMORIAL
Meyer Boulevard at the Paseo

Elementary School:

At the top of the monument and on each side you see eagles carved into the stone.

Why are these birds chosen to appear on war memorials?

Middle School:

On each side of the monument, towards the top, you see three stars. The gold one stands for the mothers whose sons died in the war. The silver one stands for mothers whose sons were wounded in the war. The blue one stands for mothers whose sons returned home safe from the war. Why were those particular colors chosen to represent those groups of the war mothers?

High School and Adult:

Almost all of the World War I monuments and memorials in Kansas City are built either on the side of a road or are set off in some other fashion. The War Mothers Memorial is an exception. It appears in the middle of a busy intersection. Why do you suppose the war mothers selected the middle of two busy streets to erect their memorial?

RELATED READINGS

M-7 Kansas City American War Mothers Memorial Fountain, pp. 63-64

"American War Mothers: The Pilgrimage to France" pp. 45-51

"Agnes Dora Fraas: The Journal of a Mount Washington Chapter War Mother's Voyage to France" pp. 52-57

"Kansas City Women at War: The Nurses of Base Hospital No. 28 and the Red Cross Nursing Service" pp. 25-30

TOUR TWO

LT. WILLIAM T. FITZSIMONS MEMORIAL FOUNTAIN
12ᵀᴴ & Paseo

Elementary School:

Why is a fountain a good way to remember a doctor who was killed in the war?

Look directly across the street from the fountain. What do you see? What does it remind you of? How is it different from how the doctor's monument remembers him?

Middle School:

There are other monuments above and behind this one. How are they similar to and different from this one?

Why is this location a good place for war memorials?

High School and Adult:

Some monuments have figures of soldiers on them. Other monuments might include the actual image of the person whom they honor. The Lt. Fitzsimons monument has neither war figures nor an image of Dr. Fitzsimons. Why do you suppose these were not included as part of the way he is remembered at the memorial fountain?

The medical symbol that appears on the monument is called a "Caduceus." It depicts the staff carried by Mercury – in mythology, the messenger of the Greek gods. Why are snakes and bird wings presented in this symbol of medicine?

RELATED READINGS

M-3 William T. Fitzsimons Memorial Fountain, pp. 20-23

"William T. Fitzsimons: That Americans Might Not Forget" pp. 13-19

"Kansas City Women at War: The Nurses of Base Hospital No. 28 and the Red Cross Nursing Service" pp. 25-30

"Lottie Ruth Hollenback: She Died that Others Might Live" pp. 31-35

Pvt. WAYNE MINER COMMEMORATIVE PLAQUE
AT BLACK VETERANS MEMORIAL
12ᵀᴴ & Paseo,

(Above and behind the Fitzsimons Memorial Fountain)

Elementary:
Look at the medallions at the base of the flagpole. What do they represent?

Middle School:
According to the inscriptions, to whom is this monument dedicated? Why do we honor these heroes? Why are they "unsung"?

High School and Adult:
Among the World War I heroes honored here is Wayne Miner. Find the flagstone dedicated to him. Read his story to find out what is especially compelling about his death. (Pages 268-272.)

RELATED READINGS:
M-19 Pvt. Wayne Miner Commemorative Plaque at Black Veterans Memorial, pp. 271-272

"Private Wayman 'Wayne' Miner: A Hero Should be Recognized at Last" pp. 268-270

FITZSIMONS-BATTENFELD MEMORIAL AT KIELY PARK
Southbound Paseo at Cleaver II Boulevard

Elementary School:

What is different about the two doctors who are remembered here?

Middle School:

Another monument that honors Lt. Fitzsimons is located at 12th & Paseo, 35 blocks north of the Fitzsimons-Battenfeld Monument. How are the two monuments, 3 miles apart on the same street, alike and how are they different from each other?

High School and Adult:

This monument commemorates two doctors who served in two different wars in two different branches of the service. Another monument on the Paseo, 3 miles north of this one, already commemorates one of these two doctors. Why do you think American Legion Post No. 8 wanted to include Lt. Fitzsimons again on this monument?

RELATED READINGS
M-4 Fitzsimons-Battenfeld at Kiely Park, p. 24
"Pvt. Thomas J. Kiely: Company E's Liaison to the 356th" pp. 252-254

MEYER CIRCLE GATEWAY—AVENUE OF TREES
Ward Parkway at Meyer Circle

Elementary:

Four memorial plaques list the names of 440 men and one woman – all from Kansas City. The writing at the top of each plaque says that this Avenue of Trees is a "living memorial to our dead of the World War." Look between the walls of the monument, past the flagpole, down the long stretch of land. Do you see the trees? In what way is this Avenue of Trees a "living" memorial to those who died?

Middle School:

The four plaques list the names of the dead in alphabetical order. Find the name of "Loretto Hollenback" on the second plaque. She is the only woman whose name appears on the plaques, and she was the first Red Cross nurse to die in the war. Read the story about her to find out when and how she died. (Pages 31-32.) Who was the first doctor, also a native of Kansas City, to die in the war?

High School and Adult:

Stand on the sidewalk and look down the long stretch of land. Trees line both sides about a mile to 75th Street. Also, on both sides of the monument you see two limestone pillars with eagles on top, both looking to the east. The eagles and the pillars are called the "gateway," and you can see a flagpole directly through the opening they make. Why do you think both of the eagles look east? Why do you think there is no actual "gate" to this monument?

RELATED READINGS

TOUR THREE

MAJOR WILLIAM J. BLAND

Gilham Road at 42nd Street

Elementary School:

Major William J. Bland is not buried here. Instead, he is buried outside of Washington, D.C., at Arlington National Cemetery, where many of our country's other war heroes are buried. Here in Kansas City, this monument to Major Bland rests between two trees. Why do you think these trees were planted here, on either side of the monument?

Middle School:

This monument was erected by the Major William J. Bland American Legion Post No. 50 and presented to the city during a ceremony on this spot on November 7, 1936. Many of the people who attended the ceremony served in the war and knew Major Bland. Joseph E. Brown, former commander of the Major William J. Bland American Legion Post No. 50 read the invocation. A veteran of the war, Joseph Brown was the brother of Sanford Brown for whom another Kansas City American Legion Post, No. 124, was named. The current post commander at the time, Dick Richardson, reminded the spectators that Major Bland had drilled troops at this very spot. Today, all the veterans of the Great War are dead. Can this monument ever have the meaning it had to those people who attended the dedication that day in 1936? (See pages 265-267.) What meaning can this monument have for us who look at it today?

High School and Adult:

The inscription on the plaque is taken from one of Shakespeare's plays, the 1593-94 tragedy, *Titus Andronicus* (Act I, sc i, lines 25-26). The inscription reads: "A nobler man, a braver warrior, lives not this day within the city walls." At the dedication of the monument in 1936, Bishop Henry Hobson, who served with Major Bland as a fellow battalion commander in the 356th Infantry, remembered his friend and comrade as possessing a keen sense of justice, honesty, unselfishness, and courage. He said that we should think of the words on the monument "not as referring to some dead hero, but as referring to one who lives today in the city of our lives." What do you think he meant? How can a monument to a dead soldier refer to someone living?

RELATED READINGS

M-18 William J. Bland Memorial, pp. 265-267

"Major William J. Bland and His Wife Mary T. Johnson Bland in the Service of Their Country" pp. 263-264

MAJOR MURRY DAVIS MEMORIAL
Main at 40th Street

Elementary:

This monument tells a lot of Major Davis' story. We learn, for example, that he was killed at Exermont, France, on September 29, 1918. We also learn that, even though he was seriously wounded, he continued to lead his men until he died. Major Davis spoke his last words to Captain Harry S. Whitthorne, who was standing right next to him. "Take care of my

men," the Major said. What other words can you find on the monument to show that Major Davis himself took care of his men before he died?

Middle School:

Sit on the bench in front of the monument. Do you notice that the arms of the monument seem to reach out to you? On the insides of the posts at the end of the arms and also on the main part of the monument itself, are the names of the places where Major Davis fought – Vauquois, Charpentry;, Chaudron Farm, Exermont, Amiens, Vosges, St. Mihiel, Meuse-Argonne. On the outside of these posts appear the names of the units in which Major Davis served. The 140th Infantry was Major Davis' regiment. It was part of the 35th Division, composed mostly of men from Missouri and Kansas. Why do you think the arms of the monument are reaching out to you with these names?

High School and Adult:

1. On each corner of the center stone we see bundled rods called *fasces*. These are used to symbolize authority. On each side of the center stone we see a sword pointing down. On both the front and the back of the center stone we see an eagle perched inside of a wreath, and at the bottom of the wreath a ribbon rippling out from each side. What do the downward sword, the eagle, the wreath, and the ribbon symbolize?

2. Murray Davis was a lawyer before he entered the service, and before his last battle, he circulated among his men helping them write their wills. What words on the monument allude to the practice of the law?

RELATED READINGS

M-14 Major Murray Davis Memorial, pp. 182-183
Major Murray Davis: " 'Take Care of My Men'" pp. 178-181

89TH DIVISION FLAGPOLE
Entrance to Liberty Memorial Mall

Elementary School:

Why do you think the people who made this monument decided to include a flagpole with it?

Middle School:

A homonym is a word that sounds like another word but has a different meaning and is often spelled differently. This war memorial contains three homonyms. Each homonym on this monument has to do with a General's name. For example, "Wright" sounds like "right." Think about General Wood and General Winn. What homonyms do their names suggest to you? Now put the three homonyms together to form a sentence, starting with "Right." What is your sentence? Why is your sentence a good way to remember what this war memorial stands for?

High School and Adult:

Kansas City men served in a number of Army divisions during the war, but most men served in one of four: the 35th Division, the 42nd Division, the 89th Division, and the 92nd Division. The 35th is commemorated in road signs along I-35. The 42nd is commemorated by a prominent arch on top of Mount Marty, overlooking the city. The 92nd Division is commemorated in the Black Veterans Memorial. The memorial to the 89th is often missed by people because it is in the shadow of the Liberty Memorial and not as conspicuous as the other Division memorials. Can you think of some ways to make the memorial to the 89th Division more notable without detracting from it?

RELATED READINGS

M-16 89th Division Flagpole, pp. 243-245
"Wood, Winn and Wright: The Midwest 89th Division" pp. 146-172
"Major Mark Hanna: To Cross the River" pp. 255-257

MEMORY HALL AT LIBERTY MEMORIAL

Elementary:

Go inside Memory Hall and look at the west wall. On each side of the door you see the names of 440 dead – all men plus one woman who died in the war. The names are listed in categories. Look through the categories and find the name of the one woman. She was a nurse who died at Camp Funston just a few weeks before she was to ship overseas. What is her name? Look at the displays of the other nurses in the glass cases:

1. Ruth Regina Shields and her identity pass, her Red Cross Service badge, her identity disc, and a convenience can. How old was she in 1918?

2. Florence Edith Hemphill was ten years older than Ruth Shields. You see her watch, her U.S. War Department identification certificate, and a letter she wrote to her brother on March 5, 1918. "So I beat you over after all," she begins. What did she mean by that?

3. Eleanor Washburn was a YMCA entertainer, one of 35,000 other artists and performers to entertain the troops. You see her straw hat, a booklet called AEF Fun in France, a YMCA Women's Bureau booklet, a souvenir booklet from Aix les-Baines, France, and a luggage tag for her trip back home. How do these artifacts tell her story? What did some of these artists and performers do to entertain the troops?

Middle School:

Look up at the west wall. Over the door you see Daniel MacMorris' mural showing the dedication of the Liberty Memorial Site on November 1, 1921. Generals Jacques and Diaz, Marshal Foch, Gereral Pershing, and Admiral Beatty appear at the top. Six young women hold flags and wreaths over the doorway and two boy scouts hold a sign that reads, "The dead we honor here made the noble sacrifice for a cause that should not be forgotten."

1. What building appears in the background? (Hint: Go out the door of Memory Hall and look north from the deck in front of the tall shaft. What building do you see?)

2. Why is that building depicted here? What was its role during the war?

High School and Adult:

On the south wall you see a woman at the bottom right holding a broken sword. Why is the sword broken? In what ways are women depicted differently than men in this mural? What do these different depictions tell us about how we as a people view war and why we continue to pursue it?

RELATED READING

"Shall I Bring My Boy Home?" pp. 3-5

All of the stories listed with the Meyer Circle Gateway Avenue of Trees, but most especially:

"William T. Fitzsimons: That Americans Might Not Forget" (see display case, north side) pp. 13-19

"Kansas City Women at War: The Nurses of Base Hospital No. 28 and the Red Cross Nursing Service" (see nurses' display cases) pp. 25-30

"Lottie Hollenback: She Died that Others Might Live" (see nurses' display cases) pp. 31-32

"Major Mark Hanna: To Cross the River" (see display case, south side) pp. 255-257

"Wright and Traub: The Santa Fe 35th Division" (see battle maps on the walls) pp. 147-172

"Wood, Winn and Wright: The Midwest 89th Division" (see battle maps on the walls) pp. 227-242

DEDICATION WALL
Pershing Road at Liberty Memorial

Elementary School:

Find the name of the road that runs east and west in front of Dedication Wall. Look at the names of the soldiers beneath the plaques on the wall. Whose name matches the name of the road? Why do you think the road was named for this man?

Middle School:

Look at the plaques dedicated to Admiral Beatty, Marshal Foch, and Generals Pershing, Diaz, and Jacques. Notice their hats. How are the depictions of the men similar? How are they different?

High School and Adult:

Speculate about why these World War I commanders of Allied forces are placed where they are across from Union Station and at the base of the Liberty memorial instead of being placed higher up on the hill where the rest of the memorial is and where you might expect commanders to be.

RELATED READINGS

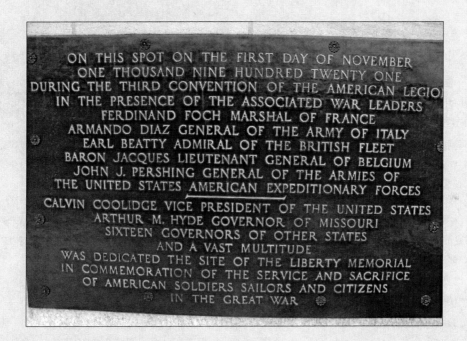

ON THIS SPOT ON THE FIRST DAY OF NOVEMBER
ONE THOUSAND NINE HUNDRED TWENTY ONE
DURING THE THIRD CONVENTION OF THE AMERICAN LEGION
IN THE PRESENCE OF THE ASSOCIATED WAR LEADERS
FERDINAND FOCH MARSHAL OF FRANCE
ARMANDO DIAZ GENERAL OF THE ARMY OF ITALY
EARL BEATTY ADMIRAL OF THE BRITISH FLEET
BARON JACQUES LIEUTENANT GENERAL OF BELGIUM
JOHN J. PERSHING GENERAL OF THE ARMIES OF
THE UNITED STATES AMERICAN EXPEDITIONARY FORCES
CALVIN COOLIDGE VICE PRESIDENT OF THE UNITED STATES
ARTHUR M. HYDE GOVERNOR OF MISSOURI
SIXTEEN GOVERNORS OF OTHER STATES
AND A VAST MULTITUDE
WAS DEDICATED THE SITE OF THE LIBERTY MEMORIAL
IN COMMEMORATION OF THE SERVICE AND SACRIFICE
OF AMERICAN SOLDIERS SAILORS AND CITIZENS
IN THE GREAT WAR

TOUR FOUR

35th DIVISION MEMORIAL HIGWAY
I-35 Southbound Mile Marker 234 & Northbound Mile Marker 0.4

Elementary School:

A number of highways go through Kansas City. Why do you suppose Interstate 35 was selected to commemorate the 35th Division?

Middle School:

Look along I-35 for another road sign similar to the 35th Memorial Highway sign, but this time blue. It has a circle of 5-stars and commemo-

rates the man responsible for creating the Interstate Highway system in our country. As Supreme Allied Commander during World War II, he was in command of the 35th and all other American and Allied divisions during that war. Who was this man, and what else do you know about him and where he came from?

High School and Adult:

In Rosedale, an arch modeled on the *Arc de Triomphe de l' toile* in Paris commemorates the 42nd Division. At the entrance to the Liberty Memorial Mall, a flagpole that displays the American colors commemorates the 89th Division. What do you know about the 35th Division that helps explain why a roadway was chosen as its memorial?

RELATED READINGS
M-12 35th Division Memorial Highway, p. 173
"Wright and Traub: The Santa Fe 35th Division" pp. 147-172

ROSEDALE ARCH
Booth Street & Memorial Drive
North of Rosedale Middle School, Kansas City, Kansas

Elementary:

Walk around the iron fence surrounding the monument. Most of the iron uprights are pointed, but a couple have figures with horns, four eyes, an open mouth, and a long beard. These are called "gargoyles," a feature of gothic architecture, sometimes found on the corners of buildings, and used as waterspouts to drain the gutters. Here they are just a decoration. To some people, they look like fanciful monsters. What do they look like to you? Why do you suppose they are used here?

Middle School:

It was said that the Rosedale Arch was modeled after the famous *Arch d'Triomph*, or "*Arch of Triumph*," in Paris. Why do you suppose the designers wanted an arch to commemorate those who lost their lives in war?

High School and Adult:

Look at the black object in front of the memorial tablet. It has a rainbow of red, white, and blue to represent the 42nd Division in which the 117th Ammunition Train from Kansas and the 117th Field Signal Battalion from Missouri served in World War

I. Nearby, Rainbow Boulevard is named in honor of this Army division, which was made up of units from 46 of the 48 states in the Union at the time. Why is a rainbow an appropriate symbol for the 42nd Division and an arch an appropriate symbol for a rainbow?

RELATED READINGS

M-15 Rosedale Arch, pp. 219-221

"Over There, Over the Rainbow: Kansas and Missouri in the 42nd Division" pp. 210-218

"Pvt. Hewitt Jordan Swearingen: Delivering Ammunition to the Front" pp. 222-223

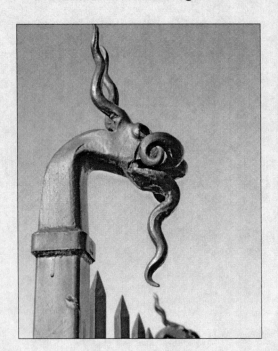 

THIS ROSEDALE ARCH IS RECOGNIZED AS A MEMORIAL OF THE 42nd DIVISION VETERANS MEMORIAL FOUNDATION

SOLDIERS AND SAILORS MEMORIAL
7th Street between Tauromee and Barnett, Kansas City, Kansas

Elementary:

Look at the words on this monument. To whom is the monument dedicated?

Middle School:

In a corner decoration you will see a shield with 13 stars. What do these stars represent? Below the stars are stripes. Where else on the grounds of this memorial would you expect to see stars and stripes?

High School and Adult:

Look at the long inscription over the top of the Soldiers and Sailors Memorial. It says, "Dedicated to the Heroes Who Fought and Died for their Country." Next to the eagle on the left the inscription reads, "Justice Actuated their Heroism, Liberty Inspired their Courage." Next to the eagle on the right, the inscription says, "Let us Resolve that These Dead Shall Not Have Died in Vain." From what the inscriptions tell us, how can we, the living, best honor these heroes who died for our country?

RELATED READINGS

M-17 Soldiers and Sailors Memorial, pp. 246-248

"Over There, Over the Rainbow: Kansas and Missouri in the 42nd Division" pp. 210-218

"Pvt. Hewitt Jordan Swearingen: Delivering Ammunition to the Front" pp. 222-223

TOUR FIVE

CAPTAIN SANFORD M. BROWN, JR. MEMORIAL
Mount Moriah Cemetery — 10507 Holmes,
Kansas City, Missouri

Elementary School:

Look closely at the monument. What images do you see? Why do you think the picture of Captain Brown appears with the eagle and the stars?

Middle School:

The American Legion Post that bears Captain Brown's name erected this monument on September 27, 1931, 13 years after the battle in which he died. Two inscriptions help us understand the reason why the American Legion Post erected the monument. The inscription on the side of the monument states: "To inculcate a sense of individual obligation to the community, state, and nation." ("Inculcate" means "to impress upon the mind by frequent repetition, to instill.") On the back of the monument, the American Legion logo appears with an inscription under-

neath, "For God and Country." Why did the American Legion Post erect this monument? What evidence can you find to show that the American Legion Post No. 124 achieved or failed to achieve that purpose?

High School and Adult:

This monument was originally erected in 1931 on the northern section of "Linwood Plaza," a park of 3,089 acres that stretched north and south of Linwood Blvd between Brooklyn and Park. This area is in the central part of Kansas City. Sanford Brown was one of the early members of the Ivanhoe Masonic Lodge, which is now just down the street from the Cemetery, at 8640 Holmes, in the south part of Kansas City. In 1963, 32 years after the monument was erected in Linwood Plaza, American Legion Post No. 124, which was named for Sanford Brown, moved the monument to Mount Moriah Cemetery. At that time, the cemetery was a burial place for members of the Masonic Brotherhood and their families. What different effects do you think such a move from the central to the south part of Kansas City might have had on the security of the statue, its preservation, and its accessibility to the public?

RELATED READINGS

M-13 Captain Sanford M. Brown, Jr., Memorial pp. 176-177
"Capt. Sanford Miller Brown, Jr. and the Attack on Charpentry" pp. 174-175

RICHARDS FLYING FIELD HISTORICAL MARKER
9063 Gregory Boulevard, Kansas City, Missouri

Elementary School:

This sign honors a Kansas City pilot who was killed on the first day of the Battle in the Argonne. The sign marks a spot named after him which now looks very different from what it looked like in 1922. Back then, it was just a field with a building that had the name "Richards Field" written on the roof. Why do you think the name was on the roof instead of on a sign like it is today? (p. 137)

Middle School:

Not far from here in Grandview, along Highway 150, was a large Air Force Base named Richards-Gebaur in honor of Lt. John F. Richards. The air base is now closed and the land is being redeveloped to be a transportation center. The land where this marker stands also used to be an airfield. It, too, was redeveloped, this time for residential housing. Why is it important for people to have a marker here when the thing the marker commemorates is gone and the person whose name appears here has been dead for 100 years?

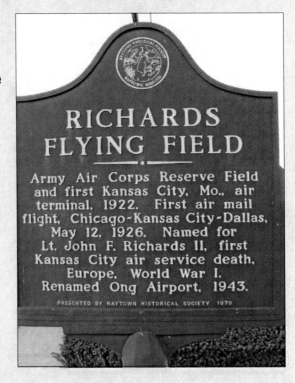

High School and Adult:

Read the story about Lt. John F. Richards included in this book. (Pages 133-134.) You will see a picture of Lt. Richards in the biplane he flew during his time at Issoudun, France. What would it have been like to fly a plane like that? What details in the picture show you how flying in a plane back then was very different from flying in a plane today? (Also see photos pp. 141-142)

Photo courtesy of National World War I Museum, Kansas City, Missouri

RELATED READINGS

M-11 Richards Flying Field Historical Marker, pp. 136-140
"Lieut. John Francisco Richards, II" pp. 132-135

LOST MONUMENTS

KANSAS CITY BAR ASSOCIATION FOUNTAIN
Old Courthouse at Missouri & Oak Street, Kansas City, Missouri

A panel of Tennessee marble, 8 feet high and 3 ½ feet wide, was carved and attached to the lobby wall of the old courthouse at a cost of $2,000. It was dedicated on April 23, 1921, and included a fountain, which became inoperable and was never repaired. The Kansas City Bar Association planned to have the fountain moved to the new courthouse at 12th and Oak, but those plans never materialized, and the fountain is now lost. It commemorated eight Kansas City lawyers who lost their lives in the Great War: Maj. William J. Bland, Maj. Murray Davis, Pvt. Lawrence W. Fulton, 1st Lt. Harry Herrod, 1st Lt. Carl W. Haner, Pvt. William T. Law, Sgt. Maj. Roswell B. Sayre, and 1st Lt. Frank L. Stauver. The inscription reads: "The heroic patriots of the Jackson County Missouri who gave their lives during the World War in Defense of Justice, Freedom & Democracy. A.D. MCMXVII" (1917).

Elementary:

The Bar Association was named after the railing, or "bar," enclosing the part of the law court where the judge sits at his bench and the lawyers sit with their clients at tables. In the picture of the monument above, the soldier represents eight lawyers who

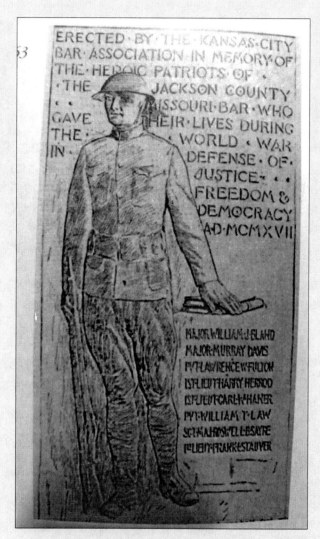

Fountains of Kansas City: A History and Love Affair. Sherry Piland and Ellen J. Ugguccioni. (KansasCity, MO: City of Fountains Foundation, 1985), Fig. 63, p. 130.

gave their lives "in defense of justice, freedom, and democracy." The soldier's right hand supports his rifle. What is his left hand doing? Why are his hands shown that way?

Middle School:

How is the soldier's pose, the action taken by his hands, and the words in the inscription especially important for men in the legal profession?

High School and Adult:

The night before the battle that killed Major Murray Davis, he was in the trenches helping his men draw up their wills. Sgt. Major Roswell Sayre served in the same battalion as Major Davis. Both died in the same battle within a day of each other. Major William Bland gave up a promising career to volunteer. Pvt. Lawrence Fulton, a graduate of the Kansas City School of Law and the Law Department of Yale, enlisted in the Canadian Army. Lt. Frank Stauver had just been commissioned a 2nd Lieutenant in aviation when he was stricken with influenza that developed into a severe case of pneumonia, from which he died. Pvt. William Law had been married just 10 days and had joined the 16th Observation Battery just 11 days before the Armistice and died in Officer's Candidate School the day after the Armistice was signed. Lt. Harry Herrod, a practicing lawyer in Kansas City, mustered out with 100 percent disability and died two months later of tuberculosis. Each man sacrificed for a higher purpose. Even though the monument to their memory is lost, their stories live on. Why is it important that they are remembered together?

RELATED READINGS

"Murray Davis: 'Take Care of My Men'" pp. 178-181
"Major William J. Bland and Mary T. Johnson Bland In the Service of their Country" pp. 263-264
"Sgt. Major Roswell Barry Sayre" pp. 187-190
"Pvt. Lawrence Fulton: To 'Die Like a Martyr'" pp. 273
"Lt. Frank L. Stauver: From Artillery to Aviation" pp. 141-142
"Pvt. William T. Law" p. 200
"Lt. Harry W. Herrod" p. 201
"1st Lt. Carl W. Haner" p. 272

CAPTAIN ARLY LUTHER HEDRICK BRIDGE
27ᵗʰ & Vine, Kansas City, Missouri

The plaque on the bridge read: "CAPTAIN ARLY LUTHER HEDRICK, 110th ENGINEERS, designer of this structure, which was his last important work before going overseas. He died in Brest, France, on the sixth day of March 1919 and was posthumously awarded the Distinguished Service Cross for extraordinary bravery in the battle of the Argonne Forest."

An early postcard showing the bridge designed by Arly Hedrick. The plaque honoring Cpt. Hedrick remained on the bridge until the bridge was dismantled in 2005, but the plaque is now lost. (Missouri Valley Room, Kansas City Public Library)

Elementary:

War heroes are most often remembered by having their names listed on a monument, and Cpt. Hedrick's name appears on two – the tablet on the west wall of Memory Hall at Liberty Memorial and the tablets at Meyer Circle Gateway Avenue of Trees listing the 441 war dead from Kansas City. A plaque commemorating Cpt. Hedrick's war service also appeared on this bridge. Read the inscription above the picture. Why was putting a plaque on the bridge the right thing to do to remember him?

Middle School:

Although Cpt. Hedrick is remembered by having his name listed at Meyer Circle Gateway and in Memory Hall at Liberty Memorial, the plaque honoring the bridge he designed at 17th and Vine has gone missing. What are some other ways he can be remembered?

High School and Adult:

Cpt. Hedrick was a member of the 110th Engineers. At the outset of the war, he recruited men for a unit of engineers and became their captain. During battle, he and his men repaired critical bridges so the heavy guns could be brought across to support the men in the front lines. He and his men inspected bridges for mines, and he personally disconnected detonators while under live fire because he thought it was too dangerous to send his own men in to do the job. For that action, he received the Distinguished Service Cross. After surviving his unit's heavy losses in battle, he died of disease four months after the war ended and before he had a chance to come home or to accept his promotion to major. Given the irony of his death, why is Cpt. Hedrick's story especially important for us to know and remember?

RELATED READINGS

"Captain Arly Luther Hedrick: Bridge Builder of the 110th" pp. 191-196

COMPARING AND CONTRASTING THE MONUMENTS

Nineteen existing monuments are featured in this book:

1. Memory Hall, Liberty Memorial p. 9
2. Meyer Circle Gateway Avenue of Trees pp. 10-12
3. William T. Fitzsimons Memorial Fountain pp. 20-23
4. Fitzsimons-Battenfeld at Kiely Park p. 24
5. Jackson County American War Mothers and Gold Star League Memorial pp. 58-60
6. Inter-City American War Mothers Memorial pp. 61-62
7. Kansas City American War Mothers Memorial pp. 63-64
8. American Legion I Fountain pp. 77-79
9. American Legion II Fountain p. 80
10. Dedication Wall, Liberty Memorial pp. 105-107

Two monuments mentioned in this book are no longer available to the public, but the names of the men they honored are included on other existing monuments (Meyer Circle Gateway Avenue of Trees and Memory Hall at Liberty Memorial).

MEMORY HALL: The Keystone to Kansas City's Great War Monuments and to Memory Itself

Memory Hall at Liberty Memorial holds a special place among the Kansas City World War I monuments. In Memory Hall, connections can be made especially to William J. Fitzsimons, 35th Division, 89th Division, the three War Mothers monuments, American Legion I and II, William J. Bland, the Gateway Avenue of Trees, and the Black Veterans Memorial. Memory Hall holds so much, in fact, that no single visit does it justice. Multiple visits focusing on specific ties to the other monuments can make the features of Memory Hall much more accessible and appreciated. Visit two or three of these other World War I monuments and then stop in Memorial Hall to see if the fol-

lowing questions help you to tie what you see there to what you observed at the other memorials.

1. What can you find in Memory Hall that relates to each of those other memorials?

2. How do the Memory Hall artifacts and depictions differ from the way the other monuments and memorials portray their subjects?

3. In what ways are the artifacts and depictions in Memory Hall similar to the portrayals the other memorials make of their subjects?

4. On the south wall at Memory Hall you see references to blue and gold stars: "Blood and mothers' tears given for a star of gold," and "Hope like a blue star kept mothers' faith alive." What other Kansas City World War I monument has blue and gold stars? Which star in that monument is missing in the Memory Hall quote?

5. In front of the fountain of the World War I Museum is a collection of stone plaques set face-up in the ground so you can read the inscriptions. At what other monument will you see similar plaques? How do these plaques continue Kansas City's practice of remembering service in war?

6. The National World War I Museum contains a number of references to the Army divisions also referenced in this book – the 35th, the 42nd, the 89th, and the 92nd. The museum also features a German field telephone captured by Lt. Col. Ruby D. Garrett, commander of the 117th Field Signal Battalion from Missouri. In another part of the Museum is a portrait of Lt. John F. Richards along with artifacts of the Army Air Service. How do the artifacts that appear with both Lt. Col. Garrett and Lt. Richards relate to their particular stories?

7. The Truman Library on Highway 24 in Independence, Missouri, contains an exhibit devoted to Cpt. Harry S. Truman's World War I service with Battery D, 129th Field Artillery Regiment, 60th Field Artillery Brigade, 35th Division. How is Cpt. Truman represented in Memory Hall at Liberty Memorial? Read the selection "Soldiers Known and Unknown" (pages 84-86) to find out the special role that Cpt. Truman played during the 1921 American Legion Convention and Liberty Memorial Site Dedication.

8. Kansas City also has memorials to other wars: the Civil War, the Spanish-American War, World War II, the Korean War, and the Vietnam War. How do the World War I memorials compare with them? Are the distinctive features of these other wars reflected in the monuments to them? Why does Kansas City have so many more monuments and memorials to World War I than to the other wars?

9. After you have taken some pictures, written some notes, or just thought about the monuments you have visited, write about what you remember most about them. In what ways do the monuments tell the stories of the men and women whose war experience they commemorate?

10. Think about ways that you and/or your family remembers important events and people in your lives. You might take a tour of your house, noting pictures, trophies, diplomas, recognition plaques, display albums, yearbooks, special decorations, or other memorabilia on display. Think about the music you play on special occasions or just to create a special mood or memory from the past. How do these various artifacts serve to keep the past alive? How do they affect the way you experience the present? Why is it important for us to share these memories with others? Which should be passed down and which should be kept personal and private?

11. Finally, who is left out? What people who served, supported, or opposed the war are not included in the various Kansas City monuments to World War I? How do you identify with those who are left out?

MONUMENTS, MEMORIALS, AND MEMORY

Webster's Third International Dictionary defines a "memorial" as "something that serves to preserve memory or knowledge of an individual or event, RELIC, TRACE; something that is kept to preserve the memory of a person or event, KEEPSAKE, MOMENTO; something designed to preserve a memory of a person or event, commemoration, RECORD, MEMOIR."

"Monument," on the other hand, is defined by the same dictionary as "something that by surviving represents or testifies to the greatness or achievement, especially of an individual or an age, a conspicuous instance, a notable example, one of unusual prominence; a distinguished figure, a structure erected or maintained in memory of the dead or to preserve the remembrance of a person, event, or action."

The word "monument" suggests something constructed in such a way that its quality of permanence and its ability to endure and withstand the elements of change will thereby preserve the memory of a person or event. The word "memorial" suggests something so closely associated with a person or event as to evoke the memory of it. A monument might be more publicly prominent, whereas a memorial something more personally preserved. Both survive through physical dimensions, either of proportion or association, but both must involve story for that survival to continue.

Using those distinctions, one might consider four of the 19 Kansas City tributes to the Great War as reference points in the continuum from "memorial" to "monument": Sanford Brown, Jr., The Liberty Memorial, Murray Davis, and finally the lost Kansas City Bar Association plaque, an example of a memorial that no longer physically exists – at least as far as we know. Considering the memorial and monumental qualities of these four war remembrances can help us to compare and contrast all the other monuments and memorials and to use the stories in this book to reflect about how Kansas City remembered and continues to remember its World War I service. To that end, the stories about the dedications of the monuments, if known, become as important as the stories of the men and women whose individual experiences the monuments and memorials commemorate. In the final analysis, however, the distinction between "memorial" and "monument" may not be at all as important as the active act of remembering itself.

As a start, one might consider the stone commemoration to Captain Sanford Brown, Jr. to be more of a memorial than a monument. From its inception, the Sanford Brown, Jr. Memorial was never fully public. Even membership in the Sanford Brown, Jr. American Legion Post No. 124 was private, "restricted from the start to members of the three Ivanhoe Masonic bodies."[35] The Masonic Lodge and American Legion Post that built the memorial requested and were granted a public name change for the park from "Linwood Plaza" to "Sanford Brown Plaza," but the memorial that the lodge and the post erected there was never formally presented to the city as most of the other monuments were.

In an interesting reversal of the private to public gift, the Jackson County government gifted two of the War Mothers memorials to the War Mothers organization itself, thus privatizing to a certain extent sites that had been public. The significance of that privatization in itself may reveal something of how the public recognized the unique role that the war mothers played in the gift of their sons, a fact that may help explain why Congress funded their trips to the graves of their sons in foreign soil. Metaphorically, the mothers' losses were so personal, and yet so necessary to the survival of our country, that the public owed them the land itself, of which their sons were now physically a part. In that sense, government recognized that the mothers had generated the land itself. As personal becomes public, public becomes personal, once again.

"Monument," on the other hand, is defined by the same dictionary as "something that by surviving represents or testifies to the greatness or achievement, especially of an individual or an age, a conspicuous instance, a notable example, one of unusual prominence; a distinguished figure, a structure erected or maintained in memory of the dead or to preserve the remembrance of a person, event, or action."

For example, the Sanford Brown marble column is distinctively personal: It contains a physical image of the man, was originally erected in the park where he and his brother played, and was near his home and the Masonic lodge where his lodge brothers and the American Legion Post that bore his name met on a regular basis. These qualities suggest the personal aspects of memorialization, and the viewer needs the story to understand why the monument was placed where it was originally.

But further evidence of the stone's memorial qualities is also illustrated in the story of its removal. From the original spot where it was erected and where its existence had so many close connections to Brown's youth, its 10 tons were removed and taken to a Masonic cemetery where many of the Lodge members are now buried and where a few blocks away the Masonic Lodge itself now stands. The marble memorial to Brown remained the same; the physical locations changed, but the story behind the change helps us understand how physical expressions of remembrance continued to be invested with elements of human emotion in order for the memorial to survive. Here, proximity and human closeness play a key role in the story. Restricted to their membership, lodge members wanted to be close to their memorial of Brown while they lived, and as they died and were buried, they continued to remain close to one another, to their lodge, and to Brown's memorial. The removal story is as essential to the memorial's role in the preservation of Brown's memory as the story of the monument's original placement is to the preservation of that memory. More critically, both stories are essential to the preservation of the memorial itself.

The stories of the memorial's locations also emphasize the importance of close relationships between those who erected the memorial and those who remember Sanford Brown. At first, they were largely the same people. However, the monument itself tells a story, as well – this one between those who built and removed the monument and who knew Sanford Brown and those other viewers who have come to Mount Moriah Cemetery for one reason or another, see the memorial, but have no knowledge of Brown at all. How can the memorial be personal to them?

The memorial itself attempts to speak to that question. Unlike many other memorials, the Sanford Brown, Jr., Memorial directly states its purpose: "To inculcate a sense of individual obligation to the community, state and nation." The memorial now stands in a more remote and semi-private place, and its relationship to the viewer is more overtly individual and consciously didactic, but its

message is still publicly oriented: The memorial invites the viewer into the example of Sanford Brown's personal story, his death in the Argonne, and the memorial's purpose is directed to the service of the common good, just as his lodge and its members were.

The tribute to Murray Davis, on the other hand, might be considered more of a monument than a memorial because it is constructed in a very public place, along Main Street of Kansas City, and seems to emphasize a more communal aspect with its arms reaching out to the visitor, the names of the battles fought by the 35th Division on its end posts, and the Major's last words, "Take care of my men," prominently displayed on the centerpiece in the middle. Where Sanford Brown emphasizes what the viewer should do for the common good, Murray Davis invites the viewer to recognize what was already done for the common good.

Other structures, like the Liberty Memorial itself, probably mix the two dimensions – public and personal remembrance. The monolithic nature of the Liberty Memorial structures, the grand elevations and vistas, the elevated language, the stylized figures, the original regional subscriptions and subsequent efforts to revitalize, and especially the prominent position in the Kansas City skyline all testify to Liberty Memorial's monumental status. But it is also a "memorial." The very word "memorial" is part of its name, and one of its buildings is named "Memory Hall." There inside, listed on bronze tablets, are the names of the 441 war dead of Kansas City. Above the tablets the inscription "We Are the Dead" expresses in first person plural the personal sacrifice those listed made individually and collectively. Personal relics are preserved in Plexiglas cases around the walls. And below ground is the National World War I Museum filled with artifacts and stories of the thousands of men and women who fought and died during the Great War.

We might best, therefore, consider the 19 structures and sites described in this book as both monuments and memorials, each containing, to one degree or another, elements both personal and public, depending on the context in which they were constructed, the care and treatment they have received since their dedications, the contemporary relevance of the features cast originally into their designs, and the accessibility to the stories which they commemorate.

Unknown, of course, is the future of these monuments and memorials. Will they cease to retain their highly personal associations once personal connections lose significance or become irrelevant to succeeding generations who have no personal memories to evoke? Will their prominence be obscured by changes in their environments? Is a necessary part of a memorial or monument always the present process of its transmission? As time goes on and social norms of inclusion change, who and what continue to be left out?

Certainly the personal responses and associations grandparents make with their children and grandchildren during a visit to a memorial or monument become part of the monument or memorial itself. Young people remember the personal responses of their elders, especially if the elder is able to attach the personal adjective "your" to the person whose own story is evoked in the event being commemorated – "your great, great grandfather served in the Army Air Corps" or "your great aunt was an Army nurse." Relationships are established there, and the memories of those relationships become invested in the physical monument itself and the memorial artifacts, allowing them to endure into another generation.

Inevitably, though, monuments and memorials are defaced, otherwise vandalized, destroyed, stolen, forgotten, or lost. But just as inevitably, something remains, and even those obliterating events can become part of the story, making the monument or memorial that much more compelling. The original plaque dedicating Richards Flying Field to the memory of Lt. John F. Richards, II, is a case in point. After being moved twice to new locations as the Army Air Corps Reserve was transferred, the plaque was finally retired when the unit was dissolved, and it was then consigned to the warehouse with other of the unit's records. However, in the process of its removal, it was – apparently unbeknownst to anyone – accidentally lost. For a number of years it was virtually forgotten.

Only when it was discovered half buried in an orchard did it take on more enduring significance. The prisoner who found it while cutting grass must have recognized the plaque's importance, or he would certainly have worked around it, never bothering to remove or report it. The commanding general who received the report could have sent the plaque to the storage area where it had originally been consigned. The former commander to whom the general wrote and wanted to give the plaque "a better home" might have just kept it for himself out of his own association with what it represented to him. But the prisoner, the general, the former commander, and the newspaper reporter with whom the commander consulted all recognized something sacred about what the plaque represented. So the plaque was returned to places devoted to remembering – war memorials and local museums. Because of its own story, the memorial plaque itself acquires a kind of demonstrated endurance that makes it monumental and iconic, but only for so long as its own story is told.

Other memorials and monuments are physically lost when major renovations or moves are involved, but the memorials and monuments can continue to exist in completely virtual ways, equally enduring. The Kansas City Bar Association plaque is a good example. It was lost when the plaque was moved from the old courthouse at Missouri and Oak to the new courthouse at 12th and Oak. However, pictures of the plaque remain, a memorial program of testimonials to the names inscribed survives in the Missouri Valley Room of the Kansas City Public Library, computer links and microfilm references provide public access to those records, and books like the present one continue to tell the stories and attempt to understand what memory itself is all about. The possibility even exists that the Bar Association plaque, like the Richards Field Plaque, may be found, and its story takes on added significance in its own right.

In the final analysis, though, whether the remembrance is a memorial or a monument matters not nearly so much as the quality of a viewer's interaction with it and the opportunity to share that response with other people, especially with the young. It is within their memories and what they do as a result of those memories that monuments and memorials truly exist.

Independence, Missouri
January 27, 2013

Endnotes

1   Kittery, Maine, is directly across from Portsmouth, New Hampshire, the official discharge site indicated on Paul Sunderland's service record on file with the State of Missouri Soldiers' Records. Paul remembered with a wry smile that Kittery was the site of one of the naval prisons. He and the rest of his band were asked to play at Kittery at the time they were discharged, and his performance prompted the offer of a job, but Paul declined. He was "ready to be free" from life in the Navy and to come home to pick up life where he had left off.

2   Soldiers' Records: War of 1812 - World War I. Missouri Digital Heritage. Service record of Paul Sunderland. http://www.sos.mo.gov/archives/soldiers/results.asp?txtName=Sunderland,%20Paul&selConflict=All&txtUnit=&rbBranch=#soldsearch. Accessed by author April 22, 2013.

3   Benedict Crowell and Robert Forrest Wilson. *The Road to France Vol II: The Transportation of Troops and Military Supplies 1917-1918.* (New Haven: Yale University Press, 1921), p. 574.

4   Ibid, p. 413, 416.

5   "All Making the Huns Humble." Photos of nine servicemen in *The Kansas City Star*, November 6, 1918, p. 3.

6   Benedict Crowell and Robert Forrest Wilson. *The Road to France Vol II: The Transportation of Troops*

and Military Supplies 1917-1918, op. cit., p. 417.

7   Ibid, p. 410.

8   Ibid, p. 422.

9   Ibid, p. 395.

10   Ibid, p. 396.

11   Ibid, p. 399.

12   Ibid, p. 406.

13   Ibid.

14   Ibid, p. 395.

15   Ibid, p. 415.

16   Ibid, p. 395.

17   Ibid, p. 415.

18   Ibid, p. 416.

19   Ibid, p. 396.

20   Ibid, p. 415, Crowell. See also, Eugene O'Neill. *Seven Plays of the Sea.* (New York: Vintage Books, 1972), p. 79-107. Eugene O'Neill's play, "In the Zone," chronicles one of these submarine scares. The Washington Square Players in Greenwich Village first produced this play on October 31, 1917. See also, Travis Bogard. *Contour in Time: The Plays of Eugene O'Neill.* (New York: Oxford University Press, 1972), p. 457.

21   Benedict Crowell and Robert Forrest Wilson. *The Road to France Vol II: The Transportation of Troops and Military Supplies 1917-1918*, op. cit., p. 604.

22   Ibid, p. 619.

23   "Paul Sunderland Interview." VHS tape of interview conducted by Doran Cart, National World War I Museum archives, 2002.

24   Benedict Crowell and Robert Forrest Wilson. *The Road to France Vol II: The Transportation of Troops and Military Supplies 1917-1918*, op. cit., p. 418.

25   Ibid, p. 414.

26   Ibid, p. 411.

27   Ibid, p 421.

28   Ibid, p. 420.

29   Ibid, p. 420.

30   Soldiers' Records: War of 1812 - World War I. Missouri Digital Heritage, op. cit.

31   "Paul Sunderland." Deaths and Funerals. *The Kansas City Star*, January 13, 2004, p. B3.

32   Danielle Hillix. "Area's Last Known WWI Vet Dies at 107." *The Kansas City Star*, January 13, 2004, p. B-1.

33   "Frank Woodruff Buckles." *The Kansas City Star*, March 6, 2011, p. A3.

34   "The Last Veteran of WWI Dies." *The Kansas City Star*, February 8, 2012, p. A3.

35   "American Legion's First Kansas City Posts Formed Thirty-five Years Ago." *The Kansas City Times*, August 19, 1954, p. 38.

Index

D

M

S

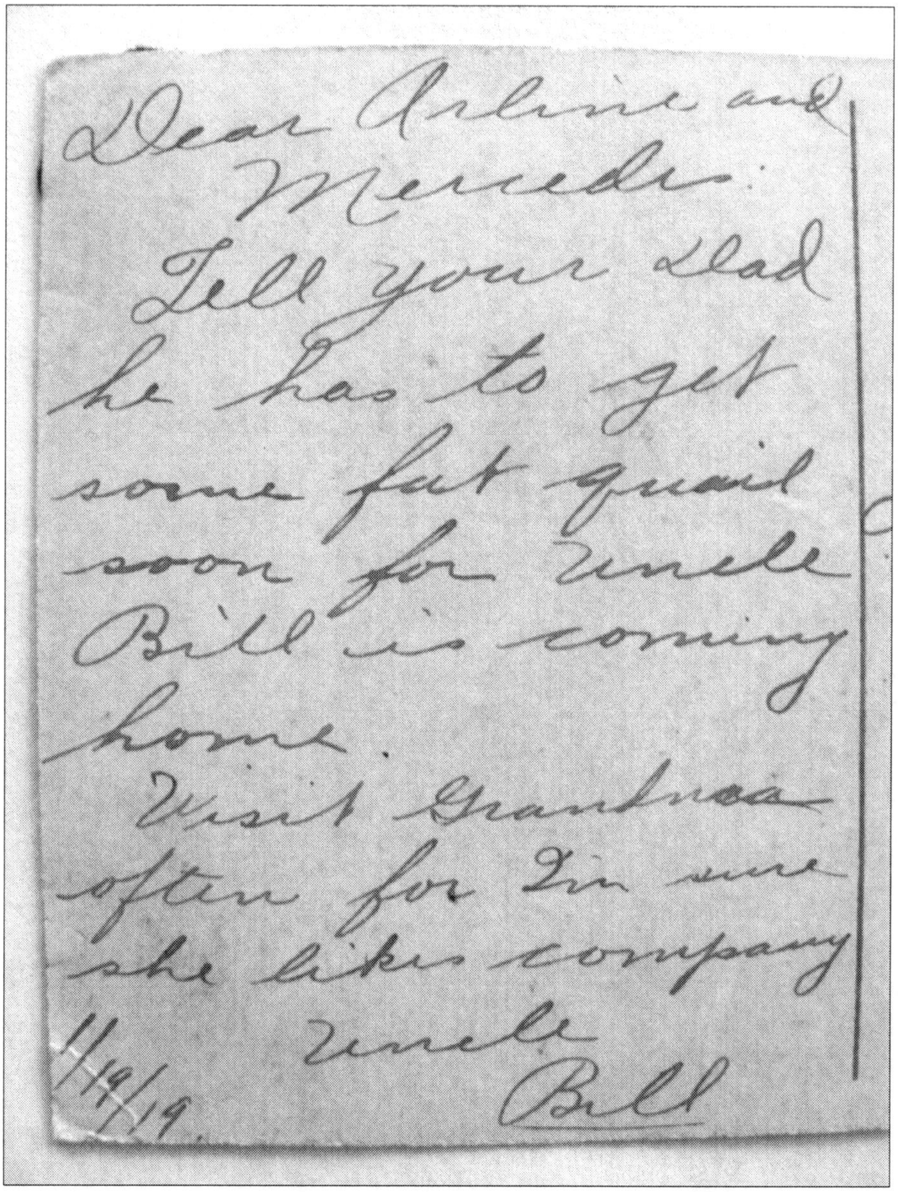

Dear Arline and
Mercedes:
Tell your Dad
he has to get
some fat quail
soon for Uncle
Bill is coming
home.
Visit Grandma
often for I'm sure
she likes company
1/9/19.   Uncle
Bill